Praise for *Women Leading Education Across the Continents*

"Too often women and leadership topics focus on the negatives—the toxicity, the issues, the sexism and misogyny. These are all true and unfortunately accurate portrayals of one aspect of the dark side of leadership for women. But there is another side to which this book draws our attention. It is a well overdue collection of chapters on the possibilities and promises of leadership and of the joy within. I read it with great enjoyment and found the stories, drawing on a wide range of women's experiences, inspiring and full of hope. In an era of Trump, this is an important message to be providing."—**Jane Wilkinson, associate dean graduate research; associate professor educational leadership**

"This book is an excellent addition to the work on women in educational leadership, with its broad perspective, and multi-cultural focus. Students of educational leadership will find it an excellent addition to the work in the field, and learn something new both about themselves as leaders, and the richness of the contexts within which women lead."—**Megan Crawford, PhD, director, Plymouth Institute of Education, Professor of Ed Leadership and Professional Learning**

"This book reflects a wealth of experience from women leaders and those supporting women leaders of education throughout the world. It includes established internationally known voices and those fresh to the field who bring new insights. In this 'Me Too' era, listening to the voices of women in so critical a field as education could not be more important. This book provides a highway to listening and understanding their experience throughout the world."—**Jacky Lumby, emeritus professor, University of Southampton, UK**

"This comprehensive collection from seminal researchers in the field, alongside emerging researchers and practitioner-scholars, from such diverse contexts, provides a powerful model of scholarship for equity. This book will be a valuable text in academic studies and will also provide insight and guidance for women, and all leaders focused on equity for women, at all levels of the system. *Women Leading Education Across the Continents: Harnessing the Joy in Leadership* builds on, but not exclusively from, a strong community of voice and research from the Women Leading Education group. It therefore provides critical perspectives, as well as offering practical strategies and hope, for equity for women's leadership in education."—**Jan Robertson, PhD, Academic Leadership Consultant New Zealand, Adjunct Professor Griffiths University Australia**

"*International Women Leading Education,* by Rachel McNae and Elizabeth C. Reilly is groundbreaking and sets the agenda for Women Leadership in Education while creating a cultural shift and empowering mechanism. The rich voices presented in the different chapters set the stage for cross-sectional understanding of women leadership and equitable education praxis in different nation states which makes the book of a global value."—**Khalid Arar, associate editor,** *International Journal of Leadership in Education*; **author,** *Arab Women in Management & Leadership*, **Palgrave**

"This collection presents a rich tapestry of women's experiences and women's theorizing of educational leadership. Woven through are voices of indigenous, minority, and majority women hailing from small Pacific island nations to large, heavily populated continents. The diversity of their storying captures the rich colors, textures, and patterns of women's leadership across the globe and reflects the strength of scholarship and knowledge building made possible by *Women Leading Education*."—**Margie Kahukura Hohepa, PhD, professor of education, associate dean Maori, University of Waikato, New Zealand**

Women Leading Education Across the Continents

Finding and Harnessing the Joy in Leadership

Edited by
Rachel McNae
Elizabeth C. Reilly

Foreword by
Jane Strachan

Published in partnership with AASA,
The School Superintendents Association

ROWMAN & LITTLEFIELD
Lanham • Boulder • New York • London

Published by Rowman & Littlefield
An imprint of The Rowman & Littlefield Publishing Group, Inc.
4501 Forbes Boulevard, Suite 200, Lanham, Maryland 20706
www.rowman.com

Unit A, Whitacre Mews, 26-34 Stannary Street, London SE11 4AB

British Library Cataloguing in Publication Information Available

Library of Congress Cataloging-in-Publication Data

Names: International Women Leading Education Across the Continents Conference
    (5th : 2017 : Hamilton, New Zealand) | McNae, Rachel, editor. | Reilly,
    Elizabeth C., editor.
Title: Women leading education across the continents. Finding and harnessing
    the joy in leadership / edited by Rachel McNae, Elizabeth C. Reilly ;
    Foreword by Jane Strachan.
Other titles: Finding and harnessing the joy in leadership
Description: Lanham : Rowman & Littlefield, [2018] | Papers originally
    presented at a conference held in 2017 in Hamilton, New Zealand. |
    "Published in partnership with AASA, The School Superintendents
    Association". | Includes bibliographical references and index.
Identifiers: LCCN 2018013021 (print) | LCCN 2018028012 (ebook) | ISBN
    9781475840728 (electronic) | ISBN 9781475840704 (cloth : alk. paper) |
    ISBN 9781475840711 (pbk. : alk. paper)
Subjects: LCSH: Women school administrators—Cross-cultural
    studies—Congresses. | Educational leadership—Cross-cultural
    studies—Congresses. | Women in education—Cross-cultural
    studies—Congresses.
Classification: LCC LB2831.8 (ebook) | LCC LB2831.8 .I67 2017 (print) | DDC
    370.82—dc23
LC record available at https://lccn.loc.gov/2018013021

Printed in the United States of America

To the cherished memory of Susanne Maezama
A woman of strength and humility and leader of many
A shining example of what it means to bring joy to others

Contents

SECTION 3: WOMEN'S LEADERSHIP EXPERIENCES
Editor: *Alice Merab Kagoda*

SECTION 4: WOMEN'S LEADERSHIP AND HUMAN RIGHTS
Editor: *Michelle D. Young*

SECTION 5: WOMEN'S LEADERSHIP STORIES
Editor: *Jacqueline Oram-Shortt*

Foreword

Women Creating a Cultural Shift in Educational Leadership

Jane Strachan

During the 30 years that I taught, worked, and researched in the area of women and educational leadership in Aotearoa New Zealand, and Melanesia, there have been very few moments of joy; interest yes, curiosity yes, satisfaction yes, challenge definitely, heartbreak certainly, and disappointment, too. However, a highlight has been my involvement with the women from the Women Leading Education (WLE) group. The support, the sisterhood, and the love have been sustaining. The WLE women including the editors and women authors in this book have been fearless in their fight for social justice for women and those belonging to marginalized groups. Some I have known for decades, others are new friends. Their work shines a spotlight on the strength of women and how they add unique and effective value to educational leadership.

A number of years ago I was at an international conference (AERA) where some Māori (Indigenous New Zealand) colleagues were giving a group presentation about the achievement of Māori school students. It wasn't a fairy tale with a happy ending; Māori were underachieving across the board. Māori children are more likely than their tauiwi (non-Māori) counterparts to live in poverty and to leave school without qualifications. This unfortunately is also evident for those students later in life; a very high percentage of New Zealand's prison population is Māori. Māori die younger and they have higher rates than tauiwi of mental ill health. Sharon Campbell's story (prologue) details much of that sad situation. The glimmer of hope in their presentation was when Linda said, "when you put a Māori teacher in front of Māori kids magic happens." She was referring here to the importance of the cultural connection in teaching. Yet, we have few teachers who are Māori.

I refer to this story as an illustration of how important it is to have people in positions of leadership that are widely diverse, who are able to relate and make connection to those with whom they serve and work. If women are denied their place in educational leadership, then a cultural shift in how leadership is practiced is very unlikely to happen. So, I am both heartened and despondent when I read the chapters in this book. They are some stories of joy, although not many. There are stories of hope, courage, optimism, hard work, and determination. What is heartening is that despite the challenges the women persevere and continue to work for social justice, no matter how exhausting that can be. This is just as well as aging feminists such as myself need to pass the baton on to our younger feminist colleagues. Many of the authors in this book are early or mid-career educational leaders, and they will go on to mentor others. Some already do.

I want to thank the women of WLE for, through their scholarship, being my role models over the decades; I have admired and used your scholarship in my work. Through WLE it has been a privilege to work with you. Some of you are very close and cherished friends as well as colleagues. I want here to pay special tribute to Susanne Maezama (chapter 3). For over a decade I worked very closely with Susanne both in the Solomon Islands and in Aotearoa New Zealand. Susanne was a woman of integrity, humility, compassion, and enormous ability. She died recently surrounded by her family, in her home in Honiara, Solomon Islands.

I want to end on a joyful note. At approximately 7 p.m. on Thursday, October 19, 2017, I leapt up from sitting on my couch, punched the air, and gave a whoop of joy and shouted "Yes"! This is not my usual behavior; however, I had been watching TV and like many in Aotearoa New Zealand, was nervously waiting to hear who our new prime minister would be. It was close, it could go either way, was it to be the old male-dominated, conservative guard? Or, would it be a vote for change?

The whoop of joy was because our new prime minister was to be Jacinda Ardern. She is 37 years of age, intelligent, articulate, and with an enormous heart, and a passion for social justice. Her rise to the most senior position in the country has been meteoric. How did that happen?

Over the subsequent weeks we learned more about this remarkable woman and much of it resonates with what the research tells us about women in educational leadership. She has extraordinary women and men as mentors and a supportive partner; she is informed and approachable; she works hard, is compassionate, and has a clear social justice vision. She is outspoken and courageous. You will come across these words as you read this book. The strategies mentioned work. They worked for Jacinda and I'm looking forward to that cultural shift, from a government led by a woman. Already there are a larger number of women, Māori, and people from minority cultures, including the lesbian, gay, bisexual, transgender, intersexed (LGBTI) community, in her government. The cultural shift is gaining momentum.

So, as you read the accounts of remarkable women from around the world (section 1) and what factors impede women's progress (section 2), and as you read their very personal stories (sections 3 and 5), and as you read how human rights (section 4) interplay with women's progress, be heartened. And, if you have been on the receiving end, as I have, of the generosity of others in your career, pay it forward and find the joy in giving.

"It's not good enough [for women] to be heard, women must be at the decision-making table" (Jacinda Ardern cited in *The Dominion Post*, 2017, p. A2).

Wahine ma	Women
Wahine ma	Women
Karanga mai, karanga mai	Speak out, speak out
Kia kaha	Be strong

REFERENCE

The Dominion Post. (2017, December 8). Prime minister makes it onto coveted Financial Times list, *The Dominion Post*, Section A2.

Acknowledgments

Waikato-taniwha-rau
He piko, he taniwha
He piko, he taniwha

Waikato of a hundred Chiefs
At every bend a Chief can be found

In Aotearoa New Zealand, specifically the Hamilton region where the International Women Leading Education Conference was held in 2015, a well-known traditional Māori proverb draws our attention to the Waikato River, the longest river in New Zealand. There is recognition that across the landscape leadership can exist as a distributed phenomenon, where work is shared and contributions to the greater purpose are to be valued. The proverb at the beginning of this section also draws our attention to the importance of acknowledging leadership in its many manifestations. That is how this book has come into being.

This book became possible because of the work of many. The foundation of this book stems from the work contributed by scholars and practitioners who attended the 5th International Women Leading Education Conference, in Aotearoa New Zealand. Alongside these authors, additional scholars and researchers from across the globe added further perspectives, bringing other exciting ideas. Sharing insights from various contexts, the work of the authors makes significant contributions to the scholarship of women and educational leadership. They shed light on the complexities, challenges, inspirational moments, and aspirational elements which comprise this research area. The valuable work by section authors—Alice Kagoda, Sister Chrispina Lekule, Pontso Moorosi, Jacqueline Oram-Shortt, and Michelle Young—has situated these contributions in the global leadership landscape and drawn together threads of comments, analysis, and provocative questioning for further consideration. New space has been carved for research about, for, and with women in the area of educational leadership, and as new agendas for scholarship have emerged, exciting ideas have materialized and powerful bodies of knowledge created.

The wealth of experience, knowledge, and skills that Jane Strachan has contributed has played a significant role in bringing this book to fruition. Jane, a retired academic from the University of Waikato, was involved in the development of the first Masters of Educational Leadership postgraduate program in New Zealand. She is a founding member of Women Leading Education (WLE) and an incredible mentor and role model for many of us leading, living, working, studying, and researching in New Zealand and beyond. Jane lives her values. She demonstrates her wealth of knowledge in the areas of socially just and culturally responsive ways of working in her daily life. Along with her attention to detail throughout the editing process, she has ensured the essence of women's leadership remains authentic and our voices remain at the forefront of each contribution.

The artwork, "Hei Tiki Heroine," which graces this cover, is the generous gift of Aimee Ratana, a talented young photographer of Ngai Tuhoe ancestry with a growing reputation as one of New Zealand's foremost indigenous artists. The art work titled "takitini" which graces the cover of the book is a generous gift of Aimee Ratana, a talented artist of Ngai Tūhoe ancestry with a growing reputation as one of New Zealand's foremost indigenous artists. This piece was part of the exhibition "Te Whatu ō Mawake" which translates to the eye of the storm, referring to the calm in the storm, the stillness found within rapid movement. Aimee believes art provides an element of tranquility, a space for withdrawal, to find joy and create. Her creation of "takitini" references the significance of existing as a collective, as people encounter ngā piki me ngā heke o te haerenga—the ups and downs of the journey. Aimee feels these ideas are extremely important for wahine (women) to consider as they embrace numerous roles and responsibilities, and develop relationships and connections to find calm within their hectic lives. We are extremely grateful to Aimee for connecting her joy and passion with the work of this project. We are grateful for Aimee's visual representation of our written work.

The unique and distinct nature of the work of WLE is supported by generous personal contributions from WLE members, along with sponsorship from the School of Education at Virginia Commonwealth University, AASA (The School Superintendents Association), and the University Council for Educational Administration (UCEA). Each time we meet at universities in host countries that support the conference. For the conference and the book, we received the generous support from the Institute of Professional Learning and Faculty of Education at the University of Waikato, New Zealand. All financial support plays an essential role in providing scholarships for women from developing countries to attend the conferences.

We would like to acknowledge the true and living partnership which forms the foundation for this publication. We have been extremely lucky to have the guidance and support from our acquisitions and production editing team at Rowman & Littlefield—especially Sarah Jubar and Carlie Wall. The work of Sarah Jerome and James Minichello has highlighted another aspect of the important role that AASA, The School Superintendents Association, plays in this collaborative endeavor.

As with leadership, the life-giving properties of water cannot be ignored as a powerful force. Water shapes and is shaped by what it encounters. The currents, eddies, snags, and rapids become part of the journey as water shifts in shape, volume, and speed: rushing, pressing, and surging in some spaces while meandering, trickling, and ebbing in others on its way to its destination. As the water fills the channels, new tributaries are created, adding to the flow and guided by the spaces that have been created. Similar to leadership, understanding the contextual forces and elements which continue to shape and influence women's leadership, along with the critical role of women leaders in education is essential—sustaining the flow becomes paramount.

Rachel McNae and Elizabeth C. Reilly
Hamilton, New Zealand and Los Angeles, California

Prologue

Kupu whakataki. Titiro whakamuri, kia pai ai te titiro whakamua

Look to the Past to Understand the Present and Prepare the Pathway Forward

Sharon Campbell

This Kupu whakataki (introduction) introduces readers to the unique and distinctive feature of Aotearoa New Zealand, the location of the fifth gathering of the group International Women Leading Education Across the Continents. A bicultural island nation located in the southern boundaries of the Pacific Ocean, the country is made up of two main islands (the North and the South Island) and a number of smaller islands, New Zealand was one of the last landmasses to be settled by humans. The first settlers to this area were the Polynesian forebears of today's Māori and as such, Māori have come to be known as the indigenous people of New Zealand. Unique with their own language, cultural customs, and protocol, Māori culture provides significant historical and cultural roots for New Zealand.

The Treaty of Waitangi (Te Tiriti o Waitangi) is considered to be New Zealand's founding document and is an important agreement central to New Zealand law and a means by which to recognize, value, and celebrate Māori culture. With an increasing number of new settlers arriving in New Zealand in the mid-1800s, a number of British Crown representatives and Māori leaders signed an agreement which espoused ideals for British settlers and the Māori people to live together in harmony. This binding treaty was created in order to protect the rights of Māori (e.g., retain access to natural resources such as land, forests, fisheries), and governance was shared with the British (Waitangi Tribunal, 2013). From this agreement, a new government was created which would be responsible for the future of New Zealand. The Crown established the right to create new laws and govern in the interests of all New Zealanders, and British settlement ensued, giving Māori the same rights and status as British citizens. Most importantly from this agreement was the commitment that Māori were to be recognized as the first people of New Zealand, having occupied New Zealand before British settlement and as such, Māori culture and heritage must be protected.

As a result of this treaty, many of the laws in New Zealand, past and present, continue to be influenced by the underlying principles of *active protection, the tribal right to self-regulation, the right of redress for past breaches, and the duty to consult form the body of the Treaty of Waitangi*. Through current understandings of these ideas, "education policy makers, leaders, educators (teachers and lecturers at all levels of the system) as well as educational researchers have a responsibility to understand, recognize, and surface the principles of partnership, protection, and participation within educational research" (McNae & Cowie, 2017, pp. x–xi).

Although simplistically represented in this summary, there is a level of complexity that stems from the interpretation of the principles and the translations of the document. One version of the treaty was written in Māori and one in English and these two versions of the treaty can be interpreted to mean different things. There is still debate to this day over how to interpret the documents (Waitangi Tribunal, 2013). Consequently, not only is educational policy required to reflect these principles and ensure they are actively addressed, but ways of working and acknowledging the cultural dimensions within and across contexts is also essential.

Therefore, the placement of this chapter is important. As through traditional Māori custom, this chapter first serves to welcome readers into Te Ao Maori—the world of Māori. Cultural protocol emphasizes the importance of beginning this way. Through this welcome, it is hoped that the significance of working in partnership is demonstrated from the position of Tangata te Whenua (people of the land) emphasizing how personal histories are an essential element of surfacing and sharing insights into others' lived experiences and cultural knowledge. This chapter also plays an essential role in contributing to the nominal research associated with Wāhine Māori (Māori women's) leadership. The origins of Wāhine Māori leadership are inextricably linked to the whakapapa (genealogy) of Papatūānuku (earth mother), Ranginui (sky father), and their progeny. Whakapapa maps relationships and intergenerational connections through the transmission of knowledge, tikanga (customs), and philosophies embodied through the legacy of the creation story to Māori currently.

The context of this research includes the impact of displacement and the decline of the Māori language and associated cultural practices, intensified by the process of assimilation of Māori through the missionary and state education system within Aotearoa New Zealand. Thereafter, heralding a polarizing political era in the 1970s led by Wāhine Māori for Māori to establish te reo me ōna tikanga Māori education initiatives outside the state system initially and subsequently integrated within the education system.

My story is inextricably interconnected through whakapapa of the Māori feminine and the colonial historical trauma exacted upon Māori. To complement the essence of this story, the Pūrākau (narrative approach) is the relevant methodology. Through the generations, Wāhine Māori have been resilient in revitalizing and preserving Māori language and practices through initiating Māori medium education within Aotearoa New Zealand.

TE OROKOHANGA ME TE UWHA MĀORI: CREATION AND THE MĀORI FEMININE

Māori cosmology and the quintessential origins of our human existence are integrally linked. For the purpose of this chapter, the Māori feminine and Wāhine Māori leadership will be examined. Although limited research sources consider the legacy of Māori femininity. In her research into the Māori cosmology of the goddesses and their great mana, Aroha Yates-Smith (1998) rediscovered the feminine in Māori spirituality, which was an acknowledgment of the legacy of the feminine, an understanding also supported by Pihama (2001) and Royal (2012). "Māori are not just joined to the land, they are an integral part of nature, with a relationship to every other living thing, defined by whakapapa" (Williams, 2004, p. 50).

The first human form Hine-ahu-one (the first human woman), fashioned from clay by the pantheon of Māori deity interrelate the esoteric and terrestrial spaces as a legacy of descent. This enduring whakapapa and relationship of Wāhine Māori and their integral connection through whānaungatanga (kinship ties and relationships), manaakitanga (caring), and aroha (love) to strengthen whānau, hapū, and iwi (Ruru, 2016).

The importance of Wāhine Māori can be further understood conceptually, and we begin to see wahine as the intersection of the two worlds: wa and hine. Wa relates

to notions of time and space, hine to a female essence. The term Wāhine designates a certain time and space for Māori women but is by no means a universal term like the term woman in English. There are many times and spaces that Māori women move through in our lives. Wāhine is one of those (Pihama, 2001).

TE ARIĀ KAUPAPA MĀORI ME NGĀ PŪRĀKAU: MĀORI THEORY AND NARRATIVES

The Māori creation story through whakapapa underpins our human existence and affirms the methodology of the kaupapa Māori theory through narratives. Intergenerational transmission of oral narratives shared over eons of time and space is now accessible through written narratives to be reflected upon by members of my whānau and with this publication the international community also. The choice of using a narrative style aligned with both a traditional mode of sharing knowledge (oral) and a contemporary style of research (writing). The purpose being to share this research as a Wāhine Māori educator, captured through the method of storytelling (narratives approach).

Māori narratives about the origins of creation "explain who we are and how we live our lives" (Reilly, 2004, p. 1), and form an important part of our worldview. Te Tirohanga Māori (Māori worldview) acknowledges 'ngā uwha atua' (feminine goddesses) and their leadership attributes and authority within oral traditions through time and currently evidenced through te reo me ōna tikanga (Yates-Smith, 1998). For example, karanga (welcome call) enacted during the creation phase when Papatūānuku was calling and appealing for Ranginui, when they were separated by their children. The karanga which is performed by Wāhine Māori continues during the welcoming rituals of encounter at pā and within nongovernment and government institutions including the many schools throughout Aotearoa New Zealand. As a practicing kaikaranga, this expression is symbolic of our origins and remains as a constant role of the Māori feminine within contemporary society. The karanga and other practices within our culture reveal that the Māori feminine and their prominence continues to be valued within hapū and iwi (King, 1992).

This expression determines how I became, who I am at different points in time and space, and how this whakapapa influences my present. This personal account of my story as a Wāhine Māori is premised on experiences gained as a daughter, sister, mother, aunt, and educator, imbued with a strong sense of culture and social justice, to contribute and strengthen the pathway of Wāhine Māori leadership and succession with an aspiration to reclaim our whakapapa and associated practices. This narrative of resilience is influenced by learning the stories of the heroic leadership modeled by my ancestress Muriwai.

LOSS OF CULTURAL KNOWLEDGE

During the 19th and 20th centuries, much valuable cultural knowledge was lost through the introduction of social structures underpinned by euro and ethnocentric attitudes of racial and cultural superiority. Europeans permeated institutions, including the mission schools of the new society, with an assimilation agenda (Walker, 1990).

Assimilation in policies and legislation further accelerated the decline of Māori knowledge and pedagogy. As Henry and Pene (2001) state:

> The Maori political economy was antithetical to 19th-century British culture, imposed by the systematic introduction of British rule. Maori social, cultural and spiritual institutions were eroded, alongside the expropriation of land and resources, the diminution of language and cultural artifacts, and the assimilation of Maori into Western society. However, traces of the traditional culture resonate in contemporary Maori beliefs and practices. (p. 235)

Despite the legacy of colonialism, appropriation, assimilation, and the ongoing tyranny of government policies, which continue to disproportionately affect Māori, a growing renaissance in Māori awareness means that consciousness of being Māori is reviving. An Auckland-based radical group, Ngā Tamtoa, declared in 1973 that assimilation had failed and detected instead "a feeling of Māoriness in the air." By then, campaigns for Māori rights had gathered great momentum (Hill, 2009, p.150).

MĀORI MEDIUM EDUCATION INITIATIVES

Traditional Māori learning rested on the principle that every person is a learner from the time they are born (if not before) to the time they die. There was an expectation to work alongside each other to achieve a goal. Theory and practice were expected to go hand-in-hand insofar as much of the learning was based on practical experiences, observation and discovery, enhanced and interpreted by highly motivated people who inspired and gained respect. The older generations had a flexible but thorough system of transmitting the cultural practices and economic lore of the tribe to their young. They taught their mokopuna (grandchildren) history, mythology, tribal and local legends, tribal sayings, waiata (songs) (variety of chants and songs), genealogy, karakia (invocations), various crafts,

hand-games, and other leisure pursuits. The parent's generation instructed the children in practical matters, such as harnessing, conserving, and storing crops and the need to know and respect the land were all part of the children's learning. The children were exposed to patterns of regular activity; for example, seasons, plants, and animal rhythms, and family and community gatherings. These patterns of learning were necessary and important (Pere, 1982).

Therefore, coming to know the past is crucial and empowers Māori to be part of the critical pedagogy of Kaupapa Māori. To hold alternative histories is to hold alternative knowledge. The pedagogical implication of this access to alternative knowledge is that they can form the basis of alternative Māori ways of doing things that are Kaupapa Māori. However, to transform our colonized views of our own history (as written by Pākeha) requires us to revisit, site by site, our history under Western eyes. This in turn requires a theory or approach which helps us to engage with, understand, and then act upon history (Smith, 1999). Wāhine Māori continue their commitment to Māori medium education initiatives. Freire (1970) suggests:

> The more radical the person is, the more fully he or she enters into reality so that, knowing it better, he or she can transform it. This individual is not afraid to confront, to listen, to see the world unveiled. This person is not afraid to meet the people or to enter into a dialogue with them. This person does not consider himself/herself the proprietor of history or of all people, or the liberator of the oppressed; but he or she does commit himself or herself, within history, to fight at their side. (p. 39)

Kaupapa Māori principles are important aspects of Māori immersion education initiatives. Principles such as manaakitanga (caring, hosting people), ako Māori (learning, teaching, reciprocity, cultural pedagogy), and kānohi kitea (the seen face) aroha (compassion, love) contribute to leadership drivers that enhance Wāhine Māori within their leadership roles. This view and the social connectedness strengthens the resilience of Māori women to navigate the ongoing changes and countless challenges they face (Ruru, 2016).

In the past 40 years, the commitment of Wāhine Māori to establish and contribute to the lifeblood of immersion Māori education initiatives in Aotearoa New Zealand, spans all sectors of the system, from Kohanga Reo early childhood centers, Kura Kaupapa Māori (Māori immersion schools), and Kura-a-iwi (tribal) primary schools, Wharekura (secondary schools), and Whare Wānanga (tertiary level education) institutions to revitalize the Māori language and associated practices and worldview.

TŌKU AKE PŪRĀKAU: MY STORY

The small Māori rural farming community in the Eastern Bay of Plenty, in the North Island of Aotearoa New Zealand, imbued in me a deep connection to place, people, and culture. The resident tribal groups Pūrākau (story) of origins within Aotearoa New Zealand, regard their whakapapa of descent stems from Hinepukohurangi (mist maiden) and Te Maunga (mountain). 'Ngā tamariki o te kohu' (the children of the mist) intermarried with their ancestor Tuhoe, a descendant from the waka tradition (seafaring ancestors from the Pacific). This legacy clearly connects them to their turangawaewae (place of belonging) and associated customs and practices as kaitiaki (guardians) to their place and people.

The connection to place and people and the associated experiences enhanced one's quality of life. The values of whānaungatanga (relationships), manaakitanga (nurturing), and wairuatanga (spirituality) are a source of continued passion and inspiration. These formative experiences enabled me to observe firsthand the multiple levels of leadership, succession, collective responsibility, and reciprocity.

These practices are visibly exercised within the community and during the formalities at the pā. The pōhiri (welcoming ceremony) is an evocation to the spiritual and physical realms symbolic of the whakapapa of creation and rendering a state of tapu (sacredness) during the formalities. The kaikaranga (women callers) are the first voices heard during pohiri; thereafter the kaikōrero (male speechmakers) reinforce the connection of whakapapa to those who have passed and the current visiting groups. The kaiwaiata (female and male singers) embellish each speaker with a lament. The hongi (pressing noses) ritual symbolizing the first human being, Hine-ahu-one (women fashioned from clay) sneezed and drew her first breath of life after Tane imbued her with hā (breath). Thereafter the formalities of the welcoming ritual rendered noa (normalized) once everyone enters the wharekai (dining hall) and partakes in food. These cultural rituals symbolic of a legacy of seamless complementary roles of leadership between the genders determined by te reo Māori me ōna tikanga (Māori language and practices). These cultural norms and experiences modeled by the many elders, aunties, uncles, and cousins, engendered the cultural lens in which I view the world.

The fun, laughter, and enjoyment as children playing at the pā surrounded by our elders, aunties, uncles, and the nannies, enriched our lives. One of my memorable aunt's voice was deeply soulful and therapeutic especially listening to her performing karanga, singing laments, and karakia and I would blissfully fall into a deep sleep within the wharepuni (meeting house). My mother was a fluent speaker of te reo Māori and was raised within the Haahi Ringatu (Upraised Church), a following which commenced in the Tairawhiti (East Coast) region and had a very strong following within Tuhoe and the local community. We were quickly embraced, as followers of this faith, by the elders and the local community.

Growing up on a dairy farm filled our home with many relatives and friends. The values of the community and associated social structures included caring for several adolescent males who were placed in my parents' care by their elders and whānau to work on the farm. The commitment to the social organization of the community is based on the practices of manaakitanga (caring) and collective responsibility to support the adolescents from the influences of a changing world. The summer holidays and hay-making season embodied the values of whanaungatanga and manaakitanga. The shared cultural responsibilities and collective will of everyone working together to support each other were embedded within the customs and practices of our daily lives. My role was to assist mum with food preparation and cooking to ensure the value of hospitality was maintained.

Returning to school after each summer break of fun and whānau was always an anticlimax. My schooling years were uninspiring, the daily routine of classroom confinement seemed like an eternity. Having to sit in classrooms for hours centered on subjects and content that were seemingly irrelevant. These memories continue to evoke a deep sense of resentment and distress. Many generations of Māori, including mine, were and continue to be educated in the dominant culture's monolingual schools. The Māori medium education initiatives were not an option in the 1970s. So, I left school at 15 years of age, with no formal qualifications. It was definitely a reprieve, with which my parents agreed. They needed someone to manage the local grocery store they purchased for my brother who decided soon after commencing that he did not want the responsibility. I welcomed the opportunity to manage the store, which was a great leadership and learning opportunity.

Lucy, a close friend, came to assist and we worked full time in the shop managing the day-to-day responsibilities. We used leadership skills in managing a small business community, and a supportive nanny guided Lucy and I through the process of mastering basic accounting skills, billing, and banking. The ordering and purchasing of goods from the myriad of traveling vendors was fun. The help from aunties, uncles, nannies, and cousins was always appreciated. However, as an adolescent, I was looking to spread my wings. I moved away from home, first to seasonal work in Gisborne, then to other employment opportunities in Wellington. My whakapapa connections helped me find accommodations with relatives and friends. However, after some time I yearned to return to the comfort of home and the associated cultural practices.

On returning home there was a quick transition into gainful employment as a result of my European father's influence. The job as a cook and part-time barmaid enabled me to gain insights into the pervading social ills rooted in our colonial past. The manifestation of this social dysfunction became evident in the 1980s when I personally witnessed generations of my people, fueled by alcohol and drugs, exact multiple acts of violence at the many social functions hosted at the pā. During this time, I knew five male victims who died as a direct result of violent acts. The ongoing violence continued and the threat of gang confrontation and retaliation was addressed at a community meeting convened at the pā. The hapū and iwi leaders called hui (meetings) by coming together kanohi ki te kanohi (face to face) to discuss the issues and reconcile the factions within our community and to strengthen whanaungatanga. The social impact of drugs and alcohol exacted within whānau are profound; my immediate whānau live with this intrusive legacy.

NGĀ TAU O TAKU ATE: MY ENDLESS LOVES

My journey from childhood to the associated responsibility of motherhood was a rude awakening. Nicholas Thomas George Seymour, of Te Whānau-a-Kai, Te Aitanga-a-Mahaki, and Ngai Tai descent, fathered our five eldest children (our second child, a son, died during pregnancy). He had multiple skills and abilities. However, debilitated by mental illness, in 1996 he took his own life. Our four children have few or no memories of their father.

My eldest son, a father of two boys who attend Kura Kaupapa Māori, and his supportive partner are both working full time in their respective careers as experienced professionals. My eldest daughter and her partner, both experienced medical doctors, are currently employed in a local hospital. My third son is challenged with managing his bipolar condition. My second daughter is living and working in Sydney.

I have a second family that includes three children. One son has an intellectual disability and attends the local secondary Independent Living Unit. My daughter attends a Wharekura (Māori immersion secondary school). My youngest son is currently in his final year at a Kura Kaupapa Māori (Immersion Māori primary school). Their father, Heke Collier, is of Ngai Tai, Whakatohea, and Te Whānau-a-Apanui tribal descent. His whakapapa includes an intergenerational skill of wood carving. His skill was enhanced when he trained at the Whakarewarewa (Arts

and Crafts Center) located in Rotorua to carve with a range of mediums including wood, bone, greenstone, and other mediums. The art of carving remains his main source of inspiration and employment.

TŌKU HUARAHI MĀTAURANGA: THE EDUCATION PATHWAY

I have a determined personal resolve to ensure my children maintain a solid foundation and connection to their Ao Māori (Māori culture) during their formative schooling years. I made a conscious decision that my children would be educated in the Māori medium education sector, which offers a conducive learning environment aligned to Māori philosophies and values. Enrolling them within the Kohanga Reo sector and continuum of Māori medium schools has and continues to be advantageous for them all.

I was encouraged to return to formal education and supported by the matriarch of our whānau. My mother, who was a full-time faculty member at the University of Waikato, enrolled me in a four-week women's bridging course. This course was designed to inspire women to return to formal university study. For me, the course raised awareness regarding various study options which included education, Māori studies, social sciences, health science, and law. This reentry into formal study as a mature student has and continues to be a fulfilling pathway.

Once I completed the bridging course, I applied to gain entry into a teacher aide course. During this course, a sense of confidence was restored to me and the basic foundational skills for further study were realized. My newfound confidence was particularly pleasing and was a source of continued inspiration. I submitted an application for an off-campus teacher education course through the University of Waikato, School of Education (Te Kura Toi Tangata). I was accepted and graduated in 1995.

Pursuing tertiary-level studies continued as a personal priority of development and in 1995 I enrolled in the Bachelor of Māori Studies. My continuing education plan intertwined with deep longing and desire to learn the Māori language. It was the unpacking of the insidious impact of colonialism and historical trauma that galvanized my resolve to learn more. The course content highlighted the importance of leadership, collective responsibility, reciprocity, and succession. The knowledge of this history defined my role as Wāhine Māori and as an educator. I was inextricably interconnected with the legacy of the Māori feminine whakapapa and continued in the footsteps of those who chartered this pathway of resilience and succession. With the encouragement of my mother, I continued onto master's level study.

A kaiako (teaching) position was advertised in a region where my principle whakapapa links were known. I started teaching in January 1998. The principal of the school was European and a fluent speaker of the Māori language. We worked collectively. We were proactive and aimed to engage the community and local iwi by hosting many school events and noho marae (staying on a marae) to gain their support and trust. These initiatives were focused on enhancing the whānaungatanga (relationships) and manaakitanga (hospitality) for all those involved. The opportunity to endear the community by demonstrating the staff's willingness to ensure the kura (school) was viewed as accessible, augmented community engagement. The community was responsive. However, without a seamless education pathway to sustain the momentum and knowing our students were going to secondary school with a legacy of failure was disappointing. After seven years my aspiration to become a principal was realized.

TUMUAKI: PRINCIPAL LEADERSHIP ROLE

In 2005, I was appointed as tumuaki (principal) of a Kura-a-iwi. The experiences and insights gained were adrenaline-charged and demanding. The school was a designated character school which was established under section 156 of the Education Act of 1989. It is a state school that has a particular character which sets it apart from ordinary state schools. The only students who may enroll at a designated character school are those whose parents accept the particular character of the school (Ministry of Education, 2010). The local Māori community expectation was to embed their tribal language, customs, and practices. The Māori-medium education sector has made a major contribution to the wider education system by giving learners a new means through which to achieve education success. The innumerable Wāhine Māori contributions to reclaiming our language and associated cultural customs continue in earnest.

This has been further enhanced by the release of the curriculum for Māori-medium schools. In 2008, Te Marautanga o Aotearoa (Māori Curriculum) brought together the wisdom and experience of a number of leading Māori educationalists who have integrated philosophical approaches including Māori pedagogy and Māori development goals. Some tribal groups in Aotearoa New Zealand, have developed their own unique curriculum. The Tuhoe tribe in which I was raised developed one of the first tribal curricula, based on te reo me ōna tikanga o Ngai Tuhoe (Tuhoe dialect and practices). This initiative is led by their women educators and elders. The following story features the cultural experiences that continue

to influence and guide me to the present day. The experience gained as a Wāhine Māori principal within a small Māori tribal community was certainly the greatest professional leadership learning and extraordinary challenge gained in a formal leadership role.

Engaging the critical mass within Māori communities impacted by the legacy of our colonial history requires fortitude and unconditional support. The school charter mission statement deeply resonated with me, 'Kia ūhia a tātou mokopuna ki te korowaitanga hei oranga mō rātou.' My interpretation being, 'It takes a whole village to raise a child,' engendered a sense of collective responsibility, an important element to enhance the pathway to succession in the kura and the associated iwi. Hence, leading a purposeful pathway of succession relevant to the expectations espoused within the school charter. This succession process requires the support and the commitment of all, the whānau, parents, and caregivers of the school community, and tribal elders. The strength of the collective advances the potential of the children to succeed in education and eventually to strengthen the succession of their language and associated practices and customs. The struggle to realize the precepts of the charter statement is expressed in the following, "Transformation is only valid if it is carried out with the people, not for them" (Freire, 1970, p. 72).

Working with and for the people was customary in traditional Māori society. However, European contact and colonialism changed the social structure and a move from collectivism to individualism was embedded. Traditional Māori social organization, language, and practices shaped and supported seamless intergenerational knowledge transmission and succession. The revitalization of the Māori language and associated practices remains the most important goal for those committed to the cause.

Although a concerted effort to work with and for the people to realize the school's charter was made, aspirations set by the community were unrealized. A legacy of division within the community culminated in my resignation and a clear sense of disillusionment. The professional leadership responsibilities were balanced with supporting my whānau in crisis. However, on reflection, the leadership experience I gained has been enduring.

NGĀ MAMAETANGA TUKU IHO O TŌKU WHĀNAU: HISTORICAL TRAUMA WITHIN MY WHĀNAU

The intergenerational social ills are entrenched and embodied within my whānau. However, as a descendant of a tenacious eponymous matriarch Muriwai and life experiences as a daughter, mother, sister, aunty, partner, and Wahine Māori educator, I am committed to strengthening our cultural connections as a pathway to overcome the legacy of social ills. Traversing the multilayered social ills and dysfunctional behaviors and associated addictions to alcohol, drugs, intimidation, and violence is symptomatic of my reality and that of many other Wāhine Māori.

In 2006, my ailing mother died from a long-term smoking habit and heart disease. Two years later my European father was imprisoned for the first time at the age of 72 for supplying and selling cannabis. During this time, and debilitated by an initial diagnosis of early psychosis at 16 years of age, my son attempted to commit suicide. My son continues to struggle to manage his condition which impacts all our whānau. The intergenerational legacy of mental illness within my whānau is endemic and many nuclear and extended whānau members are impacted by this insidious illness.

The purpose of sharing this challenging legacy within my whānau is to show the ongoing challenges many Wāhine Māori and their whānau throughout Aotearoa confront on a daily basis. I personally believe this legacy of mental illness is derived from the historical trauma of colonialism exacted upon my whānau when my ancestors were imprisoned on the Chatham Islands in the 1860s. The ancestors of the father of my five eldest children's ancestors was also wrongfully imprisoned. Recent information regarding historical trauma suggests epigenetics impacts on whakapapa. My whānau has a legacy of intergenerational mental illness which I can trace back to Raupatu (land confiscation), displacement, and wrongful imprisonment.

Regardless of this whakapapa and the legacy of historical trauma, the strength drawn from a whakapapa of creation and matriarchal heroine ancestress Muriwai reminds me of their fortitude and the legacy which gives me strength to continue regardless of the ongoing challenges. A deep passion and the fire in my belly continues to burn. The desire to continue strengthening my whānau, hapū, iwi, and others, whose aspirations advance our Māori language and associated practices to address the growing inequalities within Aotearoa continues unabated.

KUPU WHAKAKAPI: A SUMMATION

Traditional Māori leadership concepts continue to inform and permeate leadership practices in educational contexts. Valuing Māori ways of leading, while respecting traditional cultural practices is complex. Oral histories are an essential part of Māori knowledge and cultural practice. The intersection of common every-

day tasks that women undertake within the complex cultural and social structures provide challenges for identifying leadership as an explicit practice when it is embedded in the day-to-day actions and expectations of each individual. However, illuminating Māori women's experiences of leadership, and supporting other women in their leadership within these structures, can highlight the significant role women play, not only in supporting existing cultural practices and ideals, but in creating new ways of leading, when there appears to be no other way forward. The challenge in this case is to honor and respect the cultural heritage which has gone before, while balancing the new demands of what it means to be a Wāhine Māori, daughter, mother, sister, aunty, and educator into the future.

REFERENCES

Freire, P. (1970). *Pedagogy of the oppressed.* New York: Continuum.

Henry, E., & Pene, H. (2001). Kaupapa Māori: Locating indigenous ontology, epistemology and methodology in the academy. *Organization, 8*(2), 234–242. Retrieved from http://journals.sagepub.com.ezproxy.waikato.ac.nz/doi/abs/10.1177/1350508401082009

Hill, R. (2009). *Māori and the State: Crown-Māori relationships in New Zealand/Aotearoa, 1950–2000.* Wellington, New Zealand: Victoria University Press. Retrieved from http://nzetc.victoria.ac.nz/tm/scholarly/tei-HilMaor-t1-body-d7-d1.html

King, M. (1992). *Te aohurihuri. Aspects of Māoritanga.* Auckland, New Zealand: Reed Publishing Group (NZ) Ltd.

McNae, R., & Cowie, B. (Eds.) (2017). Elaborating the local. In *Realizing innovative partnerships in educational research* (pp. ix–xv). Netherlands: Sense Publishers.

Ministry of Education. (2010). OECD Review on evaluation and assessment frameworks for improving school outcomes: New Zealand country background report 2010. www.educationcounts.govt.nz/publications.

Pere, R. (1982). *Ako, concepts and learning in the Māori tradition.* Hamilton, New Zealand: Department of Sociology, University of Waikato.

Pihama, L. (2001). *Tihei mauri ora: Honouring our voices; mana wahine as a kaupapa Māori theoretical framework* (Doctoral thesis, the University of Auckland).

Reilly, M. P. J. (2004). Te tīmatanga mai o ngā atua: Creation narratives. In T. M. Ka'ai, J. C. Moorfield, M. P. J. Reilly, & S. Mosley (Eds.), *Ki te whaiao: An introduction to Māori culture and society* (pp. 1–12). Auckland, New Zealand: Pearson Education New Zealand.

Royal, T. A. C. (2012). Māori creation traditions: Common threads in creation stories. Retrieved from https://teara.govt.nz/en/maori-creation-traditions/page-1

Ruru, S. M. (2016). *Māori women's perspectives of leadership and wellbeing* (Master's thesis, University of Waikato,

Hamilton, New Zealand). Retrieved from http://researchcom
mons.waikato.ac.nz/bitstream/handle/10289/10635/thesis
.pdf?sequence=3&isAllowed=y

Smith, L. T. (1999). *Decolonizing methodologies: Research
and indigenous peoples.* Dunedin, New Zealand: University
of Otago Press.

Waitangi Tribunal. (2013). Wellington, New Zealand. Author.
Retrieved from https://teara.govt.nz/en/principles-of-the
-treaty-of-waitangi-nga-matapono-o-te-tiriti

Walker, R. J. (1990). *Ka whawhai tonu mātou: Struggle without end.* Auckland, New Zealand: Penguin Books.

Williams, J. (2004). Papa-tūā-nuku: Attitudes to land. In T. M.
Ka'ai, J. C. Moorfield, M. P. J. Reilly, & S. Mosley (Eds.),
Ki te whaiao: An introduction to Māori culture and society
(pp. 50–60). Auckland, New Zealand: Pearson Education
New Zealand.

Yates-Smith, G. A. (1998). *Hine! E Hine! Rediscovering the
feminine in Māori spirituality* (Doctoral dissertation, University of Waikato, Hamilton, New Zealand).

THE STATUS OF WOMEN IN EDUCATIONAL LEADERSHIP: GLOBAL INSIGHTS

Editor: *Pontso Moorosi*

Chapter 1

Overview

The Status of Women in Educational Leadership: Global Insights

Pontso Moorosi

Research on women in educational leadership was initiated by the low representation of women in the leadership positions despite their constituting the majority in the teaching profession. This body of research has grown significantly since the early works of Shakeshaft (1989) and Schmuck (1996) in the United States. It has spread from west to south, uncovering stories, perceptions, and experiences of discrimination, influenced by an often too familiar range of barriers. In its growth, gender research has also broadened its focus from experiences of the majority white women in Western countries to experiences of minority groups and black women across the globe.

Moreover, from focusing exclusively on gender theory, research has moved to using different theoretical frameworks that suggest a wider focus than just gender, and showing how gender interacts with other forms of identity shaping the experiences of women. Studies of gender and career development (for school leaders) have shown that while discrimination against women occurs mostly at the point of employment, there exist some barriers throughout women teachers' career paths, which affect women in different ways from men, making it difficult for them to progress (Oplatka, 2006; Moorosi, 2010).

Recent research, however, suggests that women have made significant strides leading education across continents (Sobehart, 2009). This is seen in the rising statistics on women who occupy the leadership positions in primary and secondary schools as well as in higher education, although the latter are still wanting. For example, Coleman's (2002) study found women making only 32 percent of the headteachers of schools in England, yet by 2013 women made 65 percent of headteachers (Fuller, 2013). In the United States, female principals made up 24.6 percent in the 1980s and 52 percent in 2012 (Vitterman, Golding, and Gray, 2013). This growth trend is seen and experienced in many countries including Australia, New Zealand, and South Africa. However, despite the apparent success in the quantitative gains, further

analysis shows that women have mostly made progress in lower and elementary schools, and less in the leadership of higher education institutions.

A further qualitative analysis of women's experiences shows that even where women have attained positions of leadership, they still suffer discrimination and prejudice on the grounds of gender (Moorosi, 2010), sometimes leading to high exodus from the positions of leadership. This shows that gender still remains a prevalent way in which people are marginalized in the workplace (Coleman, 2011; Strachan, Akao, Kilavanwa, & Warsal, 2010) and implies that while progress is being made on the quantitative aspect, the qualitative aspect still needs a great deal of attention.

One of the most pervasive ways in which gender discrimination manifests in the workplace is through cultural conceptions of the position of women in different societies. While research has moved from socialization theories that suggest that the male image of leadership (the public sphere) is the norm, and that women are the deficit model, one thing remains clear: the cultural and traditional stereotypes continue to dictate roles for men and women in society determining the duality of responsibilities that women bear in the home and at the workplace, affecting the way women are perceived in the workplace.

The chapters in this section illuminate the cultural aspect as a determinant for the underrepresentation of women in educational leadership in various contexts. Additionally, these chapters present insights from rarely heard contexts where voices of women are suppressed by powerful male acts and male embodiment of power, culture, and voice.

ACCESS, CULTURE, AND CHANGE

Chitra Mku's chapter provides an account of Indian women in higher education showing different enrollment figures between men and women. In this context, although women have made significant strides in enrolling for higher degrees in larger numbers, that level of participation does not seem to translate to improvements in career progression. Increasing numbers of women in higher education enrollment have been observed in many contexts, but what remains questionable is how women's participation in higher education results in improved status of life as compared to that of their male counterparts.

Indeed, Mku's analysis emphasizes this gap between men and women, but also between different groups of women who have different access to opportunities. This analysis brings to the fore factors that affect women's participation, which include social class, rurality, and poverty or lack of access to resources as factors determining the representation and participation of women in higher education which inevitably affects their representation in educational leadership and other careers.

Reilly's illustration through two case scenarios of strong and resilient women, captures how Afghan women challenge attempts to exclude their voices from civil society and from playing an important role in their country's future and in particular from liberating women so they can have meaningful lives free of fear and violence by men. Through stories of tenacity, courage, and dedication, the women lead in their different constituencies displaying strong leadership and inspiration to other women and addressing the deeply entrenched problems within the society and confronting different forms of social inequality and injustice.

In presenting these stories of courage, Reilly illustrates how misogyny and gender injustice can be tackled by a peaceful and collective effort in different sectors driven by one goal. She captures it appropriately in saying, "the degree to which these sectors have congruent goals is the degree to which authentic change can occur."

Through powerful personal narratives of Afghan women leaders, Reilly's chapter further depicts the strength of the political self. She portrays stories of courage from women who relentlessly serve their communities for social justice despite the harrowing dangers and risks they face, regardless of their position or status in society. These narratives carry a message of hope—hope that a collective effort can change the position of women even in the most difficult circumstances. In this context, change does not only need to happen in the workplace, but in the minds and attitudes of society.

GENDER, CULTURE, AND LEADERSHIP

Closely connected in contextual presence, Susanne Maezama and Daisy Walsal both write from small Pacific Island states' perspectives where little is known about the experiences of women in general and experiences of women in leadership in particular. In their chapters, the issue of culture surfaces as a barrier to educational leadership positions amidst each country's political commitment to eradicating all forms of gender discrimination. Interestingly, there also exists a matrilineal culture that positions the strength of women in decision making within the community, providing opportunities for women to have power and respect within community contexts.

However, this community power does not translate into easy access to leadership positions in organizations. Maezama shows how access to leadership positions in the educational field is constrained by a barrage of sociocultural factors, while on the contrary, women's leadership is accepted across a range of community contexts. Maezama's chapter helpfully captures the different influences on women's representation and participation in leadership, reminding us of the deeply embedded nature of the forces of women's oppression: from colonialism, Christianity, and culture, and how entangled these can be. It is this interplay and the interacting nature of these powerful forces of oppression that uphold male power and marginalize women by excluding them from key aspects of society's public life.

The exclusion of women from the public life is a phenomenon linked to the values attached to the gendered dichotomy of the notions of the public and private sphere of leadership that confines women's influence to the domestic arena (Moorosi, 2007). Maezama's chapter presents a scenario that illustrates the power of women within the community in which society allows women to enact leadership that is linked to the domestic sphere of the home—the traditional perspective that views women's role to be primarily in the home.

This traditional view dichotomizes the notions of male and female as public and private respectively (Moorosi, 2007; Reiger, 1993), upholding men as legitimately deserving of the leadership roles in the public sphere. It is here, at the cultural interface, where policy doesn't seem to have an effect leading to the questioning of the gender equity policies and the ratification of international commitments to gender equity. Both Maezama and Warsal highlight symbolic commitments made by their states, which do not seem to be met with equal commitment in practice.

The male norm of leadership is seen in the conception of the "big man" that excludes women from the leadership game. This masculinist view of leadership is present in both Maezema and Warsal's chapters, suggesting a strong cultural association of women to certain roles that confine them to the domestic space at home. This "big man" notion embodies power and leadership that completely overshadows women and silences their voices, leaving them struggling to access positions of leadership.

Paradoxically, access to employment is a point at which policy is most active and could have more effect. Yet, Maezama and Warsal's chapters show that in their contexts, access to leadership positions is constrained by social and cultural discourses that continue to sabotage women's aspirations. The literature established that the challenges influenced by cultural stereotypes are difficult to eradicate even by policy as they are not tangible, but are informal and subtle and on the surface, appear gender neutral (Moorosi, 2007).

As a result, many cultural norms and practices go unquestioned as they are often regarded as the way things are. Toh, Geoffrey, and Leonardelli (2012) posit that it is the tightness of culture—"its strength of norms and social sanctions" that provokes a resistance to changing those practices that have historically elevated men to the positions of leadership at the expense of women. They argue that the weaker the cultural practices, the less likely it is that policy measures will lead to sustained change.

It is perhaps worth acknowledging that the concept of culture in educational leadership has received some attention, albeit not enough. In their studies of women school leaders, Moorosi (2010) and Strachan et al. (2010) highlighted those deeply held beliefs that helped us understand how discrimination happens so blatantly in many of the contexts despite the advances made by equity legislation.

Almost a decade later, Walsal's chapter brings this aspect home in a very convincing way that puts the continuance of discrimination against women as informed by cultural understandings in context. These experiences are shaped by cultural experiences, Christianity, and paradoxically, black magic. While these notions are all clustered under cultural norms, they do suggest a greater deal of nuanced engagement with the concept of culture in different societies and how it affects the emergence, representation, and participation of women in educational leadership.

SUMMARY AND CONCLUSIONS

What we see in these chapters is an interplay of culture and religion—whether Christianity or Islam as presented in different contexts. In this sense both culture and religion have "a powerful influence on how women practice their leadership" (Strachan et al., 2010, p. 70). Significantly, they work against women's progression as women's place is perceived to be in a particular place in society.

The chapters in this section show that despite the decades of research on gender in educational leadership across the globe, the situation of women seems to be marginally improving. Individually and collectively, these chapters demonstrate the deeply embedded nature of cultural stereotypes that would need more than formal government policy to eliminate. Perhaps as a way forward, studies of culture, gender, and leadership can look into cultural tightness in various societies as suggested by Toh et al. (2012).

These authors suggest that aspects of culture need to be considered in view of how strong and loose the cultural norms are in different societies. They argue that instead of considering cultural norms and values to be the determinant for women's underrepresentation in leadership, perhaps an effort should be made to understand the process of change and how culture contributes to this process. In this way, the symbolic commitment to eradicating gender inequality can be seen incrementally as part of understanding the different cultures within their own context.

In previous work of Women Leading Education (WLE), Oram-Sterling (2015) noted that researchers documenting the lives of women across the globe should be cognizant of the difference in cultures, and document women's experiences from their situated perspectives. There is arguably more to learn from a cross-cultural perspective in order to enrich our understanding of the global experiences of women in educational leadership.

The complexities between women's access to education and women's progression to leadership positions are demonstrated. To this, Strachan et al. (2010) explain that the under-representation of women in educational leadership positions as well as in other formal sectors begins with gaining access to education. Where girls' access to education is limited, this may create a flow-on effect that impedes the participation of women economically and in decision making at all levels of society, including educational leadership. What this calls for is the need to interrogate perhaps in a more aggressive way, the connection between girls' access to education, their choice of subjects, and the participation of women in positions of power.

Role modeling has been identified as an aspect affecting women's interest in educational leadership positions as young women grow up seeing what they can identify with. Moreover, the presence of girls and women in education contributes toward changing gender stereotypes and sexist cultural norms. The existing cultural perception of women in the matrilineal contexts would therefore need to be viewed as an important foundation upon which to build initiatives that advance the position of girls and women in the public sphere.

Research in gender and educational leadership is thus far, and as seen in these chapters, broadly driven by one issue: the underrepresentation of women in educational leadership, when in many contexts women are in the majority in the teaching profession. This issue has been tackled from different angles for several decades now, and although there is some improvement on some levels, the majority of women continue to be victims of sexism and misogyny in various contexts. Amidst all the suffering, discrimination, and the oppression of women, there is hope, offered in Reilly's use of a powerful Afghan proverb: *There is a path to the top of even the highest mountain.* However, hope on its own is not enough to change the situation of women—it needs action.

REFERENCES

Bitterman, A., Goldring, and Gray, L. (2013). Characteristics of Public and Private Elementary and Secondary Schools Principals in the United States: Results from the 2011–12 Schools and Staffing Survey (NCES 2013–313). U.S. Department of Education.

Coleman, M. (2002). *Women as headteachers: Striking the balance.* London, England: Trentham Books.

Coleman, M. (2011). *Women at the top: Challenges, choices and change.* London, England: Palgrave Macmillan.

Fuller, K. (2013). *Gender, identity and educational leadership.* London: Bloomsbury.

Moorosi, P. (2007). Creating linkages between public and private sphere: challenges facing women principals in South Africa. *South African Journal of Education, 27*(3), 507–521.

Moorosi, P. (2010). South African women principals' career path: Understanding the gender gap in secondary school management. *Educational Management Administration and Leadership, 38*(5), 547–562.

Oplatka, I. (2006). Women in educational administration within developing countries: Towards a new international research agenda. *Journal of Educational Administration, 44*(6), 604–624.

Oram-Sterling, J. (2015). Gender status across the global education. In E. C. Reilly & Q. J. Bauer, *Women leading education across the continents: Overcoming leadership barriers* (pp. 3–8). Lanham, MD: Rowman & Littlefield Education.

Reiger, K. (1993). The gender dynamic of organisations. In J. Blackmore & J. Kenway (Eds.), *Gender matters in educational administration and policy: A feminist introduction* (pp. 17–26). London, England: Falmer Press.

Schmuck, P. (1996). Women's place in educational administration: Past, present and future. In K. Leithwood et al. (Eds.), *International handbook of educational leadership and administration* (pp. 337–368). Dordrecht: Kluwer Academic Press.

Shakeshaft, C. (1989). *Women in educational administration.* Newbury Park, CA: Corwin Press.

Sobehart, H. (2009). *Women leading education across the continents.* New York, NY: Rowman & Littlefield Education.

Strachan, J., Akao, S., Kilavanwa, B., & Warsal, D. (2010). 'You have to be a servant of all': Melanesian women's educational leadership experiences. *School Leadership and Management, 30*(1), 65–76.

Toh, S. M., Geoffrey, J., & Leonardelli, G. J. (2012). Cultural constraints on the emergence of women as leaders. *Journal of World Business, 47*(4), 604–611.

Chapter 2

Your Eyes Are Beautiful

Profiles of 21st Century Afghan Women Leaders

Elizabeth C. Reilly

In the tradition of their ancestral kinswomen, Afghan women today continue to challenge any attempt of others to exclude their voices from civil society and their role in their country's future. This study profiles the leadership of two of Afghanistan's women—Zohra Yusuf Daoud, adviser to the First Lady of Afghanistan, a television journalist, and the first and only Miss Afghanistan; and Hadisa Miokhail, a school headmistress from Kabul. Each embodies the values of 10th century poet Rabia Balkhi, and lives a life committed to building a nation where every individual enjoys basic human rights and dignity. Their stories provide insight and inspiration for addressing the seemingly intractable problems women face in Afghanistan today.

> Don't be satisfied with stories—how things have gone with others. Unfold your own myth.
>
> —Rumi

In Afghanistan, people tell the tale of a 10th century poet and princess, Rabia Balkhi, who fell in love with her Turkish slave. During their clandestine meetings, Rabia and her paramour, Baktash, would pen love poetry for each other. On discovering Rabia's illicit affair, her brother slashed her throat and left her to die. She wrote her final poems in her own blood on the walls where she was imprisoned.

The legend of Rabia Balkhi is well known to Afghans and she remains revered even in the 21st century. The recurring theme of the story with its several variations is this: Rabia Balkhi was a woman who challenged the cultural traditions and societal norms of the day. She boldly attempted to break down barriers of class, caste, and calling. She held a profession at a time in history when few women did. Not only did people of medieval Persia recognize her, but loved and respected her poetry. She did not stop there, however. She possessed the temer-

ity to engage with a man apart from the approval of her family. This was both a violation of the cultural tradition of the day and a violation of her position as royalty. She not only chose someone herself, but she chose a man outside of her caste—a foreign slave who had no standing in society.

One of the reasons the legend of Rabia Balkhi endures is that it presents a model of a strong Afghan woman who is indefatigable in the face of adversity. Nothing daunts this woman—not the specter of deprivation, not the threat of harm, and not the fear of death. Since I first began profiling the progress, successes, and challenges of women leaders in Afghanistan in 2008, I have had the opportunity to meet many of these heroines—modern-day Rabia Balkhis who dare to stand against all manner of social inequality and injustice.

It only takes one visit to the Afghan National Assembly to note that it is unlike perhaps any other parliament in the world. Amid the rows of tables and chairs are not only the names of its present members, but small memorials erected to those elected members who have been slain during their terms in office. In November 2014, prominent lawmaker Shukria Barakzai, an internationally recognized proponent of women's rights, escaped a suicide bomber's attack with slight injuries that left at least a dozen individuals wounded and three dead (Associated Press, 2014). Politics—or any highly visible attempt on the part of women to effect civil society—renders their families, associates, and themselves targets for maiming or death (Hamid, 2012; Nemat & Samadi, 2012).

On nearly any international index, the plight of women in Afghanistan is frequently highlighted as among the worst in the world (UNDP, 2012). Stories of the Taliban's draconian form of justice still abound with continual episodes of violence against women (Hamid, 2012). Two years ago, the stoning of a woman in a burqa outside the capital city of Kabul drew a large audience of men, loudly cheering and participating in her demise (Hackel, 2012). Days later, a suicide bomber assassinated a prominent female women's affairs official in Laghman province (United Press International, 2012). Not long after that, a 45-year-old criminal investigator in Helmand Province became the highest-ranking female officer to be slain just after her female superior was murdered only months before. Her status angered not only Islamic fundamentalists but also her family. "My brother, father and sisters were all against me," she said before her death. "In fact my brother tried to kill me three times" (Bambuck & Naiemullah, 2013, p. 4).

The mass poisoning of over 150 schoolgirls and the killing of teachers and school leaders presents grim news to the world of a nation teetering on the precipice of a return to the dark days from which the nation had only recently emerged (Popalzai, 2012). The news highlights tragedies that challenge Afghanistan's constitutional guarantees to women for equal rights. It further compromises the United Nations Educational, Scientific and Cultural Organization's (UNESCO) goals for women as capacity builders and leaders in education (Commission on the Status of Women, 2002).

Even so, rainbows do appear behind the dark clouds of bad news that gain much of the world's attention. Although numerous international reports present a broad view of the challenges Afghan women face, few investigators have examined the role of women in leadership in the country (Reilly, 2009; Reilly, 2011; Reilly 2013; Reilly & Bauer, 2015). While the nation's leaders face continual challenges ranging from security for their people to strengthening of the infrastructure, two of the principal challenges remain the role of women in society and the education of children (Giustozzi, 2010; Rubin, 2006).

Although progress remains slow and uneven, many women continue to emerge as leaders both within the nation and on the global stage. Their stories serve as a means of beginning a broader query that may lead to insight into the issues women leaders face in Afghanistan. Profiled here are two women whose lives embody the persistence and resilience necessary to survive war and devastation and to thrive in the midst of chronic trauma: Zohra Yusuf Daoud, adviser to the First Lady of Afghanistan, a renowned journalist, and the first and only Miss Afghanistan; and Hadisa Miokhail, a school headmistress from one of Afghanistan's most prestigious schools for girls. Each embodies the values of Rabia Balkhi, and lives a life committed to building a nation where each individual enjoys basic human rights and dignity. Their stories provide insight and inspiration for addressing the seemingly intractable problems women face in Afghanistan today.

ZOHRA YUSUF DAOUD

She sat with her child on her lap, not much more than a child herself, the brilliant orange fabric the color of the setting sun, surrounding her in cloud-like billows, her luminous dark eyes telling me more than her words. Rashida's stepfather had sold her to an abusive older man and her only means of escape was to the women's shelter where I had met her.

Zohra Yusuf Daoud, who holds the extraordinary distinction as the country's first and only Miss Afghanistan, is also one of its most respected television journalists. Through her invitation on that particular day, along with her daughter, Sara, who was on summer break from Stanford University, we met with the director of one of the few women's shelters in the entire country. As the young women shared sweet summer melon with us, more opened up and told us their stories—horrific tales of beatings, burnings, mutilations, and rape—degradation of every sort. A return to their families could result in an honor killing or their own suicide, but through the shelter, hope for a future emerged. The young women received job training, education, food, clothing, and a roof over their heads.

Zohra was born in Kabul, the daughter of an American-trained physician who was himself born in Kabul. She grew up in a family that respected education and expected her to pursue higher education. She completed a degree in French literature at the University of Kabul and became a journalist. But only a few years before that, in the 1970s when she was still a high school student, an educator from her school approached her and suggested she participate in what would become the first and only Miss Afghanistan beauty pageant ever held in the country. Poised and articulate, she competed against 100 other young women and won the title. Zohra said that until 9/11, she rarely spoke of her crown, but that the US attack on Afghanistan propelled her tiny country onto the global stage and, with it, many of its leaders.

The country's women, portrayed principally as backward and illiterate, needed a champion to balance this perspective. So, the former beauty queen stepped forward to provide insight into the Afghanistan in which she grew up. Even today, few individuals in the West understand that women enjoyed reasonable freedoms up to the point of the Soviet invasion: they frequently dressed in clothing of their choice—not in the burqa—sang, danced, and attended school. Even though the presence was small, there were women in leadership and women activists even in the 1970s—in the parliament, in the media, and elsewhere. Yes, Afghanistan was a very poor country even then, but it was in the decades to come that women's rights would devolve nearly completely.

As the international community's security forces continue to depart Afghanistan—those who have been the lead actors on the stage for so long—Zohra asks, "Who are the understudies?" While Pakistan gets most of the publicity as one of the likely nations of great influence, Iran is perhaps the bigger threat. Pakistan—or at least its militants—is to some degree the bully on the playground, creating military conflicts over the border and then slipping away. Iran, on the other hand, is more subtle in creating divisiveness. Iranians are principally from the Shia sect of Islam, while the dominant sect in Afghanistan is the Sunni. Furthermore, the dominant ethnic tribe is the Pashto, the second largest the Tajik, and the third the Hazara people. Sectarian and tribal clashes require one to ask their origin. The complex, geopolitical circumstances warrant continual monitoring. As its geographic neighbors seek greater influence in Afghanistan, will the country have the ability to contain unwanted suitors?

It was the current president of Afghanistan, Ashraf Ghani, who first referred to Afghanistan as an emerging "narco-mafia state" when he served as its Minister of Finance in 2003. Afghanistan is the greatest producer of opium poppies in the world. While there has been some success in some provinces in replacing the poppy with a more lucrative crop, the saffron crocus, even this small advance is threatened by various players. When acres of the fledgling blooms are destroyed, is it Iran, which is also a producer of saffron, is it the Taliban, whose supply chain with heroin, and not saffron, is better established, or is it both who seek its demise? Zohra wonders if the war in Afghanistan is less one of ideology and religion and more one of drugs.

Zohra identifies two critical priorities for Afghanistan during what she says may be the country's last chance at modernity. The first is establishing a clear strategic focus on development in rural communities. The second is establishing stronger international reach and relationships with nations who share similar cultural and religious traditions with Afghanistan. While it appears that these twin goals may seem contradictory, she believes they represent an approach that benefits all citizens of her country.

Rural communities in Afghanistan are complicated ecosystems. It is well established that even in the second decade of the 21st century, the Taliban and other militant groups govern areas of some provinces. If a member of the village needs redress for a problem and if those village elders happen to be the Taliban, he will receive the support through this local governance. Even so, upward to 70 percent of the population is food insecure and the government identifies around 45 percent of those in rural areas living below the poverty line. And these are problems that militants have not been able to resolve.

Zohra believes that the work in the villages should focus on establishing women's councils where the national government's leadership listen to their problems and support change. While the government cannot resolve terrorism, as this is an international problem, it can take small steps with its people to alleviate suffering. Those who undertake to work village to village, enrolling women in leadership for change, and who seek to establish schools, suitable healthcare, economic opportunities beyond growing poppies, and other hallmarks of civil society, will find open doors.

While it is difficult to find a silver lining in diaspora and war, Zohra points out that two results of these national tragedies can serve to bring change to rural Afghanistan. During the decades of conflicts, over six million Afghans have fled to other nations. While living in a refugee camp presents extraordinary hardships, the mere fact that people have seen a world not their own and possibilities for a different life awakens the imagination. Zohra says, moreover, that for all the bad publicity the West—and especially the United States—receives for its continued involvement in Afghanistan, one of the values that the West has transmitted to a fairly successful degree is that of a free press.

As a journalist, Zohra observes the changes her country has experienced and notes that print, radio, and television journalism have blossomed for the most part. Although in the past few years, journalists have experienced and reported increased incidents of violence directly related to their work, the free press remains one of the success stories. Even the rural poor have radio and television access, which gives the most remote corner of the country access to a variety of news outlets and information. Imagine, she says, if an individual in an isolated village sees her in a broadcast, advocating for education and women's rights. It is a powerful antidote to their daily plight. Even with high rates of illiteracy, listening and seeing can transform cultural values. Zohra, who regularly visits poor communities, finds a slow thawing of even the most conservative men toward education for their children and the dream of a better tomorrow.

Malaysia and Indonesia are Muslim nations that Zohra identifies as those with which Afghanistan should establish greater partnerships. These nations possess a greater open-mindedness toward women in leadership and women's rights. They can serve as much-needed role models for her Muslim nation in ways that Muslim nations which demonstrate less tolerance of women do not. Zohra wonders if progress for her country can result in Kabul looking similar to Dubai. If conservative Shia Arabs can build a jewel in the desert, are economic progress and advocacy for women possible simultaneously for her country?

The focus of Zohra's work is not to change the culture or religion of her people, but to reclaim its heritage, which at numerous times in Afghan history reflects protection of and advocacy for women. She envisions her work as a journalist to expand as a mentor to younger journalists who lack historical perspective of the country. In the memories of the past are the cherished values that should be reflected in the present. Women, above all, should be respected. That is worth advocating for.

HADISA MIOKHAIL

The principal of Rabia Balkhi High School in Kabul looks past the gardens lush with roses and pomegranates, toward the newly built library that houses a state-of-the art computer lab, a capacious conference room that frequently draws meetings of the Ministry of Education, and a growing collection of books in Dari, Pashto, and English. Rabia Balkhi is one of the most prestigious high schools in Afghanistan, serving students in grades 7–12 from families both privileged and poor, and providing a curriculum that prepares its children for college. Her charges, clad in their school uniforms of black tunic, trousers, and white hijab, surround a visitor, clamoring for help to gain scholarships at foreign universities since so few openings exist for girls in Afghanistan. Hadisa Miokhail smiles at their enthusiasm and marvels at the slow and steady progress made at rebuilding this famous school for girls that just over a decade before lay in rubble following the Taliban's relentless assault not only on it, but on the practice of educating girls.

Hadisa, who was herself a student at Rabia Balkhi many years ago, was one of the rare girls to attend Kabul University, where she studied mathematics, and subsequently returned as a teacher. Over time she became the head of the mathematics department and then the vice headmistress. Finally, she was named headmistress following the fall of the Taliban by her teachers' unanimous request to the government. She has remained at Rabia Balkhi these many years and through many conflicts—the Soviet invasion and occupation, the civil war with the Mujahedeen, and the Taliban's control of Afghanistan.

While many Afghans understandably fled the country through the decades of conflict, Hadisa remained and found a way to survive each chapter of horrors facing her beloved school. Although the story is not for the faint of heart, she believes it is essential to relay it in its graphic detail so that a visitor can appreciate fully how far the school has come in the subsequent decade. In Islam, she says, there is always light after the dark, and she believes the tale is one of hope in the midst of despair. The civil war, which took place from 1993 to 1996, was a tragic

time for Afghans—an age as dark as the age of the Taliban. The school became the epicenter of battles, drawing fighters from Pakistan and Iran, and finally was nearly completely destroyed by rocket attacks. Many fighters died on the property on which the school rests, and it remained littered with corpses. If a hanging occurred, the body would be disposed of in the well that provided water for the school. For some period of time, the school disbanded and reconvened elsewhere in the city.

When the Taliban took over her beloved school and forced her teachers, students, and her to stay home for five years, she, like thousands of women, ran an illegal school for girls and boys and continued to teach, knowing that certain imprisonment, torture, or death was her fate if she were to be discovered. Just days before the Taliban converted Rabia Balkhi into a museum whose purpose was to honor itself, the United States invaded and once again, the school became hers. The interim government requested that all teachers and administrators return to their schools and with nothing more than a signature, the faculty and staff were together once again. Amid the carnage of corpses and razed buildings, little remained but her dream to rebuild the school once again.

Even with nothing but destruction, her teachers and she were happy. While one of the larger challenges was the reality of teaching children who were five years behind in their schooling, the teachers and she worked day and night to help them catch up. More remarkably, they taught without receiving any pay. The children were their future and deserving of their help. In Hadisa's mind, she could succumb to the horror of what they had all witnessed and endured or she could use the devastation as a means to impel her to make a difference in the lives of girls. Not in the same way, but different and, Inshallah, better.

There are other Hadisas in Afghanistan in K–12 and higher education leadership, but precious few. The number of women teachers exceeds the number of women university professors, and both are still extremely few in number, but leadership positions, then, attract far fewer women candidates for consideration than men. They likely have less education, professional training, and experience than their male counterparts. Even those such as Hadisa, who do possess the qualifications to achieve national leadership roles, frequently elect to remain in positions where they can directly touch the lives of young women.

In addition, family responsibilities often preclude them from taking on roles of even greater importance. She is quick to point out that the women did not cause the wars, did not participate in them, and were solely victims or casualties. Women, instead, were those who rebuilt the schools, with an eye toward peace and security for children. She also believes that her work—and that of all women in educational leadership should extend beyond the schoolhouse door. Following the establishment of the interim government, Hadisa, who had lost everything in the war, moved into a poor neighborhood where not only were most families illiterate, but not interested in sending their children to school. Slowly over time, in conversation with the families, she convinced them to send their children to school. In the end, the work must come from the heart. The efforts of women educational leaders have helped to bring about a national conversation regarding women and leadership in Afghan society. On more than one occasion, the country's president has invited Hadisa to serve as Minister of Education for the Islamic Republic of Afghanistan—a position for which she seems eminently qualified. Each time, however, she turns down the call to serve the nation because she must care for an elderly mother. What remains unclear is if she feels she has the experience and political savvy necessary to navigate a man's world or if holding such a powerful role even matters to her. In her world of Rabia Balkhi, far fewer men tread the path to her door and make demands.

Hadisa has, however, received management training through the Ministry of Education in recent years and passed their examinations that certify her to be a principal. While the training has been of benefit, Hadisa believes that her practical experience of many years has equipped her to successfully lead her school and influence education policy and practice more broadly. When she does enter the world of men at the Ministry of Education, she commands their respect and they do attend to her recommendations. While recruiting women into prominent leadership roles remains elusive for many reasons, what is consistent among women leaders throughout K–12 and higher education is the high level of commitment to and motivation for education in general and the success of girls and women in particular.

THE ROAD TOWARD EQUALITY

Will the rise of your memories Your light blue
  memories
In the eyes of fishes weary of floodwaters and fear-
  ful of the rain of oppression become a reflection
  of hope?

—Nadia Anjuman

It is justice, not charity that is wanting in the world.

—Mary Wollstonecraft

If I were to present Zohra and Hadisa with the profiles I have penned, they would likely respond, "Your eyes are beautiful." This Pashto reply to a compliment is a way of deflecting attention from oneself, as humility is

a highly cherished Afghan value. These women do not seek personal acknowledgment for the work that they do. While appreciative of national and international recognition, they embody the spirit of that Afghan phrase and are quick to refocus attention on the seemingly insurmountable tasks at hand—education, economic opportunities, and basic respect for the human rights of women. They believe that the prestige and power resulting from their accomplishments come with a moral imperative to use them for the good of the country. Zohra and Hadisa share many common values and goals for Afghanistan. Three of those goals are the necessity of transforming cultural values and societal norms that support women; a focus on reconstruction that includes women in leadership; and tireless advocacy for gender equality and women's empowerment.

TRANSFORMATION OF CULTURAL VALUES AND SOCIETAL NORMS

In its yearly report regarding the progress made in Afghanistan to implement the Law on Elimination of Violence Against Women (EVAW law), the United Nations Assistance Mission in Afghanistan (UNAMA) asserted, "Widespread harmful practices and violence against women and girls have long prevented women from participating in public life and blocked their voices from being heard in political and decision-making forums including initiatives aimed at promoting peace and reconciliation" (United Nations Assistance Mission in Afghanistan, 2013, p. 2).

In a nation where an alarming 92 percent of women believe it is acceptable for their husbands to beat them for a variety of reasons, they unquestionably have a long way to go with transformation of cultural norms and practices, and implementation of its laws (Central Statistics Organization, 2012). Nevertheless, the country is replete with historical periods where women did enjoy some amount of freedom (Ahmed-Ghosh, 2003). It is therefore a fallacious argument that frames Afghan cultural transformation as anti-Islamic or pro-Western, when the traditions that do support gender equality and women's rights are a part of its historical tapestry. Afghans need only to appropriate what has always been part of the warp and weft of society.

RECONSTRUCTION AND THE ROLE OF WOMEN

As the combat mission of the International Security Assistance Force draws to a close and Afghanistan has increasing responsibility for its security and reconstruction, several key concerns emerge. As the top producer of opium in the world, this crop remains the centerpiece of its economic sector (Special Inspector General for Afghanistan Reconstruction [SIGAR], 2014). Opium poppies occupy only 3 percent of available agricultural land, yet it is Afghanistan's largest export. The opium economy provides over 400,000 full-time jobs and supports additional jobs in parts of the legitimate economy (SIGAR, 2014). This undermines Afghanistan's legitimacy with the international community, thereby threatening its monetary investment in the country's reconstruction. Its by-products include increased corruption and the financing of criminal entities such as the Taliban. Reconstruction efforts in rural communities that address the underlying conditions of poor security, poor governance, and limited economic opportunities are the principal means of combatting the opium economy. It is in efforts such as these that rural women, with support, can become the force for change in their communities.

Community development councils that foster women's leadership, such as the one established in Badghis Province with the support of the United Nations Development Project (UNDP), can promote and implement changes in civil society that benefit everyone (UNDP, 2012). Local decision-making regarding reconstruction and attention to local priorities that include women "ensure[s] that Afghan women benefit from stronger protection from violence and improved access to justice, better delivery of public services and representation in government institutions, a stronger voice in communities and in national political processes, and expanded economic rights and opportunities" (UNDP, 2012, p. 27). The work of women is of incalculable benefit to the community and to the nation.

While the undertaking to transform Afghanistan is daunting, its partnerships with the international community decrease the possibility of a return to a country isolated from the world. It is incumbent, however, that the international community contributes to UNDP's efforts, which are funded solely from voluntary contributions from UN member states and multilateral and other organizations. The principal donors at present are the United States (the largest donor), Japan (the second largest donor), and Germany (the third largest donor). Much room exists for support from other nation states, such as those from the nonaligned nations.

GENDER EQUALITY AND WOMEN'S EMPOWERMENT

Zohra and Hadisa do not stand alone in seeking equality and empowerment for women. It is the consistent and widespread message from a growing number within the country and from the international community (UNDP, 2013). Herein lies one of the keys for national transformation: consistency of messaging from the many sectors—government, media, nongovernmental organizations, and education. The degree to which these sectors have congruent goals is the degree to which authentic change can occur. Yet, it appears that if changes in policy or the law affect women deleteriously, it is invariably from Parliament or from one of the many ministries. This may appear to be incongruous behavior coming from the very entities that have supported equality and empowerment in the past, but the national players come from an ever-changing roster of individuals who have varied educational backgrounds, experience with human rights work, and agendas.

Unbelievably, even the debate over universal human rights has not ended in Afghanistan (Human Rights Watch, 2014). While this remains a key challenge for proponents of women's rights, the watchdog role is critical so that policies and laws that subtly, or not so subtly, attempt to erode hard-fought gains do not take hold. Common purpose requires a continual emphasis on building trust and transparency, for then each provides checks and balances to the other. The vigilance required to monitor its parliament, ministries, and other agencies is backbreaking work that never takes a holiday. Nevertheless, it is critical to stand ready to take action at any moment and to marshal the international community if elected officials put forth initiatives for neodraconian policies.

THE PATH FORWARD

> There is a path to the top of even the highest mountain.
>
> —Afghan Proverb

A few years back, Zamina, a young Afghan girl from Kandahar, would call into a talk show when people could share short poems called landays. This type of poetic form, which its authors typically share aloud, is often used to express frustrations, lamentations, and protestations. In a culture where over a third of women believe it is acceptable for their husbands to beat them for burning the meal, it is no wonder that the actions of its girls and women are subject to severe scrutiny. Family members can construe any form of public sentiment—or even private sentiment—as dishonorable. In Afghan society, little is worse than the prospect of shame raining down on a family. When Zamina was discovered writing these poems and worse still, sharing them on radio, her brothers beat her. In what would become the greatest protest of her brief life, she committed self-immolation (Richardson, 2014).

Whether poet, politician, professor, or member of the press, the women of Afghanistan remain in harm's way. Educated or illiterate, their lives are at risk. Even so, Zohra and Hadisa recognize how critical it is to keep Afghanistan in the hearts and minds of the world, however war-weary the country and the international community may be. Likewise, they strive to keep the world in the hearts and minds of their people. There is a path. There is always a path. These women work unceasingly to chart it.

REFERENCES

Ahmed-Ghosh, H. (2003). A history of women in Afghanistan: Lessons learnt for the future. *Journal of International Women's Studies, 4*(3), 1–14. Retrieved from http://vc.bridgew.edu/jiws/vol4/iss3/1

Associated Press. (2014, November 16). Suicide attack in Afghan capital wounds female MP. Reading Eagle. Retrieved from http://www.readingeagle.com/ap/article/suicide-attack-in-afghan-capital-wounds-female-mp

Bambuck, M., & Naiemullah, N. (2013, September 15). Helmand province's most senior female police officer shot in Afghanistan. *The Telegraph*. Retrieved from https://www.telegraph.co.uk/news/worldnews/asia/afghanistan/10310801/Helmand-provinces-most-senior-female-police-officer-shot-in-Afghanistan.html

Central Statistics Organization (CSO) & UNICEF. (2012). *Monitoring the situation of women and children: Afghanistan multiple indicator cluster survey 2011–2012*. Kabul, Afghanistan: Central Statistics Organization (CSO) and UNICEF. Retrieved from http://cso.gov.af/Content/files/AMICS-Jun24-2012-FINAL.pdf

Commission on the Status of Women. (2002). *Discrimination against women and girls in Afghanistan*. New York: United Nations Economic and Social Council.

Giustozzi, A. (2010, February). *Nation building is not for all: The politics of education in Afghanistan*. New York, NY: Afghanistan Analysts Network.

Hackel, J. (2012, July 11). Afghanistan: Pragmatists significant voice in Taliban, says former diplomat. Retrieved from Public Radio International website: https://www.pri.org/stories/2012-07-11/afghanistan-pragmatists-significant-voice-taliban-says-former-diplomat

Hamid, Z. (2012, October 1). Afghanistan Monitoring Report 2012. Kabul, Afghanistan: Afghan Women's Network.

Human Rights Watch. (2014). World report 2014: Afghanistan. Retrieved from https://www.hrw.org/world-report/2014/country-chapters/afghanistan?page=1

Nemat, O. A., & Samadi, A. (2012). *Forgotten heroes: Afghan women killed in impunity, ignored in justice*. Kabul, Afghanistan: Afghanistan Rights Monitor.

Popalzai, M. (2012, May 29). Official: 160 girls poisoned at Afghan school. Retrieved from https://www.cnn.com/2012/05/29/world/asia/afghanistan-girls-poisoned/index.html

Reilly, E. C. (2009, April). Women in K–12 education leadership in Afghanistan: Progress, successes, and challenges. Paper presented at the meeting of American Educational Research Association, San Diego, CA.

Reilly, E. C. (2011). Women of higher education leadership in Afghanistan: Progress, successes, and challenges. In H. Macha, C. Fahrenwald, & Q. Bauer (Eds.), *Gender and education: Towards new strategies of leadership and power*. Stuttgart, Germany: Holtzbrinck/Macmillan.

Reilly, E. C. (2013). Higher education and K–12 women leadership in Afghanistan: Prospects and challenges. *NIEW Journal, 5*, 93–110.

Reilly, E. C., & Bauer, Q. (Eds.). (2015). *Women leading education across the continents: Overcoming the barriers*. Lanham, MD: Rowman & Littlefield.

Richardson, L. (2014, March 5). The secret lives of Afghanistan's female poets. *Slate*. Retrieved from http://www.slate.com/blogs/behold/2014/03/05/eliza_griswold_and_seamus_murphy_document_afghanistan_s_landays_in_i_am.html

Rubin, B. R. (2006, March 14). Afghanistan's uncertain transition from turmoil to normalcy (CSR #12). New York, NY: Council on Foreign Relations.

Special Inspector General for Afghanistan Reconstruction. (2014, October 30). Quarterly report to the United States Congress. Retrieved from http://www.sigar.mil/pdf/quarterlyreports/2014-10-30qr-intro-section1.pdf

United Nations Assistance Mission in Afghanistan & United Nations Office of the High Commissioner for Human Rights. (2013). A way to go: An update on implementation of the law on elimination of violence against women in Afghanistan. Retrieved from https://unama.unmissions.org/sites/default/files/unama_evaw_law_report_2013_revised_on_16_dec_2013.pdf

United Nations Development Project. (2012). Afghanistan human development indicators.

United Nations Development Project. (2013). 2013 Afghanistan annual report: Results in focus. Retrieved from http://www.af.undp.org/content/dam/afghanistan/docs/APRs/UNDP%20Afghanistan%20Annual%20Progress%20Report%202013.pdf

United Press International. (2012). Afghan provincial women's leader killed. Retrieved from https://www.upi.com/Afghan-provincial-womens-leader-killed/94021355156385

Chapter 3

Women's Leadership in Santa Isabel, Solomon Islands Secondary Schools

A Case Study

Susanne Maezama

The conceptualization and value of leadership in educational organizations both represent and reproduce the gender and power relations that exist in larger society (Fine, 2007). In the international research literature, a common feature of social justice discourse with regard to women's leadership is women's lack of representation in formal educational leadership positions, even though they are overrepresented in the teaching population (Grogan & Shakeshaft, 2011; Strachan, 2009).

Embedded organizational structures, workplace policies, and cultural practices continue to marginalize women in the area of leadership and feature men, valorizing "male modes of thinking, feeling, acting, and forming identities while devaluing their female counterparts" (Fine & Buzzanell, 2000, p. 130). This observation has encouraged Fine (2007) to further posit that the gendered nature of organizations shows "a masculine bias in leadership practices that devalues women's ways of leading" (p. 179).

Further to these debates is the nature of cultural context. While the majority of literature exploring women's lack of representation draws from a Western and Eurocentric position, examples which relate to the indigenous and cultural leadership of women and, in the case of this chapter, the leadership of women from the Solomon Islands, are sparse (some recent exceptions include Akao, 2008; Elisha, 2012; Pollard, 2006). This region has lacked consideration in the current educational leadership discourses associated with women and educational leadership.

Recent scholarship (e.g., Carli & Eagly, 2012; Ely & Rhode, 2010; Grogan & Shakeshaft, 2011; Sinclair, 2013) argues persuasively that those who engage in research and work in the area of women and leadership must first seek to illuminate and then act to dismantle the emotional and physical barriers that exist for women seeking leadership roles. Similarly, Blackmore (1995) states that women leaders themselves have an obliga-

tion to make a difference, "and the lens of privilege . . . requires women leaders to consider their position, to better understand how and why they came to be in that position and how they can use that position to challenge and transform exclusive images of leadership into more inclusive ones" (p. 35).

The qualitative research study presented in this chapter investigated the leadership experiences of 10 women leaders located in one cultural context, the unique island of Santa Isabel in the Solomon Islands. Semistructured interviews and focus group discussions were engaged to explore women's leadership perceptions and experiences and how these ideas were realized in the way they practiced leadership. Findings indicated that women's perceptions of, and participation in, leadership was immersed in a cultural context which was founded on a belief of matrilineal leadership culture providing opportunities for women to have power and respect in community contexts but not necessarily organizational contexts.

However, the findings also illustrated the challenges met by these women when they sought to extend their leadership practices beyond the home and their close communities, into organizations. Although a complex concept to negotiate, extending the cultural discourses of matrilineal leadership into educational leadership contexts may provide an alternative and supporting mechanism to enhance the representation of women in formal educational leadership positions in the Solomon Islands.

WOMEN'S LEADERSHIP IN THE SOLOMON ISLANDS

A number of studies undertaken in the Solomon Islands (Akao, 2008; Elisha, 2012; Liki, 2010; Malasa, 2007; Pollard, 2006; Scales & Teakeni, 2006; Sisiolo, 2010) confirm that women's leadership is significantly influenced by notions of culture, Christianity, and colonialism. However, Akao and Strachan (2012), in particular, claim that "different cultures and Christianity also play important roles in how gender is constructed" (p. 1). This assumes, then, that the way women view and experience leadership in educational settings is highly contextual and that in the Solomon Islands it may also be different.

Cubillo and Brown's (2003) research highlights these points further, theorizing across the "macro-socio-political level, the meso-organizational level and the micro level which concerns the individual herself" (p. 281). The cultural and social structure that separates society into male and female arenas is also a major obstacle to women's access to leadership positions (Oplatka, 2006). Leadership positions are perceived as belonging to male members of society and women should refrain from attempting to attain this kind of position (Oplatka, 2006). The influence of tradition and culture has also been given as an explanation as to why women are underrepresented in leadership positions in Melanesia.

Strachan et al. (2007) argue that in the Melanesian context, "culture significantly impacts on female's ability to participate in education and decision making at all levels, including educational leadership" (p. 104). In most developing countries, women's progress into senior leadership positions has been slow and irregular (Oplatka, 2006; Strachan, 2009).

In most Melanesian cultural groups, leadership and power have been said to be traditionally a male preserve, upheld by the "big man" and "chief" and further authenticated and strengthened by both church and colonial hierarchies in every aspect of society (Akao, 2008; Kilavanwa, 2004; Pollard, 2006; Strachan & Saunders, 2007). In these societies, leadership is essentially male dominated and thus, in most cases, males are the gatekeepers to accessing education and leadership positions (Strachan & Saunders, 2007). This gate-keeping marginalizes women and generally excludes them from aspects of society such as education.

The matrilineal leadership culture depicts an alternative view that could enhance the representation of women in formal leadership positions. Viewing women to have power and respect in this context demonstrates the many roles women can play in creating change in society. The notion that the matrilineal leadership culture recognizes the importance of founding strong leadership in the home may be seen as a pillar for educational and formal leadership organizations. In this way, both women and men may be encouraged to see leadership from both patrilineal and matrilineal perspectives.

Women's educational leadership in this context refers to women's ideas around leadership and how these ideas are realized in the way women practice leadership in a range of educative contexts. This concurs with Strachan's

(2005) claim that "educational contexts are not just confined to the formal education sector: they exist in many contexts" (p. 48), such as in the village, church organization, and education institutions. Women's educational leadership in these various contexts in Santa Isabel Island forms the context for this study.

Despite the Solomon Islands having ratified the United Nations Convention on the Elimination of Discrimination Against Women (CEDAW), Solomon Islands women continue to be almost invisible in formal leadership positions because of the cultural, male, hegemonic practices that deny women access to equal participation in society. However, some researchers critique this position, arguing that this is "not wholly supported by historical evidence" (Scales & Teakeni, 2006, p. 78). Scales and Teakeni (2006) contend that in the matrilineal societies of the Solomon Islands, there were women leaders.

Bogesi (1948) explains that "Santa Isabel women are sometimes figured as chiefs" (p. 216) and, in Western and Guadalcanal Provinces, clan leaders were sometimes women (Kari, 2004). Thus, Scales and Teakeni (2006) questioned the prevailing assumptions about women and leadership in traditional society, arguing that in some "pre-colonial Melanesian societies, there was no categorical necessity for all leaders to be male" (p. 78). They further stated that the idea that only men can be leaders may well be a result of the rigid gender concepts brought about by colonialism in the village headman system and the beliefs of missionaries.

Furthermore, in Melanesian societies today, women are questioning women's roles and status. This is in large part due to the increasing number of women who have been exposed to Western values through formal education, overseas travel, mass media, and modern technologies (Pollard, 2006; Tongamoa, 1988; Tuivaga, 1988). Some women who are well educated are beginning to question and see the gender division of labor as "unfair, degrading and biased against women" (Tongamoa, 1988, p. 89).

This is in contrast to the Melanesian view that this labor division is complementary to the traditional system. Complementary or not, such labor division denies equal rights for women, thus continuously affirming their inferiority and subordination to men (Tongamoa, 1988). Interestingly, Pollard (2000) also commented that even though women's role and status are undergoing rapid change, there is still reluctance among the women themselves to abandon tradition entirely.

Female participation in education in Melanesia is highest at the primary level but, at more advanced levels, the numbers start to lessen. Generally, more males than females are represented at every educational level because opportunities for education are largely taken by men. Also, because education in Melanesia is not compulsory (Strachan, Samuel, & Takaro, 2007), females' access to education is lower because of the privileging of males' education; where males are encouraged to pursue further education and girls are not seriously encouraged (Strachan et al., 2007; Tuivaga, 1988). As Pollard (2000) posits, "The inequality of participation in higher education does not necessarily reflect official policy or bias in favor of males; rather it is the consequence of the people's traditional world view, which includes the notion that a woman's place is at home" (p. 6).

Pollard (2000) suggested that basic changes in some of the fundamental attitudes, values, and beliefs are required before full gender equality can be realized. One such change may be in the perceptions that parents have about allowing girls to attend schools. Parents need to be aware of the benefits of educating girls. Strachan et al. (2007) also raise similar sentiments and suggest that, "While it is important to preserve those aspects of culture that help sustain and enrich people, it is also important to change those aspects that limit people's opportunities based on their gender. Both males and females need to be equally valued in all aspects of their lives, including education" (p. 105).

The underrepresentation of women in educational leadership positions as well as in other formal sectors in Melanesia begins with gaining access to education. Since girls' access to education is limited, this may create a flow-on effect that impedes the participation of women economically and in decision making at all levels in the society, including educational leadership (Strachan, 2009).

While Pollard (2006), Akao (2008), and Elisha's (2012) work was informative and highlighted important issues inhibiting effective leadership and women's educational leadership participation, they did so in a very general way, and from a patriarchal culture, assuming that the views shared were homogenous. Their research focused solely on women in educational leadership settings and allows us to see into the experiences of the women leaders, as well as those who experience working with women leaders.

These experiences are unique to women in Melanesia, especially the influence of the cultural context on women leaders in schools. For example, in Akao's (2008) study, Solomon Islands women expressed that the influences of the cultural patriarchal norms impacted on their leadership and that they felt discriminated against. Akao suggests that the reason Melanesian women are still struggling to address gender equity issues is the absence of women's experiences and the silence of women's voices in a "big man" leadership society. Elisha's (2012) study, however, found that teachers valued and appreciated

the leadership of women principals. She suggests that people's attitudes toward accepting women leaders are improving, albeit slowly.

MATRILINEAL CULTURE IN SANTA ISABEL ISLAND IN THE SOLOMON ISLANDS

The absence of a patriarchal culture in Santa Isabel makes the context for this research unique. Santa Isabel Island is one of the six large islands that make up the state of the Solomon Islands. Santa Isabel has a total land area of 4,136 square kilometers (Peterson, Hamilton, Pita, Atu, & James, 2012), with a sparsely settled population of about 26,000 residing in villages that range in size from 50 to a few hundred (Solomon Islands Government, 2011).

Overland transport infrastructure is minimal, which makes reaching the interior only possible via foot tracks. Most villages lie on the coast and people usually rely on outboard motor boats, interisland ferries, and traditional canoes for transport. On the island of Santa Isabel, 96 percent of the population belong to a single church, the Anglican Church of Melanesia (Kinch, 2004), and Christianity is an important part of Solomon Islands culture.

The current political structure recognizes the importance of local leadership that comprises the family leaders, village leaders, district house of chiefs, and the Isabel Council of chiefs. This structure supports and extends leadership from the village level through to the provincial level and gives the traditional leadership in Santa Isabel a greater role and partnership with the provincial government and church leadership. Importantly, it acknowledges women and their need to reclaim their chiefly/leadership roles at the village and house of chiefs' levels, playing complementary roles to their male counterparts (Whittington, Ospina, & Pollard, 2006).

Santa Isabel has a deeply entrenched matrilineal society where women hold numerous informal roles associated with power and leadership within their communities. This understanding may relate to their cultural beliefs and practices that land ownership and descent is passed through a successive generation of women. Bogesi (1948), in particular, affirms that the existence of the matrilineal culture on the island can be traced way back before the missionaries and traders landed in the 1800s.

Similarly, Naramana (1987) concludes that "people had already firmly established themselves into three tribal systems with women ancestresses under a tribal chief" (p. 42) when traders and missionaries arrived. This suggests that matrilineal beliefs and practices in tribal connections, land ownership, and roles and responsibilities are embodied in Santa Isabellians' ways of thinking and doing.

The Santa Isabel matrilineal beliefs and practices in leadership are centered on land and kinship. It is significant that leadership is aligned with land and genealogy rituals and responsibilities. This assumption illustrates that leadership is crucial in the social structure of co-existence. It is vital for people to know their place and relationships within the extended family structure as well as within the tribal structure.

WOMEN'S LEADERSHIP IN SANTA ISABEL MATRILINEAL CULTURE

Santa Isabel women display empowering and influential leadership roles in both traditional and contemporary times (Pollard, 2006; Poyer, 1996; Scales & Teakeni, 2006; Whittington et al., 2006). Such influence is displayed through word of mouth, participation and decision making in their families and communities, and sometimes at the national policy level. For example, when Solomon Islands women became eligible to vote in 1967, Lily Poznanski, a woman from Santa Isabel, was the first elected female member in the National Parliament (Pollard, 2006). At the provincial level, there are currently two women provincial members and, at the community level, women participate in decision making.

The contention that a number of women have reclaimed leadership in contemporary instances (Pollard, 2006; Scales & Teakeni, 2006; Whittington et al., 2006) suggests much unrealized cultural potential for women in matrilineal cultures to take up leadership roles. Anecdotal evidence shows that the majority of women who take up leadership roles come from matrilineal cultures.

That said, men are usually seen as the women's spokespersons on decisions reached and often become the heads of the households. They dominate formal leadership positions in their communities, church, and provincial government. Their visibility as regional and political leaders has "influenced people to associate traditional leadership with men and has threatened to undermine women's traditional high status in Santa Isabel" (Whittington et al., 2006, p. 71).

The Educational Context of Santa Isabel

The Santa Isabel Education Authority, manages 60 early childhood centers, 20 primary schools, seven secondary schools, and two technical and vocational centers (Ministry of Education and Human Resources Development, 2009). However, although these schools exist within the Santa Isabel community context, where women claim to have power and authority in the local communities, there are hardly any women principals in the secondary schools, and very few women headteachers in the primary sector.

Also, it is not surprising to observe that there are elements of culture, colonization, and Christianity in the way education processes of curriculum, recruitment, and teacher promotion are structured. Although "sex-disaggregated data is not systematically collected" (Strachan, 2009, p. 103) in the Solomon Islands and quite difficult to obtain, the representation of women in educational leadership positions is low (Akao, 2008). For example, of the 211 secondary school principals and deputy principals, only 13 percent are female (Ministry of Education and Human Resources Development, 2009).

Whittington et al. (2006) argue that inadequate consideration of the role of culture in shaping attitudes to gender and leadership constitutes a major impediment to change. Therefore, this research intentionally engages in a process of remembering and exploring the traditional and current educational leadership experiences of women in the Santa Isabel matrilineal culture.

Research Design

This study employed an interpretive, qualitative, case study research approach to gain a rich insight into the influences of the matrilineal culture on women leaders' ideas about leadership and how these were realized in the way they practiced leadership. Individual interviews were conducted with 10 women leaders drawn from formal educational settings (schools and higher education contexts) in the Bugotu region of Santa Isabel. The questions that guided this research were:

1. What are the influences of the matrilineal culture on women leaders' leadership beliefs and practices?
2. To what extent does the Santa Isabel matrilineal culture contribute to the formation of women leaders' matrilineal leadership cultural beliefs and practices?
3. How do women leaders practice leadership in the matrilineal culture?

Women shared their understandings and experiences of leadership with regard to both their work and community involvement. The interviews were transcribed and translated into English, and then analyzed using NVivo10 and thematic analysis (Braun & Clarke, 2006; Flick, 2014) to identify emerging themes. The emerging themes guided the second phase of data generation that involved three focus group discussions with some of the participants and a second round of individual interviews.

Findings

The findings illustrated some common understandings that the women held about leadership. Based on recurring themes that emerged from individual interview data and focus group discussion, key areas of findings were associated with the impact of matrilineal culture on women's positioning as leaders in their communities and homes.

THE IMPACT OF MATRILINEAL CULTURE ON WOMEN'S LEADERSHIP

Links to the Land

All 10 women leaders interviewed in this research indicated the powerful nature of matrilineal society and how this cultural foundation was influential in positioning women with regard to having power and respect in their communities. All women indicated this through comments that linked women to the land by birth and, in particular, the connection that women have to the land and the tribe through childbirth. The burying of the placenta and cord stump is culturally significant in that the return of the afterbirth into the ground establishes a relationship between women, as mothers, the land, and the tribe.

Some women leaders commented that the connection that mothers make with people and land played a significant part in forming the foundation for personal leadership. Iona commented, "In our culture in Santa Isabel, our women are foremost, very important, the reason being that the tribal land and lineage starts and ends with women as mothers. In our view, as far as leadership is concerned, this is why women were and are able to hold positions of power and leadership in the community."

Women leaders' beliefs about leadership may have been shaped by the embodied nature of the relationships founded from women's bodies (their "being"), which aligns with current relational leadership discourses. Many of the women believed this gave them the space and right to think highly of themselves because it was through this historical ritual that they connected future generations to the land and the tribe.

Iona stated, "I have strong beliefs that our women are very important to us because it is mothers who connect us to our land and our tribe," and this was a view shared by most. Hanai expressed that the worth of women as mothers is manifested in Solomon Islands culture through the respect people have for women: "This cultural practice is still very strong in Santa Isabel. Thus, people in this society listen to women when they are told to do or not to do something. They still respect and honor women."

It was not surprising that the majority of women leaders suggested that motherhood was recognized as important leadership because of the responsibility it carries to ensure the continuity of the tribe and culture. For example, Diana commented, "In Santa Isabel matrilineal culture, mothers are thought of very highly because it is through them that the tribe and culture stays alive. . . . This, nowadays, is understood as a position of leadership and responsibility that women hold."

However, although it would appear that practices associated with matrilineal culture provided leadership opportunities for women, there were also drawbacks and significant expectations linked to this which impacted upon women's choices and freedom within their communities. These aspects were linked to the women's learning experiences of leadership.

Strong Leadership Begins at Home

For all 10 women leaders, the genesis of their leadership was at home where granddaughters were watching their grandmothers and mothers teaching their daughters. The women recognized the importance of beginning and founding strong leadership in the home first. Iona felt happy and comfortable leading from her backyard. "Although women are quiet or silent, we have a place to speak. We are quiet and silent but we are the ones that do all the leading in our village and school. Our men only speak but it is we women who do most things."

The women leaders reported that they practiced leadership that was collaborative, consensus making, and caring. Furthermore, women also perceived their leadership was founded on the notion of service and working across networks. According to seven of the women leaders, these were significant aspects of their leadership practice. They also claimed that a fundamental feature of their leadership practice was their contribution to the greater good. Diana said, "In my thinking, the way a person gets to be a leader, I do not know, but maybe to help, in those ways. . . . It is to help in the area of women. . . . In the area of our lives, our children [and] our daily living."

The women leaders also suggested that a common practice in their leadership was providing for those less fortunate. Thus, sharing what you have with those who do not have and sharing what you have with your relatives and peers was the right thing to do. As Guri said, "One thing that is different in our matrilineal culture is the way we care for others, such that when people come and ask for food or other things we just give them freely." Resource redistribution was part of their leadership practice, Diana noted. "Our roles reach those of other dioceses and worldwide too. Our collection, we take them to those who are poor, those who have nothing to eat and those who are affected by natural disasters."

Their leadership practice is based on negotiating first, before resorting to other ways of solving issues. For example, women do not participate in war, but they negotiate with men involved in the warring factions. As Me'a said, "We handle conflicts through talk. This shows how we should solve problems and is an example of showing respect for people so that we can understand each other to work together." They all stated that while, in reality, they face many leadership challenges, this does not weaken their determination to keep practicing what they believe in.

All 10 women leaders took their challenges as helping them to stay firm in their leadership beliefs and purposes. According to Anika, "We must learn to be patient in what we do. This is one of the things we see in most women leaders, we never give up."

CHALLENGES AND BARRIERS TO EDUCATIONAL LEADERSHIP

The women also acknowledged a number of barriers which influenced their access to, and practice of, leadership in their educational contexts. The two main areas included a lack of recognition of matrilineal leadership practices in educational contexts and the paucity of role models for the women who wanted to develop their educational leadership.

ABSENCE OF MATRILINEAL CULTURAL PRACTICES IN FORMAL EDUCATION

The 10 women leaders reported that although there is a long cultural practice of matrilineal acceptance in the Santa Isabel context, this does not necessarily translate into the social sphere beyond the family domain. For example, Me'a expressed that "matrilineal cultural practices are absent in the formal education system." This indicates that the challenges that women experience in educational leadership begin with leadership development in the education system. Six of the 10 women expressed that they felt less important when working with men from patrilineal societies.

Iona stated, "In our school, there are men who come from patriarchal societies. These men do not understand and respect us, which makes us feel less important when working with them." All the women leaders felt they were not professionally supported to lead in formal education. Haidu stated, "Sometimes we feel that we are not encouraged to take up leadership roles in schools."

However, the challenge was that many of the tenets of matrilineal leadership that the women experienced in the community did not transfer to the contexts of education, where male dominated discourses of leadership held prominence and continued to exclude women from leadership opportunities.

LACK OF PROFESSIONAL SUPPORT

The lack of professional support and the lack of role models in their institutions was a concern for the women. Seven spoke about having resource people who would encourage women to speak out about feeling diminished and about the patriarchal practices in educational contexts. Haidu commented, "[these] feelings could impact on women's taking up leadership in education because this is a barrier that we have." Joska explicitly stated:

> These are our strong feelings that we want to share . . . that we women can be encouraged to speak up and out because this is the main thing that some of us are really having difficulty with. We women are very capable in the way we think, care, and in carrying out our leadership roles. It is only how to stand up and talk in front of the people in gatherings and meetings that some of us women are not confident to do.

IMPLICATIONS AND CONCLUDING THOUGHTS

In Santa Isabel, leadership that was founded on the intimate connection women have with the land and kinship ties positioned women to hold elements of power and respect in their communities. The matriarchal cultural practice of burying the placenta symbolizes the relationship between people and their environment. Likewise, this embodiment of belonging forms a powerful connection in regard to people's sense of place.

Thus, as Hanai stated, continuing the matriarchal practices of burying the placenta reaffirms women's connection to the land. It is these rituals and practices which affirm women's status in the community. Ensuring that this status manifests itself in other aspects of their lives, such as leadership inside and outside of the home, is paramount.

The genesis of women's leadership starts in their homes, in their sleeping, cooking, or birthing houses, under the shady trees, in their gardens, rivers, forests, and seas, where granddaughters are watching their grandmothers and mothers teaching their daughters. Locating leadership in this way affirms that leadership and context cannot be separated (Klenke, 2011).

The women leaders in this study created a worldview of leadership that shaped their beliefs from within their context. This is supported by Sharpnack (2011) who contends that contextual thinking is the basis for appropriate leadership beliefs and practices to emerge. The connection between leading in the community and leading in their educational institutions was not upheld and there were a number of barriers and challenges that the women faced in order to establish themselves in leadership roles in their employment.

The disjuncture between the women's experiences was shaped by Western ways of defining and practicing leadership and this continued to marginalize women in their workplace. Historical and cultural ways of leading became undervalued as women struggled to find space in male-dominated institutions. Fitzgerald (2003) adds that "position[ing] indigenous ways of knowing and leading at the centre of practice and theory" (p. 20) may contribute to changing the deafening silence of indigenous women and, in particular, women from Santa Isabel's matrilineal culture. I argue that women's voices and presence in leadership can only be realized if this alternative view of leadership is integrated in Solomon Islands' national policy, legislated, and included in the school curriculum.

REFERENCES

Akao, S. (2008). *Seen but not heard: Women's experiences of educational leadership in Solomon Islands secondary schools* (Unpublished master's thesis). University of Waikato, Hamilton, New Zealand. Retrieved from http://hdl.handle.net/10289/2379

Akao, S., & Strachan, J. (2012). *A gender analysis of the education sector in the Solomon Islands.* Hamilton, New Zealand: University of Waikato Wilf Malcolm Institute of Educational Research.

Blackmore, J. (1995). Breaking out from a masculinist politics of education. In B. Limerick & B. Lingard (Eds.), *Gender and changing educational management* (pp. 34–56). Rydalmere, NSW: Hodder.

Bogesi, G. (1948). Santa Isabel, Solomon Islands. *Oceania, 18*(3), 207–232.

Braun, V., & Clarke, V. (2006). Using thematic analysis in psychology. *Qualitative research in Psychology, 3*(2), 77–101.

Carli, L. L., & Eagly, A. H. (2012). Leadership and gender. In D. V. Day (Ed.), *The nature of leadership* (2nd ed., pp. 437–476). Los Angeles, CA: Sage.

Cubillo, L., & Brown, M. (2003). Women into educational leadership and management: Inter-national differences? *Journal of Educational Administration, 41*(3), 278–291. http://doi.org/10.1108/09578230310474421

Elisha, L. N. (2012). *Exploring the perceptions of teachers on women principals in the Solomon Islands* (Thesis). University of Waikato. Retrieved from http://researchcommons.waikato.ac.nz/handle/10289/7033

Ely, R. J., & Rhode, D. I. (2010). Women and leadership: Defining the challenges. In N. Nohira & R. Khurana (Eds.), *Handbook of leadership theory and practice: A Harvard Business School centennial colloquium* (pp. 377–410). Boston, MA: Harvard Business Press.

Fine, M. G. (2007). Women, collaboration, and social change: An ethics-based model of leadership. In J. L. Chin, B. Lott, J. Rice, & J. Sanchez-Hucles (Eds.), *Women and leadership: Transforming visions and diverse voices* (pp. 177–191). Maden, MA: Blackwell.

Fine, M. G., & Buzzanell, P. M. (2000). Walking the high wire: Leadership theorizing, daily acts, and tensions. In P. M. Buzzanell (Ed.), *Rethinking organizational and managerial communication from feminist perspectives* (pp. 128–156). Thousand Oaks, CA: Sage.

Fitzgerald, T. (2003). Changing the deafening silence of indigenous women's voices in educational leadership. *Journal of Educational Administration, 41*(1), 9–23. http://doi.org/10.1108/09578230310457402

Flick, U. (2014). *An introduction to qualitative research* (5th ed.). Los Angeles, CA: Sage.

Grogan, M., & Shakeshaft, C. (2011). *Women and educational leadership.* San Francisco, CA: Jossey-Bass.

Kari, H. (2004, February). Perspectives of Solomon Island women on customary land tenure. Presented at the NGO community open workshop, discussion, SIDT Conference Room, Honiara.

Kilavanwa, B. (2004). *Women leaders in schools in Papua New Guinea: Why do women leaders labor in the shadows?* (Unpublished master's thesis). University of Waikato, Hamilton, New Zealand.

Kinch, J. (2004). The status of commercial invertebrates and other marine resources in the North-west Santa Isabel Province, the Solomon Islands (pp. 1–57). UNDP, Santa Isabel. Retrieved from https://org.uib.no/westernsolomons/docs/Kinch,%20Jeff/Kinch%20(2004)%20UNDP%20Isabel%20Mar%20Resources.pdf

Klenke, K. (2011). *Women in leadership: Contextual dynamics and boundaries.* Bingley, United Kingdom: Emerald Group Publishing.

Liki, A. 2010. Women leaders in Solomon Islands public service: A personal and scholarly reflection. *State Society and Governance in Melanesia Discussion Paper* (1). Canberra: ANU College of Asia and the Pacific, The Australian National University.

Malasa, D. P. (2007). *Effective school leadership: An exploration of issues inhibiting the effectiveness of school leadership in Solomon Islands' secondary schools* (Unpublished master's thesis). University of Waikato, Hamilton, New Zealand.

Ministry of Education and Human Resources Development. (2009). Performance assessment framework (PAF). Honiara,

Solomon Islands: Solomon Islands Government Ministry of Education and Human Resources Development.

Naramana, R. B. (1987). Elements of culture in Hograno/ Maringe Santa Ysabel. *'O 'O Journal of Solomon Islands Studies, 1*(3), 41–57.

Oplatka, I. (2006). Women in educational administration within developing countries: Towards a new international research agenda. *Journal of Educational Administration, 44*(6), 604–624.

Peterson, N., Hamilton, R., Pita, J., Atu, W., & James, R. (2012). Ridges to reefs conservation plan. Retrieved from http://www .researchgate.net/profile/R_Hamilton/publication/ 257345390_Ridges_to_ReefsConservation_Plan_for_ Isabel_Province_Solomon_Islands/links/0c960524f6bf 34cde7000000.pdf

Pollard, A. A. (2006). *Gender and leadership in "Are" Are society, the South Sea Evangelical Church and Parliamentary leadership Solomon Islands* (Unpublished doctoral thesis). Victoria University of Wellington, Wellington, New Zealand.

Poyer, L. (1996). Book review forum. *Pacific Studies, 19*(1), 148–156.

Scales, I., & Teakeni, J. (2006). Election of women in Solomon Islands: The case for local governance approach. *Journal of Pacific Studies, 29*(1), 67–84.

Sharpnack, R. (2011). The power shifting context: Becoming a contextual leader. In L. Coughlin, E. Wingard, & K. Hollihan (Eds.), *Enlightened power: How women are transforming the path to leadership* (pp. 39–54). San Francisco, CA: Jossey-Bass.

Sinclair, A. (2013). Not just "adding women in": Women re-making leadership. Retrieved from http://works.bepress. com/amanda_sinclair/6

Sisiolo, J. (2010). *Being and educational leaders in Choiseul province in the Solomon Islands: A case study of the context of leadership for principals and deputy principals* (Unpublished master's thesis). University of Waikato, Hamilton, New Zealand.

Solomon Islands Government. (2011). Solomon Islands population and housing census 2009: Basic tables and census description (pp. 1–45). Retrieved from http://www.mof .gov.sb/Libraries/Statistics/2013_12_-_2009_Census_Re port_on_Basic_Tables_-_Volumn_2.sflb.ashx

Strachan, J. (2005). Working out of my comfort zone: Experiences of developing national women's policy in Vanuatu. *Delta, 57*(1), 47–66.

Strachan, J. (2009). Women and educational leadership in New Zealand and Melanesia. In Helen Sobehart (Ed.), *Women leading education across continents: Sharing the spirit, fanning the flame* (pp. 100–113). New York, NY: Rowman & Littlefield Education.

Strachan, J., Samuel, J., & Takaro, M. (2007). Ni Vanuatu women graduates: What happens when they go home? *Development in Practice, 17*(1), 147–153.

Strachan, J., & Saunders, R. (2007). Ni Vanuatu women and educational leadership development. *New Zealand Journal of Educational Leadership, 22*, 37–48.

Tongamoa, T. (1988). *Pacific women: Roles and status of women in Pacific societies*. Suva, Fiji: Institute of Pacific Studies of the University of the South Pacific.

Tuivaga, J. (1988). Fiji. In T. Tongamoa (Ed.), *Pacific women: Roles and status of women in Pacific societies* (pp. 1–21). Suva, Fiji: Institute of Pacific Studies of the University of the South Pacific.

Whittington, S., Ospina, S., & Pollard, A. A. (2006). *Women in Government in Solomon Islands: A diagnostic study.* (pp. 1–67). Honiara, Solomon Islands.

Chapter 4

The Impact of Culture on Women's Leadership in Vanuatu Secondary Schools

Daisy Warsal

Leadership is broadly defined as having the influence over a group of people to achieve the aims and goals of the organization. In a school context, educational leadership involves leading and guiding the talents and energies of teachers, pupils, and parents toward achieving common educational aims (Strachan, 2002). Given Vanuatu's rapid modernization and with capitalism replacing the traditional lifestyles of Ni-Vanuatu (the people of Vanuatu), the government is faced with the challenge of providing good quality education for its people. Effective school leadership is the cornerstone of a good quality education for Ni-Vanuatu. With effective school leadership the aims and goals of the education system of Vanuatu, stipulated in the Education Act of 2001, could be achieved. For this to occur, gender equality in school leadership positions plays an important role.

The study presented in this chapter was carried out in 2009. Statistics from the Ministry of Education of Vanuatu in 2009 showed that Vanuatu women are greatly underrepresented in leadership positions in schools. A gender analysis of education (Strachan, 2002) revealed that women represent 8 percent of secondary school principals, yet more than 36 percent of teachers were women. Of great concern is that recent statistics from the Ministry of Education show that this figure of 8 percent has since declined to 3.9 percent (Warsal, 2009).

The decline in the number of women leaders in Vanuatu secondary schools is contrary to the nation's commitment to the Convention on the Elimination of Discrimination Against Women (CEDAW). The government committed itself to CEDAW by ratification in 1995. Following that ratification, the government of the Republic of Vanuatu, through the Ministry of Education, took further steps by formulating policies on gender equality such as the Gender Equity in Education Policy (Ministry of Education, 2005). One of the major goals of the Gender Equity in Education Policy was to increase the number of female principals in secondary

schools as well as in senior positions in the Ministry of Education. Furthermore, the Ministry of Education of Vanuatu has undertaken other affirmative actions for the implementation and development of this equity policy. These include leadership programs for women in educational leadership (McNae & Strachan, 2010) and a gender analysis of the education sector in Vanuatu. However, despite measures taken by the Ministry of Education to achieve equal representation of men and women in educational leadership positions, women are still grossly underrepresented.

Encouragingly, more recent statistics from the Ministry of Education show a steady increase in women's representation in leadership positions. For instance, in 2015, it was noted out of 89 secondary schools in Vanuatu, 10 (8.9 percent) were headed by women. Similarly, in 2016, the number of women in leadership positions at the secondary school level moved up slightly to 11. Currently, there are 16 women principals at the secondary school level. While these figures showed a slow increase, women are still greatly underrepresented in school leadership positions.

THE INFLUENCE OF TRADITIONAL LEADERSHIP AND CULTURE

Vanuatu like other Melanesian countries is a patriarchal society where leadership is a male-only domain. Narakobi (1983) describes this type of leadership as "bigman leadership." Bigmen, or a bigman, sometimes called a chief, is a self-appointed leader with a certain amount of influence over his followers and often possesses leadership qualities such as oratory skills and wealth. The subordinate followers include the women and the children. Thus, women's and men's roles are very much culturally prescribed. For example, in the villages it is rare for a woman to be seen at the "nakamal." A nakamal, in

Vanuatu culture, is a very important site or shelter where the chief and his male subordinates gather to make important decisions regarding the daily issues of the village. Women are perceived instead as child-rearers, caretakers, and homemakers.

The impenetrable invisible glass ceiling of patriarchy renders it almost impossible for Ni-Vanuatu women to be part of important decision making, at the village level and particularly at the government level, specifically in Parliament. Similarly, the chiefly systems, endowed in the village communities by long-held practices of custom, enforce the notion of bigman leadership making it impossible for women to be part of important decision making. Men are the main decision makers in each family.

Land is very valuable to all Ni-Vanuatu and is the source of their identity. Men are the main decision makers on issues relating to land matters and land disputes. Normally, the first-born male of the family is endowed with all the responsibilities of the family, including land matters. When there is disagreement over any decisions made, the matter is then taken to the nakamal to be resolved by village chiefs and other bigmen of the village.

Christianity plays a big part in the lives of Ni-Vanuatu. For example, Christian values such as love, respect, kindness, forgiveness, and humility are all embedded at each level in Vanuatu society. How Ni-Vanuatu men, women, and children live their lives, make decisions, and relate to one another is very much affected by these important Christian values. Coexisting side by side with Christianity is traditional religion, or kastom (custom). Some parts of kastom, for example, black magic or sorcery, play a big part in the lives of Ni-Vanuatu. Black magic is a silent but powerful force in Vanuatu that induces fear in the lives of the people and is practiced extensively in some islands. Vanuatu people take precautions when relating to one another, in particular, they avoid offending those originating from islands where black magic is pervasively practiced. More importantly, the fear of black magic in society affects the degree of trust in relationships and often causes people to be respectful to one another; at times this means they refrain from speaking out and are submissive.

Research suggests that in some cultures, the social and cultural expectations of women impact on their leadership and often stop them from taking up leadership positions in schools (Brown & Ralph, 1996; Celikten, 2005; Diko, 2007; Oplatka, 2006; Sanal, 2008). This is exacerbated in countries where patriarchy is prevalent (Celikten, 2005; Sanal, 2008). Brown and Ralph (1996) documented the existence of cultural and social structures that impede women from taking up leadership positions in Uganda. A more contextualized case in point is that of Kilavanwa's (2004) study looking at women in educational leadership in Papua New Guinea and how the context of Papua New Guinea affects their leadership practices in schools. The findings of that study indicated that women in Papua New Guinea find it difficult to lead and manage a school because the traditional and cultural expectations devalue them as leaders. Similarly, Akao's (2008) study of women and educational leadership in the Solomon Islands revealed that culture and traditional norms of the women leaders impacted negatively on their leadership practices.

A study of Vanuatu women and educational leadership (Strachan, Saunders, Jimmy, & Lapi, 2007) indicated that several cultural influences greatly affected women's "ability to participate in education and decision-making at all levels, including educational leadership" (p. 9). A key finding of the study was male gate-keeping and the silencing of women by men. For example, the participants commented that they were often discouraged from taking up further studies by male colleagues. The women revealed that because of the influence of Christianity and their culturally ascribed roles they often felt that they were not valued and respected as leaders.

A Feminist Research Study

This study set out to discover ways in which culture affects women's leadership in Vanuatu secondary schools and how women's leadership could be developed. Two groups of women were participants. Group one comprised three women principals and three women deputy principals from several secondary schools of Vanuatu. Group two comprised five aspiring women leaders. Group two participants were secondary school teachers who showed leadership qualities and were nominated by their school principals. Semistructured interviews and focus group discussions were used to collect data.

A feminist's qualitative lens was used to approach the issue. A qualitative feminist lens was relevant to this study for a number of reasons. According to Hesser-Biber and Leavy (2004) and Kirsch (1999), a qualitative feminist research paradigm involves the emancipation and empowerment of women because it brings the silenced voices of women to the forefront. Analysis of data was done using the thematic coding analysis and narrative or storytelling. Eleven women participated in the study.

Findings

The research revealed the existence of entrenched cultural barriers in three main areas of Vanuatu culture and society. These were the education system, the social structures in society, and the attitudes of individual men and women toward women leaders.

SYSTEMS

Several structures and processes in the Vanuatu education system served as major barriers to the participant's leadership. These included appointment processes, policies, and support. There was a lack of transparency in appointment processes. The appointment of participants in this study to positions of leadership was at times made on the preference of individual stakeholders in the education system. These stakeholders included school principals, the School Council, the Ministry of Education, and the Teaching Service Commission. This lack of transparency in appointments suggests that there was bias in the appointment process that may be an impediment to the appointment of aspiring women leaders to senior positions. Despite being aware of the difficulties of previous school principals with the surrounding school communities of rural schools, two of the women were appointed to difficult schools and in rural areas where male principals refused to be posted. This suggests that the participants were discriminated against on the basis of their gender. This could be one way the government is seen to not meet its CEDAW obligations.

There are no formal policies in place and specific criteria for the selection of school principals. Appointments are made directly by the Teaching Service Commission on recommendations made from individual stakeholders such as the Director of Secondary Education, the school principal and, at times, the school chairman. The selection of school principals restricts women's access to leadership positions in schools. Research has shown that a lack of specific selection criteria is problematic as a male could be chosen without ever questioning the basis on which the choice was made (Shakeshaft, 1987).

The women participants in this study said that there was little support for women in leadership roles. They had mixed experiences of support for their leadership from the education authorities such as the Provincial Education Office, the Ministry of Education, and the Teaching Service Commission. Some participants received more support in their leadership roles and others less. The women in the rural island schools received very little support from the Ministry of Education.

Social Structures

The social structures embedded in Vanuatu's society and culture also impacted significantly upon participants' leadership. These social structures include socialization of women into gendered roles, women's place in the society, and the wantok system.

Socialization into gendered roles greatly impacted on the participants' leadership in two ways. The lack of confidence was more obvious in the younger women leaders and in particular, the women leaders appointed to the positions of deputy principals and those taking up leadership roles for the first time. For example, one younger participant related that she initially turned down the offer to be acting principal but later gave up resisting. "He actually approached me so many times, wanting to give me this position and I refused so many times until the last time he came to see me, I decided to give in and to give it a go." Another participant used her qualification as an excuse not to take up a leadership role because she felt her experience was insufficient and that having a qualification would make her feel more confident to take up a leadership role. She explained, "Personally, I think the positions are there. I received a letter appointing me as assistant principal but I refused to take the offer. In French we say 'Je suis pas qualifier' which means I am not qualified, even if I have the experience, I am not comfortable. I am still looking into the future." This lack of confidence has been explained as due to the fear of success or failure due to socialization and sex-role stereotyping (Cubillo & Brown, 2003; Shakeshaft, 1987).

The wantok system is a powerful and intricate network of cultural values of kinship and relationships within the community that is common to Melanesia, in particular the Solomon Islands, Papua New Guinea, and Vanuatu (Sanga & Walker, 2005). This study revealed that Ni-Vanuatu women leaders are sometimes prevented from taking up and continuing in leadership roles because of the violence imposed on them by the school community. This was particularly evident in rural schools. Two of the women principals in the rural schools were physically assaulted by the big men leaders in the school community, and left their profession. This finding suggests that the rural communities did not want a woman as their school principal, they had stepped outside and challenged what was viewed as their culturally prescribed and appropriate role. The women believed they experienced discrimination and violence because of the wantok system. There was nepotism in the form of interisland and tribal rivalry particularly in the rural school communities. Some of the women participants were accused of favoring teachers from the same island which ultimately resulted in physical assault.

People's Perceptions of Women as Leaders

The individuals in the school community played a major role in transmitting to the participants of this study the norms and beliefs of how Vanuatu culture views women in leadership roles. The findings in this study showed that the impact of the various individuals who impacted on the leadership experiences of the participants involved female teachers, male teachers, chiefs and big men, such as landowners in the rural communities, and some male students.

Another finding indicated that one major obstacle to women leaders in Vanuatu is the attitude of some women. The participants indicated that they encountered difficulties with other women teachers. It would seem to be from the findings that when a woman takes up a leadership role in the school, other women tend to develop negative attitudes toward her leadership. However, the findings also indicated that many male teachers, with some exceptions, were very supportive of the participant's leadership. This is interesting, because given the patriarchal nature of society in Vanuatu one would not expect such a degree of support coming from male teachers.

This is also in stark contrast to the women's lack of support, and in some cases violent opposition, from chiefs, landowners, and some male students.

How Might Women's Leadership Be Developed?

Drawing from the focus group discussion, findings indicated that educational leadership development is needed. Socialization of the women participants compounded by their lack of exposure to the administration and management of schools impacted on their confidence to apply for and carry out leadership roles. The women took on leadership roles with little educational leadership experience. The women identified mentoring, qualification attainment, and networking as strategies that would assist them.

Mentoring is mentioned in the literature as a main tool of women's leadership development. Mentoring can help provide access to educational leadership positions for women as well as aid their professional growth. It involves a more experienced person giving professional guidance and advice to aspiring and new principals. Importantly, it provides support and care. The significant lack of support by the education authorities in Vanuatu was a source of frustration for the women in this study. The school principals and deputy principals in Vanuatu could make themselves available as mentors to aspiring and current women educational leaders. The mentors would also require training in how to provide effective mentoring for the women.

The aspiring women leaders were concerned about their lack of qualifications. Certified leadership programs for aspiring women leaders would prepare the women for leadership, increase their confidence, and provide a network of support. The Ministry of Education of Vanuatu could go some way to meeting its obligations in the

Gender Equity in Education Policy by providing leadership preparation for women, recruiting women into the program, and supporting them by approving leave and financial support.

Networking as a means of support for women leaders and aspirants is vital for women leaders in Vanuatu secondary schools. Currently, there is no evidence of such support networks for women leaders in Vanuatu secondary schools. Although support networks created by the Vanuatu National Council of Women and the Vanuatu Department of Women's Affairs exist for women leaders in politics, it is important that such networks also be available for women in educational leadership positions. Networking is important as it allows women leaders in schools to share their experiences and difficulties with other school leaders in order to find solutions.

RECOMMENDATIONS AND CONCLUSION

A number of recommendations are suggested from the findings of this study.

1. Appropriate policies should be formulated by the Ministry of Education and the Teaching Service Commission for the selection and appointment of Vanuatu school principals.
2. Formal policies that make provisions for gender equity in educational leadership positions in secondary schools should be formulated and implemented.
3. Support networks for women leaders in secondary schools need to be established.
4. Formal mentoring programs for aspiring women leaders and first-time school principals could be set in place at the school level.
5. It is also recommended that the Vanuatu Ministry of Education, in collaboration with the Vanuatu Institute of Teacher Education, integrate educational leadership programs that would assist aspiring women leaders in attaining the necessary qualifications to be able to take up leadership roles in the secondary schools of Vanuatu.

This study has shown that Vanuatu women, while sharing some similarities to Western women in their experiences in educational leadership, also have different experiences due to the cultural context. Culture had a significant impact on the leadership experiences of the Ni-Vanuatu women participants. Powerful forces in Vanuatu society such as patriarchy, gendered socialization, Christianity, and the wantok system influenced greatly how Vanuatu women led in the secondary schools. The women were obstructed and often gave up their leadership roles because of the barriers inherent in the education system, such as lack of transparency in appointments, lack of selection policies, and lack of support from the education authorities. The women experienced discrimination such as resentment, nepotism, and violence, particularly from rural school communities. Professional support for women's leadership in Vanuatu secondary schools is needed if more women are to be successful in obtaining and carrying out leadership positions. Mentoring and certified leadership preparation programs will be a good start in providing that support.

REFERENCES

Akao, S. M. (2008). *Seen but not heard: Women's experiences of educational leadership in Solomon Islands secondary schools* (Unpublished master's thesis). University of Waikato, Hamilton, New Zealand.

Brown, M., & Ralph, S. (1996). Barriers to women manager's advancement in education in Uganda. *International Journal of Educational Management, 10*(6), 18–23.

Celikten, M. (2005). A perspective on women principals in Turkey. *International Journal of Leadership in Education, 8*(3), 207–221.

Cubillo, L., & Brown, M. (2003). Women into educational leadership and management: International differences? *Journal of Educational Administration, 41*(3), 278–291.

Diko, N. (2007). Changes and continuities: Implementation of gender equality in a South African high school. *Africa Today, 54*(1), 106–116.

Hesse-Biber, S. N., & Leavy, P. (2004). *Approaches to qualitative research.* New York: Oxford University Press.

Kilavanwa, B. (2004). *Women leaders in schools in Papua New Guinea: Why do women leaders labor in the shadows?* (Unpublished master's thesis). University of Waikato, Hamilton, New Zealand.

Kirsch, G. (1999). *Ethical dilemmas in feminist research: The politics of location, interpretation, and publication.* Albany, NY: State University of New York Press.

McNae, R., & Strachan, J. M. (2010). Researching in cross cultural contexts: A socially just process. *Waikato Journal of Education, 15*(20), 41–54.

Ministry of Education. (2005). *Gender equity in education policy 2005–2015.* Port-Vila, Vanuatu: Ministry of Education.

Narokobi, B. (1983). *Life and leadership in Melanesia.* Suva, Fiji: The Institute of Pacific Studies & The University of Papua New Guinea.

Oplatka, I. (2006). Women in educational administration within developing countries. *Journal of Educational Administration, 44*(6), 604–624.

Sanal, M. (2008). Factors preventing women's advancement in management in Turkey. *Education 128*(3), 380–391.

Sanga, K.F., & Walker, K. D. (2005). *Apem moa Solomon Islands leadership.* Wellington, New Zealand: He Parekerke, Victoria University.

Shakeshaft, C. (1987). *Women in educational administration.* Newbury Park, CA: Sage.

Strachan, J. (2002). *A gender analysis of the education sector in Vanuatu.* Port-Vila, Vanuatu: Department of Women's Affairs.

Strachan, J., Saunders, R., Jimmy, L., & Lapi, G. (2007). Ni Vanuatu women and educational leadership development. *New Zealand Journal of Educational Leadership, Policy and Practice, 22*, 37–48.

Warsal, D. (2009). *The impact of culture on women's leadership in Vanuatu secondary schools* (Unpublished master's thesis). University of Waikato, Hamilton, New Zealand.

Chapter 5

Factors Affecting Women's Access to Higher Education in India

Chitra Mku

Higher education is a social necessity for women's empowerment in India. For a woman to be dynamic and growth-oriented, her education must be dynamic and proactive. Higher education ensures her claim to societal benefits and demonstrates respect for her status, paving the way for her economic growth as well as that of the broader society. The woman who is able to achieve in higher education can advance further in society. One consequence of empowerment, though, may be an increase in violence against women as they threaten societal norms that value male domination. Even as violence against women is increasing, so is enrollment of women in higher education and those seeking employment.

This research examined the challenges facing women in entering higher education in India. The empowerment of women is measured in terms of their ability to achieve an education and attain employment. The data used for the study were secondary sources from India. The results of the data suggest that women still face substantial challenges to compete with men in obtaining a higher education.

The journey toward empowerment of women is still incomplete. Indian policymakers must take steps to reduce the gap of enrollment of woman in higher education and address increasing crime against women. To awaken the people, it is the women who must be awakened. Once she is on the move, the family moves, the village moves, and the nation moves.

Women held an important position in ancient Indian society. In ancient India women enjoyed equal status with men in all aspects of life, even receiving the same education as men (Rout, 2016). Many Hindu religious books such as Vedas, Upanishads, Ramayana, and Mahabharata have mentioned the names of several women who were great scholars, poets, and philosophers of the time. A wife was regarded as half of her husband—an unmarried man was considered to be an incomplete man.

All religious ceremonies were performed by the husband along with the wife.

But in the medieval period, the status of women declined considerably. She was considered to be inferior to a man. Customs of purdah (seclusion), sati (a widow's self-immolation on the death of her husband), child marriage, restrictions on a widow's remarriage, and prevalence of joint family systems have been the factors responsible for the injustice meted out to women.

Reforms in the 19th century gave way to the feminist movement in India in the 1920s and the position of women in modern India has changed considerably since then (Sen, 2000). Women are considered equal to men socially, economically, educationally, politically, and legally. Women's sufferings from sati, child marriage, and the institution of temple prostitution no longer exist.

Today, women have the right to receive education, inherit and own property, and participate in public life (Sen, 2000). Women have become more economically independent. They can seek employment anywhere and remain free individuals (Upadhyay, 2010a). While women now enjoy equal status with men in most areas of society, broadening women's access to education and to employment remains India's principal challenge.

STATEMENT OF THE PROBLEM

Indian women face a major paradox with regard to their changing status. One of the most formidable obstacles is the absence of homogeneity among Indian women (Devi, 2003). On any given indicator of development, rural women are disadvantaged compared to their urban counterparts (Upadhyay, 2010a). The profile of a rural woman is that of a woman who is poor, ignorant, illiterate, superstitious, and suppressed, with a low level of employment skills. Her access to information, assets, and opportunities are also limited. She is underrepresented in many areas of society (Suguna, 2002) and rural women in India especially suffer from being both economically and socially invisible (Upadhyay, 2010b).

Indira Gandhi was prime minister of India from 1966 to 1977 and from 1980 to 1984. Many of the political leaders were and are willing to extend their political support to and serve under a woman leader. Tamil Nadu, West Bengal, Bihar, and New Delhi are some examples of states accepting women for leading the entire state activities more than twice. But still the status of women in India today faces challenges with their prospects for a voice in civil society. It is the discrimination toward girls and women or the criminal assaults women face that remains daunting.

On one hand, ironically, female divinities are worshipped with the greatest reverence in Indian society, but on the other hand, women have to deal with oppression and humiliation in political, social, economic, and regional aspects in their daily lives (Shettar, 2015). Hence, the need is great to examine the challenges facing, and prospects for, education and work of women in India.

Need for the Study

The primary need for this study arises from the depiction Amartya Sen offered—"missing women"—in examining the gender ratio of Indian women as compared to men and the reasons this is happening in India as well as in other countries (1990, para. 6). The adult and child (0–6) gender ratio shows a decreasing trend over the decades. Women's population per 1,000 men was the same in 1961 as in 2011. In the decades between 1961 and 2011, there was a decrease in girls' births with the exception of 2001. The child population is decreasing over the decades and currently 914 female children are born in comparison to 1,000 male children.

The gender ratio of a future India is a significant societal problem. The existing girl children who will become women have to overcome the risk of morbidity to sustain or improve their ratio of women to men. This presents significant considerations for women's health, but is beyond the scope of this investigation. Many issues such as the dropout rate of female children from school and the impact of wage differences in employment require a more detailed investigation and discussion beyond this study. I will, however, discuss the impact that increasing violence against women has on the prospects of higher education and future employment.

OBJECTIVES

The general objective of this chapter is to examine the challenges and prospects of women in India. The specific objectives are to examine the trend in female literacy rates, the status of women in higher education, the constitutional and other legal support structures that exist for women, the progress of women's engagement in the workforce, and the growing trend that crime against women causes in achieving greater parity with men in education and work. I conclude with recommendations for further consideration.

METHODOLOGY AND LIMITATIONS

The study is based solely on the analysis of secondary data sources and included no field investigation of my own. I used descriptive statistics such as percentage and annual growth rate to analyze the data in order to examine the research problem. The data are derived from the National Sample Survey Office of India (NSSO), the Office of the Registrar General & Census Commissioner, India (2011), the National Crime Records Bureau of India, and the Statistical Handbook of India (2011).

FINDINGS AND DISCUSSION

Education would surely liberate and equip women to take control of their lives. Although education is essential for everyone, in the case of women it is particularly significant. Education not only opens up vast avenues and opportunities for growth but affects families and future generations as well. It is essential to examine women's literacy rates over time because literate women become proxies for all women in advocating for their rights. The fundamental right of education is a dream too few Indian women achieve even today (Surie, 2016).

Women's literacy rates have increased considerably from 1983 to 2012. Female literacy rate growth is 0.04 and 0.02 percent for the rural and urban, respectively, for the 68th round of data collection from 2011. Even so, it remains lower for rural women. The economy of India is competing with all developing and developed economies and so at this juncture, women's literacy rate growth is critical. Indian policymakers have to take serious steps to strengthen the literacy rate of women that will impact their empowerment in all aspects.

WOMEN'S ENROLLMENT IN HIGHER EDUCATION

Availability of institutions is one of the important factors in women's enrollment in higher education. Table 5.1 reveals that the number of universities and colleges is increasing over the years to meet the demand of the

Table 5.1. Number of Institutions by Type, 2013–2014 [Provisional] (Supply Side)

Higher Education	Universities	Central University	42
		State Public University	310
		Deemed University	127
		State Private University	143
		Central Open University	1
		State Open University	13
		Institutions of National Importance	68
		Institutions Under State Legislature Act	5
		Others	3
		Total	712
	Colleges		36,671
	Stand-Alone Institutions	Diploma Level Technical	3,541
		PGDM	392
		Diploma Level Nursing	2,674
		Diploma Level Teacher Training	4,706
		Institute Under Ministries	132
		Total	11,445

Data source: For Higher Education, AISHE Portal

growing population in India. Seven hundred twelve universities, 36,671 colleges, and 11,445 stand-alone institutions suggests that India has made an attempt to satisfy the demand for higher education.

Higher education in India is a combination of private and public sectors. Middle-class Indians tend to select the private sector for primary to secondary education so their children receive a strong foundation, and prefer the public sector for higher education. The supply of higher education in the government sector is able to fulfill their sanctioned capacity for admission in all courses, and those who are not able to gain admission in the public sector, select the private sector. The cost of the private sector per semester is a minimum of 12,000 Rupees (approximately $186 USD).

In the case of undergraduate arts courses, the tuition varies from institution to institution based on its goodwill

and the course of study opted. The existing demand for higher education is greater in the public sector, but the same course, same syllabus, and same degree needs a good sum of money, which is difficult for some families to afford. The Tamil Nadu state government made the undergraduate course free and provides a laptop to the students for enhancing their access to technology.

Based on secondary data sources, Kadam (2012) attempted to address the present scenario of women in the field of higher education and recommended some suggestions for the betterment of women through higher education. The history of women in higher education demonstrates that after considerable struggle the universities opened their doors to women. Cambridge University permitted women students to read (take) examinations from 1872, London University from 1878, and Oxford University from 1884. In India, Calcutta University admitted women from 1877, followed by Bombay University in 1883.

Table 5.2 presents data on women's colleges which contributed to dramatically increased numbers of Indian women attending college beginning in 1970. Now the number of women's colleges throughout India is 12 percent according the annual report of University Grants Commission (2013) with women's enrollment at 42 percent in higher education in 2012. There is an increase yearly of women's enrollment in higher education.

The enrollment of women in higher education is examined with cross data. The cross-section data reveals that the enrollment of women in different programs differs with their men counterparts absolutely and relatively. The demand for higher education of women after their secondary education is decided by their parents in Indian society. The girl's population that is outnumbered in secondary education is drastically reduced when they come for higher education. The importance of higher education is promoted through women centers in all colleges and universities. But still the number of female enrollees in different programs is not high when compared with male enrollees in many of the programs (tables 5.3 and 5.4).

Table 5.2. Women's Colleges Throughout India, 1970–2012

Year	Total Colleges (No.)	Women's Colleges (No.)	% to Total Colleges	Total Enrollment	Women's Enrollment	Percentage
1950–51	—	—	—	396,793	43,126	10.87
1960–61	—	—	—	1,049,864	170,455	16.24
1970–71	3,604	412	11.43	3,001,292	689,086	22.96
1980–81	4,722	609	12.90	2,752,437	748,525	27.19
1990–91	7,346	874	11.90	4,425,247	1,436,887	32.47
2000–01	12,806	1578	12.32	8,000,935	3,012,367	37.65
2010–11	33,023	3982	12.06	16,974,883	7,048,688	41.52
2011–12	35,539	4266	12.00	20,327,478	8,672,431	42.00

Source: Ministry of Human Resource Development (2016)

Table 5.3. Percent of Enrollment in Different Programs in Higher Education, 2012–2013

Program	Male	Female	Total
B.A. Bachelor of Arts	28.22	37.84	32.55
B.Com. Bachelor of Commerce	11.51	11.30	11.42
B.Sc. Bachelor of Science	10.41	12.09	11.17
B.Tech. Bachelor of Technology	9.10	4.46	7.01
B.E. Bachelor of Engineering	8.07	4.06	6.26
B.Ed. Bachelor of Education	1.34	2.84	2.01
L.L.B. Bachelor of Law Or Laws	0.86	0.48	0.69
M.A. Master of Arts	3.45	5.42	4.34
M.Sc. Master of Science	1.59	2.31	1.91
M.B.A. Master of Business	2.25	1.44	1.88
M.Com. Master of Commerce	0.77	1.16	0.94
M.C.A. Master of Computer	0.92	0.75	0.84
M.B.B.S Bachelor of Medicine	0.46	0.52	0.49
M.Tech. Master of Technology	0.61	0.39	0.51
M.E. Master of Engineering	0.25	0.22	0.24
Others	20.20	14.72	17.73

Source: AISHE 2012–13 Report (All India Survey on Higher Education)

Table 5.4. Enrollment in Higher Education Through Regular and Distance Mode, 2012–13 [P]

Mode	Male	Female	Total	% of Total
Regular	14,347,637	11,748,655	26,096,292	88
Distance	1,980,666	1,552,064	3,532,730	12
Total	16,328,303	13,300,719	29,629,022	100

Source: AISHE 2012–13 Report (All India Survey on Higher Education)

Table 5.3 depicts how the absolute difference in enrollment in different programs of higher education occurs. Medicine, master of science, and master of arts women are leading in enrollment over men. The number of women in bachelor's of education degrees suggests there is a high possibility of having a female teacher in Indian schools. Table 5.4 shows that the women's enrollment in regular education is lower than men's in India. Eighty-eight percent of individuals study in regular education and 12 percent study in distance mode. Women engaged in distance education are not equal to men at this point. Distance learning presents a clear opportunity for exploration—particularly since so many rural women lack the access to higher education.

The inequality between women and men in higher education over a decade is illustrated in table 5.5. The Gender Parity Index for higher education moved in a positive direction in which women per hundred men increased from 58 to 81 between 2000 and 2013. Eight years of hard work by educators and the government reduced the gap in higher education enrollment of women. The remaining gap is hoped to be closed by 2020 per the target of policymakers, but for that to occur, citizen cooperation is essential.

The program has been designed and approved by the government and has been implemented, but choosing the accessibility for its young women remains in the hands of citizens (Nagaraja Murugan & Chitra, 2013). Parents in India must step forward to send their daughters to colleges and universities.

CONSTITUTIONAL DOCUMENTS SUPPORTING WOMEN

Today women have the right to receive education, inherit and own property, and participate in public life. They have the potential to become economically independent. Many governmental changes are responsible for the improvements in the day-to-day life of women in today's India. Most of the important statutory legislation to improve the status of women took place in the 20th century:

The Hindu Widow Re-marriage Act of 1856
The Child Marriage Restraint Act of 1929
The Hindu Women Right to Property Act of 1937

Table 5.5. Inequality of Women in Higher Education

Years	Recognized Educational Institutions (in absolute numbers)		Higher Education Enrollment (hundred thousands)			Gross Enrollment Ratio (Higher Education 18–23 years)			No. of Girls per 100 Boys in Higher Education	Gender Parity Index in Higher Education
	Colleges	University	Boys	Girls	Total	Boys	Girls	Total	—	=
2000–01	10,512	254	54	32	86	—	—	—	58	NA
2005–06	16,982	350	88	55	143	13.5	9.4	11.6	62	0.69
2006–07	19,812	371	96	60	156	14.5	10.0	12.4	62	0.69
2007–08	23,099	406	106	66	172	15.2	10.7	13.1	63	0.70
2008–09	27,882	440	112	73	185	15.8	11.4	13.7	65	0.72
2009–10	25,938	436	124	83	207	17.1	12.7	15.0	67	0.74
2010–11	32,974	621	155	120	275	20.8	17.9	19.4	78	0.86
2011–12	34,852	642	162	130	292	22.1	19.4	20.8	80	0.88
2012–13[P]	35,829	665	163	133	296	22.3	19.8	21.1	81	0.89
2013–14[P]	36,671	712	NA	NA	NA	NA	NA	NA	NA	NA

Source: AISHE 2012–13 Report (All India Survey on Higher Education)

The Hindu Marriage Act of 1955

The Hindu Succession Act of 1956

The Suppression of Immoral Traffic in Women and Girls Act of 1956–57

The Dowry Prohibition Act of 1961

The principle of gender equality is enshrined in the Indian Constitution in its Preamble, Fundamental Rights, Fundamental Duties, and Directive Principles. The constitution not only grants equality to women, but also empowers the state to adopt measures of positive discrimination in favor of women. The 73rd and 74th Amendments (1993) to the Constitution of India provided for the reservation of seats in the local bodies of Panchayats and Municipalities for women. Another Constitutional Amendment (84th Constitutional Amendment Act of 1998) reserving 33 percent of seats in Parliament and State Legislatures is still to be enacted.

Parliament passed various legislation to safeguard the constitutional rights of women. These legislative measures include the Hindu Marriage Act (1955), the Hindu Succession Act (1971), Equal Remuneration Act (1976), Child Marriage Restraint Act (1976), Immoral Trafficking (Prevention) Act (1986), and Prenatal Diagnostic Technique (Regulation and Prevention of Measure) Act (1994). Even with these laws and policies, though, there is frequently incongruence with accountability and implementation. So, while many fundamental federal laws protect women, the government must continue to work to enact them consistently across the nation.

WOMEN WORKERS' POPULATION RATIO

The National Sample Survey (NSS) provides data on employment in India. Each NSS "round" refers to a particular year. The women worker population ratio in India has in the short term decreased by about one percentage point for females in rural areas, whereas it increased by one percentage point for urban females between NSS 66th round and NSS 68th round. Between NSS 27th round and NSS 68th round, there was a prevalence of underemployment for women in rural areas.

Overall women's employment remains a national challenge (Upadhyay, 2010b). According to Surie (2016), while female literacy and education enrollment rates continue to improve, women's workforce participation is below that of many countries throughout both the Middle East and sub-Saharan Africa. Surie (2016) stated,

India ranks 127th on the gender inequality index and 108th on the global gender gap index. . . . Over the last decade, women's participation in the labor force has seen

a dramatic decline. Latest government statistics suggest that women's labor participation rate fell from 29.4 percent in 2004–2005 to 22.5 percent in 2011–2012. The gender gap in the labor force is particularly stark when we consider that in the 15–59 age group, women's participation is only 32 percent in rural areas compared to 83 percent for men, and 21 percent in urban areas compared to 81 percent for men. (para. 2)

Numerous scholars identify the reasons for the decrease in employment among women. One of these is the increase in crime that women face in India. That is described in greater detail in the next section.

CRIME AGAINST WOMEN IN INDIA

The National Crime Records Bureau (NCRB) predicted that the growth rate of crimes against women would be higher than the population growth rate by 2010. Surie (2016) stated, "Growing concerns around the safety of women is also a clear deterrent to women's employment" (para. 7). The records of NCRB depict that domestic violence by a husband or his relatives under section 498A IPC increased from 4.2 in 2009 to 4.5 in 2013. Dowry deaths under the section 304B IPC decreased over the years from 0.4 in 2009 to 0.3 in 2013. (Dowry deaths refer to the husband or husband's family killing the bride, frequently by burning her to death, due to a dispute over the adequacy of the dowry. See, for example, Greenberg [2003] for more information on dowry deaths.)

The total reported crimes against women in India is 309,546: the 25 states registered cases are 295,930 and the seven-union territory registered cases were 13,616. The crimes per day against women in India is 848 and the crimes per hour is 35.34. The cases registered under the section 376 IPC as rape are 33,707. The crime rate of rape is 5.69 over the year. There are 92 rapes per day and 3.84 rapes per hour. Domestic violence by husband and his relatives is registered as 118,866 in 2013. There are 325.66 women per day and 13 women per hour who suffer in section 498A IPC. The capital city, New Delhi, is noted for its crime registered under rape: 585 cases were registered in 2012 but it increased to 1,441 in 2013. Increased crime provides a plausible reason for families refusing to allow women to work. Upadhyay (2010b) wrote:

The gap in policy and practice in women's empowerment is most visible when it comes to the level and kinds of violence women face in India. Despite the policies, laws, and initiatives by civil society institutions, violence against women in India is widespread and the consequences for perpetrators rarely match the crime. Enforcement of laws and sentencing of perpetrators are long and arduous processes, and the gaps in these processes are further widened by corruption. (p. 4)

While written laws and policies regarding women's rights lack congruence in many areas, many factors contribute to lack of justice for women when they are the victims of crime. Greater enforcement of existing laws can move forward the overall country goal of increasing educational and employment opportunities for women.

CONCLUSION

In the 21st century, remarkably, the Indian family still to a great degree controls a woman's rights before marriage. This power to exercise control over her is transferred to the husband's family after marriage. It is an unwritten norm to which women of all castes and religions are subject. Additionally, the declining gender ratio of women to men and the ascending crime against women of India requires systemic action to protect women. The economic challenge for women is to decrease the worker population ratio gap between men and women while also increasing women's enrollment in higher education.

Sen (1990) identified the key benefits to the family when a more favorable environment exists for women: she has outside income, work that is viewed as productive, economic resources as a safety net, and societal understanding of the importance of resolving the deprivations that women face. He pointed out that education for women and political action remain the fundamental drivers to achieving the key benefits for women and their families, as well as for society.

Opportunities, however, for education and employment still leave many of India's women far behind even as we enter the third decade of the 21st century (Surie, 2016). Sen's (1990) contention that missing women will result in a crisis of incalculable proportions still goes unheeded nearly 30 years since he first penned that essay. The overall societal impact greatly affects economic growth, competition, and cooperation on the global stage, not to mention fundamental human rights. Shettar (2015) pointed out, "Government initiatives alone would not be sufficient to achieve this goal. Society must take initiative to create a climate in which there is no gender discrimination and women have full opportunities of self-decision making and participating in social, political, and economic life of the country with a sense of equality" (p. 19).

What is the role of government in India and the policymaker at this juncture? It is a challenge, unquestionably, but there is an avenue for every challenge to become an opportunity. The urgent need is to identify those challenges or limitations that are obstructing the prospects of women within higher education.

REFERENCES

Devi, U. (2003, May). Women, law, and social change. *Social Welfare, 50*, 38.

Greenberg, J. G. (2003). Criminalizing dowry deaths: The Indian experience. *American University Journal of Gender Social Policy and Law, 11*(2), 801–845.

Kadam, R. N. (2012). Empowerment of women in India: An attempt to fill the gender gap. *International Journal of Scientific and Research Publications, 2*(6), 11–13.

Ministry of Human Resource Development. (2016). *All India survey on higher education.* Retrieved from http://aishe.nic.in/aishe/viewDocument.action?documentId=239

Nagaraja Murugan, S., & Chitra, M. (2013). *Performance of secondary and higher secondary school education in India.* Delhi, India: Associated Publishing Company.

National Crime Records Bureau. (n.d.). *Crime in India.* Retrieved from http://ncrb.nic.in/

National Sample Survey Office. (n.d.). *Employment and unemployment situation in India, National sample survey, 27th through 68th round.* Retrieved from http://mospi.nic.in/sites/default/files/publication_reports/nss_report_554_31jan14.pdf

Office of the Registrar General & Census Commissioner, India. (2011). *SRS statistical report 2011.* Retrieved from http://www.censusindia.gov.in/vital_statistics/SRS_Reports.html

Rout, N. (2016, January). Role of women in ancient India. *Odisha Review, 72*(6), 42–47. Retrieved from http://magazines.odisha.gov.in/Orissareview/2016/Jan/Janreview.htm

Sen, A. (1990, December 20). More than 100 million women are missing. *New York Review of Books.* Retrieved from http://www.nybooks.com/articles/1990/12/20/more-than-100-million-women-are-missing/

Sen, C. (2000, April). *Toward a feminist politics? The Indian women's movement in historical perspective.* Retrieved from http://www.onlinewomeninpolitics.org/india/indian.pdf

Shettar, R. M. (2015, April). A study on issues and challenges of women empowerment in India. *IOSR Journal of Business and Management, 17*(4), 13–19. Retrieved from http://iosrjournals.org/iosr-jbm/papers/Vol17-issue4/Version-1/B017411319.pdf

Suguna, B. (2002, August). Strategies for empowerment of rural women. *Social Welfare, 49*, 3.

Surie, M. D. (2016, March 9). *Where are India's working women?* Retrieved from https://asiafoundation.org/2016/03/09/where-are-indias-working-women/

University Grants Commission. (2013). *UGC Report.* Retrieved from https://www.ugc.ac.in/page/ugc-regulations.aspx

Upadhyay, R. (2010a). *Women's economic opportunities in India.* Retrieved from https://asiafoundation.org/resources/pdfs/womensempowermentindiabriefs.pdf

Upadhyay, R. (2010b). *Women's empowerment in India.* Retrieved from https://asiafoundation.org/resources/pdfs/womensempowermentindiabriefs.pdf

FACTORS IMPACTING WOMEN'S LEADERSHIP

Editor: *Chrispina Lekule*

Chapter 6

Overview

Factors Impacting Women's Leadership

Chrispina Lekule

Globally, there has been increased scholarly attention on factors that have prohibited women from engaging in educational leadership positions. Some governments and nongovernmental organizations have engaged strategic interventional measures to ensure equal opportunities in leadership. According to Ndlovu and Mutale (2013), among the measures are "[an] increase of women's liberation movements, global and national agreements, and the increase of opportunities for girl's education, conventions and commitments amongst others" (p. 72). It is as a result of efforts such as these, that the world is currently witnessing a gradual increase in the number of women in top leadership positions.

However, when considering women's involvement in education overall, they remain statistically underrepresented. Women encounter multiple challenges that impact on their access to leadership and their ability to lead. These challenges are vast and complex. This chapter presents core themes which arise from the following four chapters, illustrating across these stories of leadership experiences, factors which impede women's ability to access leadership spanning societies, organizations, and personal and professional lives.

SOCIETAL FACTORS

Many societies across the world lack an inclusive leadership environment that supports and promotes women. Consequently, the few women who are in leadership positions are often viewed as strangers and face multiple challenges that arise from the societies in which they live. Wafa Hozien's study examined the experiences of "Minority Women Leaders in Higher Education."

Findings indicate that, despite the gradual increase of the number of women leaders in higher education, women still encounter setbacks which emanate from societal practices and long maintained values. This is consistent with the literature that establishes how gender bias in many societies impacts women's leadership as it contributes to inconsistencies and underrepresentation of women in educational leadership.

Wafa Hozien offers an in-depth look at the leadership styles of minority female leaders who have been successful in attaining higher education positions. She ascertains that there are multiple factors impacting women and minority women in particular. For example, minority women who are involved in higher education leadership are changing their leadership style to adopt one that is more consistent with that which is considered the norm. Akin to factors that impact women's leadership in general, Wafa Hozien argues that minority women leaders "have the same struggles as white women leaders, associated with gender, but have additional challenges associated with culture and linguistic issues."

She further suggests that barriers that women face in leadership are a result of innate prejudiced perceptions that are acquired from childhood about women's ability to be effective leaders. This is to say that the negative perceptions about women originate from sociocultural and historical norms of the given society. Based on this ground, it is not surprising that societies establish and sustain practices, which safeguard the status quo and male dominance in leadership. Shin and Bang (2013) arguing that "there are broad societal forces and policies which perpetuate assumptions and stereotypes which present challenges to women in leadership roles" (p. 3).

More societal factors impacting women's leadership have been highlighted in Samantha Mortimer's and Frances Edwards's study under the title "Scaling the Mountain to Principalship: The Barriers and the Enablers in a Female First Time Principal's Journey." The authors present a narrative of a real-life experience on how women make their journey to a top leadership position using a case of a New Zealand woman who advanced from being a kindergarten classroom teacher to a position of principal of a high school. In the narrative, gender issues and family responsibilities are highlighted as barriers while the woman's strong belief in social justice, mentors, and professional development are noted, as enables.

Mortimer and Edwards note that despite the number of girls acquiring secondary and university education around the world, women are still discriminated against by being compartmentalized into so-called women's work or roles and as a result of such stereotypical perceptions, the number of women in top leadership positions is not impressive. The reasons being doubts about women's ability to be committed to work due to their other responsibilities as wives and mothers. Lack of representation of women in the shortlisting panels for leadership positions is also noted by the authors as an obstacle to women's representation in leadership.

ORGANIZATIONAL FACTORS

Organizations across the globe are traditionally male dominated, consequently, significant decisions are made without consultation with or involving women. Hence, women aspiring for leadership positions face the challenge of making their voices heard (Priola, 2007). Tamara Jones and Deidre Le Fevre draw on the notion of women's engagement in organizations in their chapter titled, "How Perceptions of Risk Can Affect Women Who Are Leading and Engaging in Educational Change," presenting new insights into organizational factors impacting women's leadership.

The findings illustrated how women faced barriers to leadership because the organizations they were working with did not consult or involve them in the decisions when planning for professional learning. Other organizational factors impacting women's leadership as highlighted by the authors included lack of time and deprivatization of teaching practice where women could gain more experience which can boost their confidence as educators and leaders.

Double standards when judging performance that is a result of hegemonic practices and gender bias are also a hindrance to women's leadership. Women are held to higher standards than men when evaluating their work. Heilman and Okimoto (2007) explain this factor noting that women leaders in male-dominated organizations are generally faced with "social rejection and personally directed negativity, which have detrimental consequences for career-relevant organizational rewards" (p. 81).

Hegemonic practices of masculinity in many organizations jeopardize women leaders' ability to be successful. Eagly and Carli (2007) note that it is probably from this standpoint that women who make it to leadership posi-

tions often face resistance from people with outdated perceptions about women as leaders.

PERSONAL AND PROFESSIONAL FACTORS

As natural human beings, and more specifically in their position as mothers in the family, women are exposed to additional factors that negatively impact their leadership. As mothers, they have to balance work and family responsibilities which can affect their personal relationships, or their professional life depending on the choices they make.

Arceli Rosario's chapter on "Barriers and Strategies: Stories of Women's Rise to Leadership" shows evidence that some of the factors impacting women's leadership are personal while others are professional. The findings from seven women leaders in accredited higher institutions in the Philippines who participated in the study showed that the personal factors impacting women's leadership included: women's negative attitudes about self and a feeling of inadequacy. Another factor is a double burden due to inability to balance work and family life.

These findings resonate with those of Northouse (2007) who states that, "women are not less educated than men, but they handle more domestic duties which results in less work practice and more job disruptions" (p. 29). Hence depending on the ability of an individual woman leader to balance leadership responsibilities and their domestic roles, it is likely they will fail to meet deadlines or miss important meetings, thus impacting leadership (Kadaga, 2013).

Rosario identified a number of professional factors impacting women's leadership including discrimination based on gender, lack of support in mentoring and networking, and a perceived inequality in salaries. Closely related to these factors was the sense of enfeebled self-efficacy.

According to Shin and Bang (2013), women without role models or those experiencing "highly gendered professional stereotypes" (p. 4) are likely to develop low self-esteem and self-mistrust of their ability to perform as leaders. Hence, women's leadership is impacted by the sense of diminished self-efficacy which is the result of multiple factors including conscious and unconscious gender bias, underrepresentation of women in leadership, and the culture which perpetuates the hegemony of masculine values and ideologies about leadership.

Continuing on this personal theme, in their chapter focusing on the impact that stress and health has to a woman superintendent's life, Kerry Robinson and Charol Shakeshaft explore sources of stress and the possible effects they have on the lives of superintendents. The findings illustrated disturbing trends in women's experiences of stress and the detrimental impact this can have on women's health overall. They explore notions of spirituality and mindfulness as ways to reduce the impact stress may have on women and argue that a woman superintendent's health and the effective management of stress are related to her success in her role as a leader and argue if these aspects are considered and managed effectively, there is a great opportunity to harness the joy of her leadership in her daily life.

CONCLUSION AND RECOMMENDATIONS

The four chapters in this section illustrate that despite the evidence of the steady increase in number of professional women in the society, women still lag behind men in occupying top leadership positions due to persistent hindrances, which generally cut across the globe. As ascertained in the four chapters, the most common factors impacting women's leadership emanate from hegemonic practices and the struggle to maintain the status quo. Other factors are those promoted by social media such as the negative perception of women and their contribution to the society.

Similarly, organizational tendencies to segregate women in favor of men as leaders were among the most noted challenges. From the vivid life stories of these women, it became evident that there are also personal and cultural factors, which hinder women's opportunities to pave their ways into prestigious leadership positions such as principalship. Therefore, based on these findings, recommendations are made for professional women, educational leaders, and policymakers.

Given the diverse experiences women have of leadership and the factors impacting women's leadership being multiple, and culturally contextually located, it is evident that women continue to face numerous challenges accessing and participating in educational leadership opportunities. Despite the entrenched and long-standing challenges faced by women, this problem is not intractable as evidenced by recent advances in attitudes and policies that now demand employment equity and emphasize workplace rights.

Illuminating women's experiences of leadership is important as exposing these can support an ongoing dialogue where women can contribute their phenomenological experiences and shine light on progress we have made and where we still need to go and the nature of the path forward.

The studies that are hereby presented in this overview lead us to wonder about what needs to be done to completely eradicate gender stereotypes and injustices against women so that they can have equal and unbiased opportunity to influence and contribute to the well-being of the society from a position of leadership. Akin to these thoughts therefore, policymakers play a key role in implementing policies that require equal opportunity for all.

The work of Ely, Stone, and Ammerman (2014) posits that societies and organizations must be vigilant about unspoken but powerful perceptions, beliefs, and practices that constrain women's leadership practices. Women are key to this process and through exposing patriarchal practices that promote the status quo, shifts in organizations, communities, and societies can be made to create opportunities for women to be fairly represented and celebrated in their leadership.

REFERENCES

Eagly, A. H., & Carli, L. L. (2007). *Through the labyrinth: The truth about how women become leaders*. Cambridge, MA: Harvard Business School Press.

Ely, R., Stone, P., & Ammerman, C. (2014). Rethink what you "know" about high-achieving women, R1412G. *Harvard Business Review, 92*(12), 101–109.

Heilman, M. E., & Okimoto, T. G. (2007). Why are women penalized for success at male tasks? The implied communality deficit. *Journal of Applied Psychology, 92*(1), 81–92.

Kadaga, R. A. (2013). Women's political leadership in East Africa with specific reference to Uganda: Women's Leadership for Enterprise. Retrieved from www.commonwealthgovernance.org/

Ndlovu, S., & Mutale, S. B. (2013). Emerging trends in women's participation in politics in Africa. *American International Journal of Contemporary Research, 3*(11), 72–79.

Northouse, P. G. (2007). *Leadership: Theory and Practice* (4th ed.). Thousand Oaks, CA: Sage.

Priola, V. (2007). Being female doing gender. Narratives of women in education management. *Gender and Education, 19*(1), 21–40.

Shin, Y. H., & Bang, S. C. (2013). What are the top factors that prohibit women from advancing into leadership positions at the same rate as men? Retrieved August 18, 2017 from Cornell University, ILR School site: http://digitalcommons.ilr.cornell.edu/student/39/

Chapter 7

The Relationship of Stress and Health in Women Superintendents in the United States

Kerry Robinson and Charol Shakeshaft

The role of the superintendent is indeed complex and at most times, extremely demanding. The changing educational climate in the United States has brought with it numerous changes and many would attest to the fact that higher levels of stress manifest in this leadership role as leaders seek to reconcile the demands of educational change, social and political shifts, and personal circumstances. This chapter focuses on the relationship that stress and health has to a woman superintendent's life. By determining and exposing these sources of stress and the effects they have on the superintendent's life, there may be possibilities for creating greater longevity in the careers of women superintendents overall.

The position of superintendent is one that continues to evolve with layers of complexity every year (Finnan, McCord, Stream, Mattocks, Petersen, & Ellerson, 2015; Kowalski, 2005; Petersen & Fusarelli, 2008). While the position has always had to deal with complexity, many feel that the added stressors that have more recently appeared (federal policy changes, the rise of social media), make the position even more complex than even a decade prior (Lytle & Sokoloff, 2013).

As women currently make up approximately 24 percent of school superintendents in the United States (Finnan et al., 2015), the goal is not only keeping these women serving in the position of superintendent, but also finding ways to increase the percentage of women, and especially women of color, into the superintendency across the country. To do this, we wanted to understand the relationship that stress and health had to a woman superintendent's life. While we knew there would be stress related to operating in her position, we also wondered about the other aspects of her life that might be causing stress and in these different realms of her life, were they affecting her health in a negative way? By determining these sources of stress and the effects they were having on the superintendent's life, future research might explore ways to help women better deal with the stressors in their lives and allow them to remain in the position of superintendent for a longer tenure.

The issue of stress is one that most people feel they personally understand. While the sources of stress may vary, and the consequences of stress may differ, people believe they know something about the topic of "stress," although there is not a single definition of the phenomena (Kinman & Jones, 2005). The American Psychological Association (APA) has been studying stress annually since 2006. They have found that most stress in Americans comes from the following areas: money, work, family responsibilities, and health concerns (American Psychological Association, 2015). While these reports are presented in aggregate form which does not allow us to look at some specifics in detail, one thing the 2015 report highlights is that women report higher levels of stress (5.3) than men (4.9) (American Psychological Association, 2015).

Research on stress suggests looking at the topic with more of a multidisciplinary approach:

> It views stress as not just a function of being under pressure in an occupational sense but as a function of an individual's whole life situation. It includes factors intrinsic to the job (workload); relationships at work; organizational structure and climate; role ambiguity and conflict; opportunities for career development and progression; and the home work interface. (Fielden & Cooper, 2002, p. 20)

By looking at stress through these many lenses, a person is better able to navigate a life with constant conflicting pressures, both inside and outside the workplace.

Not all stress is alike, however. In *The Stress of Life*, Selye (1976) identifies a difference between good stress (eustress) and bad stress (distress).

> During both eustress and distress the body undergoes virtually the same nonspecific responses to the various

positive or negative stimuli acting upon it. However, the fact that eustress causes much less damage than distress graphically demonstrates that it is "how you take it" that determines, ultimately, whether one can adapt successfully to change. (Selye, 1976, p. 74)

What is important for a person who experiences a role that causes a great deal of stress is to develop a better understanding of how to react to the stress she experiences. The fear is when people do not learn strategies to deal with sources of stress.

Most research written on the topic of superintendent stress has occurred in dissertation research, with some dissertations focused deliberately on the topic (Carroll, 2010; Hawk, 2008; Richardson, 1998; Simonson, 2013), where others found the topic of stress appeared as a finding in a larger study (Kassebaum, 2011; Olesniewicz, 2012; Passalacqua, 2007; Robinson, 2013; Unzicker, 2012; Wheeler, 2012). Unfortunately, as with many dissertation studies, the scope is often a single state with limited participants so while contributing to the knowledge base, it leaves the need for national studies on the superintendent even more valuable.

Outside the area of dissertation studies, others have called attention to the increasing stress in the position of superintendent of schools. In some cases, the issue is addressed as a by-product of the positions continuously evolving complexity (Carter & Cunningham, 1997; Finnan et al., 2015; Glass, 2000; Lytle & Sokoloff, 2013). Others have found the exploration of coping mechanisms regarding stress to be an area in which to focus (Gmelch, 1996; Hawk & Martin, 2011). While these different works are helping to identify the issues the superintendents are experiencing, there has been nothing that attempts to link the types of stress superintendents are experiencing with the health condition of the superintendent as they are on the job. What affect does this have on a person when these stressors are constant and the superintendent is remaining in a state of distress? What affect will this have on her health?

As one might expect, there have been numerous studies linking extreme levels of stress to contributing health conditions (American Psychological Association, n.d.; Demerouti, Bakker, Nachreiner, & Schaufeli, 2001; Marin, Lord, Andrews, Juster, Sindi, Arsenault-Lapierre, & Lupien, 2011; McEwen, 2007; Selye, 1976). A recent study by Rohleder (2014) reviewed previous studies exploring the link between stress and inflammation and determined "Inflammation therefore stands out as a promising biological process to investigate in the association between stress and disease" (p. 183). This study and others (Bellingrath, Rohleder, & Kudielka, 2010; Hänsel, Hong, Cámara, & von Känel, 2010) highlight that stress-induced inflammation has been linked to cardiovascular disease, stroke, diabetes, Alzheimer's, and cancer. Liu, Wang, and Jiang (2017) noted, "[s]tress is the common risk factor of 75%–90% of diseases, including the diseases which cause the foremost morbidity and mortality" (p. 1).

In addition to stress, health can be affected in other negative ways. When women lead school districts, they often are so focused on taking care of everyone, they spend less time focused on themselves. This often manifests in poor eating habits, not exercising, and having terrible sleep habits, to name a few (Robinson, 2016). While it may be in our nature to care for those we are leading, Brock and Grady (2002) offer up important advice,

> Your health is your responsibility. No one else knows exactly how you feel or has the same level of concern. Working despite illness may be viewed favorably by your superiors, but they will not suffer the consequences of your poor health. You will. (p. 45)

To determine the link between superintendent stress and superintendent health, the purpose of this study was to examine the following three questions:

1. What are the common job stressors perceived by women superintendents? Do these stressors differ by the race of the superintendent?
2. What are the common health ailments identified by women superintendents? Do these ailments differ by race?
3. Is there a relationship between level of stress and severity of health condition? Are these relationships different by race of superintendent?

RESEARCH DESIGN

We chose to conduct survey research for this study, which would allow us to make statistical comparisons across all respondents. We constructed a survey based on findings from previous research on administrator stress (Gmelch & Swent, 1984; Hawk, 2008), as well as medical conditions previously tied to stress in literature (CDC, 2013; Horgen, 1991). We also constructed a section asking the participants to rate a list of the challenges present in their school districts at the time of the 2015 survey. These challenges were identified by reviewing publications of organizations that focus primarily on the responsibilities of superintendents (American Association of School Administrators [AASA]; National Association of School Superintendents; the Council for Great City Schools; and the National School Board Association). The survey also collected information about district and superintendent demographics. The final part of the survey development was piloting the survey with a small group of superintendents and other researchers to determine ease of use.

In order to get the largest national sample of superintendents we purchased a list from Market Data Research and asked to have a larger proportion of women and superintendents of color included in our sample which would allow us to target a larger portion of underrepresented groups in the superintendency which may not traditionally be in other national superintendent surveys like the AASA Decade and Mid-Decade studies (Finnan et al., 2015; Kowalski, McCord, Petersen, Young, & Ellerson, 2011). In January through February 2015, the survey was sent to a random stratified sample of 6,540 superintendents in the United States through an email invitation asking for superintendents to participate. We also sent three follow-up emails reminding superintendents about the survey during the survey window being open. We had a 28.5 percent response rate for all superintendents, but even with oversampling, only 13.6 percent of our total responses were from women superintendents (890) and 1.2 percent of our total responses were from women superintendents of color (79 respondents).

We are not able to determine whether our response rate is representative of all superintendents because there are no records kept on the race and sex of superintendents. The Department of Education, National Center for Education Statistics, does not collect race and sex data on superintendents. The Schools and Staff survey collects that information on teachers and principals, but not superintendents. AASA conducts a survey of members, but response rate makes those findings questionable. However, the AASA mid-decade survey conducted in the same time period as this survey, identified the following statistical representations (presented in table 7.1).

Our response rate and sample were quite different, with nearly twice the proportion of women respondents overall and a larger proportion of women superintendents of color than the AASA 2015 survey (table 7.2). We think it is fair to say that our sample overrepresents the number of women superintendents, but we are not sure by how much. We continue to call for regular counts of superintendents by race and gender. One of us first asked for those statistics from the US Department of Education in 1977; we are still waiting.

Table 7.1. AASA Mid-Decade Respondents by Race and Gender

	Percent Superintendents of Color	Percent White Superintendents	Total by Gender
Percent Female	2.2	24.6	26.8
Percent Male	3.0	70.2	73.2
Total by Race	5.2	94.8	100.0

Table 7.2. Health and Stress Respondents by Race and Gender

	Percent Superintendents of Color	Percent White Superintendents	Total by Gender
Percent Female	4.3	43.6	47.9
Percent Male	3.4	48.7	52.1
Total by Race	7.7	92.3	100.0

FINDINGS

What Does Superintendent Stress Look Like for Women?

We started by asking about stress levels of women superintendents. Stress was examined using three measures. The first is a composite scale that asked respondents to rate, never to very often, their experience of 10 different conditions. The scale range was 10 to 50, Cronbach's Alpha = 0.881. The scale was then recoded on a scale of 1 to 5, to be consistent with the overall survey scale. Four items were reverse coded so that a 1 indicated the least stress and 5 the most stress. We then examined these 10 items for district size differences (see table 7.3).

The second perspective on stress included 20 questions that asked for respondent stress about professional and personal issues. These questions were factor analyzed using principal component analysis with Varimax (orthogonal) rotation. The analysis yielded five factors explaining 63.5 percent of the variance for the entire set of variables. Table 7.4 displays those values.

Finally, we examined stress by life categories and found that personal stress for superintendents was low but that slightly more than 50 percent of superinten-

Table 7.3. Women Superintendent's Stress

	Mean	S.D.
Been upset by something that happened unexpectedly	3.10	0.87
Were unable to control the important things in your life	2.68	1.06
Felt nervous and stressed	3.38	0.96
Did not feel confident about your ability to handle your personal problems	1.73	0.81
Did not feel things were going your way	2.21	0.79
Found you could not cope with things that you had to do	2.45	1.07
Not able to control irritations in your life	2.24	0.84
Felt were not on top of things	2.26	0.81
Been angered because of things outside of your control	2.80	0.96
Felt difficulties piling up so high you could not overcome them	2.38	1.06
Stress Total: How Often Do You Feel Stress	2.29	0.58

Scale: 1 = Never to 5 = Very often

Table 7.4. Means and Percentages of Women Superintendent Stressors

Stressor	Mean	S.D.	Percent: Considerable to Extreme Stress
Time	3.54	1.14	41.3
Finance and oversight factor	3.43	1.01	32.5
Relationships with board and community	2.85	1.10	21.1
Job performance of district and building administrators	2.65	0.97	13.4
Self-confidence in ability	1.94	0.81	3.5

Table 7.5. Means and Percentages of Women Superintendent Stress by Type

Stressor	Mean	S.D.	Percent: Considerable to Extreme Stress
Professional stress	3.69	0.98	53.4
Personal stress	2.79	0.95	19.4
Day-to-day, both personal and professional	3.35	0.90	37.5

dents reported considerable to extreme professional stress (see table 7.5). We then analyzed these stressors to determine whether there were differences between women superintendents of color and white women superintendents and found no meaningful differences in the stress of the two groups.

General Health Conditions and Well-being for Women Superintendents

We developed a list of 22 health conditions (see table 7.6). We then asked superintendents if they had the condition. We also asked if the condition developed during the superintendency. The average number of health conditions for women was two, with no differences by race. More than a quarter of all women superintendents reported no health conditions (29 percent). More women of color (35 percent) reported no health conditions than did white women (28 percent). Of those who did identify current health conditions, there were seven that 10 percent or

Table 7.6. Percent Women Superintendents With Health Conditions

Insomnia	29.1
High-Blood Pressure	26.9
Gastrointestinal	22.7
High Cholesterol	21.6
Obesity	19.7
Anxiety	18.1
Chronic Headaches	17.5

Table 7.7. Health Conditions by Race

Condition	Percent Women of Color	Percent White Women	p	Phi
Heart Disease	7.6	2.7	0.02	−0.08
Obesity	30.4	18.6	0.01	−0.08
Diabetes	17.7	4.4	0.00	−0.16

more of women experienced. Table 7.6 lists those and the proportion of women who experienced this condition. These conditions have been associated in the literature with stress.

We analyzed all health conditions by race. Our cutoff for determining a meaningful difference was 8 percent of the variance explained. Table 7.7 displays the conditions for which there were differences by race of women superintendents. We were curious whether any of the conditions began during the superintendency. Conditions that at least 10 percent of women report they developed during the superintendency include:

- Insomnia
- High-blood pressure
- Obesity
- Gastrointestinal problems

Most of the women entered the superintendency with the condition already existing.

Relationships of Stress to Health

Our third research question examined the relationship between level of stress and number of health conditions. The relationship between level of stress and number of health conditions was statistically and practically significant: $r = 0.393$, $p = 0.00$, $r^2 = 0.15$. This relationship was stronger for white women ($r = 0.334$) than for women of color ($r = 0.284$)

SUMMARY

The question might be asked, what does this tell us about the stress and health of women in the superintendency? It is important to put these findings into context with other studies that have looked at the stress and health of the superintendent and determine where future study might be warranted.

In regard to stress, while our data highlight that professional stress was a greater source of stress than personal stress, what we were most taken by was that only 53.4 percent categorized their stress level as considerable to extreme. Other studies have looked at superintendent stress over time. In 2007, Glass and Franceschini took a historical look at superintendent stress over the course of four superintendent decade or mid-decade studies (1980, 1992, 2000, 2006). What they found was the group who fell into the top tiers of stress; "very great stress" and "considerable stress" had been increasing over time 43.6 percent in 1980, 50.3 percent in 1992, 51.5 percent in 2000, and 59.2 percent in 2006 (Glass & Franceschini, 2007, p. 48). This would lead researchers to believe that in future decade or mid-decade studies, these numbers would continue to grow.

Unfortunately, during the next two AASA studies (Finnan et al., 2015; Kowalski et al., 2011), there were questions that dealt with stress, but they were asked in a way that didn't allow for that historical tracking to continue. In our larger study on superintendent stress and health in regard to both male and female respondents, there were no statistical differences in the professional stress levels between the superintendent's by gender or by race, with 53.3 percent of the respondents identifying "extreme" or "considerable" stress (Robinson & Shakeshaft, 2016).

Perhaps this suggests that, on the whole, superintendents are doing a better job managing their levels of stress than superintendents have previously. It is critical that we continue to not only ask the same questions over time to be able to track these items historically, but additional items need to be added as new challenges arise and the position continues to evolve so we may better understand stress and its relation to the challenges present in the position of superintendent (Robinson, Shakeshaft, Grogan, & Newcomb, 2017).

In reviewing the findings of the principal component analysis, the five factors that emerged as women superintendent stressors contained areas that have been identified historically as challenges for female superintendents with time (Brunner & Grogan, 2007; Grogan & Brunner, 2005; Harris, 2007; Hawk & Martin, 2011; Hill, McDonald, & Ward, 2017; Robinson et al., 2017), relationship with school board and community (Brunner, 1999; Glass, 2000; Kamler & Shakeshaft, 1999; Tallerico, 2000), and finance and oversight (Brunner & Kim, 2010; Gardiner, Enomoto, & Grogan, 2000; Glass, 2000; Grogan & Shakeshaft, 2011) and the percentages of considerable to extreme stress in those areas highlight that these are still challenges for women currently in the positions. This emphasizes that there is still work that needs to be done to help current superintendents address these issues, as well as find ways to prepare aspiring women superintendents for these traditionally challenging areas.

As previously stated in the review of research, all stress does not need to be categorized as a negative (Brock & Grady, 2002; Lyles, 2005; Selye, 1976), but it can in fact be utilized in a way that can provide satisfaction and self-fulfillment for the women in the position of superintendent. As Grogan and Brunner (2005) found "some stress is necessary for self-fulfillment because 83 percent of the highly-fulfilled group [in their sample] experienced moderate or considerable stress" (p. 16). The challenge becomes how do women work to control the effect of stress on their jobs and their lives?

One promising practice is through the practice of mindfulness. In her dissertation, *Embracing Mindfulness: A Woman Superintendent's Journey*, McDonald (2012) shares the findings of how a mindfulness practice not only helped her as she navigated her superintendency, she also provides examples of where others have encouraged administrators adopting mindfulness practices into their daily lives (Gmelch, 1995; Hawk & Martin, 2011). The idea behind a regular mindfulness practice for superintendents proved to be more than just a dissertation topic (and survival strategy) for McDonald.

McDonald (2015) also applied this mindfulness framework to the challenges of a small-district superintendent, as well as researching with others the importance of adopting a mindfulness practice in addressing the various challenges of a turnaround district (Coogan, Gates, & McDonald, 2015). Additional research on the topic of mindfulness in the superintendency might provide opportunities for current superintendents to adopt practices for their own health, but may also have implications for colleges and universities that are preparing future principals and superintendents. Would providing a course in mindfulness practice be one that would benefit not only the administrator, but all of the teachers, staff, and students that she leads?

The findings regarding women superintendents and particular health conditions were also consistent with the previous literature on the health of the superintendent (Colgan, 2003; Domenech, 1996; Hawk & Martin, 2011; McDonald, 2012; Queen & Queen, 2005; Robinson, 2013). While traditionally a person would probably miss work when experiencing negative health conditions, for many women superintendents, the opposite is true where they continue to show up for work even if they are not able to function to their fullest capacity (Carroll, 2010), or until they are no longer able to function in the position. In the most recent AASA Mid-Decade Survey, Finnan et al. (2015) found that while only five (0.6 percent) of respondents resigned their superintendency for health reasons, it is interesting to note that four of the five departures were by women.

As we created our study we had hoped that there would have been more findings that could be disaggregated by race, but one of the few areas that did have some statistical differences were in the areas of health. Overall, there was a larger percentage of superintendents of color who reported no health conditions compared to the white superintendents who reported no health conditions. Previous research in the area of African American female superintendents highlights the importance of resilience in persevering in such a challenging position (Johnson, 2012; Kingsberry, 2015; Odum, 2010) with spirituality playing a large part of what keeps them focused on the work (Alston, 2005; Simmons & Johnson, 2008; Smith, 2011; Williams & Peters, 2011). The connection with spirituality has been recognized as a source of positive health outcomes for women of color (Musgrave, Allen, & Allen, 2002).

What lessons can superintendent's learn from these studies of resilience and spirituality? One thing that is critically important is that there needs to be additional research in this area. What lessons can be learned from the study of resiliency and its connection to spirituality that Simmons and Johnson (2008) identify as "her ability to draw upon an inner strength" (p. 224) and how that might help women better address these challenges with stress and health?

A more dire finding was the difference of the women superintendents of color who did have medical conditions and the higher instances of heart disease, obesity, and diabetes than the white women superintendents. Hopefully, additional research can be conducted that continues to look at the issues related to stress and health and that a larger sample of female superintendents can be surveyed so that there will be additional ways to look at this data historically.

Finally, while the topic of mindfulness was introduced in the review of stress, additional research on the topic of superintendent well-being should be conducted to identify the healthy stress management practices that are working for current superintendents. From these findings, this information can be shared with both current and aspiring superintendents, as well as school board associations, and leadership preparation programs. By identifying ways to keep a women superintendent healthy and effectively managing the stress associated with the job, we have a better chance of harnessing the joy of her leadership as she works to serve the district she oversees.

REFERENCES

Alston, J. A. (2005). Tempered radicals and servant leaders: Black females persevering in the superintendency. *Educational Administration Quarterly, 41*(4), 675–688.

American Psychological Association. (2015). Stress in America: Paying with our health. Retrieved June 30, 2016, from http://www.apa.org/news/press/releases/stress/2014/stress-report.pdf

American Psychological Association. (n.d.). Stress Effects on the Body. Retrieved June 30, 2016, from http://www.apa.org/helpcenter/stress-body.aspx

Bellingrath, S., Rohleder, N., & Kudielka, B. M. (2010). Healthy working school teachers with high effort-reward-imbalance and overcommitment show increased pro-inflammatory immune activity and a dampened innate immune defence. *Brain, Behavior, and Immunity, 24*(8), 1332–1339.

Brock, B. L., & Grady, M. L. (2002). *Avoiding burnout: A principal's guide to keeping the fire alive.* Thousand Oaks, CA: Corwin Press.

Brunner, C. C. (1999). *Sacred Dreams: Women and the superintendency.* Albany, NY: State University of New York Press.

Brunner, C. C., & Grogan M. (2007). *Women leading school systems: Uncommon roads to fulfillment.* Lanham, MD: Rowman & Littlefield.

Brunner, C. C., & Kim, Y. (2010). Are women prepared to be superintendents? Myths and misunderstandings. *Journal of Research on Leadership Education, 5*(8), 276–309.

Carroll, K. J. (2010). *Consequences of stress for public school superintendents* (Doctoral dissertation). Retrieved from ProQuest Dissertation and Theses database. (UMI No. 3422264)

Carter, G. R., & Cunningham, W. G. (1997). *The American school superintendent: Leading in an age of pressure.* San Francisco, CA: Jossey-Bass.

Center for Disease Control. (2013). *2014 Behavioral Risk Factor Surveillance System (BRFSS) Questionnaire.* Retrieved October 18, 2014, from https://www.cdc.gov/brfss/questionnaires/pdf-ques/2014_BRFSS.pdf

Colgan, C. (2003). Burned out. *American School Board Journal, 190*(4), 24–28.

Coogan, N., Gates, G., & McDonald, T. (2015). Becoming a mindful superintendent in a "turnaround" district. *Open Journal of Leadership.* http://dx.doi.org/10.4236/ojl.2015

Demerouti, E., Bakker, A. B., Nachreiner, F., & Schaufeli, W. B. (2001). The job demands-resources model of burnout. *Journal of Applied Psychology, 86*(3), 499–512.

Domenech, D. (1996). Surviving the ultimate stress. *School Administrator, 53*(3), 40–41.

Fielden, S. L., & Cooper, C. L. (2002). Managerial stress: Are women more at risk? In D. L. Nelson & R. J. Burke (Eds.), *Gender, work stress, and health* (pp. 19–34). Washington, DC: American Psychological Association.

Finnan, L., McCord, R. S., Stream, C., Mattocks, T. C., Petersen, G. J., & Ellerson, N. (2015). *The study of the American superintendent: 2015 Mid-decade update.* Alexandria, VA: AASA, School Superintendents Association.

Gardiner, M. E., Enomoto, E., & Grogan, M. (2000). *Coloring outside the lines: Mentoring women into school leadership.* Albany, NY: State University of New York Press.

Glass, T. E. (2000). Where are all the women superintendents? AASA's latest study on the profession suggests seven reasons why female numbers still lag in top district posts. *School Administrator, 57*(6), 28–32.

Glass, T. E., & Franceschini, L. A. (2007). *The state of the American school superintendency: A mid-decade study.* Lanham, MD: Rowman & Littlefield Education.

Gmelch, W. G. (1995). Administrator stress and coping effectiveness: Implications for administrator evaluation and development. *Journal of Personnel Evaluation in Education, 9*, 275–285.

Gmelch, W. (1996). Breaking out of superintendent stress traps. *School Administrator 53*(3), 32–33, 35–39.

Gmelch, W. H., & Swent, B. (1984). Management team stressors and their impact on administrators' health. *Journal of Educational Administration, 2*, 193–205.

Grogan, M., & Brunner, C. C. (2005). Women leading systems. *School Administrator, 62*(2), 1–4.

Grogan, M., & Shakeshaft, C. (2011). *Women and educational leadership*. San Francisco, CA: Jossey-Bass.

Hänsel, A., Hong, S., Cámara, R. J., & von Känel, R. (2010). Inflammation as a psychophysiological biomarker in chronic psychosocial stress. *Neuroscience & Biobehavioral Reviews, 35*(1), 115–121.

Harris, S. (2007, Spring). Motivators and inhibitors for women superintendents. *Advancing Women in Leadership Online Journal, 23*. Retrieved from http://www.advancingwomen.com/awl/spring2007/harris.htm

Hawk, N. C. (2008). *Implications of stress and coping mechanisms in the superintendency* (Doctoral dissertation). Retrieved from ProQuest Dissertation and Theses database. (UMI No. 3371061)

Hawk, N., & Martin, B. (2011). Understanding and reducing stress in the superintendency. *Educational Management Administration & Leadership, 39*(3), 364–390.

Hill, G., McDonald, T., & Ward, K. (2017). Women in educational leadership: Implications for preparation programs. *Washington Education Research Association Educational Journal, 9*(2), 55–60.

Horgen, J. E. (1991). A study of perceived stress and reported health problems: Relationships to other variables among secondary school principals of Minnesota (Doctoral dissertation). Retrieved from ProQuest Dissertation and Theses database. (UMI No. 9206422)

Johnson, B. H. (2012). *African American female superintendents: Resilient school leaders.* Retrieved from the University of Minnesota Digital Conservancy, http://hdl.handle.net/11299/120821

Kamler, E., & Shakeshaft, C. (1999). The role of the search consultant in the career paths of women superintendents. In C. C. Brunner (Ed.), *Sacred dreams: Women and the superintendency* (pp. 51–62). Albany, NY: State University of New York Press.

Kassebaum, Z. G. (2011). *Satisfied superintendents: A case study* (Doctoral dissertation). Retrieved from ProQuest Dissertation and Theses database. (UMI No. 3461340)

Kingsberry, F. S. P. (2015). Protective factors and resiliency: A case study of how African American women overcome barriers en route to the superintendency (Doctoral dissertation). Retrieved from ProQuest Dissertation and Theses database. (UMI No. 10110754)

Kinman, G., & Jones, F. (2005). Lay representations of workplace stress: What do people really mean when they say they are stressed? *Work & Stress, 19*(2), 101–120.

Kowalski, T. J. (2005). Evolution of the school district superintendent position. In L. G. Björk & T. J. Kowalski (Eds.), *The contemporary superintendent: Preparation practice and development* (pp. 1–18). Thousand Oaks, CA: Corwin Press.

Kowalski, T. J., McCord, R., Petersen, G., Young, I. P., & Ellerson, N. (2011). *The American school superintendent: 2010 decennial study*. Lanham, MD: American Association of School Administrators and Rowman & Littlefield Education.

Liu, Y. Z., Wang, Y. X., & Jiang, C. L. (2017). Inflammation: The common pathway of stress-related diseases. *Frontiers in Human Neuroscience* (pp.1–11). https://doi.org/10.3389/fnhum.2017.00316

Lyles, T. (2005). *Stress recovery manual*. Juno Beach, FL: Healthful Communications.

Lytle, J. H., & Sokoloff, H. J. (2013). A complex web: The new normal for superintendents. *School Administrator, 70*(8), 20–25.

Marin, M. F., Lord, C., Andrews, J., Juster, R. P., Sindi, S., Arsenault-Lapierre, G., & Lupien, S. J. (2011). Chronic stress, cognitive functioning and mental health. *Neurobiology of Learning and Memory, 96*(4), 583–595.

McDonald, T. P. (2012). *Embracing mindfulness: A woman superintendent's journey*. (Doctoral dissertation). Retrieved from ProQuest Dissertation and Theses database. (UMI No. 3554573)

McDonald, T. (2015). Decisions, decisions, decisions: Can using transformational leadership and mindfulness theory help you make the right ones? In G. Ivory, A. F. Hyle, R. McClennan, & M. Acker-Hocevar (Eds.), *Quandaries of the small-district superintendent* (pp. 56–71). New York, NY: Palgrave Macmillan.

McEwen, B. S. (2007). Physiology and neurobiology of stress and adaptation: Central role of the brain. *Physiological Reviews, 87*(3), 873–904.

Musgrave, C. F., Allen, C. E., & Allen, G. J. (2002). Spirituality and health for women of color. *American Journal of Public Health, 92*(4), 557–560.

Odum, R. D. (2010). *The lived experiences of female superintendents in Alabama, Florida, and Georgia.* (Doctoral dissertation). Retrieved from Electronic Theses & Dissertations 360 http://digitalcommons.georgiasouthern.edu/etd/360

Olesniewicz, J. (2012). *Balancing work and family: How female superintendents succeed at work and home* (Doctoral dissertation). Retrieved from ProQuest Dissertation and Theses database. (UMI No. 3514281)

Passalacqua, D. R. (2007). *An investigation into the impact of the superintendent/spouse relationship on longevity and success of superintendents* (Doctoral dissertation). Retrieved from ProQuest Dissertation and Theses database. (UMI No. 3283932)

Petersen, G. J., & Fusarelli, L. D. (2008), Systemic leadership amidst turbulence: Superintendent-school board relations under pressure. In T. L. Alsbury (Ed.), *The future of school board governance: Relevancy and revelation* (pp. 115–134). Lanham, MD: Rowman & Littlefield Education.

Queen, J. A., & Queen, P. S. (2005). *The frazzled principal's wellness plan*. Thousand Oaks, CA: Sage.

Richardson, L. M. (1998). *Perceived sources of stress among Connecticut superintendents: An exploratory study* (Doctoral dissertation). Retrieved from ProQuest Dissertation and Theses database. (UMI No. 9906560)

Robinson, K. K. (2013). *The career path of the female superintendent: Why she leaves* (Doctoral dissertation). Retrieved from ProQuest Dissertation and Theses database. (UMI No. 3560514)

Robinson, K. (2016). What have we learned from the departure of female superintendents? *Journal of Women in Educational Leadership, 72.* http://digitalcommons.unl.edu/jwel/72

Robinson, K., & Shakeshaft, C. (2016). Superintendent stress and superintendent health: A national study. *Journal of Education and Human Development, 5*(1), 120–133.

Robinson, K., Shakeshaft, C., Grogan, M., & Newcomb, W. (2017). Necessary but not sufficient: The continuing inequality between men and women in educational leadership, findings from the American Association of School Administrators mid-decade survey. *Frontiers in Education, 2*(12). http://dx.doi.org/10.3389/feduc.2017.00012

Rohleder, N. (2014). Stimulation of systemic low-grade inflammation by psychosocial stress. *Psychosomatic Medicine, 76*(3), 181–189.

Selye, H. (1976). *The stress of life* (Rev. ed). New York: McGraw-Hill.

Simmons, J. M., & Johnson, W. Y. (2008). African American female superintendents speaking the language of hope: Reconstructing the multi-dimensions of passion. In W. Hoy & M. DiPaola (Eds.), *Improving schools: Studies in leadership and culture* (pp. 223–249). Charlotte, NC: Information Age Publishing.

Simonson, C. R. (2013). *The relationship of stress and the physical wellness of Illinois Superintendents* (Doctoral dissertation). Retrieved from ProQuest Dissertation and Theses database. (UMI No. 3564136)

Smith, S. (2011). *The perspectives of practicing African American female superintendents in the Commonwealth of Virginia regarding the impact of spirituality on their leadership practices* (Doctoral dissertation). Retrieved from ProQuest Dissertation and Theses database. (UMI No. 3453665)

Tallerico, M. (2000). Gaining access to the superintendency: Headhunting, gender, and color. *Educational Administration Quarterly, 36*(1), 18–43.

Unzicker, T. L. (2012). *A study of the job satisfaction of Nebraska school superintendents* (Doctoral dissertation). Retrieved from ProQuest Dissertation and Theses database. (UMI No. 3539497)

Wheeler, J. J. (2012). *North Carolina superintendent turnover* (Doctoral dissertation). Retrieved from ProQuest Dissertation and Theses database. (UMI No. 3523567)

Williams, C. J., & Peters, G. B. (2011). If and to what extent spirituality impacts the leadership practices of four African American superintendents. *Delta Journal of Education, 1*(1), 1–15.

Chapter 8

Women's Perceptions of Risk When Leading and Engaging in Educational Change

Tamara Jones and Deidre Le Fevre

Women have key roles in education as both teachers and leaders. Perceptions of risk can have a significant influence on how women see and enact these roles. Recent studies have highlighted how perceptions of risk may be a fundamental barrier to change (Howard, 2013; Le Fevre, 2014; Twyford, 2016). This has important implications for women who are a significant proportion of the teaching workforce in New Zealand and abroad.

This chapter explores the concept of risk and why having an awareness of perceptions of risk may be important for women leaders in education. In this chapter, we discuss how risk-taking can influence how women shape the educational environment. The research discussed highlights how women's leadership could mitigate perceptions of risk associated with educational change. The chapter is situated in the context of educational change and, specifically, how to support teachers to change. However, concepts that are discussed are relevant to women working in other areas, as perceptions of risk are inherent in leadership and change work.

WOMEN LEADING WOMEN FOR EDUCATIONAL CHANGE

In New Zealand, and in many other countries, women dominate the primary education sector. In 2002, 82 percent of New Zealand primary school teachers were women, yet only 40 percent of these women occupied school principal positions. Seen from another perspective, 60 percent of principals were appointed from the 18 percent male pool of the workforce (Ministry of Education, 2002). Interestingly, 80 percent of the senior management positions (assistant and deputy principals) held in primary schools at the time, were held by women.

Recent statistics reveal the future looks slightly brighter for women leaders in New Zealand primary education. In 2015, the number of women teaching in New Zealand primary schools had marginally increased (83 percent); women now occupied 56 percent of the principal roles. Of concern is the fact that we do not have current data about women in leadership in education as the government funding which supported collecting this data has been cut (Ministry of Education, 2016).

Statistics show us that women leaders have a key role in working to bring about educational change. Research shows a way of doing this is through supporting professional learning for teachers. Unfortunately, however, many professional learning initiatives intended to bring about change to improve student learning are unsuccessful (Fullan, 2011; Timperley & Alton-Lee, 2008). A variety of different frameworks have been used to research the diverse and complex factors which thwart teachers' engagement in educational change. In many theories, the finger of blame for a lack of engagement in educational change has been pointed in the direction of the classroom teacher (Brody & Hadar, 2011; Hargreaves, 2005; Maskit, 2011).

Simply pointing the finger at teachers is not helpful; however, something that has promise in addressing why educational change may be difficult to implement and sustain is the idea that perceptions of risk may be a fundamental barrier (Howard, 2013; Le Fevre, 2014; Twyford, 2016). Indeed, risk-taking can influence or deter innovative behaviors and opportunities for teachers to shape the educational environment.

THE CONCEPT OF RISK

The term risk has been used numerous ways and in various contexts for many years. In the corporate world, the term "risk" is commonplace; risk management, capital risk, and systematic risk all focus on the identification, assessment, and prioritization of commercial risk (Stulz, 1996). In the education sector, the concept of risk is only beginning to be acknowledged in the context of working to understand processes of innovation and change.

A broad definition of risk includes loss, the significance of loss, and uncertainties (Aven & Renn, 2009). Loss, which can be either performance, social, psychological, or status, is considered foundational to risk-taking (Ponticell, 2003) and is often discussed in terms of significance or severity of potential loss to a person (Aven & Renn, 2009). If one perceives specific actions may lead to a greater severity of loss, then he or she will correspondingly react with higher levels of caution.

The third element associated with risk is the nature of the uncertainty of an outcome. Uncertainty is inherent to perceptions of risk (Trimpop, 1994). Scholarly literature has suggested risk-seeking or risk-averse teacher behavior may be reflective of a teacher's age and career stage (Hargreaves, 2005), based on personal practical theories (Maaranen, Pitkäniemi, Stenberg, & Karlsson, 2016), or determined by the individual's risk attitude (Baylor & Ritchie, 2002). Each of these theories acknowledges that risk-taking directly brings to the fore a person's beliefs and assumptions, which have been constructed from many and varied life experiences. Literature has also suggested groups and cultures, which have diverse social principles, may influence risk-taking behavior in education (Howard, 2013).

In a mixed methods study of 520 Israeli teachers, Maskit (2011) found that teachers in the early stages of their careers expressed the desire to extend cognitive and pedagogical knowledge, and face professional challenges. These teachers are "eager to locate better teaching methods, take risks at work, and engage actively in new projects" (Maskit, 2011, p. 858). Teachers in the early stages of their career viewed engagement in professional learning for change as an inseparable part of the teaching profession. It may be that teachers who are in the induction stage of their careers could also be overwhelmed. These teachers could perceive added expectations to implement professional learning as high risk (Hargreaves, 2005).

In contrast to findings on teachers in the early stages of their careers, research suggests teachers in the late stages of their careers feel work-related fatigue due to having already participated in numerous professional learning initiatives throughout their careers (Hargreaves, 2005; Maskit, 2011). Hargreaves (2005) found the older and more experienced a teacher was, the less willing they were to take risks and change their practice, declaring that most teachers nearing retirement "become resistant to and resilient toward change efforts outside the classroom" (p. 981). The "age and career stage" theory suggests risk-taking in an educational context is an individual, physical phenomenon. This would imply perceptions of risk when engaging in educational change could be preempted and organizational factors employed to support teachers in various stages of their careers to navigate risk.

Personal practical theories of teaching are built based on a teacher's underlying beliefs, experiences, and values regarding what constitutes quality teaching (Maaranen et al., 2016). Gess-Newsome, Southerland, Johnston, and Woodbury (2003) claim they are "formed through experience and reflection, include images of teaching and learning, the roles of teachers and students, and the purposes of and methods for content instruction" (p. 758). They play a pivotal role in teaching and may influence risk-taking behavior. Aikenhead (1984) noted the existence of personal practical theories in his earlier case study of Canadian science teachers. He concluded teachers tended "to make pre-active decisions within a frame of reference . . . with practical knowledge, teachers' rules of practice, their practical principles, and their images of basic beliefs" (Aikenhead, 1984, p. 184).

A theory of risk-taking in education which opposes the personal risk-taking theories suggests it is groups and cultures, which have diverse social principles, who guide risk behavior and judgment of what is deemed a risk and who should be allowed to take risks (Howard, 2013). This implies risk-taking in education is "domain-specific" and determined by the collective group, not the individual. The "domain-specific" theory opposes the notion that individual teachers hold a general attitude toward risk-taking. "Since identification of risks is entirely a social process, risks do not exist in objective reality, but in the collective consciousness of cultures; risk is thus a cultural phenomenon, not a physical one" (Rosa, 1998, p. 21). It could be argued the findings in Le Fevre's (2014) study align with this theory. Eleven of the 12 teachers interviewed perceived certain actions that were encouraged through a professional learning initiative to be of such high risk that it prevented them from engaging in the actions.

The four divergent theories highlight the complexities of risk-taking theories. The interrelatedness of elements in the theories suggest no singular theory underpins risk-seeking or risk-adverse teacher behavior. However, a commonality identified in the theories is that risk-taking can influence or deter innovative behaviors and opportunities for women to shape the educational environment, and likely other work environments. This is where the role of women in leadership is key. Women leaders have an opportunity to create environments and promote organizational factors that reduce perceptions of risk for teachers who are expected to engage in educational change.

WHY AN UNDERSTANDING OF WOMEN'S PERCEPTIONS OF RISK MATTERS

Some women willingly adopt or adapt suggestions for change, while many others avoid engagement or are accused of being resistant to, or reluctant to change. It has been suggested that teachers likely feel threatened or personally criticized as a change in practice assumes that current practices are no longer acceptable (McKenzie & Scheurich, 2008; Zimmerman, 2006). Teachers may fear being judged or held accountable (McKenzie & Scheurich, 2008), or may feel concerned that they are unable to implement the expected changes (Fullan, 2008; Williamson & Blackburn, 2010). In each explanation, the culpability for the lack of change tends to sit squarely on the classroom teacher.

From a different perspective, more recent studies have recognized that claiming teachers are resistant to change may be counterproductive to developing a culture of collaborative and sustainable improvement: "No one should be blamed in the process of building better schools" (Timperley & Parr, 2010, p. 17). Research suggests that teachers' perceptions of risk may be a fundamental barrier that influences teachers' engagement in professional learning for change (Le Fevre, 2014; Twyford, 2016).

A risk-perception lens has been helpful in considering the role of risk for women in educational change. Twyford (2016) explored teachers' perceptions of risk in professional learning. Her qualitative three-school case study captured the experiences of teachers as they participated in schoolwide professional learning initiatives. Twyford's analysis focused on psychological, social, and contextual factors to capture the complex phenomenon of perceptions of risk and risk-related actions. Findings point to the importance of redefining resistance as risk. What might look like resistance from the outside may in fact be due to a teacher's perceptions of a high level of risk.

Jones (2014) explored women's perceptions of risk associated with engagement in professional learning for change in a large New Zealand primary school. Organizational factors that influenced engagement in educational change and forms of support that enabled 21 women teaching in the school to navigate risk were identified. The initial quantitative aspect of the study allowed for perceptions of risk to be situated. The sequential qualitative element of the research enabled a deeper exploration into the perceived risk trends and offered women the opportunity to identify support that enabled them to navigate perceived risks.

Findings from Jones (2014) illustrate how complex theories of risk-taking combined with organizational factors can influence women's engagement in educational change. Perceptions of risk can be generated from a lack of clarity of professional learning purpose and relevance, lack of time and opportunities to engage in new practices, and when there are expectations to deprivatize practice. The implications of this research may shine a light on the potential role perceptions of risk can play. It may inform women leaders of the significance of being aware of and responsive to teachers' perceptions of risk when there are expectations to engage in educational change.

ORGANIZATIONAL FACTORS THAT INFLUENCE WOMEN'S ENGAGEMENT IN EDUCATIONAL CHANGE

The problem this chapter addresses is that engagement in professional learning has the potential to improve teaching and thus educational outcomes for students (Borko, 2004), yet school reform is often unsuccessful (Fullan, 2011; Timperley & Alton-Lee, 2008). The focus this chapter provides is that one key reason for the lack of success is the perceptions of risk teachers have about changing the way they teach. The solution we explore is how women in leadership can take intentional actions to reduce these perceptions of risk and thus potentially improve teaching and educational outcomes for students.

So how might women's leadership mitigate teachers' perceptions of risk? In this chapter, we focus on three organizational factors. These factors are women leading consultation and collaboration; time and opportunity for teachers to engage in professional learning; and supporting the deprivatization of teaching practice.

WOMEN LEADING CONSULTATION AND COLLABORATION

In this section, we draw on data from a New Zealand–based study of female leaders and teachers engaged in professional learning for change (Jones, 2014). The women's willingness to engage in professional learning initiatives was negatively influenced when change was mandated without consultation and collaboration with the leadership team. Consequently, the women perceived the professional learning lacked purpose and relevance and they were disengaged. Kelly (teacher) said, "It's a lack of direct relevance and because it's not directly relevant to what I am needing in my class day to day, and I can't see the worth of it in that context."

Teachers' engagement in professional learning is strongly influenced by the degree to which the teachers perceive themselves to be collaborating in the decision making and change process (Hargreaves, 2004). Without active discussions about the purpose of the learning, women can feel "as if change is being imposed or demanded" (Le Fevre, 2010, p. 73). Feelings that change is being mandated can result in lower levels of teacher engagement and leave teachers feeling resentful, frustrated, and overwhelmed by the workload (Gibson & Brooks, 2012; Hargreaves, 2004).

The knowledge and skills presented during professional learning sessions need to be practical and understood in principled ways for women to change their practice and be able to solve future teaching and learning challenges. One way to achieve this is through collaboration and consultation about the learning purpose. Focusing professional learning content and making explicit how the professional learning fits with what women already know and is coherent with their priorities is paramount to mitigate perceptions of risk and result in higher levels of engagement. When teachers understand the purpose of new learning and experience the benefits of the learning, either for themselves or for their students, they become committed to engaging in the new practices, and it becomes more than "just ticking boxes."

WOMEN HAVING TIME AND OPPORTUNITY TO ENGAGE IN CHANGE INITIATIVES

The amount of time required to implement a new strategy informed through professional learning alongside a teacher's level of comfort has been found to be one of the most challenging barriers to teachers' adoption of the new instructional strategy (Richards & Skolits, 2009). Professional learning is not a simple process of learning new things and then learning how to implement them. Teachers require ample time and opportunities to explore the practical implications when making significant changes to teaching practice. However, given that most primary teachers are women, engaging in professional learning while simultaneously teaching full time and attending to a raft of extracurricular activities means opportunities to engage in the professional learning can be limited.

The women in the New Zealand study were expected to engage in three mandated literacy initiatives in the same year. This resulted in them feeling "swamped" and "overloaded," which had serious implications for Sarah (teacher). Sarah explained, "It was like being dropped into a pool, and you didn't know how deep it was, and you didn't know anything. That is extreme risk, and it contributed to me dropping to part-time hours for a year and a bit."

Leaders have a key role in understanding the multiple demands on the lives of women.

Common in education is the issue of overloading teachers with too many different and sometimes conflicting change initiatives (Le Fevre, 2010). Common beyond education is for women to have multiple family and community responsibilities and roles. An implication from this is that women leaders in education, and other disciplines, would benefit from identifying what professional learning initiatives should be prioritized and which ones should cease, not only so deeper learning can be promoted but for humanistic reasons.

SUPPORTING THE DEPRIVATIZATION OF TEACHING PRACTICE

Deprivatization of teaching practice refers to making "public" the instructional practices and routines that often happen behind closed doors. Deprivatization involves sharing with colleagues what happens in your own and others' classrooms. This can lead to more open collegial interactions, collective inquiry, and conscious reflections on successful practices which can nurture the gradual emergence of professional knowledge and help teachers integrate new learning into existing practice (Hardy, 2012; Timperley, Wilson, Barrar, & Fung, 2007). However, this comes with challenges. Deprivatizing practice can evoke a range of emotional responses, from feelings of fear, uncertainty, and perceptions of risk (Francis, 2014; Le Fevre, 2014), to feelings of respect (Baskerville & Goldblatt, 2009; Boyle, While, & Boyle, 2004; Hardy, 2012).

Deprivatizing practice can result in perceptions of risk. For example, teaching in front of colleagues can create a degree of uncertainty, feelings of a lack of control and can be perceived as "threatening even to our best teachers and terrifying to our less confident teachers" (Francis, 2014, p. 24). Teachers may be reluctant to observe each other's classrooms or to have a colleague in theirs and "shared the view that it was risky to have their colleagues looking at them as they might be making judgments" (Le Fevre, 2014, p. 60). Such perceptions of risk can prevent teachers from expressing or testing their assumptions and precludes change that improves student outcomes.

In the New Zealand primary school (Jones, 2014), questions around perceptions of risk associated with deprivatization resulted in conflicting views from the women. On a questionnaire scale, the women perceived "analyzing their teaching practice with colleagues" as a relatively low-risk activity, with six women claiming there was no risk engaging in this practice. Brenda (teacher) said, "I would rather have someone come in and tell me where I can improve than to keep on going on a track and it being a disaster. So, I would rather have that because I want to improve."

However, the women readily identified colleagues who they perceived would be reluctant, even "resistant," to open their doors and make their teaching practice public. Jane said, "I can think of at least three or four who would not want anyone to come into their room, and I guess that comes from their fear." The interviewees presented two suggestions for their perceptions of collegial resistance to deprivatization. Stephanie (teacher) supported the theory of Hargreaves (2005) and Maskit (2011) and believed that willingness to deprivatize practice was determined by the teacher's age and career stage. "Teachers hate being observed, it seems to be really a huge problem for most teachers. I don't know if it is different for us because we have come out of a BT [beginning teacher] system where we were observed all the time."

In contrast, Brenda (teacher) believed risk-averse or risk-seeking behavior in a classroom is determined by the individual teacher's risk attitude. She said, "People who are a certain type of personality don't mind that stuff and other personalities are very much 'close the door and don't let anybody in.'" The women's variation in reasoning about perceptions of risk indicates that risk-taking may not be domain-specific as Howard (2013) suggests, but a personal, physical phenomenon. Whichever theory is considered, it is clear that leaders can have an influence in reducing perceptions of risk.

REDUCING PERCEPTIONS OF RISK FOR TEACHERS AND THE IMPORTANCE OF WOMEN'S LEADERSHIP

It is important for leaders to understand that teachers are diverse learners who hold varying beliefs, assumptions, knowledge, and skills, which may generate or lessen perceptions of risk when engaging in change initiatives. Specifically, the leadership of women has a central role in potentially reducing these perceptions of risk. For example, research makes visible the key role women have in organizations in building relational trust and being the relational glue that provides support and safety (Bryk & Schneider, 2003; Louis, 2007).

Women who are leaders and teachers in education are framed by gendered experiences. These experiences will influence what they perceive as a risk. If one is to believe the controllable factor that has the most impact on the success of students' learning is the teacher (Hattie, 2012), then it becomes vital that educational leaders are aware of how women's perceptions may act as barriers to teachers' engagement in educational change. Having insight and employing organizational systems that limit teach-

ers' perceptions of risk when engaging in professional learning may result in opportunities for more successful and sustainable change.

Change is an inherent feature of education, and with change in any context, perceptions of risk will exist. Women leaders who acknowledge that risk is an integral part of the change process can remove the weight of blame from women. Identifying what women perceive as a risk when engaging in professional learning for change is the next vital step. Only with this understanding can women leaders support teachers to navigate risk and engage in new learning that makes a positive difference to both student learning in schools and learning and change in other contexts.

REFERENCES

Aikenhead, G. S. (1984). Teacher decision making: The case of prairie high. *Journal of Research in Science Teaching, 21*(2), 167–186. doi:10.1002/tea.3660210208

Aven, T., & Renn, O. (2009). On risk defined as an event where the outcome is uncertain. *Journal of Risk Research, 12*(1), 1–11. doi:10.1080/13669870802488883

Baskerville, D., & Goldblatt, H. (2009). Learning to be a critical friend: From professional indifference through challenge to unguarded conversations. *Cambridge Journal of Education, 39*(2), 205–221. doi:10.1080/03057640902902260

Baylor, A. L., & Ritchie, D. (2002). What factors facilitate teacher skill, teacher morale, and perceived student learning in technology-using classrooms? *Computers & Education, 39*(4), 395–414. doi:10.1016/S0360-1315(02)00075-1

Borko, H. (2004). Professional development and teacher learning: Mapping the terrain. *Educational Researcher, 33*(8), 3–15. doi:10.3102/0013189X033008003

Boyle, B., While, D., & Boyle, T. (2004). A longitudinal study of teacher change: What makes professional development effective? *The Curriculum Journal, 15*(1), 45–68. doi:10.1080/1026716032000189471

Brody, D., & Hadar, L. (2011). "I speak prose and I now know it." Personal development trajectories among teacher educators in a professional development community. *Teaching and Teacher Education, 27*(8), 1223–1234. doi:10.1016/j.tate.2011.07.002

Bryk, A. S., & Schneider, B. (2003). Trust in schools: A core resource for school reform. *Educational Leadership, 60*(6), 40–45.

Francis, S. (2014). Feedback-the breakfast of champions. *Educating young children: Learning and teaching in the early childhood years, 20*(1), 24.

Fullan, M. (2008). *The six secrets of change.* San Francisco, CA: Jossey-Bass.

Fullan, M. (2011). *Choosing the wrong drivers for whole system reform.* Melbourne, Australia: Centre for Strategic Education.

Gess-Newsome, J., Southerland, S. A., Johnston, A., & Woodbury, S. (2003). Educational reform, personal practical theories, and dissatisfaction: The anatomy of change in college science teaching. *American Educational Research Journal, 40*(3), 731–767. doi: 10.3102/00028312040003731

Gibson, S. E., & Brooks, C. (2012). Teachers' perspectives on the effectiveness of a locally planned professional development program for implementing new curriculum. *Teacher Development, 16*(1), 1–23. doi.org/10.1080/13664530.2012.667953

Hardy, I. (2012). Teachers' professional development in special needs settings: Creating 'kid-cool' schools in challenging times. *International Journal of Inclusive Education, 16*(8), 809–824. doi:10.1080/13603116.2010.523906

Hargreaves, A. (2004). Inclusive and exclusive educational change: Emotional responses of teachers and implications for leadership. *School Leadership & Management, 24*(3), 287–309. doi.org/10.1080/1363243042000266936

Hargreaves, A. (2005). Educational change takes ages: Life, career and generational factors in teachers' emotional responses to educational change. *Teaching and Teacher Education, 21*, 967–983. doi:10.1016/j.tate.2005.06.007

Hattie, J. (2012). Visible learning for teachers: Maximizing impact on learning. New York, NY: Routledge.

Howard, S. K. (2013). Risk-aversion: Understanding teachers' resistance to technology integration. *Technology, Pedagogy and Education, 22*(3), 357–372. doi:10.1080/1475939X.2013.802995

Jones, T. K. (2014). *Theories of risk-taking and primary teachers' engagement in professional learning for change* (Unpublished master's dissertation). University of Auckland, New Zealand.

Le Fevre, D. (2010). Changing tack: Talking about change knowledge for professional learning. In H. Timperley & J. Parr (Eds.), *Weaving evidence, inquiry and standards to build better schools* (pp. 71–91). Wellington: NZCER Press.

Le Fevre, D. M. (2014). Barriers to implementing pedagogical change: The role of teachers' perceptions of risk. *Teaching and Teacher Education, 38*, 56–64. doi:10.1016/j.tate.2013.11.007

Louis, K. S. (2007). Changing the culture of schools: Professional community, organizational learning, and trust. *Journal of School Leadership, 16*(5), 477–487.

Maaranen, K., Pitkäniemi, H., Stenberg, K., & Karlsson, L. (2016). An idealistic view of teaching: Teacher students' personal practical theories. *Journal of Education for Teaching, 42*(1), 80–92.

Maskit, D. (2011). Teachers' attitudes toward pedagogical changes during various stages of professional develop-

ment. *Teaching and Teacher Education, 27*(5), 851–860. doi:10.1016/j.tate.2011.01.009

McKenzie, K. B., & Scheurich, J. J. (2008). Teacher resistance to improvement of schools with diverse students. *International Journal of Leadership in Education, 11*(2), 117–133. doi:10.1080/13603120801950122

Ministry of Education. (2002). Table S1: FTTE of state school teachers. Wellington, Ministry of Education.

Ministry of Education. (2016). Education Counts. Retrieved from https://www.educationcounts.govt.nz/statistics/schooling/teaching_staff

Ponticell, J. A. (2003). Enhancers and inhibitors of teacher risk taking: A case study. *Peabody Journal of Education, 78*(3), 5–24. doi:10.1207/S15327930PJE7803_02

Richards, J., & Skolits, G. (2009). Sustaining instructional change: The impact of professional development on teacher adoption of a new instructional strategy. *Research in the Schools, 16*(2), 41–59.

Rosa, E. A. (1998). Metatheoretical foundations for postnormal risk. *Journal of Risk Research, 1*(1), 15–44. doi:10.1080/136698798377303

Stulz, R. M. (1996). Rethinking risk management. *Journal of Applied Corporate Finance, 9*(3), 8-25. doi:10.1111/j.1745-6622.1996.tb00295.x

Timperley, H., & Alton-Lee, A. (2008). Reframing teacher professional learning: An alternative policy approach to strengthening valued outcomes for diverse learners. *Review of Research in Education, 32*(1), 328–369. doi:10.3102/0091732X07308968

Timperley, H., & Parr, J. (2010). *Weaving evidence, inquiry and standards to build better schools*. Wellington: New Zealand Council for Educational Research Press.

Timperley, H. S., Wilson, A., Barrar, H., & Fung, I. (2007). *Teacher professional development: Best evidence synthesis iteration (BES)*. Wellington, New Zealand: Ministry of Education.

Trimpop, R. M. (1994). *The psychology of risk taking behaviour*. Netherlands: North-Holland.

Twyford, K. (2016). *Risk or resistance: Understanding teachers' perceptions of risk in professional learning* (Doctoral thesis, ResearchSpace@Auckland). University of Auckland, Auckland, New Zealand.

Williamson, B., & Blackburn, B. R. (2010). Dealing with resistance to change. *Principal Leadership, 10*(7), 73–75.

Zimmerman, J. (2006). Why some teachers resist change and what principals can do about it. *NASSAP Bulletin, 90*(3), 238–249. doi:10.1177/0192636506291521

Chapter 9

Barriers and Strategies

Stories of Women's Rise to Leadership in Higher Education in the Philippines

Arceli H. Rosario

A woman's rise to a leadership position can be extremely complex as she navigates the social, cultural, political, and organizational cultures along the way. Numerous challenges exist and many women encounter personal and professional barriers. Personal barriers can include a woman's negative attitude about herself; feelings of inadequacy; and being faced with a "double burden"—describing a duality of roles, for example, maintaining a career and running a household (Moen, 1989). Professional barriers can include discriminatory experiences in the workplace such as a negative attitude of colleagues and superiors on the basis of gender, a lack of mentoring and networking, and inequality in salaries and benefits, among others.

Using hermeneutic phenomenology, this study explored the leadership experiences of seven women presidents of higher education institutions in the Philippines and investigated the barriers they experienced and the strategies they used to overcome them. The women became presidents only in their mid-50s, which shows that the ascent of women to leadership is delayed compared with men. The participants showed that while women experience barriers, they can overcome them and rise even to the highest leadership posts in higher education.

In this era of women's emancipation, women have been obtaining bachelor, graduate, and postgraduate degrees and there has been a rise in the number of women advancing toward organizational and management levels. However, women remain underrepresented in senior leadership roles in higher education contexts (Gooch, 2012; Hunt, 2007; Lapovsky, 2014; Morley & Crossouard, 2014).

Women encounter challenges in exercising their full potential at the workplace. Women who aspire to leadership roles often face barriers and frequently forfeit leadership opportunities. While research studies have shown that feminine leadership attributes are associated with effective school administration, qualified women

"still face attrition and slower career mobility particularly in higher education" (Porat, as cited in Growe & Montgomery, 2000, p. 1). Women must cross numerous barriers in order to develop their full potential and achieve higher education leadership positions. Morley and Crossouard (2014) noted that only a small proportion of women survive multidimensional barriers in higher education leadership.

Personal barriers can be categorized as (a) psychological barriers, which may include a woman's negative attitude toward herself and feelings of inadequacy in becoming a leader (Hunt, 2007; Nguyen, 2013; Oplatka, 2006) and (b) familial barriers, which refer to challenges in achieving a work-life balance (Hacifazlioglu, 2010; Lazarian-Chehab, 2017), especially for women who are raising children (Blue, 2014; Nguyen, 2013) and holding multiple and conflicting roles (Quinlan, 2012).

Professional barriers may be structural, political, and cultural. Lack of role models and networks and discriminatory hiring and promotion practices are examples of structural barriers (Lazarian-Chehab, 2017; Tiao, 2006). Political barriers include exclusion from professional networks that might support leadership aspirations and future opportunities (e.g., "good old boys'" networks) (Cosimini, 2011; Quinlan, 2012), difficulty in being heard, and having the opportunity to contribute to organizational discussions, getting recognition for work completed, experiencing double standards (Long, 2008; Nguyen, 2013), fighting against workplace politics, sexual harassment, and a lack of access to decision-making opportunities (Rabas, 2013; Tiao, 2006). Cultural barriers also exist, and women might be challenged by negative attitudes toward them because of their gender resulting in an inhospitable work climate, other women's intolerance of their success, and gender stereotyping (Tiao, 2006).

Knowing what these barriers are is extremely important if women are to engage in activities which may mitigate the effect of these barriers, or even remove them all together. Therefore, through hermeneutic phenomenology, the purpose of this chapter is to add to this growing body of literature and examine the barriers that prevent women leaders' rise to formal leadership roles in higher education contexts and, most importantly, highlight the potential strategies women engage to successfully circumvent them.

METHODOLOGY

This qualitative study employed hermeneutic phenomenology (Laverty, 2003), with the purpose of understanding and describing the "nature and meaning" (Van Manen, 1990, p. 9) of an experience. It focuses on the question: "What is this experience like?" (Laverty, 2003, p. 22). Van Manen (1990) explains that hermeneutic phenomenology is a study of experiences as they are lived and understood, how the participants make meaning of their life world within their cultural, social, and historical contexts (Munhall, as cited in Laverty, 2003). Each of the women was asked to tell their story about the barriers they encountered on their rise to leadership and the strategies they employed to overcome them. Through hermeneutic phenomenology, I captured the "story behind the glory" (Nance, 2006, para. 5), recording each encounter, and transcribing the data. From the data, narratives were crafted and analyzed and themes were generated.

The participants in the study were seven women who were presidents of accredited higher educational institutions in the Philippines.

Linda was married and had three children whose ages were 37, 34, and 32 at the time of this study. All her children were professionals. She described them as "wonderful and a source of support and inspiration" and raising them was her biggest accomplishment.

Sarah was married and did not have children. She described her husband as very supportive to her career. Although he had never complained about her schedule, Sarah was conscious of her domestic responsibilities. She said, "Sometimes I feel that I have to go home because he is there alone."

Mary Jo had two children with her late husband. When she served as president, her children were already grown up and, according to her, did not require much of her attention.

Sylvia, with her late husband, raised two children. They were already grown up when she became president.

Belinda was married and had three children, all of whom studied chemistry. She underscored that they as a family were committed to their individual professions and firm in their Christian conviction.

Rosemarie was not married. She recalled that she had wanted to enter the convent but was "pulled" into leadership work. She realized that she did not actually lose her vocation. Instead, she claimed, "I found it."

Carol was married and had two children. Her daughter was working and her son was studying toward a degree. She said her husband was very supportive and did not mind her spending long hours at the office.

FINDINGS: PERSONAL BARRIERS

The findings illustrated that the women were able to identify barriers and challenges with regard to their leadership opportunities and practice.

ATTAINING A WORK-LIFE BALANCE

Only one participant commented that women faced a double burden, or in fact, a triple burden. Five mentioned the woman's responsibility to attend to domestic duties. However, women's difficulty in balancing work and home duties was not highlighted. Instead, the women emphasized the strategies that they employed to attain a work-life balance. For example, Linda did not feel burdened with her home duties while pursuing a career. When her children were still in preschool, she worked out of the home in the morning only. She engaged in full-time employment when her children were in school the entire day. Her role as dean of a university graduate school came when her youngest child was eight years old. Living in the same compound with her parents-in-law, she found a strong support system.

Similarly, Sarah, Rosemarie, and Carol, like Linda, were not burdened with home duties. Carol married early and had her children when she was in her mid-20s. She was a hands-on mother until her children were in high school. She and her husband invested lots of family time together. The children were already in college when she took on big responsibilities.

Mary Jo's family was her source of strength. When things got tough in the workplace, she felt blessed to have a family that served as an anchor. Her husband was very supportive of her. When people asked her what her hobby was, she would answer, "I have none, only my family." She wanted to spend every spare moment that she could have with them. "That is what I enjoy," she said.

Sylvia was able to combine both home and work creatively. An excerpt from her nomination to a certain award stated, "From her laborious career and involvements, [Sylvia] invested quality time for her family. She has kept a healthy balance between her work and home. Her children . . . who are successful in their professions could attest to that" (quoted from award citation material). However, Sylvia agreed that a woman experiences a double burden, even a triple burden. According to her, a woman does most of the housework. Although she wanted to attend to her home duties full time, she decided to engage herself in gainful employment. While she could be tempted to spend her time making the house immaculately clean, she resolved to use her time on more productive pursuits.

One of the best decisions that Belinda and her husband made was to settle in the university campus where they were working. They felt fortunate to be asked to serve there because they recognized that the university was "a good place for bringing up children." When their children were small, Belinda and her husband helped each other with the housework. Also, her mother, who stayed with them, helped them look after the children. They had house helpers, too. Belinda and her husband continued their commitment to help each other. Even during the time of her presidency, they still did things together such as buying their groceries and supplies from the wet market. When she got very busy or tired at times, her husband did the house chores. Aside from housework, their support for one another extended to other areas as well. Belinda considered her husband her greatest mentor. "We share and discuss things and get ideas from one another about what is the best thing to be done under a given situation," she elaborated.

FEELINGS OF INADEQUACY

The women admitted feeling inadequate once given a new work assignment. When the institute's president suddenly passed away, Rosemarie was the choice to replace him. At that time, she felt inadequate to step into her predecessor's big shoes. Rosemarie was only 36 years old when she was thrust into the top leadership post. However, after serving for eight months as acting director, she was conferred the presidency. Her sense of inadequacy was slowly dispelled as she gained strength from prayer, guidance of a mentor, and support of people she called collaborators.

Carol admitted having felt inadequate for the positions that she applied for. She feared she would not be able to come up to the expectations of the constituents. "Nobody is ever really prepared for anything," she explained. "There are anxieties, there are reservations but if people believe that you can do it, then you give it a try." With the support of colleagues and friends who encouraged her and assured her she could make it, she

pushed through with her presidential candidacy and won. Although she felt inadequate, she did not feel inferior. She explained that "it's always good to be anxious. One can never be too overconfident. When you feel too overconfident about what you're supposed to do, that's when things will crumble. When you are anxious, then you are challenged."

Mary Jo and Carol disclosed that they also felt inadequate when they took over their university presidencies. They clarified that this inadequacy was not equated with inferiority, but it was a feeling that one is never fully equipped to do a new task. The feeling of inadequacy is true of women from other cultures as well (Morley & Crossouard, 2014). American women were twice as likely to describe themselves as not qualified even though they had the same credentials as their male counterparts (Lawless & Fox, as cited in Hunt, 2007).

When asked if she had ever felt inadequate about a new assignment, Mary Jo admitted that she had. "When something is new, I'm never quite sure if I can do a good job." She cited her chairing a committee in the United Nations which was a preparatory body for the United Nations world conference. "It was an honor for me and for the country, and I had to do well." Eventually, she was elected chair of a main committee during the United Nations world conference. As chair, she steered the discussions and consolidated points of agreement among the delegates of more than 180 nations. The committee's main goal was to come up with a blueprint that would address women's issues and improve their status worldwide (Azarcon-de la Cruz, 2007). She felt the work was intimidating because the committee had to deal with sensitive issues, and at many times the delegates took opposing stands. Moreover, many of the proposed actions were "threatening and challenge[d] the male establishment" (Azarcon-de la Cruz, 2007, p. 53). She further explained that "when women's lives change, men's lives have to change as well" (p. 53); thus, there is strong resistance to women's empowerment. From her experiences in that world conference, Mary Jo valued teamwork even more. "You should not try to do things on your own," she counseled.

FINDINGS: PROFESSIONAL BARRIERS

Gender Discrimination

While three of the seven participants said they had not experienced gender discrimination, four admitted being discriminated against. The discriminatory incidents happened when they were still in the early parts of their presidencies. The negative reactions came from some of their colleagues, not their superiors.

Linda admitted having experienced gender discrimination. However, she stated, "Those times were few and far between." At such times, the resistance arose from some of her male colleagues who felt she was not qualified to be in a leadership post because she was a woman. However, she observed that the resistance melted over time. When confronted with discrimination, Linda said she did not react. She just performed her job well, acted fairly at all times, and dealt with everyone sincerely and honestly.

In spite of her confidence and assertiveness, Mary Jo disclosed that she had experienced being discriminated against. Those were times when she promoted women's issues, and she did not get the support she expected. She felt her word was not taken seriously, and her passion toward alleviating the conditions of women was not shared by others. This apathy toward women's issues did not just come from men but also from some women. Mary Jo, however, pressed on with her agenda on women's empowerment and gender equality. She promoted global awareness on protection of women against sexual harassment, rape, domestic abuse, sex trafficking, and human rights abuses. Her contribution to a United Nations world conference was lauded as having generated policies and positive action on women's issues. Regarding discriminatory organizational structures, she admitted that they exist although administrators may not realize it. She believed the workplace should be women-friendly in terms of salaries, benefits, opportunities, and practices. Mary Jo lauded academic institutions for their generally fair and nondiscriminatory practices. She observed that, in the academy, women are empowered and enjoy the same opportunities and financial privileges as men do.

Sylvia shared that she had experienced some forms of discrimination such as not being given the same opportunities and privileges received by her male counterparts. Recognizing that gender discrimination did occur in the workplace, Sylvia employed some strategies to overcome it. She worked very hard; promoted the pursuit of common success, harmony, unity, and peace; downplayed competition and resorted to win-win solutions; and was content with whatever tasks were given to her and did them well.

Rosemarie encountered many setbacks in her leadership. One of the major incidents was when some employees opposed her leadership. She advised women leaders "not to retaliate to those who appear to be putting obstacles to [their] dreams and aspirations" and to be strong and not be intimidated. But she cautioned that women leaders should also examine themselves for their complicity in the problem. Belinda did not mention any incident where she felt discriminated against in the workplace. Her superiors and colleagues, when she was

on faculty in one university, were very supportive of her. She named two of her male superiors who gave her opportunities to grow. She worked with one of these two men on a project that paved the way for an open university of which she became its first president.

Sarah could not remember being discriminated against. Although her field was traditionally male-dominated, she had never felt intimidated, inadequate, or disadvantaged in the presence of men. Having six brothers and 16 male cousins, she always felt accepted by boys. In her professional life, gender had never been an issue to her.

On the other hand, Carol and Belinda said they had supportive institutions. Carol praised the academy, especially her university, for its nondiscriminating culture and for nurturing a classless society. She expounded that in her university "nobody is rich, nobody is poor, nobody is better than you." She asserted that "everybody is equal. Everybody can voice out what he or she wants to say and yet is not punished for it." For her, the academy is "the best place to be in."

Carol was the first woman to sit as university president and her selection was hailed as a breakthrough. Over the years the question had been asked why a woman never held the highest leadership post in the university considering the predominance of women among the ranks of middle-level administrators and faculty members. The university had also championed equality between men and women. Hence, her appointment proved that the university could act on what it advocated.

Research studies reveal that women face gender discrimination (see Liu & Li, 2010; Tiao, 2006; Ustun & Gumuseli, 2017). Specifically, Tiao (2006) found that her women participants experienced obstacles in their career advancement and skepticism and resistance. Noting these issues that women face, some institutions have taken measures to address the gender inequity and given women the chance to fill senior leadership positions. Australian universities, for example, have instituted policies to address the gender leadership gap. After two decades, women's representation in senior leadership rose from 6 percent to 31 percent (Winchester & Browning, 2015).

STRATEGIES: SOME EMERGING THEMES

The participants encountered numerous personal and professional barriers. Of the personal barriers women leaders faced, the most recurring themes were (a) feelings of inadequacy and (b) double burden. Of the professional barriers, the common recurring theme was gender discrimination. The participants did not deny the reality of other barriers, both personal and professional, but they said they were able to overcome them more easily by employing effective strategies. The experiences of the participants showed that the glass ceiling had cracked for them so that they were able to penetrate through the top leadership posts at prestigious and reputable schools in the country.

The women used several strategies to address their work and home obligations. Among these were mentoring and networking, time management, and working hard. Also, for the five participants who were married and had children, their decision to pursue leadership advancement came when their children were teenagers or young adults. Two of the participants stayed at home to take care of their children when they were not yet in school.

MENTORS AND NETWORKING

The participants learned to deal with their feelings of inadequacy. They gained confidence from being nurtured by a mentor (Brown, 2005; Dahlvig & Longman, 2014; Heath, 2012; Ligon, 2011). Specifically, one participant highlighted the help of one woman whose counsel helped her go through difficult negotiations when she chaired a committee during a world conference on women's issues. Further, the participants pointed out the significance of support from family members, friends, and colleagues.

In most cases, the participants were supported by their mentors and gained inspiration from their role models. They had networks from whom they drew encouragement and strength. Brown (2005) revealed mentorship as a reason why women rise to, and stay in, higher education presidencies. Bynum (2000) corroborated on the importance of mentors to break barriers to advancement. Batiste's (2009) findings concurred that providing aspiring women with positive role models and mentors increases their mobility to top decision-making bodies.

When Rosemarie assumed office, she chose people who supported her agenda. Her counsel was—"You have to know the people you work with. You have to build your own team. So you have to choose people who think like you and who believe in your programs."

TIME MANAGEMENT

Aburdene and Naisbitt (1992) claim that women leaders are good at balancing home duties. They are able to spend time on their careers and take time off for their families. In fact, they can even find time for recreation. Women leaders are able to find balance because "for most women, a career is not a methodical rise to power" (p. 109). The women were prepared to set aside some

years of their lives raising their children. Of the seven participants, six were married and one was unmarried. Of those married, one had no child, three had two children, and two had three children. Those who were married faced the challenge of double burden, but they intentionally put time aside for family.

To create more time all the participants engaged the services of housemaids and extended family members. Murniati (2012), who studied senior academic administrators in Indonesia, found that her participants advanced in their careers because of the support of family members. Further, in this study, all the married participants revealed that their husbands were very supportive. They helped with the housework, did not mind the long hours their wives spent at work, and shared in their commitment to their career. Astin and Leland (1991) also noted that the participants in their study received support that their work required from their husbands.

Mary Jo's commitment to her family and to work-life balance influenced the policies and programs of the institution where she served as president. She worked toward the reduction of the faculty teaching load, insisted that faculty members take their vacation leave, and granted flex time arrangements. She shared that she had always been asked how she had combined home and work. Her answer was a woman must first believe in the importance of both home and work; and second, she must learn how to put that belief into practice. In her case, the strategies she employed to enable her to meet her home and work obligations were to move close to her workplace, practice good time management, and multitask.

Mary Jo nurtured strong bonds with her children from the time they were young. One of the crucial decisions her husband and she had made was to move to a house close to her workplace. She set aside time for her children—a period in the morning before she went to work and another period after she got home. She considered those times sacred, an appointment she religiously observed. In addition, she and her husband spent Sundays with their children. When the children were in the younger grades, Mary Jo would bring them to the university, where she was employed, on weekends. She recalled, "We would bike around the parking lot."

WORKING HARD

The women worked very hard to attain competency in their leadership roles. All the participants earned doctoral degrees from reputable institutions in the Philippines and abroad. They were willing to put in more work hours than their colleagues and subordinates. Rosemarie devoted most of her waking hours to work. After attending mass at 5:15 in the morning, she would proceed to her office. Her workday usually began at 6:30. At times, she worked through lunch until late in the evening. Her sister and some nephews and nieces lived with her and her mother stayed with her until her death at age 94.

Mary Jo enjoined women to gain knowledge, strive for competence, and work very hard. She explained that it is very important for a woman leader to have the knowledge and skills for whatever tasks she will be asked to do. Further, she advised that women should take advantage of networks. "If you are organized even though it's not a woman's organization, somehow you are more empowered." Mary Jo articulated that women use another framework in establishing their credibility which is through the use of knowledge, skills, and work orientation. She explained that "women have to be very knowledgeable. They have to know whatever it is that they are doing. They have to be highly competent." According to her, women should work hard. Being the best and letting people know they are qualified, being willing to take responsibility, working hard, being an overachiever, are among the attributes women need to obtain leadership posts (Morrison, 2012; Pirouznia, 2009). Likewise, Eagly and Carli (2007) urged women to develop exceptional competence in performing their leadership functions and take on the difficult tasks. In doing so, they are able to revolutionize traditional organizational culture that favors men over women for leadership.

HIGH SENSE OF SELF

The participants did not allow gender discrimination to stop them from moving up their career ladder. Instead, they pressed on with their programs and plans to improve themselves and their organizations. Pumla Gobodo-Madikizela, who established the Truth and Reconciliation Commission and worked in grassroots nongovernmental organizations during South Africa's apartheid era, wrote that "women . . . have a degree of tolerance, an understanding that allows them to persist even when things seem to be very bad" (as cited in Hunt, 2007, p. 109). The participants did not react when they were discriminated against. Instead, they showed kindness to their detractors.

The participants attested that they were advantaged by the mentorship they received, their rich educational background, their high sense of security which emanated from a loving and nurturing home environment. All of them underscored the positive influence of their parents, especially of their empowered and empowering mothers, who instilled in them that they could do what they wanted to do and they could be what they hoped to be. They had developed a competent self (Denmark, 1993), which

equipped them with "the ability to see possibilities instead of obstacles" (p. 348). More so, they did not allow themselves to "be defined by situations, other people, and events" (p. 348). When discriminated against, they knew how to handle the situation. They were able to generate solutions to solve their problems and employ effective strategies to overcome their barriers.

CONCLUSION

The findings from this study revealed that the women experienced both personal and professional barriers with regard to their leadership. The participants experienced feeling inadequate about assuming a leadership post. However, they were able to dispel their feelings of inadequacy through the support of mentors and networking. All the participants achieved work-life balance by employing strategies such as managing time wisely, having a support system through domestic helpers and family members, and, for those who were married, having a supportive husband.

The main professional barrier that the participants experienced was gender discrimination. To address this barrier, they actively sought the support of mentors and professional networks. In addition, they attained high qualifications, worked hard, gained competence, and developed a strong and positive sense of self-identity. One of their greatest challenges was to change how they viewed themselves, from inadequate to competent. Many women have to manage feelings of inadequacy when offered leadership opportunities.

Since discriminatory incidents occurred while the women were still climbing the leadership ladder or only during the early parts of their presidencies, this pattern reveals that when women prove their worth as leaders, those they work with eventually give them the respect they deserve. However, this study affirms that gender discrimination still happens, that there are still unequal views and expectations regarding men and women in leadership, and that women have to be more highly qualified, work extremely hard, and be perceived by others as highly competent to be given the opportunity for leadership advancement.

REFERENCES

Aburdene, P., & Naisbitt, J. (1992). *Megatrends for women.* New York, NY: Villard Books.

Astin, H. S., & Leland, C. (1991). *Women of influence, women of vision: A cross-generational study of leaders and social change.* San Francisco, CA: Jossey-Bass.

Azarcon-de la Cruz, P. (2007). Breaking barriers and brackets. In O. H. Tripon (Ed.), *Shaping the women's global agenda: Filipino women in the United Nations Commission on the status of women-CEDAW committee* (pp. 49–60). Philippines: NCRFW.

Batiste, L. (2009, February 19). The perceptions of female school leaders of the obstacles and enablers that affected their career paths to educational administration. *The Academic Leadership: The Online Journal, 7*, 1. Retrieved from http://www.academicleadership.org/emperical_research/574.shtml

Blue, K. M. (2014). *Perceptions of challenges and barriers to career advancement by women administrators* (Doctoral dissertation). Retrieved from ProQuest Dissertations and Theses database. (UMI No. 3581421)

Brown, T. M. (2005). Mentorship and the female college president. *Sex Roles: A Journal of Research, 52*(9/10), 659–666. doi: 10.1007/s11199-005-3733-7

Bynum, V. (2000). *An investigation of female leadership characteristics* (Doctoral dissertation). Retrieved from ProQuest Dissertation and Theses database. (UMI No. 9990824)

Cosimini, S. H. (2011). *Female administrators in higher education: Victories, broken barriers, and persisting obstacles* (Doctoral dissertation). Retrieved from ProQuest Dissertations and Theses database. (UMI No. 3456113)

Dahlvig, J., & Longman, K. A. (2014). Contributors to women's leadership development in Christian higher education: A model and emerging theory. *Journal of Research on Christian Education, 23*, 5–28. doi: 10.1080/10656219.2014.862196

Denmark, F. L. (1993). Women, leadership, and empowerment. *Psychology of Women Quarterly, 17*, 343–356.

Eagly, A. H., & Carli, L. L. (2007). *Through the labyrinth: The truth about how women become leaders.* Boston, MA: Harvard Business School Press.

Gooch, L. (2012). *Philippines leads pack in promoting female academics.* Retrieved from http://www.nytimes.com/2012/11/26/world/asia/philippines-leads-pack-in-promoting-female-academics.html?_r=0

Growe, R., & Montgomery, P. (2000). Women and the leadership paradigm: Bridging the gender gap. National Forum, *The Phi Kappa Phi Journal, 17E*, 1–10.

Hacifazlioglu, O. (2010). Balance in academic leadership: Voices of women from Turkey and the United States. *Perspectives in Education, 28*(2), 51–62.

Heath, K. (2012). *Women in leadership: Strategies for work-life balance* (Doctoral dissertation). Retrieved from ProQuest Dissertations and Theses database. (UMI No. 3525746)

Hunt, S. (2007, May/June). Let women rule. *Foreign Affairs, 86*(3), 109–120. Retrieved from http://www.jstor.org/stable/20032353

Lapovsky, L. (2014). *Why so few women college presidents?* Retrieved from http://www.forbes.com/sites/lucielapovsky/2014/04/13/why-so-few-women-college-presidents/#17ba5e59634c

Laverty, S. M. (2003). Hermeneutic phenomenology and phenomenology: A comparison of historical and methodological considerations. *International Journal of Qualitative Methods, 2*(3), 21–35.

Lazarian-Chehab, R. (2017). *Traditions, mentoring, and Vietnamese women leaders in higher education* (Doctoral dissertation). Retrieved from ProQuest Dissertations and Theses database. (UMI No. 10257562)

Ligon, P. S. (2011). *An examination of African American female college presidents' professional ascendancy and mentoring experiences* (Doctoral dissertation). Retrieved from ProQuest Dissertations and Theses database. (UMI No. 3506921)

Liu, B., & Li, Y. (2010). Opportunities and barriers: Gendered reality in Chinese higher education. *Frontiers of Education in China, 5*(2), 197–221.

Long, J. L. (2008). *Women chief financial officers in higher education overcoming internal and external barriers to leadership* (Doctoral dissertation). Retrieved from ProQuest Dissertations and Theses database. (UMI No. 33313317)

Moen, P. (1989). *Working parents: Transformations in gender roles and public policies in Sweden.* Madison, WI: University of Wisconsin Press.

Morley, L., & Crossouard, B. (2014). *Women in higher education leadership in South Asia: Rejection, refusal, reluctance, revisioning.* Retrieved from https://www.britishcouncil.org/sites/default/files/women_in_higher_education_leadership_in_sa_-_executive_summary.pdf

Morrison, H. (2012). *Gender and leadership: Educational leadership through feminine eyes: Have the barriers in acquiring educational administrative positions for women changed in the last fifteen years?* (Doctoral dissertation). Retrieved from ProQuest Dissertations and Theses database. (UMI No. 3505473)

Murniati, C. T. (2012). *Career advancement of women senior academic administrators in Indonesia: Supports and challenges* (Doctoral dissertation). Retrieved in ProQuest Dissertations and Theses database. (UMI No. 3526852)

Nance, M. (2006). ACE conference: More research needed on experiences of minority women leaders. *Diverse Issues in Higher Education, 23*(21), 21–23.

Nguyen, T. L. H. (2013). Barriers to and facilitators of female deans' career advancement in higher education: An exploratory study in Vietnam. *Higher Education, 66*(1), 123–138. http://dx.doi.org/10-1007/s10734-012-9594-4.

Oplatka, I. (2006). Women in educational administration within developing countries: Towards a new international research agenda. *Journal of Educational Administration, 44*(6), 604–624.

Pirouznia, M. (2009, August 10). Fewer women than men in educational leadership. *The Academic Leadership: The Online Journal, 7*, 3. (Article 9). Retrieved from http://www.academicleadership.org/article/Fewer_women_than_men_in_educational_leadership

Quinlan, C. (2012). *Women's career development: The lived experience of Canadian university women presidents* (Doctoral dissertation). Retrieved from ProQuest Dissertations and Theses database. (UMI No. 3563228)

Rabas, A. (2013). *The barriers, fears and motivations encountered by women leaders in higher education leadership roles* (Doctoral dissertation). Retrieved from ProQuest Dissertations and Theses database. (UMI No. 3568093)

Tiao, N. (2006). *Senior women leaders in higher education: Overcoming barriers to Success* (Doctoral dissertation). Available at Master's Theses, and Doctoral Dissertations, and Graduate Capstone Projects at Digital Commons@ EMU. Retrieved from http://commons.emich.edu/cgi/view content.cgi?article =1103&context=theses

Ustun, S., & Gumuseli, A. I. (2017). Many lives of women rectors at Turkish universities. *Journal of Education and Training Studies, 5*(8), 123–131. http://dx.doi.org/10.11114/ jets.v518.2424

Van Manen, M. (1990). *Researching lived experience: Human science for an action sensitive pedagogy.* Ontario, Canada: University of Western Ontario.

Winchester, H., & Browning, L. (2015). Gender equality in academia: A critical reflection. *Journal of Higher Education Policy and Management, 27*(3), 269–281. http://dx.doi .org/10.1080/1360080X. 2015. 1034427

Chapter 10

Scaling the Mountain to Principalship in New Zealand

The Enablers and Barriers in a Female Principal's Journey

Samantha Mortimer and Frances Edwards

Girls are now outperforming boys in high schools and universities around the world and are currently entering the workforce at higher salaries than ever before (Slaughter, 2015). However, there have been minimal changes in the proportion of females in top executive positions in the last decade (Fitzgerald & Wilkinson, 2010; Hansen, 2014; Kelsey, Allen, Coke & Ballard, 2014) despite alterations to the law to create a more equitable practice (Shah, 2015). Consequently, leadership and the influence for change remains highly gendered (Lyman, Strachan & Lazaridou, 2012). This gendered practice translates into education, and although the majority of teachers are women in most Westernized countries, including New Zealand, the majority of principals are men (Fuller, 2013; Grogan & Shakeshaft, 2011; Ho, 2015).

For example, in New Zealand in 2017, 59 percent of secondary school (students ages 13–18) teachers are women but 30 percent of principal positions are held by women (Ministry of Education, 2017). This being the case, it is useful to reflect on the stories of women who have achieved school principal positions, in order to discover what helped and hindered them on their journey.

This chapter describes the journey to school principalship of a New Zealand woman committed to making a difference for the students with whom she worked. Janet described her journey into and through leadership. She identified the enablers and barriers she experienced along the way and the identity work that enabled her to gain her first position as a school principal. Janet acknowledged the impact of gender, being a wife, and being a mother to a school-aged child, and the gender-specific expectations others have of principals, as barriers in her journey.

She also identified enablers—the people and the processes that helped her to succeed in her career, including her strong belief in social justice; her support systems, including the mentors who guided her throughout her career path to the present day; and professional development opportunities. She talked about a gestalt shift in

her identity and its collision with circumstances which gave her the confidence to apply for her current job as a school principal. Janet showed she was capable of making workable, manageable, and balanced judgments in relation to her work and life, including finding people and activities that could support her. Building on the work of Mahmood (2015), we present a visual metaphor that encapsulates Janet's journey.

RESEARCH DESIGN

This research was designed to elicit the lived experiences of a woman leader, who had been recently appointed to her role. Purposive sampling was engaged to find a first-time female principal who was willing to share her experiences about entry into formal leadership of a school. Janet, a New Zealand European first-time principal, was appointed to her leadership role in her 50s, and when approached was willing to share her story through a dialogical, ethnographic interview (Le Fevre & Farquhar, 2015; Lyman et al., 2012). The interview took place at her school, and through the use of a guided interview schedule Janet was supported to share her story into and through the early stages of her leadership.

FINDINGS

The findings shared in this section will outline Janet's personal background and upbringing as a significant influence along with the barriers and enablers she identified as critical to her success as a first-time principal.

JANET'S PERSONAL BACKGROUND

Janet was a fifth-generation teacher in New Zealand. Her mother was a kindergarten teacher and her mother's father was a principal. After the school day finished, Janet and her brothers spent a lot of time at their mother's kindergarten as it was only three doors down from where they lived, so teaching was the norm. Janet also used to mark both of her brothers' homework after school and "although she wasn't a good speller" she liked to "use the red pen." Janet's mother often said to her when she was young that "teaching was in her blood."

In the early 1980s Janet attended Teachers' College. According to Janet, "[at that time] experience was more important than your qualifications," she was qualified to teach with a diploma not a degree. She taught at an intermediate school (10–12 year olds) in an isolated rural area in the central North Island with a high percentage of Māori in the community. Later, she met and married her husband, had a child, and stayed in that community. Janet soon moved to teach in the local secondary school. At that time secondary school teachers were paid more than their primary school colleagues, who were seen as having lesser value. As Janet articulated, her colleagues did not know about her background and qualifications, and made assumptions about her. Over the years, Janet applied for and was appointed to more senior positions. She gained a deputy principal position at a larger school in a different town and after 13 years returned to her first high school as principal.

PERCEIVED BARRIERS TO PRINCIPALSHIP

When reflecting on her career progression, Janet identified a number of barriers that she believed slowed her journey to principalship.

Gender: Women Teach and Men Lead

Janet identified the stereotypes of men and women in education as a major barrier to her leadership progression. The stereotypical characteristics of teachers, such as caring, patience, creativity, and so on, are often seen as female traits, but Janet found, in her experience, the features of leadership were typically linked to masculine traits (Litmanovitz, 2011). Women do not reflect the stereotypical image of a high school principal (Coleman, 2005; Coleman, 2007). They struggle to be shortlisted for principal positions because some people doubt women's commitment to their work, due to the demands upon them as wives and mothers, and doubt their ability to lead others, particularly men (Coleman, 2007; Hewlett & Luce, 2005). Asking for help, being seen as too kind, too gentle, overly emotional and sensitive, and a person who cannot make difficult decisions may also add to the

stereotype that women are incapable of being leaders (Bassett, 2009; Fuller, 2013).

It has been suggested that women and men may differ in their leadership style and skills (Eckman, 2004) as "feminist educational leadership is educational rather than managerial" (Strachan, 2009, p. 123). However, Fuller (2013) questions this as she argued that women can use power to control and men can use it to empower. Janet does not conform to the expected male norms for principalship but deliberately uses a collaborative approach and gives "responsibility and authority" to her senior leadership team (Lyman et al., 2012).

Alongside her collaborative approach Janet is not afraid to show her vulnerabilities and says, "It is a female principal thing. I haven't come across any male principal doing this. Like if I talk to a male principal and I don't know something then I want an answer. Very rarely will they admit they don't know whereas I am the first one to say, well I don't know but I will go and find out for you."

Similar to other female educational leaders who have gone before her, Janet moves dynamically and fluidly across binary gender norms, even if these are linked to stereotypes (Christman & McClellan, 2008; Coleman, 2009). She said, "I can play the dumb female, help me, help me I don't know what I am doing." But she also takes on the role of "I am actually a woman and I have got to this position and I don't need any of you men to help me. I can stand up in my own right." Janet tries to find "a balance of those two" because "you need their [the male principals] support a lot of the time." Through thoughtful projections of herself, she negotiates the relationships involved in principalship in order to get what she needs.

Whānau/Family and Motherhood

Janet found that whānau/family acted as a barrier to her career development, especially at a specific time in her career. Women principals undertake multiple roles, maintaining their professional role as well as acting as homemakers/mothers/caretakers of young children, teenagers, and older parents (Hansen, 2014). Women often put their needs of their partner and family ahead of their own career aspirations (Coleman, 2009; Neidhart, 2009). An example of this is the prioritization to relocate to take up new employment. Research shows that few women have the luxury of relocating (Neidhardt, 2009; Robinson, 2015). However, in Janet's case, she and her husband had "looked at moving but house prices were absolutely phenomenal [and she was] quite happy to travel" for around 45 minutes each way when she was appointed to a new school as a deputy principal.

Janet also understood that principalship "does put pressure on relationships, marriages." This made her less willing to make the sacrifice of home/career balance, including time spent away from her husband and daughter. Janet wanted to wait until she had more time and fewer responsibilities before moving into principalship. Her goal of being a good wife and mother was stronger than her goal of becoming a principal, and Janet waited until her daughter had left school before she pursued the role of principal. Janet felt it more important to put time into her role as mother while her daughter was still living at home. This resonates with the opinions of a number of female leaders in the United States (Kelsey et al., 2014). However, more recent research has detected that a new generation of women appear ready to access leadership positions at a younger age as they accept compromises in their home and work life (Sperandio, 2015).

PERCEIVED ENABLERS TO PRINCIPALSHIP

Janet was able to identify a number of enablers that helped her eventually become a school principal. These included her very strong beliefs in social justice for the students she was working with, and the support she received.

Passion for Social Justice

Janet's mother was a deacon in the Anglican Church and also a Justice of the Peace, so Janet "saw her dealing with many social issues." Janet applied these family values as her moral "guiding compass" (Lyman et al., 2012, p. 83). She affirmed that these values guided her throughout her teaching career, directing her decisions as she moved into a principalship position. Social justice remained an ongoing motivator as she continued in her role as principal.

Janet has a true passion for her school community. She talked about the students she worked with as her "extended kids." She truly believes that society "can't have any more kids falling through the cracks and doing nothing." This personal commitment to working for equity and positive outcomes for disadvantaged students has been reported by many other principals and leaders both male and female (Brown, 2002; Harris, James, Gunraj, Clarke, & Harris, 2006; Theoharis, 2007). Subsequently, social justice compelled Janet to make the journey from deputy principal to principal.

Personal and Professional Support

Janet attributed her successful journey to principalship to the support of a range of people. She acknowledged that her husband was "a great support" throughout her career.

She talked about the way he shared childcare duties as well as helping around her school. Family connections and support are of the utmost importance to both Janet and her husband. When setting up as a new principal, Janet had "aunties and uncles, nieces and nephews coming in hanging up curtains and putting them into classrooms." International research identifies the importance of a husband's backing when a woman becomes a principal or takes on a similar leadership role (Kelsey et al., 2014; Masters, 2015; Rosario, 2015; Young & McLeod, 2001).

Support for Janet also came from female colleagues with small children who also used the school's daycare center. Janet reminisced, "it was nice that a lot of teachers had their children there, had that empathy and quite often one of us would go and pick up four kids, while their mothers were still working."

Mentors and Role Models

Janet was given "professional endorsement" (Young & McLeod, 2001, p. 485) by two male mentors who encouraged her and gave her confidence to apply for promotions. Research has found that gender is not necessarily a factor in mentoring, in terms of positive and understanding relationships (Kinnersley, 2009; Lyman et al., 2012). Janet's first mentor was a senior teacher who identified her potential early in her career. Her other mentor was the principal at her first high school teaching post. She talked about how important it was to have someone in a position of authority who actually believes in you. "He believed in me, I didn't believe in me but he did." He gave her responsibilities in the school, which is seen as a vital element in pre-principalship training (Weindling & Dimmock, 2006). He continued his mentoring role and also supported Janet when she took on her first principal position.

Participating in Professional Leadership Learning and Development

Janet was encouraged by her mentor to study for a diploma in School Management. This meant traveling a considerable distance to Auckland every holiday. This course included learning about things such as personnel management including conflicts in staffing, dealing with open to learning conversations, and so on, and Janet speaks very highly of it. Professional development such as this course helped Janet develop a sense of self-belief. Taking on the role of acting principal provided another avenue for professional learning and is one of the most valuable ways to prepare for a principal position (Weindling & Dimmock, 2006). Janet had the opportunity to do this, and it gave her the confidence to think that she could become a principal in the future.

Being in an acting principal position increased Janet's confidence. She found that she could manage the role, and although it was stressful, it was a great learning experience.

CONCLUSIONS AND REFLECTIONS

This investigation documents Janet's career path and therefore her life journey (Jones & Le Fevre, 2015). From very early on in their careers women need to be aware of the barriers that may stop or slow them down on their trek toward principalship. Simultaneously, women must grow the enablers that will support them in any future expeditions. Individual women do have to take responsibility and champion themselves (Kelsey et al., 2014), but society also needs a political shift to incorporate these ideas (Grogan & Shakeshaft, 2011).

One of the key elements in Janet's journey was her confidence in her own ability and to contemplate applying for principalship. Men often just take a chance on a promotion whereas women may feel like they need to tick all the boxes before they can confidently apply for a role (Future Leaders Trust as cited in Tickle, 2015, September, 29). This would indicate that society must find ways to develop confidence in female leaders by building up the enablers and minimizing or breaking the barriers to guarantee an increase in the number of female principals in schools as well as male principals who do not fit into a constricting masculine construct (Moorosi, 2015).

Someone asked Janet, "What's your next project?" and she replied, "I haven't finished this one yet." She continued by saying, "This school is definitely my swansong. I'm fifty-five now, I was fifty-two when I took on my first position as principal and now at fifty-five I sort of look at it and think this is my home. I'm going to give it the next ten years so, basically, to me, this is it." She is challenged yet content with her role as principal in her own community and will continue to work in this until the end of her career.

Figure 10.1. Janet's Climb to Principalship—the Barriers and the Enablers as a Visual Metaphor. Drawn by Jenni Bayliss

ADVICE FROM JANET

We end this chapter with Janet's voice, as this is her story. The three pieces of advice she would give women who are considering becoming principals are:

- A lot of people wouldn't agree but it has huge implications on your time with your family so wait until they (the children) are older. At least when they are already in high school to be able to cope and do both [be a mother and be a principal].
- Find yourself a good mentor when you are a DP (deputy principal).
- Don't ever be ashamed to say you don't know. There is no such thing as a dumb question. I ask them all the time because I don't know how you can find out if you don't ask. (Janet)

Her final words ring true as she describes her views on what it means to be a women leader, stating, "I have to be honest, I would say to anybody, yourself included, if you're thinking about it, a principal's position is not a job, it's a life, you actually live it 24/7."

REFERENCES

Bassett, D. (2009). Overview for part 1. In H. C. Sobehart (Ed.), *Women leading education across the continents: Sharing the spirit, fanning the flame* (pp. 9–12). Lanham, MD: Rowman & Littlefield.

Brown, K. M. (2002, November). *Leadership for social justice and equity: Weaving a transformative framework and pedagogy.* Paper presented to the University Council for Educational Administration Annual Convention, Pittsburgh, PA.

Christman, D., & McClellan, R. (2008). "Living on barbed wire": Resilient women administrators in educational leadership programs. *Educational Administration Quarterly, 44*(1), 3–29. http://dx.doi.org/10.1177/0013161X07309744

Coleman, M. (2005). *Gender and headship in the twenty-first century.* Nottingham, England: National College for School Leadership. Retrieved from http://dera.ioe.ac.uk/7260/1/download%3Fid=17191&filename=gender-and-headship-in-the-21st-century.pdf

Coleman, M. (2007). Gender and educational leadership in England: A comparison of secondary headteachers' views over time. *School Leadership & Management, 27*(4), 383–399. http://doi.org/10.1080/13632430701562991

Coleman, M. (2009). Women in educational leadership in England. In H. C. Sobehart (Ed.), *Women leading education across the continents: Sharing the spirit, fanning the flame* (pp. 13–20). Lanham, MD: Rowman & Littlefield.

Eckman, E. W. (2004). Does gender make a difference? Voices of male and female high school principals. *Planning and Changing, 35*(1–2), 192–208.

Fitzgerald, T., & Wilkinson, J. (2010). *Travelling towards a mirage? Gender, leadership and higher education.* Mt Gravatt, Australia: Post Pressed.

Fuller, K. (2013). *Gender, identity, and educational leadership.* London, England: Bloomsbury Academic. Retrieved from http://site.ebrary.com/lib/waikato/Top?id=10775526

Grogan, M., & Shakeshaft, C. (2011). *Women and educational leadership.* San Francisco, CA: Jossey-Bass.

Hansen, J. (2014). *A qualitative study of women high school principals' career life histories* (Doctoral dissertation, Utah State University). Retrieved from http://digitalcommons.usu.edu/etd/2158

Harris, A., James, S., Gunraj, R., Clarke, P., & Harris, B. (2006). *Improving schools in exceptionally challenging circumstances. Tales from the frontline.* London, England: Continuum.

Hewlett, S. A., & Luce, C. B. (2005). Off-ramps and on-ramps. *Harvard Business Review, 83*(3), 43–54.

Ho, E. S. C. (2015). Overview: Confronting the barriers of women leaders around the world. In E. C. Reilly & Q. J. Bauer (Eds.), *Women leading education across the continents: Overcoming the barriers* (pp. 85–90). Lanham, MD: Rowman & Littlefield.

Jones, T., & Le Fevre, D. (2015, September). *Exploring women's perceptions of risk when engaging in professional learning.* Paper presented at the 5th International Women Leading Education Across Continents Conference, Hamilton, New Zealand.

Kelsey, C., Allen, K., Coke, K., & Ballard, G. (2014). Lean in and lift up: Female superintendents share their career path choices. *Journal of Case Studies in Education, 6*, 1–11.

Kinnersley, R. T. (2009). *Mentoring relationships of female administrators in Tennessee higher education* (Doctoral Dissertation, Tennessee State University). Retrieved from http://gradworks.umi.com/33/56/3356142.html

Le Fevre, D., & Farquhar. (2015, September). *Re(cognising) and en(couraging) women's leadership.* Paper presented at the 5th International Women Leading Education Across Continents Conference, Hamilton, New Zealand.

Litmanovitz, M. (2011). Beyond the classroom: Women in education leadership. *Kennedy School Review, (11)*, 25–28.

Lyman, L. L., Strachan, J., & Lazaridou, A. (2012). *Shaping social justice leadership: Insights of women educators worldwide.* Lanham, MD: Rowman & Littlefield Education.

Mahmood, A. (2015, September). *The path of leadership for women in Pakistan.* Paper presented at the 5th International Women Leading Education Across Continents Conference, Hamilton, New Zealand.

Masters, Y. (2015, September). *The good little woman at home: Being a female principal in a Catholic school.* Paper presented at the 5th International Women Leading Education Across Continents Conference, New Zealand.

Ministry of Education. (2017). Teacher headcount by designation (grouped), gender and school type in state and state integrated schools. https://www.educationcounts.govt.nz/statistics/schooling/teaching_staff

Moorosi, P. (2015). "Breadwinners" and "homemakers": how constructions of masculinities affect women's progression in leadership. In E. C. Reilly & Q. J. Bauer (Eds.), *Women leading education across the continents: Overcoming the barriers* (pp. 21–26). Lanham, MD: Rowman & Littlefield.

Neidhardt, C. (2009). *Speed bumps and l-plates: Female deputy principals' perceptions of the barriers in aspiring to primary principalship* (Master's thesis, University of Waikato, Hamilton, New Zealand). Retrieved from http://hdl.handle.net/10289/4314

Robinson, K. (2015). Why do women leave the superintendency? In E. C. Reilly & Q. J. Bauer (Eds.), *Women leading education across the continents: Overcoming the barriers* (pp. 55–62). Lanham, MD: Rowman & Littlefield.

Robinson, V. (2009). *Module 3: Building trust in schools through open-to-learning conversations. First-time principals programme.* University of Auckland: New Zealand. Retrieved from http://www.educationalleaders.govt.nz/content/download/4919/39711/file/Background%20Paper%20for%20OLC%20module%2020090721.pdf

Rosario, A. (2015, September). *Barriers and strategies: Stories of women's rise to leadership.* Paper presented at the 5th International Women Leading Education Across Continents Conference, Hamilton, New Zealand.

Shah, S. (2015). Where does the power lie? Gender, leadership, and positional power. In E. C. Reilly & Q. J. Bauer (Eds.), *Women leading education across the continents: Overcoming the barriers* (pp. 165–171). Lanham, MD: Rowman & Littlefield.

Slaughter, A. (2015, September 18). A toxic work world. *New York Times.* Retrieved from http://www.nytimes.com/2015/09/20/opinion/sunday/a-toxic-work-world.html

Sperandio, J. (2015). Where are all the women superintendents? A case study of Pennsylvania, USA. In E. C. Reilly & Q. J. Bauer (Eds.), *Women leading education across the continents: Overcoming the barriers* (pp. 35–42). Lanham, MD: Rowman & Littlefield.

Strachan, J. (2009). Women and educational leadership in New Zealand and Melanesia. In H. C. Sobehart (Ed.), *Women leading education across the continents: Sharing the spirit, fanning the flame* (1st ed., pp. 100–109). Lanham, MD: Rowman & Littlefield.

Theoharis, G. (2007). Social justice educational leaders and resistance: Toward a theory of social justice leadership. *Educational Administration Quarterly, 43*(2), 221–258. http://dx.doi.org/10.1177/0013161X06293717

Tickle, L. (2015, September 29). The teaching glass ceiling: Women fight to be heard in a sector that's 62% female. *The Guardian.* Retrieved from http://www.theguardian.com/education/2015/sep/29/teaching-glass-ceiling-women-campaign-nicky-morgan

Weindling, D., & Dimmock, C. (2006). Sitting in the "hot seat": New headteachers in the UK. *Journal of Educational Administration, 44*(4), 326–340.

Young, M. D., & McLeod, S. (2001). Flukes, opportunities, and planned interventions: Factors affecting women's decisions to become school administrators. *Educational Administration Quarterly, 37*(4), 462–502.

WOMEN'S LEADERSHIP EXPERIENCES

Editor: *Alice Merab Kagoda*

Chapter 11

Overview

Experiences of Women in Educational Leadership

Alice Merab Kagoda

High quality education transforms the lives of children, youths, and adults (Global Monitoring Report, 2016), with the potential to be a positive force for social, economic, and environmental change. As education can influence how people think, perceive, and act, it plays a key role in developing human potential and capability, ultimately contributing to the political, social, economic, and cultural resources of societies. While there is the aspiration to "empower children and adults alike to become active participants in the transformation of their societies" (UNESCO, 2017a), there is evidence that women are poorly represented in statistics showing access to education, even though they make up slightly more than half of the world's population. This is especially prevalent in the area of higher education.

Higher education is one of the prerequisites for gaining administrative and leadership positions in the education sector. While teaching can be an entry point into the education sector, few women are given the opportunity to rise up the leadership ladder (UNESCO, 2017), with Killingsworth, Cadezas, Kensler, and Brooks (2010), among others, highlighting the significant influence of contextual, social, cultural barriers, and perceptions (Crosby-Hillier, 2012), which prevent women from entering into leadership in educational contexts.

BARRIERS TO WOMEN ASPIRING TO EDUCATIONAL LEADERSHIP

Using a feminist theory perspective in research illustrates and brings attention to the ways in which women in educational leadership have been discriminated against. This perspective uncovers the politics of gendered and nonsexualized representation including the historical, social, and political context in which they were produced. Crosby-Hillier (2012) asserts that feminist theories are committed to challenging patriarchy, racism, power, and oppression, which helps to explore broader questions of social justice and multiple forms of structural inequality. It fosters empowerment, liberation, and emancipation for women and other marginalized groups.

The feminist theory focus on the advancement of women interrogates the sources of gender inequality in order to bring about the goals and aims of gender justice. Women in leadership help transform society, they advocate for girls and women because male interests are widely represented. Scholars such as Morley and Crossouard (2015), Crosby-Hillier (2012), and Killlingsworth et al. (2010) have identified barriers to women aspiring to educational leadership.

Many feminist scholars, like those mentioned previously, identify the power of the sociocultural process as the reason that prevents women moving into educational leadership positions. Women argue that they are still identified with the domestic sphere and with caring/nurturing of extended family roles. The socioeconomic backgrounds and sociocultural belief systems constrain women from pursuing academic careers, for example, women should not be in authority over men. Women from privileged socioeconomic backgrounds often reported family support and cultural capital as helping them climb up the education ladder, consequently, employment.

The metaphor of a glass ceiling emphasizes the notion that invisible and unseen structural patterns of gender discrimination prevent women from ascending into the most prestigious well-paying senior leadership positions. The glass ceiling and walls are constructed systematically as a consequence of cultural beliefs and behaviors. They explain that leadership positions within educational institutions are an outcome of the glass ceiling. A psychological glass ceiling is a concept used to explain how women themselves have internalized a patriarchal gender ideology, which undermines their women who do not engage in self-promotion or assertive behaviors or seem unwilling to take risks. Fear of failure is a great hindrance to their assertiveness (Crosby-Hillier, 2012; Killingsworth et al., 2010; Morley & Crossouard, 2015).

Women often experience difficulty in attaining a work-life balance. Positions of leadership require high educational levels which women may not be able to get once they start family. Also, women tend to have more responsibilities at home. Women lack career guidance, resource monitoring, and socialization in academic leadership positions. Many women may not have professional networks and connections to support them in their career advancement.

Exclusion from social capital and mentoring hinders their access to organizational power. Another factor leading to exclusion of women are the employers who look favorably upon those who possesses leadership attributes and traits commonly associated with men. The male-dominated power structures exclude women; men tend to recruit people like them. This reproduces male dominance in educational leadership.

THE CHAPTERS

The chapters in this section offer us alternative narratives for how women experience and practice educational leadership for social justice, they challenge the norm. They are stories of joy, hope, challenge, and courage.

Karen Barbour's chapter, "Dancing Into the Unknown: Learning Leadership" narrates her journey into a leadership position in higher education. She narrates how she "tried to understand ways in which I can engage in leadership with integrity, upholding the values, encouraging the voices, and growing shared visions with those I work with." She relied on feminist education leaders, leadership practices, role models, and research. Her story is about her personal history of learning leadership; she reflects on her school and undergraduate period when at times she did what her parents expected her to do. She refers to the inspiration of role models and describes them as "people who demonstrate appealing and appropriate behaviors, characteristics, qualities, and attitudes." She relates that her mother demonstrated through her own actions how to translate ideas and passions into action. Her mother conveyed values relating to honesty, justice, healthy and active lifestyles, family education. She narrates her life history in learning leadership using her passion for dancing as a vehicle.

Karen makes some observations about leaders, "they are people who work with and inspire others to follow them" and realized that working with people involves a wide range of relationships including collaboration, facilitation, and participation. Her academic role model inspired her to speak up for what she valued, to listen to others, and to respect their values. Most interestingly,

she draws on her experience as a dance artist to help her understand, interrogate, and find joy in her own academic leadership. She concluded, "processes I value are initiating, negotiating, contributing, and sharing, within interactive social processes and attempting to engage with a nurturing, mentoring, often shared authorship approach. Active experience and participation in process is important and for me characterizes effective leadership."

Linda McGinley and Diane Reed in their chapter, "Know Thyself: The Influence of Career Orientations on Women Education Leaders' Career Decisions," focuses on district level leaders, Assistant Superintendents for Instruction (ASI), who are pivotal in creating a culture that supports students' learning and facilitates sustainable improvement and student performance in the United States.

The authors contextualize the conditions under which these participants in their study operate, "changing demographics, a growing diversity, deregulation, power decentralization, and increased accountability; the changing roles of superintendents and increased policy expectations; the requirement for commitment to improve teaching and performance." The ASI role requires a person with skills to implement student learning cultures, greater decision making, and knowledge construction throughout the organization and to build capacity for research-based instruction. They stress the value of collaboration, shared leadership, and trust among leaders at all levels.

Their study reveals that women prefer to work as ASI where they find joy and less stress than in other leadership roles. They conclude that women ASI's career decisions may be driven by self-perceived values, talents, and needs.

Rachel McNae's chapter, "Women Leading for Social Justice in Higher Education," presents research based in the New Zealand context, where women leaders in the university context were the participants. This chapter reports on research that engaged educational theory that centered on a strength-based paradigm. She argues that hope generates the understanding that the future is open and can be influenced and through working from a paradigm of hope, organizational change can be created and sustained. Findings of her research highlight ways in which women were leading with hope which helped to counter barriers and limitations that marginalized and impacted on their leadership experiences. A sense of belonging and the notion of sisterhood were developed together, leading to career development, mentoring, and professional learning. Rachel argues that the hope paradigm empowers women leaders to develop their self-esteem that energizes them to take on challenges and constraints they might encounter as they develop their leadership skills.

The final chapter in this section by Wafa Hozien examines the experiences of minority women leaders in higher education. She explores the tensions and experiences which the women navigate in their daily lives as they practice and demonstrate their leadership across a range of contexts. Central to this research is the illumination of their support systems, engagement in education, opportunities for networking, and professional development, which supported them to overcome significant challenges and cherish the opportunity for leadership overall.

CONCLUSION

Although each of these contributions illustrates different cultural contexts, it is apparent that across each of these educational settings women show significant resilience when faced with immense challenges. Their ways of working demonstrate powerful and deep leadership of the self and others which support women to actively seek enjoyment in their work.

The world is changing and becoming more complex. There is a critical mass of highly educated women from which leaders can be drawn. The chapters in this section provide insights into how women can successfully navigate their way into leadership positions and how they can successfully occupy those roles.

REFERENCES

Crosby-Hillier, K. (2012). *Women and educational leadership: Exploring the experiences of current and aspiring female educational administrators* (Master's thesis, University of Windsor, Ontario, Canada). Retrieved from http://scholar.uwindsor.ca/etd

Killingsworth, M. F., Cabezas, C. T., Kensler, L. A. W., & Brooks, J. S. (2010). The gender dynamics of educational leadership preparation: A feminist postmodern critique of the cohort experience. *Journal of Research on Leadership Education, 5*(12), 531–567.

Morley, L., & Crossouard, B. (2015). Women in higher education leadership in South Asia: Rejection, refusal, reluctance, revisioning. University of Sussex. Centre for Higher Education and Equity Research. Retrieved from https://www.britishcouncil.org/sites/default/files/british-council-women-higher-education-leadership-south-asia

UNESCO. (2017). Learning to live together. Retrieved from: http://www.unesco.org/new/en/social-and-human-sciences/themes/fight-against-discrimination/role-of-education/.

Chapter 12

Dancing Into the Unknown

Learning Leadership

Karen Barbour

In this chapter I explore the ways in which understandings of women's leadership intersect with critical feminist pedagogies and with my practice as a dance artist. Combining narrative and theorizing, I retrace my dancing steps in becoming a leader and begin to imagine future leaps and turns as my leadership evolves within the new roles in which I find myself.

The intersections between women's leadership styles and leadership theory as described in the literature (Airini, Collings, Conner, McPherson, Midson, & Wilson, 2010; Barsh, Cranston, & Craske, 2008; Coleman, 2011; Fitzgerald & Wilkinson, 2010; Franken, Penney, & Branson, 2015; Lyman, Strachan, & Lazaridou, 2012; Sinclair, 2007), critical feminist pedagogy as applied in tertiary dance education (Barbour, 2011; Butterworth, 2004; Shapiro, 1998), and community dance practice (Barr, 2013; Hunter & Gladstone, 2009) provide a rich source of understandings that assist me in growing as a leader.

In seeking to understand ways in which I can engage in leadership with integrity, upholding the values, encouraging the voices, and a growing shared vision with those I work with, I turn to where I find most joy—dance. Dance is where my passion lies and where I nurture well-being for myself and those I work with.

Reflecting on particular trigger events and critical incidents I understand how my interest in, and embodiment of, leadership has grown. Thus, I draw on arts models for engaging with others to understand leadership differently through development of honest relationships and trust, sharing of responsibility, and respect for difference. Ultimately, I think of leadership as requiring dancing into the unknown.

INTRODUCTION

Throughout ongoing processes of learning leadership, I have been reflecting on my experiences and searching for intersections between leadership theory and the practices more familiar to me as a critical feminist pedagogue and dance maker. As I will share in this chapter, I have discovered relationships between my own experiences, leadership theory, and women's leadership styles as described in the literature (Airini et al., 2010; Barsh et al., 2008; Coleman, 2011; Fitzgerald & Wilkinson, 2010; Franken et al., 2015; Lyman et al., 2012; Sinclair, 2007).

However, it is to my passion and work in dance that I turn for sources of understandings to assist me in growing as a leader (Barbour, 2011; Barr, 2013; Butterworth, 2004; Hunter & Gladstone, 2009; Shapiro, 1998). Combining narrative and theorizing, I retrace my dancing steps in becoming a leader, beginning by reflecting on personal history and trigger events as well as identifying role models in learning leadership (Lyman et al., 2012).

In seeking to understand ways in which I can engage in leadership with integrity, upholding the values, encouraging the voices, and growing shared visions with those I work with, I respond most strongly to research in which leading within higher education is acknowledged as "about building relationships so as to create a deeper sense of connection whereby the person has not only a clearer appreciation of their organizational reality but also a stronger sense of their part in how it functions and develops" (Franken et al., 2015, p. 3). Further, I begin to imagine future leaps and turns as my interest in, and embodiment of, leadership has grown within the new roles in which I find myself.

However, I find greatest inspiration when I turn to where I find most joy—in dance. Dance is where my passion lies and where I nurture my own well-being and the well-being of those I work with. Critical feminist pedagogy as applied in dance education (Barbour, 2011; Butterworth, 2004; Shapiro, 1998) and community dance practice (Barr, 2013; Hunter & Gladstone, 2009), both provide rich sources of understandings that assist me in growing as a leader. Thus, I draw on contemporary leadership research (Hernandez, Eberly, Avolio, & Johnson, 2011; Lyman et al., 2012) as well as arts models for engaging with others to understand leadership differently through development of honest relationships and trust, sharing of responsibility, and respect for difference.

Feminist educational leaders Lyman, Strachan, and Lazaridou (2012) consider women's leadership practices and argue that "taking a developmental perspective, a leader's personal history (family, friends, early experiences, educational and work encounters, and role models) as well as trigger events (crises, positive and negative experiences) are catalysts for the development of authentic leadership behaviors and skills" (Lyman et al., 2012, p. 103). Therefore, I begin my story about learning leadership with a little personal history that allows me to reflect on my early experiences and roles models, as well as trigger events.

REFLECTING ON THE ROLE OF EARLY PERSONAL HISTORY IN LEARNING LEADERSHIP

While some people may be considered "born" to fulfill leadership roles, through family genealogy or community expectations, many others grow into leadership (Hernandez et al., 2011; Lyman et al., 2012). Particular childhood and early adult experiences may support growth into leadership roles, in that personal values and passions may be identified, working in a range of different relationships with others may develop skills, and curiosity about social processes and collaborations may prompt reflection. Reflection and self-awareness of participation in different contexts, along with support from others and willingness to accept opportunities offered to take up leadership roles may then lead to a recognition of personal leadership potential (Branson & Gross, 2014).

Reflecting on my own childhood experiences, I had not seen myself as a leader early in my life. My childhood was not full of stories of leadership or recognition of leading roles within peer groups. While I was the eldest sister of four girls (arguably something of a leadership role), I did not play team sports in our small rural New Zealand community in which sport was a big focus. Sport was valued in our community as a context in which children (although mostly boys) learned about leadership as team captains and valued players.

Instead, I was somewhat solitary (even among my sisters), preferring to express myself through contemporary dance, and to participate in individual pursuits such as athletics, swimming, and gymnastics. While I did join the debating team and I did coach gymnastics as a teenager, my solitary focus marked me as rather unusual in my small

community. I was neither socially popular nor very involved in children's group activities. Further, as the eldest child of two school teachers, being accepted by, and feeling comfortable with my peers, was simply challenging.

As a very naïve young woman, I moved to study at our regional university, partly because my parents expected me to, and also because I expected to, having taken comfort in my academic capabilities when social acceptance was harder to achieve. Part way through my undergraduate degree in philosophy and psychology, I realized that there were no dance courses or dance activities on the campus. Driven by my passion for dance, I decided to start teaching contemporary dance classes myself on campus, believing that if I wanted to dance for expression and creativity, there were likely other young women who did too. Talking the idea over with my mother, we developed an overall philosophy for dance classes and planned exercises and I simply began.

Teaching dance classes was a necessary leap that allowed me to dance and to share my passion. My health and well-being depended on expressing myself through dancing and so I did not see this as a leadership role. Teaching was about my passion for dancing although I certainly hoped that I would inspire and empower other women through dance. Many women came to join me; we enthusiastically choreographed and performed together, and it was not long before the group evolved into a student dance club that still functions more than 25 years later. As I reflect, I wonder if this was my first informal leadership role.

Throughout my undergraduate degree, and then master's in philosophy, niggling concerns about the lack of women philosophers in our studies and the disconnect between my embodied expression in dance and the written traditions of Western philosophy became more and more unbearable (Barbour, 2011). I felt that I was rehearsing the arguments of dead white men in my philosophy essays, and yet at the same time I was creating dances about my personal experiences as a woman. This growing feminist consciousness led me to some quite uncomfortable and also rather amusing experiences.

For example, I challenged one of my philosophy lecturers to a public debate about his use of sexist language (I believe I won the debate). As another example, I approached a lecturer in psychology about tutoring in undergraduate papers, only to be told that my grades were not good enough and I would never be a university tutor. These experiences occurred during an era when there were policies relating to sexism, discrimination, and equal opportunity in New Zealand universities, but enacting such policies in practice was still to come.

While I did go on to tutor in both philosophy and psychology, and I participated in and contributed to my university environment in a range of ways, these were not formal leadership roles. Again, when I reflect, I wonder if these experiences as a student at university were early "trigger events" in my learning leadership. Certainly, these were significant experiences that nurtured my feminist consciousness and my desire to pursue dance as an academic career.

Another crucial aspect in learning leadership is the inspiration that role models provide. Role models are people who demonstrate appealing and appropriate behaviors, characteristics, qualities, and attitudes. Often parents are "the first and most powerful" role models, and throughout childhood and young adulthood we develop our identities through imitating various role models we encounter in different contexts (Scarnati, 2002, p. 181).

Reflecting on my role models, I acknowledge my family members and particularly my mother. My mother demonstrated through her own actions how to translate ideas and passions into action. She conveyed core values relating to honesty, justice, healthy and active lifestyles, family, education, and creativity. As I described earlier, it was my mother who supported me in developing my passion for dance through teaching, and we continue to imagine and plan together, discussing philosophies and pedagogical approaches in movement.

It was my mother who taught me through her example to remain grounded and engaged in grassroots community activity. I also acknowledge my father, who showed me through the lessons he learned by slogging through graduate and doctoral study while teaching in schools, and negotiating research and higher education politics, how to be an academic. His values relating to education, social justice, and research shaped my desire for academic achievement and teaching in higher education.

As the eldest of four, I also acknowledge my sisters for each embodying an academic life in their unique ways, for setting standards of behavior I aspire to and providing a crucial network as we each seek fulfilment in our academic, community, and family lives. While my passion for dance led me on a different career trajectory from my sisters, our parents' valuing of education, justice, and research influenced us all in our different academic areas.

Thus, reflecting on the role of my early personal history in learning leadership, I emphasize three observations: first, that many of us grow into leadership. Working in education myself now, I recognize that we have a responsibility to identify and support young people to grow as leaders. Arguably, we are much better in New Zealand in schools at identifying and developing young leaders (McNae, 2010). Second, passion matters in learning leadership. For me, motivation for, and willingness to take on, informal leadership roles was clearest when it was driven by my passions: in my case, my passion for

dance and for women's voices to be heard in education. And third, our early role models may provide ways for us to learn about leadership as we observe and imitate their behavior as we grow into adulthood.

REFLECTING ON "TRIGGER EVENTS" IN LEARNING LEADERSHIP

Identifying personal leadership potential and learning while growing into leadership roles necessitates deepening self-awareness and reflection. Reflection may arise as the result of a particular experience—a "trigger event" or "critical incident"—that creates tension or conflict (Lyman et al., 2012). Such discomfort may occur because personal values and required behavior no longer align in a particular context. "Trigger events" thus prompt self-reflection, identification of options, and decision making about how to behave.

Throughout university study, my passion for dance continued to grow, and in my mid-20s I leapt away from university into the world of full-time professional contemporary dance training. During this time I also started reading feminist theory to satisfy my own curiosity, and I began to develop a vision for new ways to empower and inspire women through professional dance. At the time professional funding for the arts was particularly scarce and most of the dance funding in New Zealand was going to well-known male choreographers.

As most of my peers and dance teachers were women, the number of female dancers training for, and working in, professional dance outnumbered males at least 10 to 1. With the development of a new professional men's dance company, suddenly there were actually more jobs available for men in professional dance companies, too. I despaired about my own and my peers' opportunities, and I wondered how I could improve this situation.

Taking the initiative, I again talked ideas over with my mother and I wrote a funding proposal for a professional contemporary dance project with the explicit aim to create space for women in dance. I was successful in obtaining funding and I employed my peers. We quickly established collective working relationships, had a wonderful debut performance season, and received positive critical reviews. I felt that perhaps I had created a space for myself within the professional dance community.

At the same time, I was also working as an academic administrator for a dance program. There were very limited dance offerings in higher education in New Zealand at the time, and this particular program aimed to shift from a training focus into the higher education context. I saw this as an innovative and exciting development that I could be part of, and I was also relishing tutoring dance in this program. I imagined that the combination of leading within a collective of professional dancing women with feminist agendas, and working as a tutor and administrator in a higher education dance program was the realization of my vision for an integrated life in academia and dance.

However, two trigger events or critical incidents occurred, almost at the same time. First, as women in the professional dance project began planning for ongoing projects, we began to argue, in particular about employing high-profile male choreographers to work with us. I realized that my peers did not fully share my feminist values to create space and prioritize opportunities for women, and I felt that the agenda for the group was already shifting away from my aspirations for women's empowerment.

Coupled with the challenge of writing applications and actually obtaining funding, marketing and producing performances, and performing myself, I seriously questioned whether I could sustain my involvement in the collective I had initiated. Disheartened, I wondered if I even had a place in this collective if my core values did not align with my peers.

Alongside this, the dance program in which I was working was advertising for a leader for the new innovative degree program I had contributed to developing as an administrator. During the appointment process, I discovered my colleagues supported the applications of professional dancers, who, while being wonderful artists themselves, did not have substantial academic backgrounds. I voiced my concerns about the necessity of academic knowledge and reputation in this leadership role, and took a stand against the appointment of a dance professional without an academic qualification. I was devastated to be told to be quiet or leave the program.

On reflection, these trigger events led to one of the lowest points in my life. Almost at the same time, I recognized that the vision I had nurtured for empowering women in dance was not shared by my peers, and that my aspirations for the development of dance in higher education were at odds with the program I was working in. Suddenly, my vision for an integrated life in academia and dance seemed unobtainable. I withdrew from the collective and resigned from my job in the dance program. Needing a break I traveled overseas for a time, doubting what I was capable of doing or should be doing.

These trigger events prompted reflection at the time, and in that moment my decision was to walk away. However, taking time to reflect while traveling and to identify other options, I came to the conclusion that I would need to continue my academic study. I needed to engage with feminist theory and praxis, and to embrace the diversity of research in dance, so that I could more fully contribute and become an academic leader in dance myself.

Thus, I emphasize two more observations: first, that leaders work with others, and second, that personal values matter in leadership. One of the simpler ways of thinking about leaders is that they are people who work with, and inspire, others to follow them. Communicating effectively, raising awareness of social issues, strategic development, and responding to change are all significant leadership skills that can be developed. However, contemporary leadership is not strictly, nor ideally, theorized as a simple relationship of leader to follower (Hernandez et al., 2011).

Working with people involves a wide range of relationships including collaborator, facilitator, participant, supporter, and more. Leaders are "for the people" and work with people, even when leading. Leadership then, is about relationships, and within relationships, ideas and practices have greater currency at certain times.

We develop and clarify personal values as we grow, influenced by early experiences and role models. Tensions between personal values and those of individuals and groups we work with are challenging to resolve. When we do what we can to raise concerns and advocate for change, and we are unable to be effective, there is a point at which we have to make a choice. As Lyman et al. (2012) state, "Leaders around the world take risks through speaking out to challenge the status quo and to protect their rights. Speaking out is an action central to descriptions of social justice leadership" (p. 139). Both speaking out and remaining true to personal values are important in leadership.

My journey took me into doctoral study in dance, feminist theory, and praxis, and during this time I developed a crucial relationship with my supervisor Jane Strachan (Lyman et al., 2012). Jane became and remains a key role model for my work in higher education in general, and her work in feminist educational leadership has become a significant inspiration to me. Jane embodied the necessity of retaining personal values as a leader and working with others in positive relationships:

> Aligning behaviours and actions with the true self is at the heart of authentic leadership. . . . Furthermore, authenticity cannot be forced; authentic individuals express their core feelings, motives, and inclinations freely and naturally (Kernis 2003). Rather than use the words of others, leaders must find their own true voice to gain credibility with followers. They must develop and follow personal moral compasses. (Lyman et al., 2012, pp. 122–123)

Jane modeled for me how to speak up for what I valued, to listen to others, and to respect their values. Her actions in feminist educational leadership remind me to think beyond the personal into the political, beyond university into the community, and into issues for women nationally, as well as in the Pacific region. Jane taught me, from early in my doctoral study and into my job as an academic, to value the work of women and to cite feminist contributions in research. She encouraged me to make a conscious choice to engage with the politics of knowledge production, to challenge what knowledge counts and who can be a knower. In particular, Jane embodied a quality I admire most in leaders—that of "walking the talk."

Thus, in reflecting on personal history and the role of trigger events, the potential for growing into leadership is supported by early experiences and significant role models. Both following passions and retaining personal values matter as we work in varied relationships with others, leading formally and informally.

LEARNING LEADERSHIP WITHIN HIGHER EDUCATION

In my learning of leadership within my career as a dance academic, the process of applying for, and participating in, the New Zealand Universities Women in Leadership Programme (NZWiL) provided another opportunity for me to reflect on particular trigger events and the ways in which these events had shaped my decision making as an adult. The NZWiL program was an innovative professional development opportunity offered to a small group of women nationally, and I participated before I had taken up formal leadership roles in the university. The program aimed to both recognize and enhance women's leadership capacities and influence within universities (NZWiL, 2013).

I did have, however, some experience in informal leadership roles at university and in the wider dance community, including involvement in our national tertiary dance education network. In attending the NZWiL program I also had rather limited knowledge of leadership theory. However, I was particularly interested to understand more about what leadership in the higher education sector might look like, and I had one simple question in my mind: Would my experiences of leadership from working in dance in the community and professional sectors be relevant for a potential shift into academic leadership?

As an academic I draw on my experiences as a dance artist involved in typically social practices of dance, recognizing that varied communication and problem-solving skills and genuine interest in relationships with others are integral to everything I do. It seemed to me that leading was an extension of the commitment I had to dance, to

the people I worked with and a kind of authentic response to the joy I found in this work.

Most particularly, I had grown into informal leadership roles in dance in which I was committed to the aims and evolving identity of the group, and able to see the relationships between the group and the wider context (Haslam, Reicher, & Platow, 2011). I already recognized that motivation for, and willingness to, take on leadership roles was strongest for me when it was driven by my passions. As an academic I believe that dance education,

> can be a place where students make connections between the personal and the social; develop their perceptual, imaginative, and sensual abilities; find their own voices; validate their feelings and capacity for compassion; and become empowered through affirmation of their ability to be co-creators of their world. (Shapiro, 1998, p. 18)

Dance is my passion, and not for the purpose solely of making dances or nurturing dance teachers, but for growing engaged, response-able people capable of contributing to their own communities. But I wondered how this passion would translate, if it did at all, into ways of working with other academics and administrators within universities.

During the innovative NZWiL program we engaged in many activities that were reflective, inspirational, and educational and were not based on the development of individual skills or competencies. Knowing something about the history of academia as a Western enlightenment project, until recently the domain of men (Barbour, 2011), I had not been optimistic that general leadership theory would assist me much. It is something of an irony that,

> universities, across their 600-year history, have promoted differences of thought, the creation of new knowledge, intellectual freedom and acted as the critic and conscience of society. Yet, equitable practices and outcomes have not been achieved. Women are, and remain, predominantly located in the lower rungs of the academic hierarchy and are considerably under-represented in senior positions. Gender equity is not solely about a quantitative change; it also includes the elimination of structural and material inequalities. In a market economy, however, this is more, not less, difficult. (Fitzgerald & Wilkinson, 2010, pp. 16–17)

However, I did have key role models (such as Jane Strachan) who offered me examples of ways to lead in higher education. I was attracted to transformational and authentic leadership theories in which understanding and leading self was a key component, and in which reflection and self-awareness about personal values and behavior was necessary. I was committed to empowerment for women, and people in minority and indigenous groups, and the potential for a leader to work collaboratively through relational practices with others so that individuals and groups could understand options and make decisions in order to respond to the changing and dynamic nature of contemporary life (Hernandez et al., 2011; Lyman et al., 2012).

Colleagues Margaret Franken, Dawn Penney, and Chris Branson commented that "leading a learning organization, or part of an organization, is about building relationships so as to create a deeper sense of connection whereby the person has not only a clearer appreciation of their organizational reality but also a stronger sense of their part in how it functions and develops" (Franken et al., 2015, p. 3).

However, such aspirations for building relationships with colleagues may also challenge women academics. Many women in education have multiple roles and responsibilities that impact on leadership. Parenting and care-giving roles and community involvement are often part of the regular commitments of women in educational leadership positions. Taking time out of teaching and research commitments, or life outside work, to foster collegial relationships requires difficult choices and may compromise an already difficult balancing act.

A key concern is always the notion of balance in roles and responsibilities both within the working context and also with community and family commitments. Fortunately, some have argued that the elusive "work-life balance is a myth" and have instead turned attention to the more sensible goals of managing energy and allowing life and work to enrich each other (Barsh et al., 2008, p. 40).

Research on centered leadership also suggests that talented women acknowledge the impact of positive emotions. Such women find meaning in utilizing strengths toward an inspiring purpose; understanding where energy comes from and how to manage it; developing a constructive, positive framing of the world; connecting through strong relationships and belonging, and engaging voice to become self-reliant and confident in working with others (Barsh et al., 2008). Awareness of strengths and positive emotions is particularly crucial, and our strengths and positive emotions as women are as likely to be embodied in family and community activity as in higher education commitments at work:

> There is a need to give equal weight to personal aspirations such as attaining self-acceptance, effective management of one's life, maintaining positive relationships, sustaining personal growth, and assuring autonomy or self-determination. In this connection role models and mentors are once again important. But at least equally important are organizational values, policies, and structures that respect personal rights and moral agency and do not make personal needs subservient to organizational needs. (Lyman et al., 2012, p. 115)

Nevertheless, much of the leadership literature I had encountered previous to the NZWiL program, as well as some shared during the program, was not particularly stimulating in working out how I might act in leading myself.

Crucial for me was a clear understanding of my own values and the application of practices from my experience and knowledge, to leading in an academic context. While I was not convinced that I had done well as a leader in the women's dance collective or the dance administration role I had previously left, I did have experience working as a choreographer and teacher (often understood as the clearest leadership roles in dance), in professional, educational, and community dance settings. In the broadest sense, I understand choreography as the art of organizing people in space and teaching to empower students to become active in communities. I imagined I could apply some of my arts-based practice to the academic setting.

On completing the NZWiL program, I felt that my experiences of leadership from working in dance did offer some basis for this potential shift. However, I first needed to understand and reflect critically much more on what I actually did in dance choreography and teaching to know how this might inform my leadership practice. Thus, the focus of this discussion shifts not to leadership theories (such as transformational and authentic leadership (Hernandez et al., 2011; Lyman et al., 2012), nor remains on myself as a leader (Haslam et al., 2011), but shifts to the dancing practices in which I find joy.

LEARNING LEADERSHIP THROUGH DANCING

Seeking to understand dancing practices as inspiration for leadership, I turned to Joanne Butterworth's (2004) "Alternative processes continuum" for theorizing the role of a choreographer. In her original model, Joanne developed useful ways of understanding the roles and methods of choreographers working with dancers in professional and in community dance contexts that moved well beyond any narrow understanding of choreographer as autocratic leader (Butterworth, 2009).

She identified a series of processes from choreographer as expert at one end of the continuum, to choreographer as author, pilot, facilitator, and choreographer as collaborator at the other end of the continuum. In my adaptation of her model, I have replaced the word "choreographer" with "leader" to help me think through leading

78 — Chapter 12

as a dancer. In this model, associated with the range of different leader roles, are identified skills and methods.

For example, the leader as expert would involve the leader controlling the concept, style, content, structure, interpretation, and generation of all material, with a passive (sometimes impersonal) form of social interaction requiring participants to conform, receive, and process instructions. Such a description typifies the traditional approach in dance, particularly of professional male choreographers, teachers, and company directors, and embodies an authoritarian leadership style.

At the other end of the continuum, the leader as collaborator shares with others, involving research, negotiation, decision making about content and intention, and requiring social interaction across the group, leading to shared authorship and an experiential approach with participants who contribute fully to concept, style, content, form, process, and discovery. I have adapted Butterworth's (2009) continuum (see table 12.1) for considering leadership.

It is perhaps no surprise that I value leadership practices to the right of this continuum, in the categories of piloting, facilitating, and collaborating. Processes I value are initiating, negotiating, contributing, and sharing within interactive social processes and attempting to

engage with a nurturing, mentoring, often shared authorship approach. Active experience and participation in process is important, and for me, characterizes effective leadership.

Interestingly, the way I was thinking about choreography relating to leadership also aligned well with my critical feminist pedagogy in dance education. It seemed to me, and this was quite a joyous and liberating realization, that choreographing, teaching dance, and leadership could all be connected. Emboldened by this perspective, I have been reexamining my dance pedagogy, which I had identified as critical and feminist in general (Barbour, 2016). I am interested in articulating embodied ethical principles that sit alongside my general dance pedagogy.

I have come to articulate these ethical principles as follows: Meet where we are; Affirm and respect personal, family, and cultural identities; Celebrate the wealth of (embodied) knowledge we bring; Invite us all to extend our existing (embodied) knowledge; Move and learn together; Foster relationships and dialogue; and, Do no harm (Barbour, 2017). Now I seek to practice these principles as a feminist authentic leader, as well as a critical feminist pedagogue and choreographer. Thus, understanding the practices of leading from within my

Table 12.1. Alternative Processes Continuum

Process One	Process Two	Process Three	Process Four	Process Five
Leader role				
Leader as expert	Leader as author	Leader as pilot	Leader as facilitator	Leader as collaborator
Leader skills				
Control of concept, style, content, structure, Interpretation. Generation of all material.	Control of concept, style, content, structure, interpretation in relation to capabilities of others.	Initiate concept, able to direct, set, develop tasks, shape the material that ensues. Facilitate process from content generation to macro-structure.	Provide leadership, negotiate process, intention, concept. Contribute methods, style, develop/share/adapt content, structure.	Share with others research, negotiation, decision-making about concept, intention.
Social interaction				
Passive but receptive, can be impersonal.	Separate activities but receptive, with personal qualities stressed.	Active participation, from all, interpersonal relationships.	Generally interactive.	Interactive across group.
Leadership methods				
Authoritarian.	Directorial.	Leading, guiding.	Nurturing, mentoring.	Shared authorship.
Participant approaches				
Conform, receive, process instruction.	Receive, process instruction, utilize own experience.	Respond to tasks, contribute to discovery, replicate material from others.	Respond to tasks, problem-solve, contribute to discovery, actively participate.	Experiential. Contribute fully to concept, style, content, form, process discovery.

Adapted from Jo Butterworth's Didactic-Democratic spectrum model for choreographic process (Butterworth, 2009, pp.187–188).

arts context as a dancer has been most helpful for me in learning leadership.

LEADERSHIP AS DANCING INTO THE UNKNOWN

In conclusion, I do not have many answers and I do not wish to propose a new theory of leadership. I do have lots of questions. However, I am thinking about leadership and learning by doing. I do believe that passion matters and that values matter, and I appreciate the insights of leadership theory and models. But most of all, it is the joy I find in my relationships with others that matters most. While expressed a little differently in dance, there is joy for me in initiating, negotiating, contributing, and sharing within interactive social processes and attempting to engage with a nurturing, shared approach.

Active experience and participation in process are crucial and relate easily to my own core values and ethics. Again, while I might express my embodied ethical principles a little differently within leading and teaching roles, there is much that is in common. And finally, I have come to embrace the different ways I can lead, with joy, dancing into the unknown.

REFERENCES

Airini, Collings, S., Conner, L., McPherson, K., Midson, B., & Wilson, C. (2010). Learning to be leaders in higher education: What helps or hinders women's advancement as leaders in universities. *Educational Management Administration and Leadership, 39*, 44–62.

Barbour, K. N. (2011). *Dancing across the page. Narrative and embodied ways of knowing.* Bristol, England: Intellect Books.

Barbour, K. N. (2016). Embodied values and ethical principles in somatic dance classes: Considering implicit motor learning. *Journal of Dance and Somatic Practices, 8*(2), 189–204.

Barbour, K. N. (2017). Dance on campus: Partnerships and participation in tertiary dance education and community dance practice. In B. Cowie & R. McNae (Eds.), *Realizing innovative partnerships in educational research* (pp. 197–209). Rotterdam, Boston, Taipei: Sense Publishers.

Barr, S. (2013). Learning to learn: A hidden dimension within community dance practice. *Journal of Dance Education, 13*(4), 115–121. http://dx.doi.org/10.1080/15290824.2012.754546

Barsh, J., Cranston, S., & Craske, R. A. (2008). Centered leadership: How talented women thrive. *The McKinsey Quarterly, 4*, 35–48.

Branson, C. M., & Gross, S. J. (2014). *Handbook of ethical educational leadership.* New York, NY: Routledge.

Butterworth, J. (2004). Teaching choreography in higher education: A process continuum model. *Research in Dance Education, 5*(1), 45–67.

Coleman, M. (2011). *Women at the top. Challenges, choices and change.* London, England: Palgrave Macmillan.

Fitzgerald, T., & Wilkinson, J. (2010). *Travelling towards a mirage? Gender, leadership and higher education.* Mt. Gravatt, Australia: Post Pressed.

Franken, M., Penney, D., & Branson, C. (2015). Middle leaders' learning in a university context. *Journal of Higher Educational Policy and Management.* http://dx.doi.org/10.1080/1360080X.2015.1019120

Haslam, S. A., Reicher, S. D., & Platow, M. J. (2011). *The new psychology of leadership: Identity, influence and power.* Hove, England: Psychology Press.

Hernandez, M., Eberly, M. B., Avolio, B. J., & Johnson, M. D. (2011). The loci and mechanisms of leadership: Exploring a more comprehensive view of leadership theory. *The Leadership Quarterly 22*, 1165–1185.

Hunter, V., & Gladstone, P. (2009). Dance and social inclusion: Facilitating the process, developing graduate employability. *International Journal of Arts in Society, 4*(2), 150–159.

Lyman, L., Strachan, J., & Lazaridou, A. (2012). *Shaping social justice leadership: Insights of women educators worldwide.* Lanham, MD: Rowman & Littlefield Education.

McNae, R. (2010). Young women and the co-construction of leadership. *Journal of Educational Administration, 48*(6), 677–688.

New Zealand Women in Leadership (NZWiL). (2013). *NZ Women in leadership programme objectives.* http://www.waikato.ac.nz/pod/wil/vccwil.shtml

Scarnati, J. T. (2002). Leaders as role models: 12 rules. *Career Development International, 7*(3), 181–189.

Shapiro, S. B. (1998). *Dance, power and difference: Critical and feminist perspectives on dance education.* Champaign, IL: Human Kinetics.

Sinclair, A. (2007). *Leadership for the disillusioned.* Crows Nest, Australia: Allen & Unwin.

Chapter 13

Know Thyself

The Influence of Career Orientations on Women Education Leaders' Career Decisions

Linda L. McGinley and Diane E. Reed

The research reported here investigated the career orientations of 171 assistant superintendents for instruction in New York State, 118 (69 percent) of whom were women. Career orientations represent an individual's self-perceived talents, needs, and values, and address the question of what drives and gives direction to a career over the long term and shifts the responsibility for career planning from the organization to the individual (Schein, 1996). The internal career is regarded as a stable, long-term definition of work identity focusing on a person's self-identity.

This study probed for the association between career plan and gender and the relationship between career orientation and career plan. Specifically, do women whose career plans are to remain in assistant superintendent roles or to ascend to superintendent roles differ in their career orientation? The findings suggest that women assistant superintendents' career decisions may be driven by self-perceived values, talents, and needs. The career orientation may provide a lens for gaining insight into what brings joy and career fulfillment to the women.

District leaders are pivotal in creating a culture that supports student learning and facilitates sustainable improvement in student achievement (Fullan, 2005). The No Child Left Behind Act (NCLB) has accelerated and intensified the need for districts to demonstrate effects of standards-based reform as measured by high-stakes assessment results (Kim & Sunderman, 2005). Building the capacity for district-wide improvements in instruction and student achievement requires significant involvement and service by district office leaders. District-level leaders must exercise essential leadership throughout the system to bring about these sustained improvements (Honig, Copland, Rainey, Lorton, & Newton, 2010).

The assistant superintendent for instruction is the district-level leader responsible for school improvement and for building others' capacity in the system to strengthen and sustain improved performance achievement. Little

is known about the career orientations of district-level leaders (Leach, 2009), and why a substantial number of these leaders choose to remain in this role, opting not to ascend to the role of superintendent (Cetorelli, 1997). In the national study of women assistant/associate/deputy superintendents, 60 percent of 472 central office administrators, nearly half of whom were hired as assistant/associate superintendents for curriculum and instruction, indicated that they did not aspire to the superintendent role (Brunner & Grogan, 2007).

The primary reasons women cite for not aspiring center around work conditions, benefits, or personal satisfaction. The top three reasons included happiness in the current position and lack of interest in changing jobs, and being dissuaded by the politics of the superintendent role and stress (Brunner & Grogan, 2007). Considering that the assistant superintendent position is a direct career pathway to the superintendent role, yet a majority decide not to seek the position, it is important to understand the assistant superintendent for instruction's (ASI) career orientations.

Career anchors (table 13.1) represent an individual's internal (as opposed to external) career and describe what motivates and shapes direction over time (Schein, 1996; Van Vuuren & Fourie, 2000). While career anchors of teachers have been studied, there have been no studies of district-level administrators' career orientations. Studying the career anchors of women assistant superintendents for instruction would explain the underlying motives, needs, and values that assistant superintendents for instruction hold and would inform the research base about these district-level leaders' career choices.

This investigation was guided by the following questions:

1. What are the career orientations of New York State ASI, excluding those in New York City?
2. What is the relationship between career orientation and gender?

Table 13.1. Definitions of the Nine Career Anchors

Anchor	Definition
General Managerial Competence	Excited by analyzing and solving organizational problems that are overarching, uncertain, and complex. Likes mobilizing others toward common goals. Energized by crisis situations.
Technical Functional Competence	Excited by developing depth of content expertise. Prefers advancement only in area of technical expertise.
Entrepreneurial Creativity	Motivated by the ability to create and initiate their own projects or new ventures.
Geographic Security	Needs opportunities to remain in stable or fixed locations.
Job Security	Needs long-term stability and good benefits and is willing to embrace organizational values and norms.
Lifestyle	Needs balance of career and personal life. Prefers organizations that have flexible family programs and values.
Autonomy	Needs situations free of organizational constraints. Desires freedom to set own schedule and work pace.
Service to a Cause	Motivated by sense of service for impacting a greater good. Desires to align work activities with personal value of improving society.
Challenge	Motivated by overcoming major obstacles and competing to win. Defines career in competitive terms, solving problems that are almost unsolvable.

Note: Adapted from *Career anchors: Discovering your real values,* by E. H. Schein, 1990, San Diego, CA: Pfeiffer & Co.

3. What is the relationship between career orientations and career plan?
4. What is the difference between career orientations of women who intend to remain in the ASI role and women who intend to ascend to the superintendent role?

DATA GATHERING AND SAMPLE

The study involved surveying 364 New York State (NYS) assistant superintendents for instruction or district-level administrators responsible for K–12 instruction. The participants were drawn from NYS public school districts, excluding New York City. For purposes of this study, those currently practicing and holding titles of ASI or curriculum, or titles demonstrating district-level oversight of K–12 curriculum and instruction leadership, were included in the sample.

The first step in the data collection included emailing an invitation to participate in the survey. The invitation letter contained a link to the online survey. The electronic invitation letter outlined the requirements of the study as well as one's right to withdraw at any time. The letter of consent, in electronic format, assured participants of voluntary participation and anonymity to the researcher. To increase the response rate, a follow-up email was sent to each assistant superintendent for instruction one week after the initial invitation and then one week later for continued nonresponses. The survey was open during a 48-day period. Of the 364 potential respondents, 171 completed responses were received, a final response rate of 46 percent. Of the respondents, 118 were women ASIs.

RESEARCH INSTRUMENTS

For this study, career orientations were measured using a 25-item, short-form Career Orientations Inventory (COI) developed by Igbaria and Baroudi (1993). The short-form COI survey tool was selected because of its streamlined process that does not require each respondent to apply an additional weighting to their responses. This survey tool is based upon nine career orientations, which include those developed by Schein (1978). In this survey, the security orientation is split into two separate anchors: geographic and job security. All 25 items contained on the short form are taken from the original COI survey (Schein, 1985) and are considered to be of equal value. A five-point Likert scale is used to measure the nine career orientations.

Items 9 to 23 range from 1 (of no importance) to 5 (centrally important). Items 24 to 33 require respondents to indicate the extent that each of the items relates to their career preferences, using a five-point Likert scale ranging from 1 (not at all true) to 5 (completely true). The 25 items are categorized in the following manner: three statements correspond to technical/functional, general managerial, entrepreneurial/creativity orientations; two statements each correspond to job security and geographic security; and three statements correspond to autonomy, lifestyle, challenge, and service orientations. The order of the items within each orientation is determined on a random basis. Total scores obtained for each of the nine subscales of career anchors are summed and averaged to yield a mean score for each career anchor or orientation. The orientation that yields mean scores above 3.0 are regarded as dominant career orientations.

DATA ANALYSIS

To determine the relationship between the orientation scales, a bivariate Pearson's Product Moment Correlation test was conducted. Pearson's correlation coefficient (r) is a measure of the strength of the association between the two variables (Huck, 2008). This test indicates the strength of the relationship between variables in the sample. Correlation coefficients can range from –1.00 to +1.00, and a value of 0.00 represents a lack of correlation. The size of the value of the coefficient indicates the strength of the relationship between variables. Cohen (1988) suggests a value from 0.10 to 0.29 indicates a small relationship, a value from 0.30 to 0.49 indicates a moderate relationship, and a value of 0.50 to 1.0 indicates a large relationship.

Research questions two and three were answered using a one-way multivariate analysis of variance (MANOVA) test. The relationship between career orientation scores (dependent variables) and gender, and career plan (independent variables), were identified by calculating a MANOVA. The MANOVA is used to test the significance of a linear relationship of independent variables on explaining more than one related dependent variable. In this study, when conducting the analysis, there is only one independent variable and nine dependent variables. This test is necessary when we use more than one dependent variable which is correlated, provided some basic assumptions are met. If the MANOVA is significant, it is customary to interpret the univariate analysis of variance (ANOVA) tests to know which of the dependent variables (career orientations) are determined by the independent variables (participants' characteristics).

Research question four compared the career orientations of female ASIs who remained in their position (remainers) and those who intended to ascend to the superintendency (ascenders). The standardized mean difference in career orientations was calculated between female ASIs who intend to ascend or remain in their role.

RESEARCH FINDINGS

Demographics

The most prevalent number of years worked for participants in this study was between 21 years and beyond. Nearly three-quarters of respondents (71.2 percent) worked in public education for 21 years and beyond, and nearly all (89 percent) worked for 16 years and beyond. These findings indicated that women assistant superintendents for instruction in this study were an experienced group of educators (table 13.2).

Table 13.2.   Frequencies for Women ASI's Total Number of Years Worked in K–12 Public Education

Range of years (n = 118)	Totals
21 years and beyond	84 (71.2%)
16 to 20 years	22 (18.6%)
11 to 15 years	9 (7.6%)
6 to 10 years	2 (1.7%)
1 to 5 years	1 (0.8%)

The data indicate that the majority of respondents have worked in their role for 10 years or less. Nearly half of the respondents (48 percent) worked for only 1 to 5 years, and just over one-quarter of the respondents (29 percent) worked for 6 to 10 years in the role. For this group of women assistant superintendents or district-level leaders for instruction, 89 percent have served as educators for 16 or more years, while 77 percent of respondents have served in the role of ASI for only 10 years or less. While possessing many years' experience in education, as a group, more than three-quarters of women ASIs are relatively new to their role as the district's leader for instruction.

Slightly more than one-quarter have earned their doctoral degree (27 percent) and the majority (60 percent) have earned their Certificate of Advanced Study, a degree beyond the master's level. The data indicate that the female ASI population in this study is a highly educated group of administrators. The ASI population in this sample is nearly split in their desire to remain in the role or to ascend to the superintendent role. Only 35 percent of women ASIs plan to ascend to the superintendent role. The majority of women ASIs plan to remain in their role (50 percent) or plan other opportunities (14 percent).

The majority of women participants (83 percent) were 45 years of age or older, and one-third (37 percent) of the participants were of retirement age in NYS. Slightly less than one-quarter (21 percent) were under the age of 44. Of the 169 respondents to survey question eight, the majority were white/Caucasian (76 percent) and 1 percent were African American. None of the female ASIs were Hispanic and only 1 percent were "other." The other category was not defined in the survey but may include multiracial respondents.

Career Orientations of ASIs

The first research question was, what are the career orientations of New York State assistant superintendents for instruction, excluding New York City? Career Orientations Inventory (COI) mean scale scores were calculated for each of the nine career orientation scales (technical functional, general managerial, autonomy, geographic security, job security, entrepreneurial creativity, service, challenge, and lifestyle). The results indicate that, for all ASIs and for women ASIs, four of nine career orientation means (SV, SEJ, GM, and SEG) were above 3.0. Orientation scores above an average rating of 3.0 were selected as dominant because they represented the orientations about which participants felt were most important or true.

Career Orientation, Gender, and Career Plan

What is the relationship between gender and career orientations? This research question was addressed in the results of a one-way MANOVA examining how males and females differ on career orientations. No statistically significant differences were found between males and females on career orientation. As a result, further univariate analysis was not tested.

The research question, what is the relationship between career orientation and career plan?, was explored using a multivariate analysis of variance test. A significant multivariate effect was found. Follow-up univariate ANOVAs were conducted to determine if there was a statistically significant difference in mean scores between each career orientation and the mean scores for the career plan.

Technical functional (TF) and job security (SEJ) scores were higher for those who intended to remain in the ASI role compared to those who intended to ascend from their role. In contrast, general managerial (GM) scores were higher among ascenders than remainers. Effect size statistics show that the difference in career orientations between these two groups of ASIs were not trivial.

Association Between Career Plan and Gender

A post-hoc test was conducted to determine if there was an association between career plan (intent to remain or ascend) and gender. A Pearson chi-squared test was used to determine whether differences between observed and expected frequencies of variables were statistically significant. For this population males and females differ in career plans greater than one would expect. The data indicate that females desire to remain in their roles more than expected (see table 13.3). Likewise, males desire to ascend more than expected.

To compare the career orientations of female ASI remainers and ascenders, the standardized mean difference in career orientations was calculated between female ASIs who intend to ascend or remain in their role. Effect size statistics show that the standardized mean difference in career orientations between female ASIs who decide to ascend or remain in their role is not trivial.

DISCUSSION OF FINDINGS

Overall, the group of women ASIs in in this study were an experienced group of educators, a majority having worked public education for 16 years and beyond, yet nearly half were fairly inexperienced in the ASI role having served in the role for only one to five years. A majority of women ASIs were 45 years of age or older, and one-third were of retirement age. Most participants in this study were of white/Caucasian ethnicity (see table 13.4) and, as a group, they were highly educated with a third having attained a doctoral degree. Half of the women ASIs desired to remain in their role and one-third desired to ascend to the superintendent role.

The results of this study indicated that ASIs in NYS possessed all nine career orientations, four of which were dominant for all ASIs and for women ASIs: service to a cause, general managerial competence, job, and geographic security. In examining the relationship between certain demographic and professional profile characteristics and career orientations, results indicated that gender had no significant effect.

A significant association was found between gender and career plan. Though the effect size is small, a greater percentage of females in this study intended to remain in the role of ASI while a greater percentage of males intended to ascend to the role of superintendent. A comparison of career orientations of women ASIs who intend to ascend and those who intend to remain in the role showed significant differences. Women remainers had higher technical functional and job security career orientations and these effect size statistics were not small. Female ascenders scored higher on the general managerial career orientations scale and the effect was medium.

The findings of this study provide a lens for understanding what drives and gives direction to the women ASIs' careers over the long term, including what influences their decisions to either remain in the role or ascend to the superintendent role. We now explore the implications of the findings of this research study in comparison

Table 13.3. Career Plan Frequencies for Female ASI's

Career plan (n = 118)	Totals
Remain in position of ASI	59 (50%)
Ascend to superintendent role	41 (35%)
Other	17 (14%)

Table 13.4. Women ASI's Race/Ethnicity Frequencies

Race/ethnicity (n= 118)	Totals
White/Caucasian	114 (97.0%)
African American	1 (0.9%)
Hispanic	0 (0%)
Other	1 (0.6%)

to previous theory and research on career orientations of professionals, including those in educational settings. We will conclude with recommendations for professional practice and policy.

Assistant Superintendent for Instruction Dominant Career Orientations

NYS women ASIs in this study held all nine career orientations and four of the orientations were dominant for this population. Dominant orientations ranged between mean scores of 3.3 and 4.5. The service to a cause, general managerial competence, job, and geographic security mean scores were 4.5, 3.6, 3.5, and 3.3, respectively (see table 13.5). Feldman and Bolino (1996) categorized Schein's (1978) orientations into three distinct groupings: talent based, need based, and value based. Talent-based orientations center on an individual's work talents and the type of work one is involved in on a day-to-day basis. General managerial competence, technical functional competence, and entrepreneurial creativity orientations were identified as talent based. Need-based orientations center on an individual's motives and needs and involve how one desires to structure a career to fulfill basic personal desires in their lives. Geographic security, job security, lifestyle, and autonomy orientations were described as need based. Finally, value-based orientations center on an individual's attitudes and motivations involving how one identifies with the purpose of their career. Service to a cause and challenge orientations were identified as value based.

The dominant profile identified in this study suggests that women ASIs, as a group, hold talents in the area of general managerial competence, values consisting of service and dedication to a cause, and they exhibit needs for both job and geographic security. This study revealed the most dominant orientation held by women ASIs was service to a cause. Schein (1990) described

service-oriented individuals as holding self-directed interests to contribute to the lives of others, seeking out and embracing opportunities for influence even if it involves a change of employment. Our research findings suggest ASIs rely on their service-to-a-cause orientation to create a culture of commitment throughout the district, so they may employ system-wide strategies to improve teaching and learning for all students. The orientation of service to a cause enables ASIs to move beyond mandate compliance and meaningfully frame the reform as a call to duty, drawing upon and appealing to teachers' sense of service and commitment to students.

General Managerial Competence

The general managerial competence was the second highest dominant orientation, yielding a mean of 3.6 on the COI. Schein (1990) described general managerial, competence-oriented individuals as desiring complex, multifaceted, interconnected work with high levels of responsibility and authority. Described as a talent-based orientation, general managerial employees are willing to solve complex, system-wide issues and possess inter- and intrapersonal skills that enable them to effectively do so.

The results of this study suggest differences between ASIs and principals in their self-perception of talents that give direction and anchor them to their respective administrative roles. This may be explained by the broader context within which ASIs must currently lead. Assistant superintendents for instruction are primarily responsible for implementing NCLB's (2001) policy goals and responding to the accountability provisions. The policy context demands district leaders who are willing to confront the challenges and mediate the resistance of constituents in order to achieve short- and long-term performance improvements (Hess, 1999). Schein's (1990) talent-based general managerial competence orientation is consistent with the skills an ASI must exercise in the current complex accountability context.

Career Plans and Career Orientations

Findings from this study appear to suggest that career orientation is a significant factor in differentiating NYS ASIs' decisions to remain in the role for the duration of their career or to ascend to the superintendent role. In answer to research question three exploring the relationship of career orientation to ASIs' career plans, ASIs intending to remain in their role were significant for holding the technical functional career orientation compared to those who held the general managerial orientation and intended to ascend to the superintendent role. The effect size statistics showed that the difference between orientations of

Table 13.5. Means and Standard Deviations of Career Orientation Scale Scores for Female ASIs

COI Scale	Items per Scale	N	Mean (SD)
SV	3	116	4.5 (0.55)
GM	3	117	3.6 (0.80)
SEJ	2	117	3.5 (0.97)
SEG	2	116	3.3 (1.26)
CH	3	117	2.9 (0.84)
LS	3	117	2.7 (0.80)
TF	3	117	2.5 (1.15)
AU	3	117	2.5 (0.87)
EC	3	118	2.1 (0.88)

Note: SV = Service to a Cause, GM = General Managerial, SEJ = Job Security, SEG = Geographic Security, CH = Challenge, LS = Lifestyle, TF = Technical Functional, AU = Autonomy, EC = Entrepreneurial Creativity.

Table 13.6. Univariate Analysis of Variance for Relationship Between ASI's Career Plan and Career Orientation

| Anchor | p | F | Career Plan | | |
			Remain	Ascend	Cohen's d
TF	0.002**	(1,148) = 9.50	2.80 (1.12)	2.27 (1.00)	.47
GM	0.000**	(1,148) = 12.80	3.35 (0.85)	3.80 (0.64)	.59
SEJ	0.013*	(1,148) = 6.32	3.77 (0.80)	3.41 (0.98)	.41

Note: F ratios are Wilks's approximation of *F*s.
*p< .05, **p<.01.

these two groups of ASIs was not trivial; medium effect sizes were calculated for both groups (see table 13.6).

Leach (2009) studied assistant superintendents in NYS and found that only one-third desired to ascend to the superintendent role. The New York State Council for School Superintendents' (NYSCOSS) most recent 2009 snapshot survey researching the superintendent role in NYS integrated findings and the authors of the report, Terranova, Rogers, Fale, and Ike (2010) posed the following research questions when they further extrapolated the core ideas:

> Given the stress and increasing challenges inherent in the superintendency, the steadily increasing trend in satisfaction with the superintendency as a culminating career choice is counterintuitive. Does this indicate that the people who chose to enter the superintendency are "special" personalities? Individuals who invite and enjoy the stress and challenge of the position, who gain satisfaction and gratification from solving difficult problems? People who work with a variety of constituents and are motivated by seeing their vision come into reality no matter the personal stress and frustration that may incur? (Terranova et al., 2010, p. 30)

This study's findings may serve to inform the scholarly literature to explain reasons for the shrinking applicant pool for superintendents, despite the ASI role serving as a direct pipeline to the superintendent role. Schein (1990) described general managerial competence-oriented individuals as those who "will not give up an opportunity to climb to a high level in the organization to enable themselves to integrate the efforts of others and be responsible for the output of the organizations" (p. 530). Desiring the power and achievement of top roles and positions, general manager–oriented individuals were described as perceiving that their "competencies lie in their ability to analyze problems and remain emotionally stable and interpersonally competent" (DeLong, 1982, p. 52). In contrast, technical functional competent orientations "are more concerned with the intrinsic content of their work and will not give up the ability to apply their skills in an

area of expertise and to continue to develop those skills to a higher level" (Tan & Quek, 2001, p. 531).

Gender and Career Plan

A post hoc test was conducted to determine the effect of gender on ASIs' career plans. Findings suggest that, for this population, males and females differ in career plan greater than one would expect. More than expected, females desire to remain in their role, and more than expected, males desire to ascend, and the association was significant. A greater percentage of females intend to remain in the role of ASI, and a greater percentage of males intend to ascend to the role of superintendent, and this association is significant as well. These results corroborate previous findings related to the 2009 NYS Superintendent Snapshot Survey conducted by the New York State Council on School Superintendents where 63 percent of superintendents in NYS are male. Women as a proportion are growing in their entry to the superintendent role as evidenced by an increase of 7 percent to 37 percent between 2000 and 2009 (Terranova et al., 2010).

Women ASI Remainers' and Ascenders' Career Plan and Career Orientation

Findings from this study appear to suggest that career orientation is a significant factor in differentiating women ASIs' decisions to remain in the role for the duration of their career or to ascend to the superintendent role. Women ASIs intending to remain in their role were significant for holding the technical functional career orientation and the job security orientation compared to those women ASIs who held the general managerial orientation and intended to ascend to the superintendent role. The effect size statistics showed that the difference between orientations for ascenders and remainers was not trivial; a large effect size was shown for remainers holding the technical functional orientation and medium effect sizes were shown for remainers and job security orientations and ascenders and general managerial orientations.

In a nationwide study commissioned by the American Association of School Administrators, women central office administrators were studied to understand stated reasons for aspiring and not aspiring to the superintendent role (Brunner & Grogan, 2007). The primary reasons women gave for not aspiring to the superintendency were career-focused and centered on work conditions, benefits, and personal satisfaction. The top reason for not aspiring was happiness in their current position and possessing no interest in changing jobs (58 percent).

The technical functional-oriented female ASI may be satisfying her need for ongoing development of technical expertise in matters of curriculum, instruction, assessment, and student learning by remaining in the ASI role. She may be excited by the opportunity to further develop deeper knowledge and application of practices related to instruction and learning, and may only prefer advancement if it affords her the opportunity to continue to develop that expertise in depth.

General managerial–oriented women ASIs may aspire to the superintendent role in order to bring their background in curriculum and instruction to bear as they promote student achievement in a context of high accountability and stakeholder resistance. The superintendent role requires solving organizational issues that are overarching, uncertain, and complex. General managerial–oriented female ASIs are excited, rather than exhausted by crisis situations and solving organizational issues.

While studies describe three dominant roles of the superintendency as instructional, managerial, and political, Nestor-Baker and Hoy (2001) assert that superintendents spend most of their time and energy in the managerial and political dimensions, skills directly associated with the general managerial competence career orientation. As a result, superintendents' interpersonal and emotional competence skills are exercised regularly to minimize conflict and successfully negotiate with multiple constituencies to seek approval for increased fiscal resources and programs.

General managerial–oriented ASIs use their well-developed interpersonal skills to build coalitions between and among stakeholders, leading to sustained change. Moreover, the study revealed that women superintendents experienced satisfaction and fulfillment in leading change and reform activities and the challenges of reform were perceived as providing opportunities for action and growth of complexity. This study reveals that general managerial–oriented women ASIs are motivated by the opportunity to mobilize others toward common goals, especially in a context of uncertainty and complexity, and are excited, rather than exhausted, by the opportunity to do so.

CONCLUSION

This was the first research study on the career orientations of ASIs. The findings suggest that women assistant superintendents for instruction's career decisions may be driven by self-perceived values, talents, and needs. The career orientation provides a lens for gaining insight into what brings joy and career fulfillment to the ASI. Our results reveal that career orientations may be a differentiating factor for women ASI's career decision to remain in the ASI role or to ascend to the superintendent role.

In this study, women ASIs who intend to remain in the ASI role possess technical functional career orientations or job security orientations that enable them to meet their individual talents and needs for career fulfillment. In contrast, women ASIs possessing a general managerial orientation may aspire to the superintendent role in order to fulfill a talent for analyzing and solving organizational problems that are overarching, uncertain, and complex. The general managerial–oriented ASI may view the superintendent role as an opportunity to mobilize others toward common goals. A future research study involving aspiring women educational leaders would be warranted in order to support their knowledge of their talents, beliefs, and values so they can be better positioned to make stronger career decisions. Doing so would enable them to thrive, experience satisfaction in their career, and possess joy in their leadership.

REFERENCES

Brunner, C. C., & Grogan, M. (2007). *Women leading school systems: Uncommon road to fulfillment*. Lanham, MD: Rowman & Littlefield Education.

Cetorelli, N. D. (1997). *Assistant, deputy, and associate superintendents in Connecticut and their pursuit of the superintendency* (Unpublished doctoral dissertation, University of Hartford, CT). Retrieved February 1, 2010, from Dissertations & Theses: Full Text database

Cohen, J. (1988). *Statistical power analysis for the behavioral sciences* (2nd ed.). New York, NY: Academic Press.

DeLong, T. (1982). Re-examining the career anchor model. *Personnel*. May–June, 50–61.

Feldman, D. C., & Bolino, M. C. (1996). Careers within careers: Reconceptualizing the nature of careers and their consequences. *Human Resources Management Review, 6*(2), 89–120.

Fullan, M. (2005). Resiliency and sustainability: Eight elements for superintendents who want to make a difference and have the resolve to do so. *School Administrator, 62*(2), 16–18.

Hess, G. K. (1999). Expectations, opportunities, capacity and will: The four essential components of Chicago reform. *Educational Policy, 13*(4), 495–517.

Honig, M. I., Copland, M. A., Rainey, L., Lorton, J. A., & Newton, M. (2010). *Central office transformation for districtwide teaching and learning improvement*. Seattle, WA: Center for the Study of Teaching and Policy.

Huck, S. W. (2008). *Reading statistics and research* (5th ed.). New York, NY: Pearson.

Igbaria, M., & Baroudi, J. J. (1993). A short-form measure of career orientations: A psychometric evaluation. *Journal of Management Information Systems, 5*(4), 609–915.

Kim, J. S., & Sunderman, G. L. (2005). Measuring academic proficiency under the No Child Left Behind act: Implications for educational equity. *Educational Researcher, 34*(8), 3–13.

Leach, D. F. (2009). *The assistant school superintendent in New York State: Sense of job satisfaction, job efficacy, and career aspirations.* (Unpublished doctoral dissertation, Fordham University, NY). Retrieved May 24, 2018, from PDQT Open (Publication No. 3361469), https://pdgdtopen.proquest.com/pubnum/336149.html.

Nestor-Baker, N., & Hoy, W. K. (2001). Tacit knowledge of school superintendents: Its nature, meaning and content. *Education Administration Quarterly, 37*(1), 86–129.

No Child Left Behind Act (NCLB). (2001). P L 107-110, 20 U. S. C. § 6301.

Schein, E. H. (1978). *Career dynamics: Matching individual and organization needs.* Reading, MA: Addison-Wesley.

Schein, E. H. (1985): *Organizational Culture and Leadership.* San Francisco, CA: Jossey-Bass.

Schein, E. H. (1990). *Career anchors.* San Diego, CA: Pfeiffer.

Schein, E. H. (1996). Career anchors revisited: Implications for career development in the 21st century. *Academy of Management Executive, 10*(9), 80–88.

Tan, H. H., & Quek, B. C. (2001). An exploratory study on the career anchors of educators in Singapore. *Journal of Psychology, 135*(5), 527–545.

Terranova, M., Rogers, T., Fale, E., & Ike, R. (2010). *Snapshot 2009. New York State Council of School Superintendents.* Albany, NY: NYSCOSS, 1–58.

Van Vuuren, L., & Fourie, C. (2000). Career anchors and career resilience: Supplementary constructs? *SA Journal of Industrial Psychology, 26*(3), 15–20.

Chapter 14

Women Leading for Social Justice in Higher Education

Surfacing Hope in Challenging Times

Rachel McNae

At a time in higher education where many universities face significant challenges and uncertain futures, it is an immense challenge to reposition leadership so that it is future-focused in its conception and practice. Aligning academic leadership with global shifts toward performativity, corporatization, and managerialism have changed the nature of academic work (Blackmore & Sachs, 2007). However, in these shifts some aspects are particularly relevant to women leaders.

The intensified division between academic career pathways and management positions has led to a paucity of women at senior leadership roles in higher education. Ongoing discussions and a growing body of literature continues to examine these women's experiences as they navigate these changing circumstances (Airini, Collings, Conner, McPherson, Midson, & Wilson, 2011; Ramsay, McGregor, & McCarthy, 2014). What is noticeable in this growing body of scholarship, however, is that the reporting on these experiences frequently problematizes women's leadership, outlining limitations, challenges, and struggles women continue to face as they strive for parity in their leadership opportunities, recognition, and remuneration.

This is indeed essential and important scholarship. However, with little attention paid to the enjoyment that women experience in their leadership, or the agency they create from their work, there may be potential avenues for activism which have been overlooked. Scholarly attention on women's leadership experiences continues to direct attention to the underrepresentation of women in formal leadership roles yet rarely considers the embodied and contextual practices women draw on and the joy they experience from the work they do.

This research explored leadership as an embodied and joy-filled activity providing insights into women's experiences of leading from a paradigm of hope in one higher education context. The purpose of the research was to examine women's experiences of leadership and investigate the different ways in which women found agency and demonstrated activism in their own leadership development and practice.

WOMEN'S LEADERSHIP IN NEW ZEALAND HIGHER EDUCATION

As the first country in the world to include women in the parliamentary voting system in 1893, work toward acknowledging and valuing the contributions and leadership of women has continued in New Zealand. Change (albeit at glacial rates) to the legal system and policies which champion the rights of women has been supported through the integration of international conventions and national policies aimed to further support progress towards gender equity in New Zealand. In 2013, the World Economic Forum's Global Gender Gap Index ranked New Zealand as seventh out of 136 countries with regard to gender equity. In the early 1980s New Zealand ratified the International Convention on the Elimination of all forms of Discrimination Against Women (CEDAW), and International Labour Organisation (ILO) Convention 100 and 111 on Equal Remuneration and Opportunity.

Under these conventions women have the right to equal pay with the promotion of equal opportunities for both women and men to engage in decent work in conditions of freedom, equity, security, and human dignity (Ministry of Women's Affairs, 2014). While considerable attention has been paid to issues of social justice and gender representation, many of these goals remain out of reach and women's lack of representation in the upper levels of leadership in education is still very much a concern (McGregor, 2012).

The context of higher education in New Zealand is no different and continues to evidence women's underrepresentation in positions of academic leadership. With regard to employment in New Zealand universities, the overall figures are worrying with only a small number of women represented in senior academic roles compared to their male counterparts. Statistics, presenting the employment of academic women in New Zealand universities, show women hold only 25 percent of the senior leadership positions (e.g., dean of school or faculty, chairperson of department).

Intensive attention has been directed toward this area and the development of interventions such as the New Zealand University Women's Leadership Programme, a nationwide initiative that has had a small, but positive impact on supporting women's academic leadership. The 2012 Census of Women's Participation in New Zealand illustrates that "overall the percentage of female senior academic staff has increased across all universities from 22.45% in 2010 to 24.38%" (McGregor, 2012, p. 142). All eight universities in the country improved their proportions of female senior academic women by an overall 8.56 percentage points since reporting began in 2003 (McGregor, 2012).

However, in their detailed account of institutional policy and policy discourses in New Zealand higher education, Fitzgerald and Wilkinson (2010) contend that gender equity could never really be achieved and is in fact, a mirage. In their work which examined the absence of women in senior leadership positions across Australia and New Zealand, it was found that although more women were enrolling in universities in these countries, the gender gap continues to exist at top levels of leadership.

Blackmore (2008) highlights that simply increasing the numerical representation of women in these roles is inadequate, and to really address this issue of underrepresentation she argues, shifts in the structural, cultural, relational, and political architectures are required to "advance thinking and research about gender and leadership in the context of emerging challenges to contemporary education" (p. 73).

Creative solutions and reimagining what might be possible in education and what might be the leadership required to meet these complex times becomes essential. Therefore, in this case, it is argued that hope becomes an important element of advancing this thinking as it encourages us to reconceptualize leadership, in a future-focused way which may open up possibilities to address issues associated with women and leadership.

WORKING FROM A PARADIGM OF HOPE

In times of uncertainty, the alignment of theories centered on hope appears to be an obvious connection, however, it is only recently that this association has gained

prominence in the educational leadership setting (Helland & Winston, 2005). A reliance on traditional leadership theorizing has continued to marginalize women's experiences of and in leadership. This research furthers the exploration of how hope and leadership might interrelate and provide opportunities to carve out new spaces for investigating women's leadership experiences from a strength-based position.

The past decade has seen a growth in areas of theory that align positive psychological traits to organizations. Bodies of literature pertaining to theories that emanate from a strength-based paradigm (e.g., positive organizational behavior developed by Luthans (2002), among many) continue to permeate organizational change literature, with little consideration of how such work might align with leadership practice overall. Snyder's (2000) Hope Theory is one such theory which might provide opportunities to locate women's leadership in higher education from an agentic perspective.

Snyder, Harris, Anderson, Holleran, Irving, and Sigmon (1991) define hope as "a positive motivational state that is based on an interactively derived sense of successful (a) agency (goal directed energy) and (b) pathways (planning to meet goals)" (p. 8). They consider that positioning hope in this way shifts hope as a concept of being a vague emotion, or wish, to a powerful cognitive construct. Snyder (2000) also refers to hope as a guiding influence in any situation, signifying hope as being more than a personal virtue, but rather "the sum of perceived capabilities to produce routes to desired goals, along with the perceived motivation to use those routes" (p. 8).

Hope is internally generated and relies upon two key attributes—an individual's willpower (agency) to accomplish a given goal and their way power (alternative pathways) to envision the pathways to attain the goal. Although two conceptually distinct constructs, both elements of hope are iterative, additive, and positively related (Youssef & Luthans, 2007). Drawing on the work of Ludema, Wilmot, and Srivastva (1997) there are key elements which underpin how hope might be conceived.

With an understanding that "the future is open and can be influenced, sustained by dialogue about high human ideals, and generative of positive action" (p. 9), it makes sense that leaders are turning toward new ways of attempting to reframe and conceptualize leadership in all its many guises. Hope is powerful in organizations because "it energizes and propels people forward even when the odds are against them. It helps people find innovative ways to work around their constraints. Hope helps people rise above their circumstances" (Blatt, 2014, para. 6).

Engaging Snyder's (2000) Hope Theory encompasses notions of goal setting, pathway creation, and generating agency to examine the key attributes of the women's leadership. This was a useful framework to examine the women's leadership experiences as they led in, through, and with hope within their university context, providing a useful framework to analyze and make sense of the findings.

METHODOLOGY

The key aim of this research was to investigate the perceptions and experiences of women academics who held formal leadership positions in higher education in New Zealand in order to develop a sense of contextual meaning behind these experiences. As such, this was qualitative research that took place in one university setting in Aotearoa New Zealand.

Three focus questions guided the overall research: What are the leadership experiences of women in their institutions and what influenced these? What influences women's access to leadership positions within higher education and their career advancement within the formal university leadership structure? In what ways did women find and demonstrate agency with regard to their leadership development and practice? This chapter focuses attention on the third question, illuminating aspects of agency within the women's leadership practice, and Hope Theory (Snyder, 2000) was engaged as the key theoretical framework to explore the women's experiences of leadership.

The research study engaged in semistructured interviews with seven women who held formal leadership positions within the university. Purposive sampling was employed using the following criteria: Participants were to identify as being a woman, to have held current leadership position for longer than two years, and been employed in an academic leadership role considered to be in the senior management tier. Invitations to be involved in the research were sent to the identified female academic university staff. Seven women employed across four different university faculties indicated interest to be involved in the research. The women came from various disciplines and held senior leadership positions in their school or in the broader university structure (e.g., head of school, head of committee, associate dean, and program leader).

Data was generated through semistructured interviews with each participant approximately 45–90 minutes in duration. These interviews were digitally recorded, transcribed by the researcher, and shared with the individual women to ensure accuracy and affirm meaning. Transcripts were then analyzed and through the process of thematic analysis (Braun & Clarke, 2006), significant

themes could be identified across and within the data generated from each woman's contribution.

The recurring themes related to women's experiences of educational leadership were compared and contrasted, exploring emerging groups of data and observing differences, absences, and similarities of content. Pseudonyms are used to protect the participants' identities. As there is a small number of women represented in leadership positions, the location of the women's specific roles, and their schools will not be reported in order to minimize the likelihood of the women being identified.

FINDINGS

Findings related to the question addressed by this chapter illustrated that the women were faced with multiple challenges, and they recognized numerous contextual and organizational barriers as deeply entrenched and difficult to change. The women identified systematic oppression based on their gender as significant barriers that impacted on their leadership. Many of the women described the pervasive and interwoven nature of this phenomenon within the hierarchal structures that worked to preserve men's position at the top of the hierarchy in the organization leaving women to congregate at the bottom.

Mia's comment highlights the frustrations the women felt overall as they sought to address these aspects, stating, "It's like a finger in a dike. Plug one hole, another pressure point builds somewhere else . . . and all these pressure points seem to be at ground level [meaning not high up the leadership hierarchy]. It keeps the women busy at the lower levels of the uni[versity]." It would appear from Mia's comments, that when women do make an attempt to address forms of gender inequality within the organization, other areas that require addressing are also revealed.

SURFACING HOPE THROUGH LEADERSHIP IN THE ACADEMY

Although the women acknowledged a range of aspects within the university context which impacted on their leadership, the findings also illustrated that in their leadership practice, they worked to surface and resist these in their leadership overall. This research highlighted the ways in which women led in, through, and with hope to counter barriers and limitations that marginalized and impacted on their leadership experiences. Core features of their accounts of leadership provided insights into moments of their work which filled them with a sense of joy and hope overall.

LEADING IN HOPE: A VISION FOR THE FUTURE

The women believed that when leading with the hope things could be different, they had the opportunity to create powerful change for women's leadership overall. While Mia acknowledged that this did focus many women leader's efforts on menial managerial tasks, she commented that it also provided opportunities to learn more about university systems more broadly and this valuable knowledge was used to embed change in other areas. Mia said that in her leadership she was often motivated by the belief that things could change. She stated, "things aren't always like this and the status quo does not need to remain . . . we can improve our lot if we know where we are heading."

Similarly, Denise stated, "I want other women to know that things can be different." Through her leadership Denise actively worked to disrupt traditions that continued to marginalize women. For example, she changed the department meeting times which happened during the late afternoon, often making it difficult for some women who were picking up their children from school and daycare. When pressed for her rationale for doing this, she stated, "we need all voices, their voices at the table . . . why make it hard?"

One other participant, Sarah, stated:

I believe in my role I have the opportunity to further agendas which invite women in. I see what's happening here and I know things can be different . . . maybe that's my point—I'm always hoping things will improve . . . get better around here simply from the decisions I make and the actions I take.

Likewise, Shona stated:

My leadership contributes to the bigger picture, it has to. Otherwise, there is never any traction to shift our culture. As a leader, I need to be aware that I might not see the changes now . . . but they might be shown long after I have moved on. I think that's the hardest thing about leadership, there's a lot of faith that actions create a better future and it's are not always immediate, it's playing the long game.

All of the women acknowledged the importance of having a view of what leadership should be like for women within their institution. They also felt it was important to ensure that the vision of the university was understood, and that women could see their clear role within the overall scope within the organization. For example, Rebecca stated:

I need to know what place my school has in the wider plans for the organization. This helps me to align my own ideas with [the Vice Chancellor's] vision for the future. I need to know I have a place in that and that I am actively creating space for me and other women in there. But we also need men in there to champion the work of women too. They need to be on board. So, I know overall—when I lead, I am thinking to the future and how each and every little thing I do contributes to the bigger picture.

Leonie also stated, "You need a plan, an idea where you are heading as a leader. This way, you align your thoughts, your people, your time to reaching those big ideas. That's what keeps you in the job when times are tough, when the chips are down—knowing it's shit now, but will be better."

LEADING THROUGH HOPE: CREATING PATHWAYS AND OPPORTUNITIES

All of the participants believed that through their leadership actions they had a key responsibility to demonstrate hope and create pathways and opportunities for themselves and others within the organization. In all examples reported, relationships formed the foundation for these pathways, especially in times of adversity as shared by Shona:

We have had some tough times. We've lost a lot of people [redundancies]. Those that have stayed are "heads down" and there was a point it felt like I was the only one here. It was lonely. I worked hard behind the scenes . . . we had no leadership from the top, so we just worked hard to reestablish the connections. We grieved together, because we have never had a chance . . . and we got mad. How dare they take this [our collegiality] away from us. We fought back. Together. We all had to make an effort to remain positive. To not let the sad stories dominate our conversations. Soon, glimmers of hope came from everywhere . . . they got bigger and brighter, and before we knew it . . . things were starting to be different around here. People were actually turning up and smiling. I was proud of that.

Similarly, Aroha commented:

It's like we have to seize the light and do something with it. How can people feel good about carrying on when there is nothing to look forward to? I know I need the light, so I think in my leadership, providing light for others is critical. They don't want to hear about my doldrums . . . they want to know that theirs can get better.

The women also identified ways in which their leadership could deliberately demonstrate optimism in times of challenge, and collective agency in a time of isolation.

For example, when asked to describe moments in her leadership practice, Denise recognized, "It's easier once you have a critical mass. Going it alone is dangerous and hard. If we are all looking for improvement, all expecting improvement . . . then we know we can change and this place can change with us."

Hope was engendered through the formation of professional relationships and the women actively sought ways to support each other within the university context. Mentoring was an essential relational practice the women leaders participated in with most of the women currently interacting with professional career mentors from within their university. This was a deliberate action outside of the formal university mentoring program that was also provided for all staff.

Aroha spoke about the benefits of mentoring and stated, "Sometimes you need to be able to see where you can go. It's not always visible and it's good to know someone has your back." Rebecca spoke about the importance of championing the work, the research, and teaching of other women, and stated, "We should be doing this all the time. We need to support, provide opportunities for other women, highlight their successes as they probably wouldn't do it themselves, especially the young ones."

Six out of the seven women interviewed had regular meetings with a mentor on campus, and in all cases the mentor was a woman. Two women, both with a young family, expressed the therapeutic and sometimes cathartic nature of the relationship with their mentor. Mia stated, "It's important being able to vent, and be safe when you do it. You don't want people to realize you are not coping, you don't want them to see you floundering when times are tough."

Five of the women also mentored other academic women. Many of the women spoke about the importance of "paying it forward," as they, themselves had been the recipient of a mentoring relationship and acknowledged the support they received from other women, mostly through informal means. For example, Aroha stated,

> I would have never done it [promotion application]. I had been brought up to be humble, and maybe even to believe I am not good enough. Having a shove forward and upwards from [Lisa], got me going . . . I'd never be here now if she hadn't pushed me forward.

One experienced woman leader shared her observations and some of the changes she had observed over the course of her tenure showing how women were increasingly seeing the value of forming professional relationships with other women, in order to generate networks of support and advance their careers into senior leadership roles. Having been in higher education for over 20 years and employed at the university for over a decade, Shona stated:

> It's a man's place . . . it's not easy for women. You could say some things are changing. Women are getting better at playing the game . . . by the game—I mean, the big boys game. Women are better informed. We are better at asking questions. We see the value [of] coming together. We are getting better at supporting other women . . . and some of us are getting better at standing up. But that's not to say that creates any great change.

Within the university context each of the women was able to identify a number of groups that supported women to advance their leadership, most belonging to or attending two or more groups. Examples included the Women Professors, the Gender Research Network, along with a range of professional learning opportunities, such as promotion workshops. All of the women identified the need to connect with others and create hope through the relationships they formed.

Women deliberately aligned themselves with other women who had similar visions for the future and were keen to, as Sarah stated, "make a difference together." The nature of their leadership highlighted the desire for collective agency whereby the women carved space for each other within the organization. Denise shared, "we make room for each other at the table, they may need their own chair, but we create the space." In this way, aspects such as developing a sense of community and collective responsibility for unity became central to their work.

Feeling a sense of belonging within the organization was important for each of the women. For many of these senior leaders, the notion of sisterhood was an important part of their academic activism assisting them to generate this sense of place within their institution and counteract the chilly climate that many experienced. Sisterhood was an active and deliberate approach many of the women employed to gather support with regard to career development, mentoring, and professional learning.

Evidence of women's activism in this area was located in examples of groups of women generating and joining formal and informal networks. Planned and deliberate opportunities for women to meet became a powerful opportunity for many women academics and through these instances they were able to develop their personal and professional networks. For example, when speaking about a network group she belonged to, Aroha stated, "I was teaching across two faculties . . . I felt ungrounded . . . men would not speak to me, and in fact went out of their way to ignore me completely. Now I have a place to belong . . . when I gather with them [the Gender Research Network], it shows me how great things can be possible . . . it also reminds me that there is still work to be done."

The networks provided many of the women with a sense of place and belonging and a way to counter what some women described as "a chilly climate" that "did not readily accept women."

LEADING WITH HOPE: AGENTIC LEADERSHIP

The women described numerous ways in which they felt their leadership reflected elements of agency and decision making. It was through these actions that their leadership became a collaborative endeavor which permeated the organizational culture, further than they originally anticipated. There was evidence that the women worked against the gate-keeping practices that they perceived operated in their institution. In demonstrating agentic leadership, some of the women admitted to becoming more politically aware of the broader university contexts so they felt more confident discussing issues at the university-wide level.

For example, Sarah stated, "I had to do a lot of reading up on things, policies and processes. Once I made sense of it, I then taught others. Just the need-to-know stuff really." Many believed that being well informed of the operating political structures would enhance women's understandings of the decision-making process associated with promotions and appointment processes. This would better position women so they could plan and work strategically to advance within their chosen fields. Aroha stated, "promotion for me was a big thing. Having [mentor] there beside me pointing things out that I did not see as important was critical. I had undervalued what I did."

Some women took on the responsibility to run workshops for women on topics such as negotiating employment conditions, having courageous conversations, and writing promotion applications. Other women, for example, Denise, deliberately and strategically nominated women for opportunities and leadership roles, rallying support for the nominees. They strategized meeting content and outcomes as Leonie stated, "I've learnt that meetings don't just go on in the boardroom. Before agenda items even reach the table, there have been at least two other encounters in places like car parks, corridors, and bathrooms. I've learnt this the hard way and now I realize I need to play this way too."

Other women also sought camaraderie through social events, planning and attending university and public community functions together in groups, and sharing contacts and networks over. For example, Leonie stated,

"When we go together, people notice. It gets to a point where people expect us and are not surprised to see us like they used to. . . . We are slowly carving out a space and we are quickly filling it with our connections and ourselves . . . like a growing force."

Sarah stated how she enjoyed the opportunity to mix with groups of women in the university that she would not normally mix with in social situations. She spoke of her surprise at the diversity of her colleagues and shared, "I used to feel quite different about my leadership. More solo and having to go it alone. I now connect with a wide range of people and I have learnt so much from them. We are all so different in our backgrounds, but face similar issues. Coming together like we do, it's the bonding, our togetherness."

All of the women acknowledged the importance of trust in developing a sense of agency. This notion of trust manifested itself as trust in self—for example, self-confidence. Leonie commented, "Leadership for me has come from within because I have recognized and trusted my own skills. It's something that has taken time, but it builds." Agency also came from trusting others and Mia spoke about the importance of being trusted by others when she stated, "It's not something you can force, you earn this and it comes as a gift from others. It is this trust which helps us create opportunities and challenge what's there already."

All of the participants also identified beneficent actions in their leadership and in the leadership of some of their colleagues, with the purpose of being focused on leading for future change. However, they were also aware that change took time and the benefits might not be immediate but they understood that through their actions, their willingness contributed to a greater picture even if they were not the immediate beneficiaries. For example, Aroha shared, "I'm not doing this for me. I'll be gone soon. I'm doing this for the other wahine,[1] the strong ones who come after me. I can till the soil and plant the seeds, they will be the ones to eat the kai."[2]

DISCUSSION AND FUTURE DIRECTIONS

This research has highlighted the ways in which women can lead in, through, and with hope to counter barriers and limitations which marginalize their leadership and impact on their leadership experience. Although not necessarily equally distributed, nor distinct in their entirety, the blending of these leadership actions provided shared metaphorical spaces whereby the women were able to surface enjoyment and hope in their leadership ideals overall. This research also identified that although women are constrained by a number of barriers within their organizations, they also work in ways to resist cultures that suppress and marginalize their leadership.

Examining leadership from a paradigm of hope provided insights into the ways women leaders deliberately and strategically worked together to generate agency within their leadership contexts. By leading in the hope of things being different in the future, through modeling hope in their leadership, and by forming relationships that support women leaders, the women in this research illustrated the powerful potential for women's leadership in the university when aligned with conceiving their leadership from a strength-based position.

High levels of hope can also be associated with deriving more courses of action to accomplish the same goal (pathways), which is associated with achieving goals more often. However, what is interesting about these findings is that, although hope is frequently portrayed as an individual construct deeply embedded in the personal psyche, in terms of this group of women leading in higher education, hope appeared to be an endeavor which existed in more of a collective sense rather than a personal aspiration.

As such, Snyder's (2000) Hope Theory was a useful theoretical framework to support the conceptualization of each woman's individual leadership in action, from a strength-based position, however, it would appear to be less suitable when utilized at more a collective level. The relational aspects of leadership were an important part of women's leadership experiences in higher education. The relationships formed between academic women in higher education support aspects such as identity construction, developing research agendas and research strategies, and addressing feelings of being isolated in women's professional work (Newcombe, 2014).

While Coleman (2010) outlines many of the complexities associated with women-only groups for educational leaders, she also highlights the benefits of offering "opportunities that mixed groups did not, providing a special type of support as a network of women who can speak honestly and openly in a way that a mixed forum does not allow" (p. 779). However, Harris, Ravenswood, and Myers (2013) state that informal networks are just as "important for mentoring, information, decision making on appointments and research collaborations" (p. 232).

CONCLUSION

Change is inevitable in higher education if universities are to remain contextually relevant and useful in the modern age. Innovation and adaptation become critical aspects of organizational culture as universities seek to remain aligned to the needs of their communities. Sitting

alongside this change is the potential for a diverse array of responses to change—in response to and in order to generate change overall. Women's presence in this change is paramount if the social, cultural, and political architectures are to shift and women are to flourish in their leadership in higher education contexts.

The presence of hope in an organization can be harnessed by women as a potent anchor for stability, a powerful tool for creativity, and a possible driver for innovation and change. The challenge will be sustaining hope in impoverished, disappointing, and challenging times. Stories of hope also encourage us to examine the organizational stories that we share, affirm, and redistribute in their many forms. This way, working from a paradigm of hope offers opportunities to examine women's leadership from an alternative position, as they seek to interact with, and generate change within their organization.

NOTES

1. Indigenous New Zealand Maori word for women.
2. Indigenous New Zealand Maori word for food.

REFERENCES

Airini, Collings, S., Conner, L., McPherson, K., Midson, B., & Wilson, C. (2011). Learning to be leaders in higher education: What helps or hinders women's advancement as leaders in universities. *Educational Management Administration & Leadership, 39*(1), 44–62.

Blackmore, J. (2008). Re/positioning women in educational leadership: The changing social relations and politics of gender in Australia. In H. C. Sobehart (Ed.), *Women leading education across the continents: Sharing the spirit, fanning the flame* (pp. 73–83). Lanham, MD: Rowman & Littlefield Education.

Blackmore, J., & Sachs, J. (2007). *Performing and reforming leaders.* New York, NY: State University of New York Press.

Blatt, R. (2014). *Leadership through hope.* Retrieved from https://www.forbes.com/forbes/welcome/?toURL=https://www.forbes.com/sites/ruthblatt/2014/07/31/leadership-through-hope-lessons-from-reggae-music/&refURL=&referrer=#4d2e96e91554.

Braun, V., & Clarke, V. (2006). Using thematic analysis in psychology. *Qualitative Research in Psychology, 3*(2), 77–101.

Coleman, M. (2010). Women-only (homophilous) networks supporting women leaders in education. *Journal of Educational Administration, 48*(6), 769–781.

Fitzgerald, T., & Wilkinson, J. (2010). *Travelling towards a mirage? Gender, leadership and higher education.* Queensland, Australia: Post Pressed.

Harris, C., Ravenswood, K., & Myers, B. (2013). Glass slippers, holy grail and ivory towers: Gender and advancement in academia. *Labour and Industry: A journal of the social and economic relations of work, 23*(3), 231–244.

Helland, M., & Winston, B. (2005). Towards a deeper understanding of hope and leadership. *Journal of Leadership and Organizational Studies, 12*(2), 42–54.

Ludema, J., Wilmot, T., & Srivastva, S. (1997). Organizational hope: Reaffirming the constructive task of social and organizational inquiry. *Human Relations, 50*(8), 1015–1052.

Luthans, F. (2002). Positive organizational behavior: Developing and managing psychological strengths. *Academy of Management Executive, 16*(1), 57–72.

McGregor, J. (2012). *New Zealand census of women's participation 2012.* Wellington, New Zealand: Human Rights Commission.

Ministry of Women's Affairs. (2014). *Strategic Intentions 2014–2018 New Zealand Universities.* Wellington, New Zealand.

Newcombe, W. (2014). Collaborative feminism at work. In W. Newcombe & K. Mansfield, (Eds.), *Women interrupt-ing, disrupting and revolutionizing educational policy and practice* (pp. 193–209). Charlotte, NC: Information Age Publishing.

Ramsay, E., McGregor, J., & McCarthy, D. (2014). *New Zealand's experiment: Closing the gender gap in higher education leadership through cumulative cultural change.* 8th European Conference on Gender Equality in Higher Education held at Vienna University of Technology, Vienna, Austria, September 3–4, 2014.

Snyder, C. (2000). Hypothesis: There is hope. In C. R. Snyder (Ed.), *Handbook of Hope* (pp. 3–21). New York, NY: Academic Press.

Snyder, C. R., Harris, C., Anderson, J. R., Holleran, S. A., Irving, L. M., & Sigmon, S. T. (1991). The will and the ways: Development and validation of an individual-differences measure of hope. *Journal of Personality and Social Psychology, 60*, 570–585.

Youssef, C., & Luthans, F. (2007). Positive organizational behavior in the workplace: The impact of hope, optimism, and resilience. *Management Department Faculty Publications, 36*, 774–800.

Chapter 15

Minority Women Leaders in Higher Education

Wafa Hozien

Minority women in leadership positions in higher education are underrepresented. This chapter examines the predominant leadership styles of minority women who have achieved leadership positions in higher education and explored intentional changes in their leadership styles. Primarily, this study sought to determine if these leaders had similar leadership styles and whether they have intentionally changed their leadership styles in their attempt to attain their positions. The results showed that minority women in leadership positions in higher education do, in fact, have predominantly transformational leadership styles, and that a majority of minority women in these positions have intentionally changed their leadership styles in an effort to achieve advancement.

It is important to understand how minority women navigate between the two cultures. Once we understand their successful journey, we will have a better idea of how to develop more minority female leaders in order to increase role models and representation in higher education. The findings indicated that the participants described their route to their leadership roles as challenging. However, their support system, education, networking, and professional development allowed them to overcome all the challenges they encountered along their path to be able to attain their leadership roles.

The glass ceiling (Frenkiel, 1984; Hymowitz & Schellhardt, 1986), which is defined as an invisible barrier that holds a person back from further advancement due to one or more prejudices, remains for women in higher education administration because of traditional gender perceptions of leadership. Women, however, in higher education administration have broken through this barrier. Eagly and Carli (2007) spoke of a woman's journey into the upper levels of leadership as a maze, where the traveler must identify the turns in the road ahead in order to continue the journey. This qualitative study identified trends in the leadership styles of women in public and private higher education institutions who have broken

this barrier and achieved advancement and included both an established leadership survey and researcher-developed open-ended questions.

Because the percentage of minority female leaders in higher education is very low and because there is little research on their challenges or experiences in higher education, their paths, processes, and patterns to leadership are not clearly understood. The disproportional representation, between the size of the minority population in the United States and the percentage of minority female administrators in higher education, demonstrates a need to develop more minority female leaders. How can we develop more minority female leaders if we do not understand their paths to leadership? Conceivably, career development of minorities for leadership positions could increase the number of minority leaders in higher education.

PURPOSE AND PROBLEM STATEMENT

The purpose of this chapter is to present data on minority women who have broken the glass ceiling and determine the leadership styles they shared that have been most beneficial to their success. Guiding this study is the assumption that a majority of minority women who have achieved leadership positions in higher education exhibit a common leadership style.

As the number of women working within leadership positions in the higher education system increases, there becomes more of a need to research these positions. Specifically, it is important for researchers to attempt to better understand the personal reasons and motivations that account for why women are taking these positions and the concerns (e.g., balancing work and life obligations) that come along with them.

The role of a woman within a leadership position is complex and is influenced by her gender and life experiences (Murphey, Moss, Hannah, & Wiener, 2005). With the number of women holding leadership positions within higher education organizations increasing in a still-male dominated field, these women are frequently expected to exhibit the same leadership styles as men. The result of this is frustration and various obstacles (e.g., glass ceiling, lower pay) that women must overcome in order to succeed in their positions. There is a dearth of research toward understanding the various ways minority women navigate this challenging path to leadership in higher education.

Women in Leadership Positions

Women in general have struggled to obtain and maintain leadership positions in the world of academia. Androcentrism, defined as the "elevation of the masculine to the level of the universal and the ideal, and the honoring of men and the male principle above women and the female" (Shakeshaft, 1990, p. 94), fosters a belief in male superiority and a masculine value system, one in which female values, experiences, and behaviors are viewed as inferior. The intersectionality of the experiences of minority women presents particular challenges in the predominantly white male world of higher education. Issues associated with racism, sexism, and tokenism create an often chilly climate for minority women leaders in postsecondary institutions. In addition, demands placed upon minority women from their external communities, create a web of complexities that only further complicates matters. In the often openly oppositional environments of higher educational administration at predominantly white colleges and universities, minority women must find a way to balance their personal and professional priorities, while remaining cognizant of the dilemmas that they will confront as a result of racial and gender discrimination.

PARTICIPANTS

The participants in the study included leaders who held a position above chairperson, including deans, vice provosts, provosts, vice chancellors, chancellors, vice presidents, and presidents. In addition to the Multifactor Leadership Questionnaire (MLQ) (Bass & Avolio, 1994), the participants completed a questionnaire to provide a qualitative overview of their leadership traits and experiences while achieving higher education leadership positions. Subjects' leadership tendencies were determined using the US-based scale the authors of the MLQ provided. Leaders' own perceptions of their leadership styles were determined through the answers provided in the open-ended portion of the questionnaire.

The open-ended answers ascertained whether participants had intentionally altered their leadership styles while they worked toward leadership positions, and whether there were additional barriers that existed for them as they sought leadership positions within private or public colleges and universities. Three hundred MLQ and open-ended question surveys were emailed out to minority women in higher education leadership positions in the United States. Eighty-five surveys were returned, with 65 completed with all questions answered. Ten participants replied that they would be willing to participate in a one-hour phone postsurvey interview.

GUIDING QUESTIONS

The following question guides this chapter: Did the majority of minority women who have achieved leadership positions in higher education exhibit a transformational leadership style?

The following research questions supported the investigation of this guiding question:

1. Is there a commonality in the leadership styles exhibited by minority women achieving leadership positions in higher education?
2. Did the minority women who attained leadership positions in higher education intentionally change their leadership style in order to achieve advancement?

METHOD

This study was not intended to compare the assorted adaptations employed by women with those utilized by men. Further, this study was not designed to determine the differences between the ways in which minority and white women adapt to the dissonance experienced in their leadership capacities. Instead, this study focused specifically on the selected adaptations devised by minority women in leadership positions at predominantly white colleges and universities.

In examining this problem, I collected data using the Multifactor Leadership Questionnaire (MLQ). Bass and Avolio developed the MLQ in 1994 as an assessment of leadership style. The MLQ assesses leaders' tendencies toward transactional, transformational, or laissez faire leadership styles by examining a full range of leadership traits. Corporations often use this instrument to identify the extent of these leadership behaviors and their impact on a given organization (Bass & Avolio, 2004).

Analytical Methods

The scoring of the MLQ was the first step in the analysis of the data. The Rater Form of the MLQ was the portion intended for leaders' self-reporting. Each of the items on the survey was scored using the scoring key provided in the MLQ 5X Manual. Responses to the items on the MLQ determined leaders' tendencies based on the following descriptive categories: Idealized Influence (Attributed), Idealized Influence (Behavior), Inspiration Motivation, Intellectual Stimulation, Individual Consideration, Contingent Reward, Management-by-Exception (Active), Management-by-Exception (Passive), Laissez-Faire Leadership, Extra Effort, Effectiveness, and Satisfaction (Bass & Avolio, 2004).

The MLQ contains approximately four items designed to measure each of the different categories, and each of these descriptors falls into the categories of transactional, transformational, or laissez-faire leadership styles. Transformational behavior indicators included the Idealized Influence (Attributed), Idealized Influence (Behavior), Inspiration Motivation, Intellectual Stimulation, and Individual Consideration categories. Transactional behavior indicators included the Contingent Reward and Management-by-Exception (Active) categories. Laissez-faire leadership behavior indicators included the Management-by-Exception (Passive) and Laissez-Faire Leadership categories. To score the questionnaire, I grouped the corresponding items for each category and calculated the average. Afterward, the averages were compared to the normed averages for the United States (both men and women), which yielded a percentile based upon those national averages for self-reporting.

The calculated percentiles indicated that the participant tended either more or less toward exhibiting that behavior. Through these percentiles, a portrait of the leader as either more transactional or more transformational emerged. Leaders who showed a tendency in one or two of the categories opposite to their basic trend were categorized as exhibiting some traits of either transactional or transformational. Leaders who showed a tendency in more than two of the categories opposite to their basic trend were categorized as both transactional and transformational. Table 15.1 shows the numbers and percentages of these categories.

Once determination of the leaders' primary tendencies of leadership styles was established, I coded the open-ended portion of the survey for specific descriptive terms. For analysis of the one question that could not be narrowed to a specific either/or answer, the researcher looked for repeated or synonymous words or phrases that could be categorized as common.

The first open-ended question was, "Do you consider your personal leadership style to be transactional or transformational?" The responses were coded as either transactional, transformational, or both. Analysis for frequency of each of the answers was run. A chi-square test between the results of the MLQ and the leaders' determination of their leadership style showed there was no significant difference, X squared (1, N=51) = 3.00, although it was approaching significance, p = 0.083. Table 15.1 shows the full results.

Another open-ended question asked, "What specific behaviors do you exhibit which help you classify yourself as one or the other?" The answers were varied. However, there were common terms describing behaviors among the respondents that were coded to allow for measurement. Common words among responses were: organize, delegate, vision, empower, team, mission, praise, servant, and relationships. These common behaviors were then categorized using the definitions of transactional and transformational leaders provided by Cuadrado, Morales, and Recio (2008) into types of behaviors considered either transactional or transformational. The researcher compared the data provided by this extrapolation to the women's self-description of their leadership styles and with those revealed by the MLQ as their leadership tendency. This helped provide a more complete picture of the leaders' styles.

ANALYSIS

Understanding minority female leadership styles and exploring the paths to leadership of successful minority women in leadership positions in colleges and universities in the United States is critical work for the future. It is important to understand how they navigate between the two cultures. Once we understand their successful journey, we will have a better idea how to increase the representation and the number of minority female leadership role models in higher education. The scoring of the MLQ was the first step in the analysis of the data. The Rater Form of the MLQ was the portion intended for leaders' self-reporting. Each of the items on the survey was scored using the scoring key provided in the MLQ 5X Manual.

Table 15.1. MLQ Results

Self Results	Transactional		Transformational	
	n	*%*	*n*	*%*
Transactional	3	75.00	1	25.00
Transformational	5	31.90	32	68.10

INTERPRETATION OF THE FINDINGS

Most of the minority women who participated in this study described themselves as transformational in their behaviors as leaders. The chi-square test run to determine if the leaders' determinations of themselves were the same as the results the MLQ showed that there was no significant difference. However, according to the participants' answers to the open-ended questions designed for this study, a majority of the participants answered that they intentionally changed their leadership behaviors to incorporate more transformational behaviors in order to attain their positions as upper-level leaders in their institutions.

Additionally, though many of the minority women employed by private, religious institutions answered that they felt their success in achieving upper-level leadership positions presented for them barriers those working in the public sector did not face. There was no discernible pattern to their answers. It was not possible to conclude that being employed by a private, religious institution created any additional barriers to achieving upper-level leadership positions in higher education.

Further, this research suggests that minority women seek opportunities for internal support both from other minority women and white men in higher educational administration. External sources of support are critical for these minority women, and family and spirituality stand as the most important resources. Although marriages sometimes collapsed, these generally strong systems of support help minority women maintain the high levels of self-confidence and self-assurance necessary to their survival.

Finally, this study indicates that minority women leaders at predominantly white colleges and universities should not expect to receive rewards for their work in traditional ways, rather, there will be times when they should recognize and accept the rewards found in working for the greater good.

Implications and Recommendations

The responses gathered through the MLQ and the researcher-developed questions did answer the research questions posed by the researcher. From the results there was a clear majority of women who have achieved upper-level leadership positions in higher education who exhibit predominantly transformational leadership behaviors. Since women tend to be transformational in their approaches to leadership (Cuadrado et al., 2008), it was evident that by using their natural talents and character traits in leadership in upper levels, these women were not disadvantaged.

From the data collected, minority women often feel that their natural tendencies must be tailored or added to in order to achieve the positions in leadership to which they aspire. With a large percentage of upper level leaders who are primarily transformational and a large percentage of those participants who indicated that they felt their leadership style had to be changed to incorporate some transactional types of behaviors, it is possible that minority women who seek advancement must add to their leader behaviors in order to attain the positions they seek. Particularly, according to the data from this study, women who seek to advance have had to add or hone the transactional behaviors described as organizing and delegating.

CONCLUSION

Educational leaders across racial and gender lines must become more fully aware of the challenges that confront women and African American administrators at their institutions. As we continue into a millennium in which currently underrepresented populations will move from minority to majority status, it becomes critical for educational administrators to think carefully about how these demographic changes will affect their institutions and plan accordingly. Without continued interest in and research on the issues affecting African American women in higher educational administration, their futures look bleak.

Institutions and organizations need to tap the resources of mature minority women leaders and provide new roles to involve experienced voices. Educators and those interested in the leadership of minority women need to assist women and minority women with transitions and encourage engagement in dialogue, teaching, mentoring, and coaching of new cohorts of potential leaders. In some instances, this could mean doing more of what some institutions are now doing in inviting emirate professors to continue research, teaching, and administration, while providing opportunities for them to mentor their colleagues. Likewise, women need to seek out other women leaders. It is clear from this study that minority women are knowledgeable and competent in the leadership competency skill areas. Women need to utilize their strengths, power, and influence to support other women.

In addition to identifying skill competencies, procedures for follow-up and training are necessary to continue to develop and support minority women administrators. As stated in the study, formal and informal training, such as course work, participation on committees, mentoring and modeling, are important strategies for competency skill development.

Although more than 30 years have passed since the ratifications of antidiscriminatory measures, such as Title VII, Title IX, and Affirmative Action, it appears that very little progress has occurred. Minority women continue to struggle with racism and sexism, and other policies and practices that exclude them from the very highest strata of higher educational administration.

This is not to suggest that no change has occurred. Minority women who obtained positions in higher educational administration prior to the ratification of this antidiscrimination legislation were the rare exception. Today, however, change still comes slowly, and minority women continue to be discriminated against and discouraged in their attempts to rise to positions of power within higher educational administration.

In addition, a type of Darwinian attitude prevails within many institutions, which find it unnecessary to extend internal professional support to women and minorities at their institutions. Many top-level administrators and policy makers are of the opinion that those most worthy will rise to the top, this despite the fact that systemic discrimination aimed at women and minorities prevails. So focused on survival, the women often find themselves forced to function reactively as opposed to proactively, thus inhibiting their ability to further pursue their own interests and develop their own goals.

Minority women in higher educational administration find themselves in a similar position. Having nothing to fall back on, they too must be willing to invent themselves in ways that are theirs alone. They must demonstrate drive and determination, a willingness to work hard, and an awareness that they can and should remain true to themselves. To that end, the three minority women in this analysis can and do function as models of excellence for those who will follow.

REFERENCES

Bass, B. M., & Avolio, B. J. (1994, Winter). Shatter the glass ceiling: Women may make better leaders. *Human Resource Management, 33*(4), 549–561.

Bass, B. M., & Avolio, B. J. (2004). Multifactor leadership questionnaire. Retrieved from https://www.mindgarden.com/16-multifactor-leadership-questionnaire.

Cuadrado, J., Morales, F., & Recio, P. (2008). Women's access to managerial positions: an experimental study of leadership styles and gender Isabel. *Spanish Journal of Psychology, 11*(1), 55–65.

Eagly, A. H., & Carli, L. L. (2007). *Through the labyrinth: The truth about how women become leaders.* Boston, MA: Harvard Business School Press.

Frenkiel, N. (1984, March). The up-and-comers: Bryant takes aim at the settlers-in. Adweek. Special Report. *Magazine World.*

Hymowitz, C., & Schellhardt, T. D. (1986, March 24). The glass ceiling: Why women can't seem to break the invisible barrier that blocks them from the top jobs. *Wall Street Journal*, p. 1.

Murphey, K., Moss, G., Hannah, S., & Wiener, R. (2005). Women in educational leadership: Finding common ground. *Journal of Women in Educational Leadership, 3*(4), 273–284.

Shakeshaft, C. (1990). *Women in educational administration.* Newbury Park, CA: Sage.

WOMEN'S LEADERSHIP AND HUMAN RIGHTS

Editor: *Michelle D. Young*

Chapter 16

Overview

Women's Rights Are Human Rights

Michelle D. Young

"Women's rights are human rights." This phrase, which was frequently asserted by early feminists, was popularized in 1995 when Hillary Clinton used it in a speech she delivered to the United Nations Fourth World Conference on Women in Beijing. In her speech, Clinton argued against practices abusing women around the world, such as dowry deaths and China's one-child policy. Clinton called out governments, organizations, and individuals for ignoring or silencing women and their concerns.

What are the implications of this notion for women leaders in educational institutions? In many different societies, women have been relegated to the position of "other" by various forms of patriarchal domination. Many share an intimate experience of the politics of oppression and repression that compounds oppressions associated with poverty, race, culture, nation, and religion. While leaders are often held accountable for interrupting the politics of oppression and repression, they too are impacted and in many cases implicated by these forces.

Like Clinton, the contributing authors for this section on women's leadership and human rights, each, in their own way, make the case that:

> As long as discrimination and inequities remain so commonplace everywhere in the world, as long as girls and women are valued less, fed less, fed last, overworked, underpaid, not schooled, subjected to violence in and outside their homes—the potential of the human family to create a peaceful, prosperous world will not be realized. (Clinton, 1996)

The chapters engage directly with the issue of human rights and the implications of this fundamental notion for leaders and leadership practice. While the focus of each of the chapters differs dramatically, from affirmative action to perceptions of gender equality, there is a common thread about the social construction of reality by, for, and concerning women. As Guba (1990) pointed out, "All social realities are constructed and shared through well-understood processes. It is this socialized sharing that gives these constructions their apparent reality, for if everyone agrees on something, how can one argue that it does not exist?" (p. 89)

THE CONTRIBUTING CHAPTERS

The first contribution to this section is by Saeeda Shah, "Gender Equality and Situated Constructions: Perceptions of Muslim Women Educational Leaders From Malaysian Universities." Like Rogena Sterling in chapter 18, Shah references the International Declaration of Human Rights and reflects on whether and how the goals and principles of the declaration play out within Malaysian society and higher education institutions.

In her chapter, Shah makes the case that although the nature and degree of subordination differs depending on national and cultural context, "Women's subordination to men is a historical phenomenon common across societies . . . perpetuated by powerful norms, discourses, and social practices." She notes that this is particularly true in many religious societies, explaining that in such societies, "interpretations of religious texts are often aimed at presenting women as 'less than' and subordinate to men, whose primary role is to attend to male wishes and commands."

Operating from this understanding, Shah shares how gender equality was understood, experienced, and practiced by the Malaysian Muslim women academics who participated in her study. She describes their self-perceptions, leadership aspirations, and career progressions as well as their conceptualizations of equality as influenced by their understandings of religious teachings. Although gender inequality is often considered more pronounced in Muslim societies, and is generally attributed to their cultural and belief systems that define gender roles and practices, Shah found that Malay Muslim women academics perceived their position as equal. That is, they did not see themselves as being discriminated against or marginalized.

In her discussion of these findings, Shah explains that the beliefs regarding women's place and role are so much a part of their own belief system that women find it difficult, if not impossible, to think outside of it. Shah argues that neither the lack of women in top leadership despite the large number of women employees nor the obviously inequitable distribution of resources and work conflicted with their understandings of equity because their belief system was so ingrained that it made it virtually impossible to think outside of it.

This second contribution is by Rogena Sterling, "Adopting a Paradigm Shift of Equality for Leadership: Equality Through Human Rights." In this piece, Sterling provides a philosophical exploration of equity. She explores the roots of the very notion of equality and how the idea has been applied with varying degrees of success and failure to break down hierarchies, including inequitable access to power, voice, influence, and resources.

Sterling considers a variety of statuses and their intersection in her exploration, while providing particular attention to the status of gender. She argues that focusing on status only encourages division and competition; whereas, the equity principal of the International Bill of Human Rights (UN General Assembly, 1948), shifts the focus from status to human dignity. The International Bill of Human Rights, which Sterling and several other authors in this section refer to, consists of the Universal Declaration of Human Rights, the International Covenant on Economic, Social and Cultural Rights, and the International Covenant on Civil and Political Rights and its two Optional Protocols and begins with the following language: "Whereas recognition of the inherent dignity and of the equal and inalienable rights of all members of the human family is the foundation of freedom, justice, and peace in the world." Sterling uses the notion of inherent equity to press the reader to consider a future in which a community of equals based on respect for human dignity supplants the current hierarchical and competition-driven status-based society. She asserts, "Inequality is not natural, but part of the system by which society is organized."

Considering the implications of her perspective for leadership practice, Sterling argues that educational leaders should strive to develop a community of equals in which each individual is valued for who they are and equality is based in humanity, not characteristics or status, and equality of outcomes is achieved by providing each person what they need to flourish.

The third contribution to this section is authored by Katie Higginbottom, "Affirmative Action: An Effec-

tive Policy for Gender Parity in Leadership in Ontario's Public Education System?" In this chapter Higginbottom explores the influence of PPM 102 Affirmative Action/Employment Equity for Women Employees, a piece of legislation introduced in Ontario in 1993 that is credited as having contributed to greater gender equity at the school principal level.

Higginbottom opens her case with a review of a consequential report, Report of Commission on Equality in Employment, which laid the foundation for Canada's Employment Equity Act of 1986 and led to the development of the affirmative action legislation. This report provided evidence that four groups were systemically discriminated against: women, people with disabilities, Aboriginal people, and visible minorities. Although data on women in leadership positions in Ontario school boards, before and after the affirmative action policy was introduced, demonstrates greater gender parity following the introduction of the legislation, Higginbottom found that many women leaders felt that it had little or no effect on their careers. Of the 12 study participants, four indicated PPM 102 had no effect on their careers, and seven indicated that PPM 102 may have had an indirect effect on their careers; only one indicated that PPM 102 had a direct effect on her career.

In her discussion of these findings, Higginbottom explained that the fact PPM 102 was not well known among educators in Ontario public school boards may help explain why 11 out of 12 participants did not feel PPM 102 had a direct effect on their careers. However, like Shah in a previous chapter, she also noted that since many women deny gender discrimination even when it is occurring, her participants may not have seen themselves as in need of affirmative action/employment equity, and therefore did not see themselves as ever having directly benefitted from it.

The obscurity of the legislation was also of interest to Higginbottom, who asserted that the Ministry of Education seemed to have downplayed the role of affirmative action in achieving greater gender parity. One potential explanation offered by Higginbottom involved the "stigma" associated with the concept. According to Higginbottom, one argument against affirmative action/employment equity is that those who benefit from such policies may be thought to be less competent. As such, she argued, neither the ministry nor the participants in her study would have wanted women's success directly attributed to affirmative action/employment equity.

The fourth contribution to this section is by Victoria Showunmi, "Interrupting Whiteness: An Auto-Ethnography of a Black Female Leader in Higher Education," shifts the focus from gender to race. In this chapter, Showunmi uses critical incidents to illustrate how whiteness, racism, and the concept of white privilege have influenced her experiences as a black middle-class female in higher education. Reflecting back on her formative years as a young black female raised by a middle-class Jewish family, Showunmi explores her socialization and the formation of her identity. She contrasts this experience to being a grown black woman in the academy.

Showunmi's exploration of her own identity and experiences provides helpful insight into the experience of othering that occurs in organizations, noting how her white and black colleagues and friends defined her, sharing the assumptions they made about her background and abilities, and explaining how these beliefs influenced her work and interactions as a scholar and leader in higher education. In her discussion of these experiences, Showunmi demonstrates how racism is embedded within and thus operates through institutional policies and practices.

Considering the implications of her perspective for policy and practice, Showunmi articulates the complexity of identity, particularly how whiteness and blackness are defined and serve as limiting forces in one's personal and professional lives. Showunmi points out that while a "plethora of research on race in compulsory schooling abounds, higher education remains largely and inconspicuously absent from the debate," particularly as it pertains to the implications for leadership in higher educational organizations.

CONCLUSION

> Feminists focus on the ways that gender-social construction of masculinity and femininity—organizes political, personal, and intellectual life. The feminist assumption is that gender divisions of work, pleasure, power, and sensibility are socially created, detrimental to women and, to a lesser degree, to men, and therefore can and should be changed. (Ruddick, 1989, pp. 234–235)

Although feminists, women's rights advocates, and researchers, among others have sought to bring the issue of women's equality and basic human rights to the forefront of international policy and discourse, women and girls continue to experience stark inequalities. Even in countries with official state feminism, "Real progress toward dismantling the system of male privilege . . . remains an elusive goal" (Skrla, 2000, p. 298). Furthermore, what counts as equality, just as with what counts as gender, is socially constructed, making it a moving target for women's and human rights advocates. As Shah pointed out in her research on Malaysian Muslim women:

> The constitution offers freedom of religion for all and promises equal rights, but the policies, such as Malay Economic Policy (1971) and National Development Policy (1991) that propose affirmative action for Malay ethnic population (bumiputras) to advance their political primacy and economic welfare, raise questions about how equal rights and equality are widely conceptualized and practiced in that context and how these perceptions and constructions may vary.

What then are the implications of the idea that "Women's rights are human rights" for educational leaders? Given the number of individuals that leaders interact with and are responsible for serving, it is important that leaders not only have a strong understanding of gender and racial identity, how it is developed and how it is reinforced by individual practices and organizational structures, but it is also important that they be able to hold courageous conversations with their colleagues that enable a collective interrogation of social constructions and identity politics and to build strategies that counter inequity.

REFERENCES

Clinton, H. R. (1996). Beijing and beyond: Toward the twenty-first century of women. *Women's Studies Quarterly, 24*(1/2), 98–101. Retrieved from https://www.jstor.org/stable/40004518?seq=1#page_scan_tab_contents

Guba, E. (1990). Subjectivity and objectivity. In E. Eisner & A. Peshkin (Eds.), *Qualitative inquiry in education: The continuing debate* (pp. 74–91). New York, NY: Teachers College Press.

Ruddick, S. (1989). *Maternal thinking: Toward a politics of peace.* Toronto, Canada: Random House.

Skrla, L. (2000). The social construction of gender in the superintendency. *Journal of Educational Policy, 15*(3), 293–316.

UN General Assembly. (1948). *International bill of human rights.* Retrieved from: http://www.ohchr.org/Documents/Publications/Compilation1.1en.pdf

Chapter 17

Malaysian Muslim Women Academics and Gender Equality

Situated Constructions

Saeeda Shah

This investigation examined Malaysian Muslim women academics' constructions of gender equality within a specific ethnoreligious context. The study was designed to explore how gender equality was understood and experienced by senior women leaders in that Muslim society and its implications for their progression to leadership roles and practices therein. Findings examine how gender equality was understood and experienced by the Malaysian Muslim women academics and its implications for their leadership roles and practices, supported by the evidence from the interview data. I discuss the participants' understandings of their family roles and the implications for work-life balance, as well as the restrictions on female mobility in Malaysia that explore how these context specific perspectives and practices interacted with women's professional journeys. Situated constructions of gender equality in this research context may influence participating women leaders' career progressions.

Gender equality is a widely debated issue, high on many national and international agendas. An explicit statement about equality of men and women in the Universal Declaration of Human Rights (Draft Committee, 1948) proved a major catalyst for ensuing debates and developments that gradually led to many improved policies and practices in different parts of the world, and more recently get reflected in the prioritization of gender equality in Sustainable Development Goals (United Nations, 2015). However, it is debatable to what extent these have actually changed the women's experiences and even perceptions of equality across the world.

Human societies continue to be gendered and male dominated in most parts of the world, and therefore, translating gender equality policies into practice remains a persistent challenge. Furthermore, gender inequality is so embedded in cultures and societal structures that even when policies are in place, they are limited in their impact on practices, specifically because these policies and strategies "do not seek to challenge social structures of

male domination, and only aim at improving the situation of women within the societal framework of subordination of women to men" (Jeffreys, 2011, p. 94).

Although the nature and degree of subordination differs, depending on national and cultural context, it is perpetuated by powerful norms, discourses, and social practices emphasizing gender stereotyping both in the public and the private spheres. Female marginalization is a common phenomenon in both spheres across societies (Kenschaft, Clark, & Ciambrone, 2015), may be with some variation in the level or nature of marginalization. The United Nations Development Programme report (2016) admits that "there continue to be pronounced imbalances across genders, reflecting local values, social traditions and historical gender roles" (p. 11).

There is extensive international literature available now that highlights the marginalization and devaluation of women and their contributions (Bandiho, 2009; Kagoda & Sperandio, 2009; Shah, 2016; Strachan, Akao, Kilavanwa, & Warsal, 2010). Mostly this marginalization is embedded in societal structures, and cultural traditions and patterns of behavior. However, religion also emerges as an added factor in religious societies, where dominant discourses with claims of being religious commands act as a powerful marginalizing force limiting women's access to equal rights. As men have historically enjoyed control over religious knowledge and they continue to dominate the positions of religious interpretations and discourse formation, the resulting discourses are often circulated as God's words or religious teaching making high claims on complete submission from the followers.

These discourses tend to present women as "less than" and subordinate to men, whose primary role is to attend to male wishes and commands. Studies from within various religious traditions acknowledge that women in all major religious traditions such as Buddhism (Starkey & Tomalin, 2013), Christianity (Martos & Hégy, 1998), Hinduism (Joshee & Sihra, 2013), Islam (Shah, 2013),

Judaism (Rapoport, 2013), and others continue to experience marginalization because of the given interpretations of religious texts and the powerful gendered discourses produced by those occupying the positions of interpretation (Foucault, 1980) within these religious traditions. Such gendered discourses define gender roles and power relations in societies shaping the conceptualizations of gender equality and the practices in the private and the public spheres.

This chapter is developed from the data collected from Muslim women academics working in three different universities in Malaysia. The research participants were in senior leadership positions including deans, heads of departments, directors, and a deputy vice chancellor. The study was designed to explore how gender equality was understood and experienced by these senior women leaders in that Muslim society and its implications for their progression to leadership roles and practices therein.

The first section briefly introduces the country context to locate the study. The next section deliberates on how gender equality was understood and experienced by the Malaysian Muslim women academics and its implications for their leadership roles and practices, supported by the evidence from the interview data. Following that, I discuss the participants' understandings of their family roles and its implications for work-life balance, while the next section debates restrictions on female mobility in this Muslim society to explore how these context specific perspectives and practices interacted with women's professional journeys. The concluding section pulls together the discussion around situated constructions of gender equality in this research context deliberating how these constructions might influence participating women leaders' career progressions.

THE STUDY AND THE COUNTRY CONTEXT

The study investigated Muslim women academics' progression to leadership positions and explored the factors that shaped their career trajectories. It was designed as a qualitative study, placed within interpretive paradigm because of the exploratory nature of the research, seeking to gain some understanding of an un-researched phenomenon (Cohen, Manion, & Morrison, 2007). The intention was to engage the participants in conversations to share their perspectives and experiences (Elliot, 2005) of women academics' leadership roles and how they interpreted these in the context of gender equality.

The sample consisted of nine women senior leaders from three public universities in Malaysia. The sampling strategy was purposive and the sample selection was supported by two Malaysian colleagues I have known previously (these colleagues were not included in the research participants). My being a Muslim woman academic also facilitated access through shared gender and faith identity, and helped sharing of personal and professional histories and experiences. This shared faith identity (Muslim *Ummah*) and shared gender also helped to conduct interviews in a relaxed and "sisterly" atmosphere where the participants responded to probes in some detail, adding to the richness of the data.

To engage with this data meaningfully it is important to understand the relevant country context. Malaysia is a South East Asian country and Islam is its state religion; however, freedom of religion and equal rights are promised to all in the constitution irrespective of their faith or ethnicity. Nevertheless, some later policies such as Malay Economic Policy (1971) and National Development Policy (1991) proposed affirmative action for the Malay ethnic population (referred to as bumiputras, meaning children of the soil) to advance their political primacy and economic welfare.

The Malay community welcomed these preferential policies as ensuring "a just and equitable distribution of national wealth in the economy" (Yusoff, Abu-Hasan, & Jalil, 2000, p. 66), and justified these policies in the historical backdrop of Malay marginalization that had resulted in their economic deprivation and political marginalization. Explained in that historical and political context, these policies were explained as positive steps to ensure economic and political equality for the Malay ethnic group. However, other communities critiqued these policies as discriminatory "resulting at various times in emigration, capital flight and ethnic mobilization" (Jomo, 2004, p. 11). These policies favoring Malay community not only may conflict with the constitutional promise of equal rights to all, but also raise questions about how equal rights and equality are understood and practiced in that society.

However, the pro-Malay policies or affirmative action, as these were defined, resulted in a substantial increase in the numbers of Malay population in the country from around 52 percent in 1971 to 67.4 percent in 2010. These policies also emphasized the need for educating the Malay population to facilitate their economic and political mobilization, and put systems and processes in place to achieve that. In education, one example is the Malaysian Matriculation Programme, a one- to two-year pre-university preparatory program that is offered by the Malaysian Ministry of Education and needs to be taken by all students aiming for higher education. Within the framework of National Development Policy (1991), selection for joining this program has been through a race-based quota system, where 90 percent of the places were reserved for bumiputra students while the remaining 10 percent were open for non-bumiputras. Such measures have been critiqued by many as discriminatory against the non-Malay population but the Malay ethnic population welcomed these as ensuring equal opportunities for this ethnic group that has previously been deprived and marginalized socially and economically; they refuse to see this as an expression of inequality.

Malay women also benefitted from these policies resulting in their increased access to higher education leading to employment and economic participation. However, as Islam is the state religion of Malaysia, Islamic teachings not only guide sociocultural practices but are also recognized in the Malay constitution as the source of law guiding Muslims' lives. The constitution is explicit that Muslims's lives will be governed by Sharia laws, and therefore Sharia courts work along with the civil courts dealing with different aspects of Muslims' lives including moral values, gender relations, marriage, family, inheritance, divorce, and child custody. Cultural interpretations of Sharia laws often shape gender roles and responsibilities in Muslim societies (Shah, 2013) and Malaysia is no exception. Adherence to Sharia laws at the state level in Malaysia therefore emerges as a powerful discourse shaping Muslim women's participation in the public sphere.

All ethnic Malays are considered Muslims by Article 160 of the constitution of Malaysia. This identification with religious identity in the State discourses and documents has promoted association with given Islamic symbols and practices and is reflected in sociocultural patterns of behavior, gender roles, and associated responsibilities and visible symbols such as dress (full body covered) and head covers (men wearing cap or *kopiah* and women wearing a scarf, etc.). All participating Malay female academics were dressed Malay and wore headscarves.

The use of traditional Malay dress and headscarves among Muslim Malay women started following the introduction of affirmative action and was widely embraced because of its association with Malay Muslim identity. There was a political incentive because this association with Malay Muslim identity opened opportunities for education, employment, and career progression. However, this identification with the Muslim identity and conflation of the religious and ethnic identities also unveils the power of religious discourses that influence how gender is experienced in proclaimed Muslim societies and how Muslim women in these societies function in the professional and the private spheres. The next section briefly explains the position of women in Islam drawing upon religious texts and sources, and then discusses how gender is generally experienced in Muslim societies.

GENDER EQUALITY: SITUATED CONSTRUCTIONS

The data collected for this study was rich and fascinating, providing insights into the Malaysian women academics' professional experiences and personal lives as well as unveiling their self-perceptions as Muslim women academics in a specific societal context. What surprised and intrigued me as a Muslim woman researcher was that all the participating women academics' first response to the question about gender equality was the claim of perfect gender equality in their work context. This unequivocal emphasis on gender equality in their work context was expressed by each one of them, maybe with some variations of expressions but reflective of very similar perspectives. Second, they all emphasized that equality was an essential principle propounded by their religion. They mentioned role differences associated with men and women in their society but did not interpret this as inequality but as appropriate role distribution. Third, they emphasized the primacy of their role and responsibilities as wives/mothers, justifying this as a religious requirement, and explained submission to the husband's authority and decision making as obligatory for a "good Muslim woman."

The participating women academics were unequivocal and emphatic regarding their claims of gender equality in their workplaces. They linked this to their religious beliefs and teachings emphasizing that in Islam women and men are equal. In response to a probe regarding the practice of equality in the workplace they claimed that "We are treated equally. We have no issues with gender." They further elaborated that there was "no mention in policies that women could not apply for any post or could not work in any position."

Interestingly, the emphasis was on equal opportunity policies in their institutions and at the government level as evidence of gender equality and they claimed that in the context of such policies there was *no scope for inequality*. However, when asked specifically about practices and examples from practice, one head of department argued that, "No colleague ever complained of any gender related issues in work or career progression." The paralinguistic message was that absence of any such complaint from any colleague was evidence enough that there was no gender inequality.

They further argued that there was no mention in policies that women could not apply for any post or could not work in any position, as if trying to convince the obtuse interviewer how the system worked for equality. To what extent these policies were effective in creating conditions where equality of opportunity across all divides including gender could not be compromised was perhaps not on the agenda for critical engagement. The question that arises here is, are equal opportunity policies enough in themselves to ensure equality of practice? Hornosty (2000) points to this distance between policies and practices when she emphasizes the "need to create an equality of condition, not merely an equality of opportunity" (p. 42).

Apparently, the gender equality policies in spite of the claims that the national policies "did not bar women from applying for any leadership role," did not ensure gender equality, particularly in senior leadership positions and roles. The data unveiled that it was predominantly men who occupied top leadership positions not only in the research participants' employing universities but in all universities across the country. Although women outnumbered men in academia, they were mostly concentrated in teaching and middle management roles. Interestingly, participating women themselves admitted in response to probing that "men with similar qualifications not only moved faster toward the top position," but also they "occupied almost all positions of power." This raised questions about the effectiveness of equality policies and transference of these policies into practice. The research participants admitted that in their institutions there were very few women in top leadership positions, and even these were often tokenistic such as a deputy vice chancellor or a director with portfolios such as students' affairs.

An interesting observation was that women did not criticize this predominance of men in top leadership positions. In fact, they tried to explain this phenomenon as an appropriate distribution of roles in view of women's domestic responsibilities emphasizing that, "We look after homes and children while men have more time for the professional life" and "are free to network." They further explained that women's responsibilities within the family were a religious obligation, and therefore not open for critique or challenge. Their acceptance of different gender roles for men and women endorsed by religion was explained as submission to religious teachings as "good Muslim women."

They emphasized, referring to the Quranic teachings, that their first priority as Muslim women was their families, particularly husbands and children, and in case of any conflict between their domestic responsibilities and career progression, "good Muslim women" should and would prioritize the family; this was not an issue of equality or inequality. These comments and perceptions raised questions about how equality was understood by these women academics and its implications for their aspirations and progression to top leadership.

The participating women academics generally expressed a sense of pride in their role and responsibilities as Muslim women which required them to prioritize their family responsibilities. They were not bothered to critically explore if these given roles were actually embedded in religious teachings or were social constructions promoted by discourses discursively produced by those in positions of religious interpretation. They perceived themselves as good Muslim women and willingly acted upon the teachings of their faith as they understood it. The seductive power of religion discouraged criticality, commanding a willing submission, "Power operates visibly and invisibly through expectations and desires. It operates visibly through formal, public criteria that must be satisfied. It operates invisibly through the way individuals think of themselves and operate" (Cherryholmes, 1988, p. 35).

There were clear messages in the data that gendered roles were a reflection of accepted social practices and patterns of behavior, however, all participants were emphatic in associating these roles with religious teachings and thus justified their decisions to prioritize their domestic responsibilities even when it meant not aspiring for leadership or giving up leadership positions. Apple (2013) explains religious women's submission to religious discourse as grounded in a call to act on their duty as religious women irrespective of how this impacted on their aspiring, accessing, and practicing leadership in a professional domain.

Gender roles and practices are embedded in cultures and contexts. Islam being the state religion and the association of Malay ethnicity with Islam as well as policies associated with affirmative action prioritizing Malay political, social, and economic enhancement invested Malay Muslim identity with a seductive power. The primacy of their religious/ethnic identity and the given discourses of being a good wife, a good mother, and a good Muslim woman commanded and received submission making "it virtually impossible to think outside of them; to be outside of them" (Ball, Rollock, Vincent, & Gillborn, 2013, p. 20). There were no complaints and no criticism of the cultural systems that might have acted as barriers to their aspiration for or progression to leadership roles—career was important but secondary to their responsibilities as good Muslim women. The projection of ethnoreligious identity and observance of associated symbols and discourses was significant for their sense of self as good Muslim women.

MUSLIM WOMEN AND WORK-LIFE BALANCE

The participating women academics were proud to be Malay Muslims and willingly submitted to the associated religious-cultural codes of behavior to emphasize their association with this specific identity. They dressed Malay and wore headscarves, which was a powerful visual message of their identity. During interview conversations they emphasized their role as Muslim women and the associated responsibilities toward family. There was no indication of any doubt about where their loyalties were due; they were Muslim women and in their view Islam prioritized domestic responsibilities for women and as good Muslim women they submitted to their religion.

The centrality of family as the essential unit of Islamic societal structure (Shah, 2016) reinforced gendered role constructions that contributed to female marginalization through "commentaries and interpretations which interpret Islam in ways they want to see it" (Ed-Din, 1982, p. 223). In spite of claims of gender equality in Islam, women's access to equal opportunity in practice is often controlled by powerful discourses of female association with the domestic role and family responsibilities. Esposito (2011) argues that, "The status and roles of women in the Muslim world vary considerably, influenced as much by literacy, education, and economic development as by religion. Men and women in Muslim societies grapple with many gender issues ranging from the extent of the women's education and employment to their role in the family" (p. 102).

In spite of the fact that the women participants were all highly qualified—all with a PhD from a Western university—and worked in senior leadership positions, they acknowledged the primacy of their domestic role and family responsibilities when/if they had to choose between family and career. This created complications in managing work-life balance; they admitted this but did not complain. Queries about the work-life balance and how they managed its demands unveiled that the domestic, as constructed in the Malay Muslim culture was the priority for women with implications for their participation in the professional. They were good Muslim women and looking after the family was their responsibility; if at times family role was a barrier to their progression to leadership role they did not hesitate to make the "right choice."

The research participants acted the social roles and observed the gendered norms of behavior. For example, they all mentioned cultural norms with regard to networking across gender divide. When meeting or speaking to male colleagues they observed cultural norms and protocols to avoid physical contact such as shaking hands or sitting next to with bodies touching. Furthermore, they believed in male authority over women in the family and this got transferred to the professional space where they deferred to men by not challenging male authority. They were reluctant to voice their opinions in mixed-sex meetings. They avoided confronting male colleagues at work,

and at home they submitted to the head of the house (often a husband or father) even when making professional decisions. They were women and whether in the professional or the domestic space, they observed the gender associated norms and patterns of behavior.

All participants considered it their religious duty to obey the husbands. They argued that the Quran mentioned men as "a degree above women" (The Qur'an, 2.228), taking this line out of its context where it mentions the male role in family finances, and applying it as evidence of absolute male superiority. They all emphasized that a wife would obey her husband in whatever he said because it was her role as a good Muslim woman that, "Whatever he said she would support and obey." They referred to the Islamic teachings making claims that, "Islam tells us to obey husbands; we look after homes and children." They argued that, "We are Muslim. Family is first for us women."

Two of the participants mentioned rather proudly that they stepped down from their senior leadership roles as these were hindering them in their family responsibilities. There were no complaints or regrets. When asked why family was first for women and not men even when both were in full-time work, the answer was "our religion says this." They were probably thinking of the verse which mentions that "Men are the protectors and maintainers of women, because Allaah has made one of them to excel the other, and because they spend (to support them) from their mean" [al-Nisa' 4:34], but there was no awareness of debates among Muslim scholars who argue that such claims may apply when man is "protector and maintainer" but not where women are working and looking after themselves.

There are many other *ayahs* in the Quran which emphasize equality such as, "Women have rights over men similar to those of men over women" (The Qur'an, 2:228). Or, "The believing men and believing women are allies of one another. They enjoin what is right and forbid what is wrong" (The Qur'an, 9:71).

The power of dominant religious discourses couched in patriarchal traditions and practices seduced even educated women into believing that "obeying husbands" was an absolute and unqualified command. Some participants did mention that their husbands were cooperative and occasionally helped them in their household responsibilities or relieved them of some responsibility if needed for work. However, they did not see this as two working professionals equally sharing in domestic responsibilities but appreciated this "kindness" of their husbands as a special favor.

There was no expectation from men to share the domestic responsibilities that reflected a gendered mind-set produced and promoted by patriarchy that aims at disciplining and controlling women. Mies, Bennholdt-Thomsen, and von Werlhof (1988) discuss this as colonization of women who learn from powerful discourses to believe in male superiority, which then gets transferred to other spheres of activity. Women tend to submit, knowingly or unknowingly, to this colonization, "At the heart of the colonization of women is a belief in the superiority of men, in the infallibility of male judgment and authority and in the absolute priority given to achieving male approval and validation" (Aptheker, 1989, p. 8).

The women participants considered this a religious duty to keep their husbands happy, but there was also an underlying message that if a husband was not happy he had the power to stop his wife from continuing with her career. Husband was the authority in the household not just with regard to domestic matters but with equal authority to control the wife's professional life. Household and family responsibilities were associated with women, while men had the authority and the decision-making powers and women learned this socially from an early age by listening to discourses of how good Muslim girls/women should behave and conduct themselves. All women participants, except one, were married and had between four and seven children.

Although these women had home-help, either hired or from family, they did acknowledge that looking after children and being solely responsible for family added to their workload. This cultural learning was so deeply ingrained that these senior women leaders who were highly educated and foreign qualified did not even drop a hint of challenging these practices. In response to the query how their family responsibilities impacted on equal opportunities for career progression, the undisputed response was that they were Muslim women, and performing their family responsibilities and obeying their husbands was their religious obligation.

FEMALE MOBILITY AND *MEHRUM*

Constraints on female mobility are a common practice in many Muslim societies. A dominant discourse is that a Muslim woman must be accompanied by a male *mehrum* (an unmarriageable kin) when she travels. In its extreme form, this practice functions in Saudi Arabia but is observed, to varying degrees, in other Muslim societies as well. Interestingly, there is no mention in the Quran that women cannot travel without a *mehrum* but the Muslim societies where it is observed emphasize that it is an Islamic practice. My research participants also argued that the requirement for a female being accompanied by a male *mehrum* when traveling is Islamic teaching.

Female mobility is a complex issue in Muslim societies and it is partly linked with gender segregation. One risk in women's traveling alone is that they might come in contact with men who are not *mehrum*, and this is discouraged in Islam. Although all women participants worked in coeducational universities and their colleagues and students included men, there was a social prioritizing of segregation which required women to avoid moving into mixed-gender spaces. When work required this, then the appropriate code of conduct was observed for conversations and for maintaining the right distance. This limited networking opportunities for women. Although the women participants did not criticize or challenge segregation or constraints on mobility as such, they did mention that because of segregation and constraints on mobility they could not engage in networking and research activities and this slowed their career progression.

Networking and mobility are important elements of today's higher education scenario. In the Malaysian context, the women participants had limited mobility because they needed a *mehram* to accompany them when traveling or visiting public spaces, or they needed explicit permission from their husbands when going out unaccompanied by a male *mehram*. They admitted that such barriers slowed their career progression but tried to justify these constraints as Islamic teachings: "In Islam women cannot travel without husband's permission. My husband accompanies me when I have to travel for research."

When I pointed out that there was no such mention in the Quran, they chose to ignore it. In fact they appreciated their male *mehrums* (husband, father, or brother) who made appropriate arrangements when these women needed to travel. Such constraints on mobility and a preference for segregation restricted networking and professional socializing for women academics affecting their progression to senior leadership positions and adding to the challenges of working in leadership roles.

Even though women did not directly complain about these constraints, they did mention that men's progression to top leadership positions was facilitated by their extensive networking. They also mentioned problems in engaging with research activities because of mobility issues. In view of the growing emphasis on research and publications for career progression in higher education this emerged as seriously problematic. Even when traveling for data collection locally or out of city or country, they generally needed to be accompanied by a *mehram* which often was problematic because the *mehram* may not be available when needed. Their mention of constraints on mobility with regard to networking, research activities, and career progression clearly indicated that these women were aware of the issues, but interestingly they did not see these as factors affecting the equality agenda; the good Muslim women accepted and acted the given gender roles as their religious responsibility.

CONCLUSION

Gender equality is a highly complex and contentious issue. The concept of equality itself is riddled with contending explanations and even in this research context the policies for affirmative action to facilitate Malay ethnic populations' enhanced participation in economic and political domains have been critiqued as racial discrimination. The long-standing and ongoing debates about equality highlight that the concept is differently constructed and understood across societies and therefore the practice of equality cannot be disassociated from the contextual histories and the complex social, economic, religious, and other intersecting elements. When equality is conceptualized with reference to gender, many more elements including biological gender and power relations intersect to add to the complexity of these conceptualizations. It can be argued that biological differences, traditional gender roles, economic division of labor, religious scripts, and many other factors contribute to the given interpretations of gender equality or inequality and inform practices in a given society.

Muslim societies are often criticized for gender discriminatory practices (Griffin, 2006), while, as discussed previously, many Muslim and even non-Muslim scholars argue them Islam advocates gender equality but the practices in most Muslim societies tend to be gender discriminatory. Gross (2013) argues that gender is "a political-social category that addresses the influence of culture and the environment and how they construct inequality, discrimination and oppression" (p. 8). In Muslim societies, gender roles are often constructed at the intersections of religious and cultural discourses, and because men have traditionally and historically controlled spaces for discourse formations, these discourses invest men with a natural right to leadership, relegating women to secondary and subordinate roles, and associating them primarily with the domestic sphere. The data highlights that these professional women prioritized their family roles and submitted to the religious discourses of "obeying the husbands" even in the professional matters and choices. For example, if a husband or family did not approve for a women to take on a demanding leadership position because that might negatively affect her family responsibilities, she would submit to their decisions.

Women's career aspirations and access to leadership positions were influenced by the gendered discourses and associated societal expectations. The affirmative action policies focusing on enhancing the Malay population's political and economic participation, offered opportunities to Malay women along with men to seek higher education and share the employment market. However, the dominant discourses of gender roles validated by religion and the contextual constructions of women's role in the family and society continued to define this participation, which was reflected in academia also.

Differential patterns of career progress across the gender divide, considerably less female engagement with research, and very low presence of women in top leadership positions in spite of an almost equal female presence in the universities were some of the findings underlining the inequalities of practice. As mentioned earlier, the participating women academics emphasized that there was no inequality in the workplace, but their own comments provided evidence of inequalities. These women's refusal to acknowledge the barriers, their submission to dominant discourses, and their complacency or self-righteousness in observing the teachings of their faith can be invisible and therefore a more challenging barrier to their career progression to top leadership positions because the barriers that are not recognized and acknowledged would not get challenged. The participants accepted the gendered work division as natural and divine and therefore were unable to appreciate its negative implications for equality. They believed that being Muslim women, their primary role was to be good wives and mothers and as Yusof (2013) argues, these women leaders' progression to top leadership was negatively affected because of their "succumbing to social and cultural, not to mention biological pressures on the way to the top" (p. 6).

Gender equality policies are not always enough to ensure gender equality. More importantly, the conditions that ensure that women and men enjoy the same rights and opportunities, and where their different behaviors, aspirations, and needs are equally valued and favored need to be established. If equality of condition is not ensured in a society, the equality policies cannot satisfactorily address gender inequality. In this research context, the powerful discourses of male authority and the association of women with family roles created conditions that compromised gender equality. The data highlighted the power of cultural and belief systems in shaping women's professional roles, practices, and aspirations and the resulting self-constructions of Muslim women academics that influenced their professional trajectories and experiences.

Educational leadership is conceptualized and shaped by societal beliefs, values, and knowledge sources (Shah, 2006). The acknowledged and unacknowledged challenges facing women leaders highlight the power of cultural and religious discourses. Because of the male occupation of the places of religious leadership and religious interpretations, the social structures and resulting discourses reinforce male power contributing to female marginalization from positions of authority and leadership in the domestic and the professional spheres. The discourses of male authority and female subordination have generally been validated through given interpretations of religious texts impacting on women's self-perceptions as well as professional aspirations. Wadud (2006) argued that the male control over religious interpretation and discourse formation has been exercised historically to subjugate women and strengthen patriarchy by providing it legitimacy through religious validation.

In religious societies, discourses validated by religion exercise high power and control, which appears to hold true in the case of my research participants, who were Malay-Muslim women. They did acknowledge that their family responsibilities as Muslim women and the societal expectations and norms for conducting themselves as Muslim women hindered or slowed their progression to top leadership positions, but they did not believe that this was an inequality issue. There was a clear reluctance to aspire for top leadership if that interfered with their family responsibilities or if husbands did not approve—good Muslim women obey the husbands.

Blackmore (2010) argued that "women struggle with their own professional and personal aspirations within their own cultural and religious contexts" (p. 49). The participating women academics explained constraints on mobility and networking as well as their family responsibilities as religious obligations and therefore they did not even consider challenging practices that they believed were religious obligations. They emphasized the high significance of their perceived religious obligations and emphatically defended prioritizing the domestic over the professional. My research participants constructed gender equality within a specific ethnoreligious context and if that conflicted with widely accepted concepts of equality, they had no problem with it. Blackmore and Sachs (2007) argue that because of women's location in a gendered division of labor, "societal and organizational expectations and responsibilities are different" (p. 130), which negatively impact the equality agenda.

The research participants' constructions of gender equality aligned with their religious beliefs and cultural practices and each interviewee, in very clear terms, emphasized that there was perfect gender equality in their workplace. Even when they explained to the researcher that most top leadership positions were occupied by men and women's career progress to leadership positions was significantly different from that of men, and men with similar qualifications moved faster to top positions, it

was a statement of their social and professional reality which they were sharing, not complaining of.

Muslim women leaders or aspiring leaders are often caught between the given religious discourse of what it means to be a "good Muslim woman" and their career aspirations as professionals. Tensions between responsibilities of demanding top leadership positions and the role of a committed Muslim woman, or the dominant religious discourses advising Muslim women to remain invisible and the aspirations for or functioning in a visible leadership role could result in physical and emotional stresses. The context specific constructions of equality offered by these research participants were perhaps their way of dealing with the tensions.

REFERENCES

Apple, M. (2013). Gender, religion and the work of homeschooling. In Z. Gross, L. Davies, & K. Diab (Eds.), *Gender, religion and education in a postmodern chaotic world* (pp. 21–39). New York, NY: Springer.

Aptheker, B. (1989). *Tapestries of life: Women's work, women's consciousness, and the meaning of daily experience.* Amherst, MA: University of Massachusetts Press.

Ball, S. J., Rollock, N., Vincent, C., & Gillborn, D. (2013). Social mix, schooling and intersectionality: Identity and risk for Black middle class families. *Research Papers in Education, 28*(3), 265–288.

Bandiho, H. (2009). Status of educational leadership and female participation: The case of Tanzania. In H. Sobehart (Ed.), *Women leading education across the continents: Sharing the spirit, fanning the flame* (pp. 43–48). Lanham, MD: Rowman & Littlefield Education.

Blackmore, J. (2010). 'The other within': Race/gender disruptions to the professional learning of white educational leaders. *International Journal of Leadership in Education, 13*(1), 45–61. http:dx.doi.org/10.1080/13603120903242931

Blackmore, J., & Sachs, J. (2007). Performing and reforming leaders: Gender, educational restructuring, and organizational change. Albany, NY: State University of New York Press.

Cherryholmes, C. (1988). *Power and criticism: Poststructural investigations in education.* New York, NY: Teachers College Press.

Cohen, L., Manion, L., & Morrison, K. (2007). *Research methods in education,* 6th ed. New York, NY: Routledge.

Draft Committee. (1948). *Universal declaration of human rights.* Paris, France: United Nations.

Ed-Din, N. Z. (1982). Removing the veil and veiling: Lectures and reflections towards women's liberation and social reform in the Islamic world. *Women's Studies International Forum, 5*(2), 221–226.

Elliot, J. (2005). *Using narrative in social research: Qualitative and quantitative approaches.* London, England: Sage.

Esposito, J. (2011). *What everyone needs to know about Islam* (2nd ed.). Oxford, England: Oxford University Press.

Foucault, M. (1980). *Power/knowledge: Selected interviews and other writings (1972–1977)*. Brighton, England: Harvester Press.

Griffin, R. (2006). *Education in the Muslim world: Different perspectives*. Providence, RI: Symposium Books.

Gross, Z. (2013). Introduction. In Z. Gross, L. Davies, & K. Diab (Eds.), *Gender, religion and education in a postmodern chaotic world* (pp. 1–17). New York, NY: Springer.

Hornosty, J. (2000). Academic freedom in social context. In S. Kahn & D. Pavlich (Eds.), *Academic freedom and the inclusive university* (pp. 36–47). Vancouver, Canada: UBC Press.

Jeffreys, S. (2011). *Man's dominion: The rise of religion and the eclipse of women's rights*. Routledge Studies in Religion and Politics. New York, NY: Routledge.

Jomo, K. S. (2004). *The new economic policy and inter-ethnic relations in Malaysia*. UNRISD Programme on Identities, Conflict and Cohesion. Paper number 7. Geneva, Switzerland: United Nations Research Institute for Social Development. Retrieved from http://www.unrisd.org/80256B3C005BCCF9/(httpPublications)/A20E9AD6E5BA919780256B6D0057896B

Joshee, R., & Sihra, K. (2013). Shakti as a liberatory and educative force for Hindu women. In Z. Gross, L. Davies, & K. Diab (Eds.), *Gender, Religion and Education in a Postmodern Chaotic World* (pp. 73–82). New York, NY: Springer.

Kagoda, A. M., & Sperandio, J. (2009). Ugandan women: Moving beyond historical and cultural understandings of educational leadership. In H. Sobehart (Ed.), *Women leading education across the continents: Sharing the spirit, fanning the flame* (pp. 49–56). Lanham, MD: Rowman & Littlefield Education.

Kenschaft, L., Clark, R., & Ciambrone, D. (2015). *Gender inequality in our changing world: A comparative approach*. New York, NY: Routledge.

Martos, J., & Hégy, P. (1998). *Equal at the creation: Sexism, society, and Christian thought*. Toronto, Canada: University of Toronto Press.

Mies, M., Bennholdt-Thomsen, V., & von Werlhof, C. (1988). *Women: The last colony*. London, England: Zed Books.

Rapoport, T. (2013). Holiness class: "Constructing a constructive woman" in a Zionist religious *Ulpana*. In Z. Gross, L. Davies, & K. Diab (Eds.), *Gender, religion and education in a postmodern chaotic world* (pp. 151–171). New York, NY: Springer.

Shah, S. (2006). Educational leadership: An Islamic perspective. *British Educational Research Journal, 32*(3), 363–385.

Shah, S. (2013). Islam, education and gender: discourses and practices among Pakistani Diaspora in the UK. In Z. Gross, L. Davies, & K. Diab (Eds.), *Gender, religion and education in a postmodern chaotic world* (pp. 241–252). New York, NY: Springer.

Shah, S. (2016). *Education, leadership and Islam: Theories, discourses and practices from an Islamic perspective*. London, England: Routledge.

Starkey, C., & Tomalin, E. (2013). Gender, Buddhism, and education: *Dhamma* and social transformation within the Theravada tradition. In Z. Gross, L. Davies, & K. Diab (Eds.), *Gender, religion and education in a postmodern chaotic world* (pp. 55–72). New York, NY: Springer.

Strachan, J., Akao, S., Kilavanwa, B., & Warsal, D. (2010). You have to be a servant for all: Melanesian women's educational leadership experiences. *School Leadership and Management, 30*(1), 65–76.

United Nations. (2015). *Sustainable development goals: 17 goals to transform our world*. Retrieved from http://www.un.org/sustainabledevelopment

United Nations Development Programme. (2016). Human development report 2016: Human development for everyone. Retrieved from http://hdr.undp.org/sites/default/files/2016_human_development_report.pdf

Wadud, A. (2006). *Inside the gender jihad: Women's reform in Islam*. London, England: Oneworld Publications.

Yusof, R. (2013). *The current landscape of women in leadership and challenges in university management*. Keynote Address at International Higher Education Women in Leadership Summit, March 12, 2013, The Ritz-Carlton, Kuala Lumpur.

Yusoff, M. B., Abu-Hasan, F., & Jalil, S. A. (2000). *Globalisation, economic policy and equity: The case of Malaysia. Poverty and income inequality in developing countries: A policy dialogue on the effects of globalisation*; November 30–December 1, 2000, published by OECD Development Centre: 94, rue Chardon-Lagache, 75016 Paris. Retrieved from http://www.oecd.org/countries/malaysia/2682426.pdf

Chapter 18

Adopting a Paradigm Shift of Equality for Leadership

Equality Through Human Rights

Rogena Sterling

Leadership that implements equal treatment—that is, those who are equal be treated in an equal manner (Craven, 1995)—has failed communities. Leadership correlates with (in)equality. Under such a paradigm, leadership has the propensity to maintain or enhance inequality of the same or different groups. This is exemplified through gender inequality that persists despite the policies and programs that have been implemented. This chapter serves as an opportunity to introduce a paradigm shift in the understanding of equality to that of the Equality Principle from the International Bill of Rights. It is hoped that by illuminating core aspects associated with gender status and inequality, that opportunities for conversations and action in and through leadership can support all leaders regardless of their gender identity, to flourish in their work.

The connection between leadership and (in)equality is not due to it being hierarchical per se, but through the effect and impact on people's lives. Both directly and indirectly, leaders create or shape one's economic and social reality (Maak & Pless, 2006). This impacts on their public, private, and domestic lives.

This chapter illustrates that inequality has been perpetuated through certain leadership structures and social systems based on statuses. This is illustrated through the impact of gender inequality. Although over time, leadership may have adopted formal equality determined and measured by equal treatment, as it is based on statuses, inequality remains entrenched within society. Formal equality and the equal treatment paradigm has left gender equality elusive. The chapter recommends another method of understanding and determining equality: the equality principle (EP) based on the International Bill of Rights (IBOR).

This chapter argues that to improve equality, including gender equality, it must move away from equal treatment of equals or statuses to the EP as provided for through international human rights law. The EP provides a framework by which everyone can be equally valued, not in status and good, but in one's dignity of being. This enables and empowers individuals to their potentiality, and thus enables a community to flourish. When leadership not only acknowledges this but adopts this, it will enable all individuals to flourish as well as their community or organization.

LEADERSHIP AND FLOURISHING

The effect and impact on (in)equality can either enhance, inhibit, or deny flourishing. Flourishing (Eudaimonia or human flourishing from Aristotelian philosophy) is the mark of one's pursuit of a good life or the most desirable life (Dunn & Brody, 2008; Ostenfeld, 1994). It is an objective state, one marked by contentment and described as "doing well and living well" (Dunn & Brody, 2008, p. 414). The impact of (in)equality on flourishing not only affects individuals, but the community as well. As such equality, or the lack thereof, has a direct relationship with flourishing of both individuals and of communities.

Flourishing is an objective state which is chosen for itself (Ostenfeld, 1994). It is the mark of one's pursuit of a good life or the most desirable life (Dunn & Brody, 2008; Ostenfeld, 1994). It is always in a process and never complete, may be achieved in part, yet never achieved as a whole (Ostenfeld, 1994). The type of leadership and the environment in which the leadership operates determines the extent of flourishing. Moreover, equality is meaningless if there is no practical effect on people's lives. The practical effect comes through the enabling of flourishing. It is for this reason that if leadership is to focus on equality, it must enable people and communities to flourish.

The mark of a flourishing individual or community is well-being. Vicki Grieves's (2007) description of indigenous well-being illustrates this, "the social, emotional,

115

and cultural well-being of the whole community in which each individual is able to achieve their full potential as a human being, thereby bringing about total well-being of their community" (p. 109). Similarly, John Eekelaar (2002) writes that well-being includes "physical and mental health, the opportunity to establish and maintain important relationships, the ability to benefit from educational, social, and economic activity, to integrate into society and to achieve life plans" (p. 185).

These comments indicate that first the social, emotional, cultural, spiritual, and physical dimensions are interconnected within one's being and must be autonomously developed; and second, such development occurs in and through the community, and thus enhances the overall well-being of the community. As such, well-being and relatedness are integral to each other (Marshall, 2014). Hence, well-being can be considered as a barometer of a flourishing society. When all individual's well-being is increased, the overall well-being of the community is improved and the community flourishes.

The aim of flourishing is the actualization of potentiality. Potentiality requires the "cultivation and exercising of virtues that include personal growth, autonomy, and self-acceptance" (Dunn & Brody, 2008, p. 414). Flourishing that unlocks one's potentiality aims at a well-adapted and well-functioning life both socially and psychologically.

LEADERSHIP AND INEQUALITY

Leadership, in practice, does not always lead to flourishing individuals and communities. Leadership and its correlation to inequality is embedded within the structure and systems in which it operates and includes both individualist-based and collectivist-based societies. Understanding the connection between leadership and inequality explains how status and inequality are interconnected. Inequality subordinates people within the established or emerging system. It is an active process in which leaders are either directly or indirectly involved, creating and shaping people's economic and social reality which affects all aspects of a person's life. This reality is understood through a collective "what" of humanness (Becker, 2012) distinguished by statuses that provide positionality and power within such systems. It is through these statuses that people understand their economic and social reality.

STATUSES AND INEQUALITY

The statuses are normative categories (Becker, 2012) such as gender, race, and class. Each status is assigned

to one's physiological and psychological being usually at birth, based on lineage, gender, and social status (Guibernau, 2013). Status categories inhibit individuality and uniqueness (Guibernau, 2013) and deny the ability for a person to have "control over one's capacity to experience and express the self; to shape and direct personality, both socially and sexually; and to realize one's being and fate" (Valdes, 1996, p. 170). As such, statuses affect one's positionality and social functionality within society. The distinction through status, determines recognition (Chirkov, Ryan, Kim, & Kaplan, 2003) of who would be counted as equals (Griffin, 2001). It also enables or restricts the entitlements and duties available to such a status (Chirkov et al., 2003). In doing so, it leads to competition of status recognition through identity politics, one is pitted against another, for recognition and rights and entitlements.

Gender Status

Gender has been assumed to be based on two natural categories of male or female. Naoko Otobe of the International Labour Office states: "We are born as males and females, but we become girls, boys, women and men by learning from our families and societies" (Otobe, International Labour Office, & Employment Policy Department, 2014, p. 81). This wording is significant as it assumes that all humans can be divided into one of two categories biologically from which gender is established. However, this is far from the truth.

As with other human identities, gender has many variations and is a product of historical, political, and cultural human activity and forces and is "a set of arrangements by which the biological raw material of human sex and procreation is shaped by human social intervention" (Rubin, 1975, p. 165). Gender is thus the political means of organization that attributes political and economic significance to physiological and psychological characteristics to define male and female.

Although there are physical sex elements, they do not neatly fit into a sex binary of male and female. Rather there has been a sociopolitical fiat of gender status. As gender status has been established according to a sociopolitical construct, it has already created inequality by excluding those who do not fit into the binary of male and female. Examples of those who do not fit such a binary are people who are sexually diverse, including transgender or intersex. Serious inequality is experienced by intersex people.[1] They can be forced into surgery and medical treatments as young infants to make their bodies conform to an assigned sex given to them by medical professionals so as to uphold a gender status binary. Not only do they suffer the effects of this medical treatment for the rest of their lives, but they are expected to live in this gender status that may not match who they are. They can face discrimination by both males and females, and ultimately, they become outsiders.

People are coerced into one of the two categories that are assigned at birth and in which people are expected to live accordingly. It is here that the difference-blind system affects gender. On one hand, they are expected to be equal, or gender-blind, yet on the other, they are expected to live the gender status assigned. Moreover, as the gender status categories have been clearly demarcated, identity politics mandates a new category "other," sometimes referred to as gender identity. For example, this is to distinguish transwomen from "real" women. This segregates and subordinates transwomen. As such, despite all of the attempts to improve gender equality, any improvement has been at the expense of others, especially those at the margins and intersections of other identities. Under such a system, few individuals will flourish as autonomous beings. Only when people are recognized as and respected for who they are as dignified sex-diverse beings will it be possible to remove sex inequality.

FORMAL EQUALITY AND THE "EQUAL TREATMENT APPROACH"

Even as societies have realized the need to improve equality, the focus has been on only two areas: power relations and access to resources. Status has been ignored in much of the discussion. In fact, status has often been used to measure and determine equality. Where one's identity does not fit a particular status, a new status must be made to remedy issues of exclusion, discrimination, and inequality. Statuses have been the key area to determine equality in power relations and access to resources.

However, equality is not a new concept. It has been around for hundreds of years, yet it is not something that is simple to conceptualize, and as such has had many different understandings and variations over the years. Therefore, there has been little agreement on its meaning and aims (Fredman, 2002). It has variously been understood as:

> 'equality of treatment,' 'equality of access,' 'equality of result or achievement,' 'equality of opportunity,' 'absolute equality,' 'relative equality,' 'precise equality,' 'formal equality,' 'de facto equality' and 'de jure equality.' (Craven, 1995, p. 154)

Since the Enlightenment there has been a widespread adherence to the ideal of equality (Fredman, 2002, p. 4) that has been codified in nation-states as "formal equality."[2] Predominantly, formal equality has been understood as "equals must be treated equally" (Craven, 1995; Knight, 2009). These equals are understood as having equal status, for example, equal gender status. In considering distribution and fairness, the "good" or the "what" had to be equally distributed (Anderson, 2012), those of the same require the same.

However, gender inequality still persists today as an ordinal hierarchy between men and women in material resources, power, and status (Ridgeway, 2011). As Cecilia Ridgeway states, "Gender has many implications for people's lives, but one of the most consequential is that it acts as a basis for inequality between persons" (p. 3). Despite formal equality in the law of many nation-states, gender inequality is still pervasive. According to the United Nations Development Programme, "Gender inequality remains a major barrier to human development" (United Nations Development Programme, 2015). In all areas of their life, women and girls "are discriminated against in health, education, political representation, labour market, etc—with negative repercussions for development of their capabilities and their freedom of choice" (United Nations Development Programme, 2015).

THE EQUALITY PRINCIPLE

Inequality has thus been recognized as a big issue that can lead to conflict and war (Simma, Mosler, Paulus, Chaitidou, & United Nations, 2012). Numerous nation-states have codified formal equality as law but this has not substantively improved individuals' lives and cannot be effective in removing inequality while people are divided into statuses. To assess equality, nation-states use statuses to distinguish people. There are an increasing number of status groups, each one competing for recognition and access to power and resources. The equal treatment system understood and assessed through statuses has not remedied inequality. It has become apparent that equality had to be more than deserving equals having equal treatment.

For this reason, it is appropriate to turn to the IBOR for inspiration. The IBOR became the substantive principles by the Human Rights Committee and has become the conscience of the world (Slaughter, 2004; UN Secretary-General, 1955). It became the normative framework by which the world could live and operate together through a new legitimacy. This legitimacy was established in the UN Charter of the United Nations: "to reaffirm the faith in fundamental rights, in the dignity and worth of the human person, in equality and equal rights" (United Nations, 1948, Preamble).

The foundations of dignity and equality underpin each right or freedom, and the phrases therein, and become the guiding principles of the IBOR (Mårtenson, 1992). Dignity and equality became the new normative of the human person and essential in the formation of the human rights person within international human rights (Fredman, 2007). As such, equality is both one of the general principles and also an interpretive basis of the IBOR (Skogly, 1992). More attention has been paid to it than any other single category of rights (Skogly, 1992). It is through equality and dignity that the purpose is attained, the free and full development of one's personality. The rights and freedoms contained in the IBOR are inalienable. That is, although they could be violated, and thus requiring remedy, they could not be denied, transferred, or withdrawn, not even by a government (Morsink, 2009).

Dignity and equality are relational (Fredman, 2007). Anne Becker illustrates, "Human rights are relational as individuals can only claim rights in relation with, and to others" (Becker, 2012, p. 84). Relationality was introduced by the concept of fraternity into the Universal Declaration of Human Rights (UDHR) in the Preamble and Articles 1, 29, and 30 as a concept of "human family" or "spirit of brotherhood" (UN General Assembly, n.d.-b, Preamble, Article 1). Fraternity was a concept of reciprocity toward others to enable dignity and equality for others. This ensures that the rights and freedoms cannot be construed as to exclude particular groups or individuals from the application of international human rights (Lindholm, 1992). Thus, fraternity, equality, and dignity (Skogly, 1992) became the interpretive principles that underpin each right and freedom of the IBOR.

Equality within the IBOR was more of a moral than a legal entitlement. It became a principle running right through the heart of international human rights (Craven, 1995; Nowak, 2005), it is the EP. The EP states that the UN shall promote, "universal respect for, and observance of, human rights and fundamental freedoms for all without distinction as to race, sex, language, or religion" (United Nations, 1945 Art. 55 (c)).

At the San Francisco meeting of the Third Committee,[3] two key principles were laid out: all individuals should enjoy basic rights, and those rights should be enjoyed without distinction as to race, sex, language, or religion (McKean, 1983). The EP held prime position throughout the UN Charter (Skogly, 1992). The EP became enshrined within the International Bill of Rights (IBOR) (Conte, 2004; Craven, 1995; Skogly, 1992). The phrase "for all without distinction" can be broken into two parts. The term "for all" universalizes equality and establishes it as a basis of humanity without exception. The term "without distinction" establishes respect of persons, individuals, irrespective of difference as the central element of equality. This enabled equality to apply to everyone, no matter who they were.

The EP universalizes equality; there are no exceptions. The dignity and moral value of being human is the only thing that exists universally and can be equally distributed socially. The EP requires respect of all human beings and maintains the philosophy of no distinction in statuses. This was a rejection of status as a basis for understanding and resolving inequality. Specific articles of the IBOR provide mechanisms for protection from interference in the free and full development of personality, the goal and purpose of human rights.

LEADERSHIP AND FLOURISHING OF EQUAL BEINGS

As stated earlier, either directly or indirectly leadership creates and shapes one's life. The more traditional views of leadership, especially that of "leading the followers," can exacerbate inequality. Inequality is not a natural state, but it is created through a system that leaders uphold and maintain. Even if leadership uses formal equality and instruments such as equal treatment, inequality will remain. While leading for the greater good, or some other good, may lead to a subjective state of happiness or pleasure it is usually of a short duration (Dunn & Brody, 2008) and does not necessarily lead to flourishing.

The difference-blind approach has not challenged inequality; rather it imposes particular status ideals backed up by an ideology of what people are and what they require. Colleen Larson and Khaula Murtadha (2002) wrote about this in relation to educational leadership stating, "Researchers have also found that our enduring belief in stable, universal, and difference-blind systems of education has contributed to the profession's failure to challenge inequality based on class, race, ethnicity, and gender" (p. 138).

CONCLUSION

There is a need for a new generation of leadership that will enable individuals and communities to flourish. Such leadership respects people for who they are, not for the statuses they have been assigned and requires a shift in the paradigm of equality toward the EP. Aristotle advocated that leadership that enables flourishing is the most desirable life. It is the objective end state enabling the actualization of one's and the community's potentialities resulting in a state of well-being.

The paradigm shift of equality does not universalize identities such as gender. Rather it celebrates gender (and sex) in its diversity. There is no universalized distinction of gender categories, it enables people to flourish whether they are male, female, or nonbinary gender. There is no distinction, irrespective of the diversity of sex and gender. When leadership begins to apply the EP only then will people flourish.

NOTES

1. Intersex people are those who have sexual characteristics that cannot clearly be defined as male or female. As such, they have characteristics of both sexes.

2. The majority of nation-states have some reference to formal equality in their constitution or within a piece of legislation.

3. Referring to the UNCIO Documents: pp. iv, 13.

REFERENCES

Anderson, E. (2012). Equality. In D. M. Estlund (Ed.), *The Oxford handbook of political philosophy* (pp. 40–57). New York, NY: Oxford University Press.

Becker, A. (2012). Identity premised on equality of difference as a fundamental human right. In C. Roux (Ed.), *Safe spaces* (pp. 83–95). Sense Publishers. Retrieved from https://link .springer.com/chapter/10.1007/978-74-6091-93-6-6

Chirkov, V., Ryan, R. M., Kim, Y., & Kaplan, U. (2003). Differentiating autonomy from individualism and independence: A self-determination theory perspective on internalization of cultural orientations and well-being. *Journal of Personality and Social Psychology, 84*(1), 97–110. https:// doi.org/10.1037/0022-3514.84.1.97

Conte, A. (2004). Privacy, honour and reputation. In A. Conte, S. Davidson, & R. Burchill (Eds.), *Defining civil and political rights: The jurisprudence of the United Nations Human Rights Committee* (pp. 201–218). Burlington, VT: Ashgate.

Craven, M. C. R. (1995). *The international covenant on economic, social, and cultural rights: A perspective on its development.* New York, NY: Oxford University Press.

Dunn, D. S., & Brody, C. (2008). Defining the good life following acquired physical disability. *Rehabilitation Psychology, 53*(4), 413–425. doi:10.1037/a0013749

Eekelaar, J. (2002). Personal rights and human rights. *Human Rights Law Review, 2*(2), 181–197.

Fredman, S. (2002). *Discrimination law.* New York, NY: Oxford University Press.

Fredman, S. (2007). Redistribution and recognition: Reconciling inequalities. *South African Journal on Human Rights, 23*(2), 214–234.

Grieves, V. (2007). What is indigenous wellbeing? In J. S. Te Rito (Ed.), *Mātauranga Taketake—traditional knowledge: Indigenous indicators of well-being: Perspectives, practices, solutions, 2006.* Auckland, New Zealand: Ngā Pae o te Māramatanga.

Griffin, J. (2001). First steps in an account of human rights. *European Journal of Philosophy, 9*(3), 306–327. https://doi .org/10.1111/1468-0378.00139

Guibernau, M. M. (2013). *Belonging: Solidarity and division in modern societies.* Cambridge, UK: Polity Press.

Knight, C. (2009). Describing equality. *Law and Philosophy, 28*(4), 327–365.

Larson, C. L., & Murtadha, K. (2002). Leadership for social justice. *Yearbook of the National Society for the Study of Education, 101*(1), 134–161. https://doi.org/10 .1111/j.1744-7984.2002.tb00007.x

Lindholm, T. (1992). Article 1—A new beginning. In A. Eide, T. Swinehart, G. Alfredsson, G. Melander, L. A. Rehof, & A. Rosas (Eds.), *The Universal Declaration of Human Rights: A commentary.* Oslo, Norway: Scandinavian University Press.

Maak, T., & Pless, N. M. (2006). Responsible leadership in a stakeholder society—A relational perspective. *Journal of Business Ethics, 66*(1), 99–115. doi:10.1007/s10551-006-9047-z

Marshall, J. (2014). *Human rights law and personal identity.* New York, NY: Routledge.

Mårtenson, J. (1992). The preamble of the universal declaration of human rights and the UN human rights programme. In A. Eide, T. Swinehart, G. Alfredsson, G. Melander, L. A. Rehof, & A. Rosas (Eds.), *The Universal Declaration of Human Rights: A commentary.* Oslo, Norway: Scandinavian University Press.

McKean, W. A. (1983). *Equality and discrimination under international law.* New York, NY: Oxford University Press.

Morsink, J. (2009). *Inherent human rights: Philosophical roots of the universal declaration.* Philadelphia, PA: University of Pennsylvania Press.

Nowak, M. (2005). *U.N. covenant on civil and political rights: CCPR commentary.* Kehl, Germany: N. P. Engel.

Ostenfeld, E. (1994). Aristotle on the good life and quality of life. In L. Nordenfelt (Ed.), *Concepts and measurement of quality of life in health care* (pp. 19–34). Netherlands: Springer. doi:10.1007/978-94-015-8344-2_2

Otobe, N., International Labour Office, & Employment Policy Department. (2014). *Resource guide on gender issues in employment and labour market policies working towards women's economic empowerment and gender equality.* Geneva: International Labour Office.

Ridgeway, C. L. (2011). *Framed by gender: How gender inequality persists in the modern world.* New York, NY: Oxford University Press.

Rubin, G. (1975). The traffic in women: Notes on the "political economy" of sex. In R. R. Reiter (Ed.), *Toward an anthropology of women* (pp. 157–210). New York, NY: Monthly Review Press.

Simma, B., Mosler, H., Paulus, A., Chaitidou, E., & United Nations (Eds.). (2012). *The Charter of the United Nations: A commentary* (vol. 1). Oxford, England: Oxford University Press.

Skogly, S. (1992). Article 2. In A. Eide, T. Swinehart, G. Alfredsson, G. Melander, L. A. Rehof, & A. Rosas (Eds.), *The Universal Declaration of Human Rights: A commentary.* Oslo, Norway: Scandinavian University Press.

Slaughter, J. (2004). *The textuality of human rights: Founding narratives of human personality.* Interdisciplinary Law and

Humanities Junior Scholar Workshop Paper. Unpublished. Retrieved from http://ssrn.com/abstract=582021 or http://dx.doi.org/10.2139/ssrn.582021

UN Secretary-General. (1955, July 1). *Annotations on the text of the draft international covenants on human rights.* UN General Assembly, Official Records.

United Nations. (1948). *Yearbook of the United Nations 1946–1947* (No. 1947. L 18). Retrieved from http://www.un multimedia.org/searchers/yearbook/page.jsp?volume=1946-47&page=1

United Nations Development Programme. (2015). *Gender inequality index (GII).* Human Development Reports. Retrieved November 30, 2016, from http://hdr.undp.org/en/content/gender-inequality-index-gii

Valdes, F. (1996). Unpacking hetero-patriarchy: Tracing the conflation of sex, gender & (and) sexual orientation to its origins. *Yale Journal of Law & the Humanities, 8*(1), 161–211.

Chapter 19

Affirmative Action

An Effective Policy for Gender Parity in Leadership in Ontario's Public Education System?

Katie Higginbottom

This chapter examines the role of policy in supporting women educational leaders in Canada. Women are being promoted to principal positions within Ontario, Canada's K–12 public education system more today than ever before. In light of Ontario's progress toward gender parity among middle managers and principals in publicly funded school boards, this chapter aims to explore women in educational leadership, above the level of the principal, in the organizational hierarchy in Ontario's publicly funded school boards.

More specifically, this chapter describes the influence, if any, of the 1993 PPM 102 Affirmative Action/Employment Equity for Women Employees legislation, which is credited as having contributed to greater gender equity at the level of principal (Richter, 2007), had on women in top leadership positions in Ontario school boards. PPM 102 was revoked in September 2009, yet the number of women in the principalship continued to climb. The influence of PPM 102 is judged by the percentage of women who rose to top leadership positions after the policy was implemented, and as told by women directors of education.

The Ontario Ministry of Education takes pride in their efforts toward equity. In 2009, the Ontario Ministry of Education issued Ontario's Equity and Inclusive Education Strategy aimed at all schools in all Ontario school boards. This resulting strategy called for:

> the ministry to provide direction, support, and guidance to the education sector, so that every student has a positive learning environment in which to achieve his or her highest potential; each school board to develop and implement an equity and inclusive education policy and guidelines for the board and its schools; and each school to create and support a positive school climate that fosters and promotes equity, inclusive education, and diversity. (Ontario Ministry of Education, 2009, p. 11)

Since Ontario's Equity and Inclusive Education Strategy was released in 2009, the same year that PPM 102 was removed, it is possible that this strategy was seen as sufficient in addressing gender equity among employees as well, though no section of this document directly addresses gender equity among employees.

In Ontario, the director of education position is the highest non-elected leadership position in school boards, followed by associate directors, superintendents, principals, and vice principals. The director of education answers to a publicly elected board of trustees, as well as to a publicly elected Minister of Education.

GENDER IN LEADERSHIP POSITIONS IN ONTARIO SCHOOL BOARDS

Nine years ago, it was argued that gender parity among public school principals was close to being achieved in Ontario (The Learning Partnership, 2008). However, educational administration scholars noted women's underrepresentation in administrative positions; women are not represented in leadership positions in schools proportionate to their representation in the teaching profession (Grogan & Shakeshaft, 2011; Smith, 2011).

Data provided by the Ontario Ministry of Education support this claim. In the 2012/2013 school year, women held 81 percent of the elementary teaching positions, yet held only 65 percent of the vice principal/principal positions; likewise, in the secondary school panel, women held 55 percent of the teaching positions, yet only 48 percent of the vice principal/principal positions (Ontario Ministry of Education, 2013). Even though women hold more than half the leadership positions in schools in the elementary panel (65 percent), males, who comprise only 19 percent of the elementary teaching staff, hold 35 percent of the leadership positions in the elementary system (Ontario Ministry of Education, 2013). Conversely, women hold 65 percent of the elementary leadership positions yet 81 percent of the elementary teaching positions (Ontario Ministry of Education, 2013). Further, women principals tend to have more teaching experience (15 years) than their male counterparts (five years) (Pigford & Tonnsen, 1993; Young & McLeod, 2001), yet teaching experience is devalued in the process of being hired in administration (Pigford & Tonnsen, 1993; Young & McLeod, 2001).

Movement toward gender parity has increased radically in the past 35 years. For example, in 1980 women comprised 67 percent of the elementary teaching positions but only held 7 percent of principal positions and 20 percent of vice principal positions in Ontario (Richter, 2007). How did such progress, from 1980 to today, occur? In 1993, in an effort to promote women in educational leadership in Ontario, the provincial government passed legislation put forward by the Ministry of Education (PPM 102: Affirmative Action/Employment Equity for Women Employees), "which required school boards to have employment equity plans in place for women" (Richter, 2007, p. 4). In Canada, affirmative action is defined as "a policy designed to increase the representation of groups that have suffered discrimination" (Alexandrowicz, 2004, p. 217). In Canada, affirmative action is defined as "a policy designed to increase the representation of groups that have suffered discrimination" (Alexandrowicz, 2004, p. 217).

The Education Act was revised to "develop and implement a policy of employment equity for women and other groups designated by the Minister, to submit the policy to the Minister for approval and to implement changes to the policy as directed by the Minister" (Ministry of Education, 1993, p. 12). Along with the hard work of the Federation of Women Teachers' Association of Ontario (FWTAO) during the 1980s, this legislation is cited by the Elementary Teacher's Federation of Ontario (ETFO) as contributing to the large increase in women principals in Ontario in the 1990s (Richter, 2007). By 1996 women held 60.4 percent of the vice principal positions and 42 percent of the principal positions in elementary public schools (Richter, 2007). These numbers have continued to rise, even though the legislation was revoked in September 2009.

This research explored gender above vice principals, principals, and superintendents in the organizational hierarchy in Ontario school boards. Given the ample data surrounding women in leadership and the pressures they experience in their leadership roles, contextual findings are important and this work sought primarily to understand how women Directors of Education in Ontario have managed pressures associated with leadership.

In analyzing results, two unexpected findings emerged: first, there is a fairly high number of women who are currently serving as Directors of Education (42 percent) in

Ontario school boards; and second, the majority of their testimonies indicated that women Directors of Education in Ontario did not experience pressures associated with their gender (Higginbottom, forthcoming). Both of these findings contradict the majority of literature about women in leadership (Eagly & Carli, 2007; Ely, Ibarra, & Kolb, 2011). The purpose of this chapter is to describe these findings, and to discuss the impact, if any, PPM 102 had on women in top leadership positions in Ontario school boards, as judged by the women who made it to top leadership positions after the policy was implemented, and as told through their perspectives.

PPM 102: AFFIRMATIVE ACTION/EMPLOYMENT EQUITY FOR WOMEN EMPLOYEES

Throughout Canadian history as a result of official organizational policies, certain groups, such as women, have been discriminated against in the workplace. Additionally, women have been discriminated against through the day-to-day interactions of an organization (Alexandrowicz, 2004). According to Abella's (1984) Report of Commission on Equality in Employment, which laid the foundation for Canada's Employment Equity Act of 1986, four groups were systemically discriminated against: women, people with disabilities, Aboriginal people, and visible minorities. According to the report, the goal for women under an employment equity law would be as follows:

> For women, equality in employment means first a revised approach to the role women play in the workforce. It means taking them seriously as workers and not assuming that their primary interests lie away from the workplace. At the same time, it means acknowledging and accommodating the changing role of women in the care of the family by helping both them and their male partners to function effectively both as labour force participants and as parents. And it means providing the education and training to permit women the chance to compete for the widest possible range of job options. In practice this means the active recruitment of women into the fullest range of employment opportunities, equal pay for work of equal value, fair consideration for promotions into more responsible positions, participation in corporate policy decision-making through corporate task forces and committees, accessible childcare of adequate quality, paid parental leaves for either parent, and equal pensions and benefits. (Abella, 1984, p. 4)

The Employment Equity Act, implemented in 1986, and later amended in 1995, "require[s] positive efforts on the part of employers to reduce disparities in employment and workforce representation between designated groups [women, people with disabilities, Aboriginal people, and visible minorities] and the general workforce regardless of its causes" (Jain, Lawler, Bai, & Lee, 2010, p. 304).

Unlike Human Rights law which requires people to file a complaint to a Human Rights Commission or Tribunal to enjoy the equal rights promoted by the Canadian Human Rights Act, the Employment Equity Act is recognized as a strategy to overcompensate with the purpose of correcting past discrimination (Jain et al., 2010). Unlike the Canadian Human Rights Act of 1978, employment equity laws go beyond reactively protecting human rights to proactively reducing or eliminating workplace discrimination. It is important to note that federal employment equity only has regulatory jurisdiction over banking, communications and transportation, and most federal governments departments and agencies (Jain et al., 2010). Therefore, there are many Canadian employers who are not required by law to follow the Employment Equity Act. School boards in Ontario only began proactive reduction of discrimination after employment equity was adopted by the Ontario provincial government.

Employment equity, or affirmative action policies, have passionate proponents and ardent critics. Proponents argue that past discrimination is able to be rectified through employment equity laws that require selection processes to be more transparent and fair (Crosby & Clayton, 2004; Crosby, Iyer, Clayton, & Downey, 2003), preventing future discrimination while allowing for a more diverse workplace (Miller, 1997; Moscoso, Garcia-Izquierdo, & Bastida, 2010). Opponents of these policies argue that they are unfair because they preference one group over another, failing to consider meritocracy in selection processes, resulting in the discriminated against group having their competence questioned when hired (Moscoso et al., 2010; Sowell, 2004; Zelnick, 1996). Critics claim affirmative action policies are reverse discrimination, which run contrary to principles of fairness (Crosby, Iyer, & Sincharoen, 2006).

Additionally, those against employment equity may charge that the people benefitting from affirmative action policies are not the same people who were disadvantaged by the original discrimination, nor are those disadvantaged as a result of affirmative action policies those responsible for the original discrimination (Alexandrowicz, 2004). Along this rationale, some critics argue that "today's middle-class, heterosexual, white males are paying the price in the workforce for attitudes and behaviours of their ancestors toward the poor, homosexuals, non-white races, and women" (Alexandrowicz, 2004, p. 220). Proponents of affirmative action dismiss these arguments, claiming critics' opinions are prejudiced (Moscoso et al., 2010).

In the 1980s and early 1990s, grassroots advocating by the FWTAO brought gender disparity in leadership in Ontario public school boards to the attention of the Ontario government. As a result, in 1993 the Ontario government's PPM 102: Affirmative Action/Employment Equity for Women Employees demanded that school boards put in place employment equity plans for women (Richter, 2007). In turn, the Education Act was revised to "develop and implement a policy of employment equity for women and other groups designated by the Minister, to submit the policy to the Minister for approval and to implement changes to the policy as directed by the Minister" (Ministry of Education, 1993, p. 12).

According to Oliver (1991), organizations must respond to competing external demands and expectations; because of this competition among multiple external demands there is a range of strategic responses organizations can take in response to pressure to conform. These responses include acquiescence, compromising, avoiding, defying, and manipulating. It is possible that, dependent on the degree to which movement toward gender equity was in demand, Ontario public school boards went from acquiescing, to compromising, to avoiding over the 23-year span since PPM 102 was initially implemented. Acquiescence, which can include "mimicking institutional models [and] obeying rules and accepting norms" (Oliver, 1991, p. 152), can be thought to have happened initially after the implementation of PPM 102. It is likely the external pressure to take action toward gender equity at least partially came from other institutional models, and Ontario public school boards' desire to fit into the widely occurring equity movement. Obeying rules and accepting norms that came as a result of PPM 102 likely followed.

In 2009, PPM 102 ended. As gender parity among administrators became apparent in Ontario public school boards, it is possible that the boards moved toward the response of compromise including "balancing the expectations of multiple constituents . . . [and] negotiating with institutional stakeholders" (Oliver, 1991, p. 152). Something more pressing than gender parity likely took precedence over PPM 102 once progress was apparent. A negotiation among the Board of Trustees may have occurred at this time to make the decision to remove PPM 102.

Finally, today it could be said that avoidance is the response Ontario public school boards use when it comes to gender parity. Avoidance involves "disguising nonconformity [and] loosening institutional attachment" (Oliver, 1991, p. 152). By not making the details of PPM 102 publicly available, the Ontario Ministry of Education disguises what action it took (and is no longer taking) toward gender equity. By not keeping publicly acces-

124   *Chapter 19*

sible data that documents the gender statistics among top levels of leadership, the Ministry further loosens institutional attachment to the goal of gender parity. Is it possible that the term "affirmative action" carries such stigma (Abella, 1984) that the Ministry would like to distance itself as far away from it as possible?

RESEARCH METHODOLOGY

In order to answer the preliminary research question, "What percentage of the Director of Education positions in Ontario's 60 (English) publicly funded school boards have women filled since 1990?" a table was created listing the 60 English-speaking school boards in Ontario in the left-hand column, and the school years from 2016/2017 back to 1990/1991 across the top. Unfortunately, several boards did not respond, several boards did not have all of the information, especially the more distant history, readily available, and a few boards would not comment on the gender of any of their directors citing ethical reasons. In cases where gender was not commented upon or confirmed by school boards, I used my own judgment to assess gender based on first names or photos online.

This case study was conducted using qualitative research methods. Rather than seeing case studies as a research method, Stake (2005) sees a case study as a unit of study or "a choice of what is to be studied" (p. 443). Women Directors of Education in Ontario's English school boards were chosen largely because of Ontario school boards' adoption of PPM 102. The implementation of this employment equity policy 23 years ago makes the case of women Director of Educations' experiences within Ontario's English school boards potentially quite different from the experiences of Directors of Education in other Canadian provinces.

The Ontario (English) public school board was very purposefully selected as it offers insight into the effects of the 1993 employment equity movement on the leadership experiences of those who arguably benefited from the movement, even decades later. Participants needed to identify as women, and currently work as or have very recently retired from the Director of Education position in an Ontario English school board. The group from which to draw potential participants was small to begin with, limited to 25 individuals, of whom I aimed to interview 12 to 15. Women Directors of Education who were brand new to the position that year were included in the invitation to participate and in the final sample.

Of the 12 participants who completed the interview in person or over the telephone, five had spent their careers in an Ontario English Catholic school board, while seven had spent their careers in an Ontario English public school board. Participants ranged in age from their mid-40s to late 60s, with their average age being 57.8 at the time of the interview. The average length of time participants had served as director was 6.04 years. One participant was single and the rest were married; all but one had between one and six children or stepchildren, ranging in age from eight to 41 years old. Four had grandchildren.

Semistructured interviews were engaged as the primary research tool as using interviews accomplishes one of the goals of feminist research, that being to give women a voice (Butler, 2004; Walby, 2011). Using semistructured interviews goes a step further, empowering women Directors of Education to share ownership over the direction of the research due to the flexibility the format afforded the participants and researcher.

RESEARCH FINDINGS

In the 1993/1994 school year, only 10 of 60 (16.6 percent) school boards were able to offer the gender history data of their directors. Notably, in the 1993/1994 school year, the year PPM 102 was implemented, all 10 directors were male. By the 1996/1997 school year, 28 out of 60 (46.6 percent) school boards provided gender history data of their directors, and four of those 28 (14.3 percent) were women. One year later, in the 1997/1998 school year, 32 of 60 (53.3 percent) school boards provided gender history data of their directors, five of those 32 (15.6 percent) were women. Five years later, in the 2002/2003 school year, 54 of 60 (90 percent) school boards provided gender history data of their directors: 13 of those 54 (24 percent) were women. Ten years after PPM 102 was implemented, in the 2003/2004 school year, 54 of 60 (90 percent) of school boards were able to offer gender history data of their directors, 17 of those 54 (31.5 percent) were women.

Fifteen years after PPM 102 was implemented, in the 2009/2010 school year, 59 of 60 (98.3 percent) school boards were able to offer gender history data of their directors, 25 of those 59 (42.3 percent) were women. Twenty years after PPM 102 was implemented, in the 2014/2015 school year, each of the 60 school boards (100 percent) were able to offer gender history data of their directors, 23 of them (38.3 percent) were women. In the school year immediately prior to this study, the 2014/2015 school year, all 60 schools were able to offer gender history data of their directors: 25 (41.6 percent) were women.

Finally, using the most recent data from the 2015/2016 school year, all 60 school boards were able to offer gender history data of their directors, and 26 (43 percent) Directors of Education were women. This data shows a slow but steady increase, beginning in 1993/1994, when

0 percent of the directors were women, to 2015/2016, when 43 percent of directors were women. This data suggests that PPM 102, implemented in 1993, did have a positive impact on the number of women in the directorship position in Ontario school boards.

Of the 12 study participants, four indicated PPM 102 did not have any influence on their career, seven indicated that PPM 102 may have had an indirect effect on their career, and one indicated that PPM 102 had a direct effect on her career. As such, I have organized this section into the following categories: No Effect, A Possible Indirect Effect, and A Direct Effect. In the following sections, explanations provided by participants that fell into each of these categories are shared.

No Effect

One-third (four) of all participants did not believe that PPM 102 had any effect on their own career success. Some of the older participants had been promoted long before 1993, when PPM 102 was implemented. For example, one participant was promoted to a superintendent position in the late 1980s, and when asked whether affirmative action had any effect on her career her response was:

> No that was ages ago! NO! I don't think that was helpful at this level . . . I'm sure it was helpful to many people in many areas. It was neither helpful nor prohibitive because once you get into senior management it's about competency. You cannot have quotas based on gender in senior management. You might be able to have that in some jobs, but the person whom you work for has to sleep at night. I would not hire anybody based on any of those isms, because I didn't have such and such kind of a person. I would hire the best person.

Not only did this participant not believe affirmative action had helped her in any way, she expressed a skepticism that affirmative action could effectively be used to hire for senior leadership positions at all. When I asked this same participant whether she recalled the affirmative action movement in the 1990s, she explained her role in helping to develop affirmative action plans:

> I remember it because I had a committee and I developed policies and an implementation plan. . . . I can't remember what was in my plan but it had to do with increasing the number of women administrators in the secondary path because that is where we didn't have them. . . . So I got more women into being high school principals, which was a job class which was under represented by the female gender.

The contradiction between stating she would hire the best person and then stating that she helped more women into being high school principals through affirmative action policies are, to say the least, juxtaposed.

Two other participants brought up timing. After one participant replied that affirmative action policies had not helped her in her career success, she elaborated, "I seem to always be just far [enough] ahead of the curve that things are developed after I'm already there. My whole career has been like that. . . . Yeah, and see that would really bother me if I got hired because I was a woman. If everything was equal and I got hired because I was a woman, I would rather not have been hired."

Another participant claimed, "In my situation, there were not any affirmative action policies in place. And, I certainly would want to have been hired to be a leader based on my skills and experience, not because I am of a certain gender." For these participants, the idea of being hired because of their gender was not a welcome idea.

One participant was first promoted just a few years prior to PPM 102 beginning. When I asked whether any grassroots movements, which led to the affirmative action movement, had perhaps helped her, she said, "honestly it didn't." When I elaborated, asking whether she may have been aware of the movement as a vice principal or principal and asked to identify appropriate women candidates and suggest they begin the leadership training to become a principal, she replied:

> No. It was always, "what's the criteria?" And that is where I loved when the frameworks came in because [before that] our criterion wasn't that clear. And I think that we have made great strides . . . and I think that we can improve them but just the idea that there are actually some specific knowledge, skills and practices that you expect of a school and system leaders—is really a very, very good thing.

This comment emphasizes this particular participant's belief that leadership frameworks, rather than any sort of affirmative action movement, should guide hiring processes. For each of these participants, in addition to rejecting the notion that affirmative action could have helped them in their career success, they expressed a preference for a meritocratic approach to hiring over any affirmative action movement.

A Possible Indirect Effect

Though indicating a specific occasion during which affirmative action helped their career was not easy for most participants, the majority (56 percent) reported that in some way, perhaps indirectly, affirmative action policies likely helped them. For example, one participant reported, "It might have at very senior level because it would've brought awareness. . . . It brings a level of awareness to the senior team and the Director that perhaps wasn't there before, but I don't have a recollection of me benefiting directly from affirmative action strategies."

Another participant echoed the point that affirmative action policies bring awareness. "It would be hard to say, but I'm a big believer in having the frameworks in place to support the work so I would say policy is really important for that. . . . I think that having a framework in society to move our thinking along—because it takes a long time to move our thinking along—is really helpful. So [affirmative action] really in the background, supported me along the way."

This participant believes that frameworks, such as the leadership frameworks (which guide the work of educational leaders), are very helpful in changing the way people think about an issue. During her interview, she compared leadership frameworks to affirmative action policies, in that, though helpful, they do not entirely resolve all issues surrounding leadership. This participant acknowledged that the policy likely supported her all the way along her leadership journey by changing (progressing) the way others thought about leadership and who could be a leader.

Participants in this group, who recognized affirmative action played an indirect role in their career success, generally replied with a comment similar to:

> I don't know if [affirmative action] directly helped. Certainly, I don't think that it hurt. Absolutely didn't hurt. I know the board had affirmative action policies in place, as well as a steering committee and the goal at the time was to have more women principals because the board was still predominantly male in that position. So certainly, that must have contributed to the pathway that unfolded. But to say directly that I got to the position I got to because of affirmative action, I don't think that I could say that.

This participant acknowledged that the affirmative action policy Ontario had in place from 1993 to 2009 "may have contributed to the pathway that unfolded," though she did not see a direct relationship between affirmative action and her getting any leadership position. For women in this category, it was very important that their own merit be acknowledged. One participant claimed, "I think it partially had to do with gender but also a great deal of competence." The participants' emphasis on their competence illustrates how central equal ability (competence) was throughout PPM 102's application in Ontario (English) public school boards. Participants were almost never able to identify a direct effect of affirmative action on their career.

A Direct Effect

In response to a question about whether she would say that affirmative action played a role in her career success, one participant was clear:

Yes I would. One day my principal, who was a fantastic guy, a really good mentor and supporter, and a very good leader, gave me a letter of encouragement to go into administration, saying that we need female principals. Apparently, the principals had been requested at a district meeting to put forward the names of potential future female leaders from their schools. He said to me, "You are amazing and I'm putting your name forward to the board. You need to do this."

Of all 12 participants, there was only one whose experience with affirmative action was so transparent.

DISCUSSION AND CONCLUSION

Of the 12 study participants, four indicated PPM 102 had no effect on their careers, seven indicated that PPM 102 may have had an indirect effect on their careers, and only one indicated that PPM 102 had a direct effect on her career. There are a number of potential reasons why so few participants saw a direct effect of affirmative action.

It is important to note that during interviews it became apparent that PPM 102 as a policy was not well known among Directors of Education in Ontario public school boards. This may help explain why 11 out of 12 participants did not feel PPM 102 had a direct effect on their careers. If the Ministry of Education is aiming to downplay any role affirmative action performed in their history because of stigma associated with the concept, it is possible that those working in the organization understood and adopted this stigma at a personal level.

One argument against affirmative action/employment equity is that those who benefit may be thought to be less competent (Moscoso et al., 2010; Sowell, 2004). It is likely that participants did not want to identify their success directly with affirmative action/employment equity. There is evidence to suggest this was the case as 11 out of 12 participants expressed preference for meritocratic hiring, rather than hiring based on affirmative action. It is also possible that since most women deny gender discrimination even when it is occurring (Crosby, 1984), participants did not see themselves as in need of affirmative action/ employment equity, and therefore did not see themselves as ever having directly benefitted from it. Finally, it is possible that participants truly did not benefit from the affirmative action/employment equity movements in their school boards.

The pros of affirmative action/employment equity, as revealed in this case study, mostly surround the steady increase of women in directorship positions over the 20 years following the implementation of PPM 102. Though the policy was meant to help get women in the principal position in Ontario school boards, the effects of the policy can be seen higher up the leadership hierarchy. The cons of affirmative action/employment equity, as revealed in this case study, mostly surround the fact that there seems to be a prevailing assumption that affirmative action negates competence. The majority of women Directors of Education refused to acknowledge any direct role that PPM 102 played in their careers, which may reflect the notion that affirmative action negates competence. Additionally, while some women Directors of Education acknowledged that PPM 102 likely helped their careers in an indirect way, many felt the need to ensure their competence was not questioned, which again reflects the limited understanding that people have of affirmative action.

More case study research is needed in contexts where an affirmative action/employment equity policy has been adopted. The interesting question is, if affirmative action has increased the number of women in administrative positions, why do some women in those positions resist acknowledging its role in their career paths?

REFERENCES

Abella, R. S. (1984). *Report of the commission on equality in employment.* Ottawa: Government of Canada. Retrieved from https://archive.org/details/reportofcommissi00cana

Alexandrowicz, G. W. (2004). *Dimensions of law: Canadian and international law of the 21st century.* Toronto, Canada: Emond Montgomery Publications.

Butler, J. (2004). *Undoing gender.* New York, NY: Routledge.

Crosby, F. J., & Clayton, S. (2004). Affirmative action and the search for educational equity. *Analyses of Social Issues and Public Policy, 4*(1), 243–249.

Crosby, F. J., Iyer, A., Clayton, S., & Downey, R. A. (2003). Affirmative action: Psychological data and policy debates. *American Psychology, 58*(2), 93–115.

Crosby, F. J., Iyer, A., & Sincharoen, S. (2006). Understanding affirmative action. *Annual Review of Psychology, 57,* 585–611.

Crosby, P. B. (1984). *Quality without tears: The art of hassle-free management.* New York, NY: McGraw-Hill.

Eagly, A. H., & Carli, L. L. (2007). *Through the labyrinth: The truth about how women become leaders.* Boston, MA: Harvard Business School Press.

Ely, R. J., Ibarra, H., & Kolb, D. M. (2011). Taking gender into account: Theory and design for women's leadership development programs. *Academy of Management Learning and Education, 10*(3), 474–493.

Grogan, M., & Shakeshaft, C. (2011). *Women and educational leadership.* San Francisco, CA: Jossey-Bass.

Higginbottom, K. (Forthcoming). *Strategies women directors of education use to manage the pressures of leadership* (Un-

published doctoral dissertation). Ontario Institute for Studies in Education, Toronto, ON.

Jain, H. C., Lawler, J. J., Bai, B., & Lee, E. K. (2010). Effectiveness of Canada's employment equity legislation for women (1997–2004). *Implications for policy makers. Industrial Relations, 65*(2), 304–329.

Miller, F. (1997). The political rhetoric of affirmative action: Infusing the debate with discussions about equity and opportunity. *American Behavioural Science, 41*(2), 197–204.

Ministry of Education. (1993). The status of women and affirmative action/employment in Ontario school boards: Report to the legislature by the Minister of Education. Toronto: Queen's Printer for Ontario.

Moscoso, S., Garcia-Izquierdo, A. L., & Bastida, M. (2010). Reactions toward affirmative action measures for women. *Revista de Psicología del Trabajo y de las Organizaciones (Journal of Work and Organisational Psychology), 26*(3), 211–221.

Oliver, C. (1991). Strategic responses to institutional processes. *The Academy of Management Review, 16*(1), 145–179.

Ontario Ministry of Education. (2009). Realising the promise of diversity: Ontario's equity and inclusive education strategy. Toronto, ON: Queen's Printer for Ontario. Retrieved from http://www.edu.gov.on.ca/eng/policyfunding/equity.pdf

Ontario Ministry of Education. (2013). *Quickfacts: Ontario schools 2012–13.* Retrieved February 1, 2015, from http://www.edu.gov.on.ca/eng/general/elemsec/quick facts/2012-13/quickFacts12_13.pdf

Pigford, A. B., & Tonnsen, S. (1993). *Women in school leadership: Survival and advancement guidebook.* Lancaster: Technomic.

Richter, B. (2007, June). It's elementary: A brief history of Ontario's public elementary teachers and their federations. *ETFO Voice* (Magazine of the Elementary Teachers' Federation of Ontario), 1–8.

Smith, E. (2011). Teaching critical reflection. *Teaching in Higher Education, 16*(2), 211–223.

Sowell, T. (2004). *Affirmative action around the world: An empirical study.* New Haven, CT: Yale University Press.

Stake, R. E. (2005). Qualitative case studies. In N. K. Denzin & Y. S. Lincoln (Eds.), *The Sage handbook of qualitative research* (pp. 443–466). Thousand Oaks, CA: Sage.

The Learning Partnership. (2008). *Succession planning: Schools and school boards.* Retrieved August 15, 2013, from http://live.iel.immix.ca/storage/2/1284604374/Succes sionPlanningReport.pdf

Walby, S. (2011). *The future of feminism.* Cambridge, MA: Polity Press.

Young, M. D., & McLeod, S. (2001). Flukes, opportunities and planned interventions: Factors affecting women's decisions to become school administrators. *Educational Administration Quarterly, 37*(4), 462–502.

Zelnick, B. (1996). *Backfire: A reporter's look at affirmative action.* Washington, DC: Regnery Publications.

Chapter 20

Interrupting Whiteness

An Auto-Ethnography of a Black Female Leader in Higher Education

Victoria Showunmi

In recent years, there has been a burgeoning literature on race and ethnicity in the British education system. While the plethora of research on race in compulsory schooling abounds, higher education remains largely and inconspicuously absent from the debate. Increasingly, however, the nature and extent of racism in the structure of academia in the United Kingdom are emerging in more recent literature.

The central focus of this chapter is not only to document and critique concepts of racism, embedded in institutional policies and practices, but to utilize auto-ethnography to explore my, as a black female academic's, experience in higher education. It examines notions of whiteness from a critical race perspective (CRT) and issues of multiple identities. It explores the shifts in identities and how these are enacted within the context of predominantly white higher education institutions in the United Kingdom. A comparative analysis of my journey and experiences in UK higher education will provide the backdrop for the discussion. Whiteness interrupted by blackness vis-à-vis the narratives of a black female leader will examine British higher education institutions as sites that remain the province of mainly white men and to a lesser extent women. My experience as a black female leader in higher education prompted the research reported in this chapter, which explores identity and leadership.

with a particular emphasis on my own experience living and working in the UK. Exploring race in the context of this study could suggest race is simultaneously an interpretation, representation, and/or an explanation of racial dynamics which adds to the challenge in the reorganization of one's thinking along particular racial lines. This study presents "race" as a particular discursive practice, in a way in which social structures and everyday experiences are racially organized based on their meaning. The research is not the first to explore BME women's experiences of leadership. However, it is the first piece of research seeking to add insights into leadership and the way in which cultural identity influences perceptions and experiences within the UK context.

The research emerged through my lens. I wanted to find answers to my recent leadership experience. The research design is on the boundary between autobiography and auto-ethnography. Ellis and Bochner (2000) define auto-ethnography as "autobiographies that self-consciously explore the interplay of the introspective, personally engaged self with cultural descriptions mediated through language, history, and ethnographic explanation" (p. 742). Similarly to ethnography, auto-ethnography pursues the ultimate goal of cultural understanding underlying autobiographical experiences.

WHO AM I? WHERE DO I BELONG IN ACADEMIA?

According to Montecinos (1995) members of a group may not always recognize themselves:

> The use of a master narrative to represent a group is bound to provide a very narrow depiction of what it means to be a Mexican-American, African-American, White and so on. . . . A master narrative essentialises and wipes out the complexities and richness of a group's cultural life. . . . A monovocal account will engender not only stereotyping

WHAT DOES NARRATIVE HAVE TO DO WITH EDUCATIONAL LEADERSHIP?

> The social function of narrative is not limited to "primitive" people sitting around the fire telling each other where Fire came from and why they're sitting around it (Ursula K. Le Guin, 1976)

This research study used an autobiographical lens and auto-ethnographic framework to focus on leadership and identity among Black Minority Ethnic (BME) women but also curricular choices that result in representations in which fellow members of a group represented cannot recognize themselves. (Montecinos 1995, 293–294)

As an academic in higher education I have often asked myself the questions, "Who am I?" and "Do I belong in the academy?" There is a significant gap in the literature in exploring individuals such as myself who address notions of whiteness through the lens of a "black" skinned person socialized in a white world due to adoption by German Jewish upper-middle-class parents. The complexity is that, as a black person, I am perceived (by some white and some black people in the UK) as having the same shared experiences as all other black people. However, being socialized white sets me apart.

To illustrate, I draw reference to a discussion I had with a fellow black academic with whom I was recently sharing my work. It was pointed out that my usage of the term "set me apart" could be pejorative, in that it could infer superiority although it was far from my intention. My use of language can be problematic if one draws on Bourdieu's (2001) ideas of signification in understanding language and power. To some fellow black individuals, the term could, at an unconscious level, be seen as acting white and to some white individuals it could be perceived as desiring to be on the same equal footing as them. It of course begs the question, why? In this chapter I will attempt to provide some answers through the use of the critical incidents and discussion that is used in this section.

A recurring issue that gets in the way of many of my professional relationships is the display of unconscious whiteness that irritates my colleagues. As a black person that has been raised as a white person I find myself constantly justifying my existence. If I am among a group of colleagues who are white or black some may be surprised when there are gaps in my understanding of what is perceived as cultural blackness. For example, we may be having an everyday conversation on certain issues such as family encounters whereby my contribution to the conversation is seen as very different. I note that I am indeed being "othered" from both sides, but in different ways using different approaches and styles. Othering is a process that identifies those that are thought to be different from oneself or the mainstream, and it can reinforce and reproduce positions of domination and subordination (Johnson, Murphy, Zewdie, & Reichard, 2008).

For me the notion of blackness is experienced through the lens of whiteness and all that whiteness bestows upon a person by virtue of being white, as such I am unable to relate my racial experiences through the framework of CRT but instead use whiteness theory and intersectionality as both "blackness" and "whiteness"

form part of my psychology. Both form part of the recurring question of what it means to be white and what it means to be black.

Identity for me is a complex issue, as a black person having been socialized from birth until young adulthood as white. I know that my so-called white behavior and or disposition will cause many people to think that I am a "self-hating Negro" who is not happy with who they are. This is not the case. I have not lost my way or spent my entire life "acting white." Neither am I a "mis-educated Negro" to use Woodson's (1990/1933) words. Instead, I have not chosen to "act white," but rather I have been raised and socialized as white—a situation which inevitably has caused confusion to myself and misjudgment by others, who assume that I am "acting white" through choice, as opposed to understanding my actual identity. Perhaps the psychosocial and intersectional framing of Ann Phoenix's (2009) work would be a useful way to examine more closely the multiple identities that contribute to being black as a woman in the academy?

One could question whether my white privilege came about from taking from others, and/or if my life has been more about giving up my white privileges either consciously or unconsciously. This raises the question, How does one come to terms with white socialization as perceived advantage and at the same time "blackness" which is often experienced as a disadvantage? The use of cultural dissonance assists us to further unpick the complexity of my story. In its simplest form dissonance means a fundamental lack of agreement. Differences between cultures, and class, are inherent. Cultural dissonance is the term commonly used to describe a sense of discomfit, discord, or disharmony arising from cultural differences or inconsistencies which are unexplained and therefore difficult for individuals to negotiate. Dissonance can be explained by all parties in the cultural interchange and attempts to resolve discordant issues can be bewildering or distressing (Gordon & Yowell, 1999).

The two critical incidents discussed next illustrate how "whiteness" and the concept of "white privilege" have influenced my experiences as a black middle-class female in higher education. Each incident forms an integral part of my multiple identities. I draw on Steele's (1988) early work where he dares to interrupt the thinking that middle-class black Americans are "somehow expected to celebrate the black underclass as the purest representation of African American identity" (p. 261). Interestingly, Steele maintained that he had more in common with middle-class Americans than underclass blacks. There are indeed some parallels with my own experiences in the story that he shares about the discussion he has with a friend about being black middle class. The following extracts capture the essence of the conversation:

Not long ago, a friend of mine, Black like myself, said to me that the term "Black middle class" was actually a contradiction in terms. Race, he insisted, blurred class distinctions among Blacks. If you were Black, you were just Black and that was that. When I argued, he let his eyes roll at my naivete. Then he went on. For us, as Black professionals, it was an exercise in self-flattery, a pathetic pretension, to give meaning to such a distinction. Worse, the very idea of class threatened the unity that was vital to the Black community as a whole. After all, since when had White America taken note of anything but color when it came to Blacks? He then reminded me of an old Malcolm X line that had been popular in the sixties. "Question: What is a black man with a Ph.D.? Answer: A nigger." (Steele, 1988, pp. 680–681)

The use of the this quote starts to illustrate the journey that I encountered as I engaged with each of the differing stories.

CRITICAL INCIDENT ONE: CULTURAL DISSONANCE

I started working in academia when asked to consider a position as part of a national initiative to increase the number of black and minority ethnic students entering teacher training programs within English universities. The project involved both quantitative and qualitative research to identify the support needs that black and minority ethnic students may have. What was apparent was that they were looking for a black researcher—not any black researcher, but one with the qualities they believed would "fit" in the academy.

These were the attributes that were not written into the role specification but communicated through nonverbal agreement prior to or during the interview: the hidden questions, "Will they fit with the team?" and "How do they look and present themselves?" The questions have both class and race undertones. The notion of bringing difference to the team could be seen as desirable, encouraging inclusion or creating a greater understanding in the workforce. In this instance, it may have been tokenism.

I fully accept that my socialized white upbringing will have perhaps made it easier for me to display the attributes that they desired for the post but there was certainly no "acting white" from me, I was simply being myself. I attended a very informal interview with the dean of faculty. I was being employed on the basis of an oral reference from the principal of my college, who happened to be a friend of the person who wished to employ me. This experience contradicts that of many black intellectuals who often do not have the networks or social contacts that my upbringing had afforded me.

The job raised a number of racial and class issues for me, from a completely unexpected source. I had started to date a black male of Jamaican descent whose upbringing and awareness of being black was very different to mine. I am black African/English but raised as a white, having been adopted as a baby by white upper-middle class parents. He came from a poor working-class Jamaican family in England. He knew that education was his way out of poverty. He was in his third year of his PhD and was finding it very difficult to find meaningful employment. He was extremely resentful and upset that I ("some white coconut," a name he called me because of my privileged "white" upbringing) should be granted the opportunity to work in the academy without the need to apply formally.

At the time, I had no idea why he would display such negativity toward me; I thought he would be pleased. However, I enquired with my new boss whether I could bring another person into the project as an adviser. There were many questions that occurred from this difficult and challenging situation. Why did I feel the need to entertain his abusive insults and at the same time provide a network and connections similar to what I had but he lacked? Was I trying to compensate for my "whiteness"?

I did not understand that I was dumping down and passing over my own opportunity to a frustrated and angry man who wished for the entry into academia that I had been given and, perhaps, the experience of white privilege that he purported to detest. Was this an act of sexism or racism or both, or was it his perception of my upper-middle-class privilege that was tearing him apart? Whatever it was, the experience spurred my process of questioning who I was and whether I was "black" enough to work on such a project. I had always been surrounded by a very middle-class white community, my accent and behavior were very "white."

It was agreed that my Jamaican friend would be an adviser to the project but it soon became clear that his intention was to take over the project. However, this did not happen as he wanted the status but was unable to complete the work. The contribution that he made to the project was to constantly remind me that my history got in the way in this particular role. I was not "black" enough, and I did not even have a black way of thinking. Until this moment, I had not had any problem with who I was. Was working hard for social justice at the heart of my work being viewed as an example of whiteness at work? It is an interesting question which I intend to explore another time.

The opportunity that had arisen at the university would enable me to help black and minority ethnic student teachers. It was a privilege I was happy to share with my Jamaican friend. He, however, believed that the position should have been given to someone like him;

someone who was far more black (black in the sense of understanding the cultural dimension of blackness) than I was. Taking a closer look at what was happening I believe revealed his own insecurity about not finding work in his chosen field.

In the next academic year two new appointments were made, two black academics. Was the thinking within the department now that it was time for a change? Had the first appointment of a black researcher helped to pave the way for these new appointments? I remember being excited until the welcome I received from one of the black academics was not what I had expected. Had the same recurring question returned: "Is this the kind of black we are expected to be?" Yet again I had been misunderstood and hung out to dry while the two "proper" black academics established their position within the academy.

The mismatch between my race and my class led to questions from all quarters—from the white staff about my race; and from the new black staff and my Jamaican friend for not being "black" enough. This experience highlighted for me the added difficulties encountered by black people who have been socialized as white. I realized that it is very possible that my socialized white behavior may have played some part in my being offered the job. But it also contributed to a degree of hostility from one of the recently appointed black staff members. The job had made me aware of an extra form of discrimination that I had to learn to navigate from black and white faculty staff.

REFLECTIONS ON CULTURAL DISSONANCE

Being socialized as white can cause problems. I remember having a discussion with another black staff member who believed black people socialized as white were part of the problem, as we were seen by other black people as "Uncle Toms" who were easily accepted in the academy. What they failed to understand is that "blacks" in my position are not acting white to move up the system: they have been socialized white, which is entirely different. There is also a failure to recognize that just as black people experience racism from white staff who feel they do not fit in the academy, black staff who are socialized white may doubly experience rejection from other black staff who equally feel they do not belong in the academy.

While one understands the difficulty in attempting to conceptualize what is being said, some, including black colleagues, confuse the notion of being socialized white as the same as "acting white." It is completely different. The notion of being socialized white takes place from a time when a baby has been given away by their biological parents to people who are not from the same ethnic

origin. The baby is raised into the culture(s), class, and lifestyle of the new adopted parents. Is this where cultural dissonance begins? In other words, the notion of whiteness is central to who I am.

It may not be clear to readers how I have benefitted from "white" middle-class privileges. I accessed private education and the unspoken code of whiteness, that is knowing what is required and/or how to behave in certain situations without this being spelt out. I argue that this is reflected in my everyday mannerisms/behavioral patterns and deployment of cultural, linguistic, and social capital, for example, being prepared to enter and negotiate schooling/higher education/professional employment in professional spheres. I also acknowledge that through an invisible knapsack of "unearned assets" (Leonardo, 2004), I have been able to convert whiteness as a way of enhancing my higher education progression.

Collins (1998) encourages women to define themselves. My identity is complex, multiple, and intersecting and I realize it is difficult to accept that this could be anything but an authentic/my story. I believe that my socialized behavior is very different from what Harris (1993) portrays in her paper on "Whiteness as Property" in which she writes about her grandmother who deliberately passes as white in order to find employment, forcing her to live two different lives, a life of being black with her family and a life of being white while at work. For Harris's grandmother, "acting white" gained her access to a set of privileges, in contrast, my own behavior was unconsciously developed through my being parented by a white privileged/well-to-do family. It was not adopted deliberately in order to gain access to white privileges.

My university appointment represented the first black staff member appointed to the Faculty of Education. The dean accepted me as a member of the faculty, highly recommended through a very good source. However, I had a different reception from many of the staff. They had been in their positions for many years—and were not about to submit themselves to scrutiny by a recent appointment who happened to be "black." There was a firm view that the reason that black students were not visible on the teacher education programs was either because they had not applied, or when they did apply they were not good enough. In their minds, this project had been inflicted on them without prior consultation.

Much of their anger was directed to me, "Who is she and who invited her to the scholarly table?" It was difficult to know whether the staff were questioning the appointment because of how they felt about black students not being good enough, or because of their overall perceptions of "black" people. Can black people not aspire to the same things white people in England take for granted? This is something that Cose (1993) discusses within his book *The Rage of a Privileged Class*. Many black professionals interviewed in the book were constantly being questioned and made to jump through hoops that did not appear necessary for advancement. The black professionals worked harder at proving themselves and winning acceptance. White professionals' experiences were different as they did not have the racial tensions that were part of the "black" experience.

CRITICAL INCIDENT TWO: IDENTITY AND LEADERSHIP

During 2008, I started work at another elite UK university as a senior manager. I was recruited to a department renowned for leadership development. However, the majority of the leaders were white and all the black staff, except two, held positions of low responsibility. My role was to head up a section of five white members of staff and 20 associate staff members who were out in the field delivering executive education. Most of the outer and inner team consisted of retired head teachers, deputy heads, and senior school administrators.

In this case, I achieved the post very much through my own efforts, and not because of who I knew. When I received the notification that I had been appointed, I was ecstatic that I had been chosen to take on this enormous task. I can recall the very first day. I asked the question, "Will there be an induction?" and was informed, "You would be lucky. Ask the team members and they will induct you," and then there was a laugh, "You are a senior member of staff after all."

I set up meetings to understand and establish the purpose of the work that the team was doing. Prior to these meetings I had been aware that this team was deemed dysfunctional and my appointment was to ensure that the group would start to work together as a team. My role was to make change happen. However, I had not been prepared for the rejection that lay ahead. The team was not only resentful, but had not had a chance to prepare itself for a leader of my background. They clearly had inbuilt prejudices about the ability of a black person to be a leader of their team. Much of the resentfulness, in my opinion, could only be attributed to my race. They made numerous criticisms about my ability to do the job which could not be substantiated.

Working there was a miserable experience for me. Some of the white staff members isolated me, criticized me behind my back, refused to offer me any assistance, did not socialize with me, and made out that it was me being unsociable. They took no account of the fact that I was completely new to the role and made no attempt to accommodate me. They told me nothing about the work,

and then criticized me for not knowing. I questioned and reflected again and again on whether I was to blame, and frequently changed my approach, but nothing changed. The situation that I had experienced in the department had been torturous and traumatic. However, what was even more concerning is that it appeared to be an accepted form of behavior within that particular department. People did not complain, instead it was seen as part of the institutional culture. The culture of the department was toxic, which provided an environment in where racism was able to flourish.

Eventually, after a difficult meeting with my team and senior management, I was given the option of moving to another department, which I accepted. Racism had won the day. I went on to achieve success in other roles despite the challenging and racist context. I was told by several managers both black and white that I had handled the situation with dignity. I was left with unanswered questions though; what did that experience mean? I believe the experience was extremely insightful in terms of how institutional racism is enacted. It is these subtle and often unconscious processes that are operationalized, which often cause some black academics to leave the academy. As previously discussed, questions of identity are multilayered. It could be argued to some extent that there may be an idealized notion of blackness. This begs the question: How can institutions enhance the environment to retain black academics? The study indicates the need for further work to be carried out in organizations to unlock the barriers that potentially stop black women leaders from moving ahead as fast as their white counterparts. Further research is needed to explore the leadership positions of BME leaders.

REFLECTIONS ON IDENTITY AND LEADERSHIP

Much has been said about corporate leaders and what defines them as successful or effective. However, current leadership models are usually devised within a homogeneous (North American) Westernized, white male-oriented paradigm (Lumby, 2007). Theorists have noted the inadequacy of many leadership perspectives, urging a move from colonial models of managing otherness, to incorporate minority ethnic voices (Lopez, 2003; Osler, 2006).

As the weeks unfolded, I began to realize that the team's perception of a leader was different to that of the person that had been appointed to lead, me. Much of their interpretation of a leader and leadership was drawn from their own experience, which was located in the context of whiteness. I had not realized the extent that gender and race would play in the role. Instinctively, I knew it was essential that I was able to lead and yet still hold on to my own identity. This prompted further learning and relearning of my own understanding of leadership.

I came to the conclusion that leadership is one of the most debated aspects of business and contemporary organizations. Other significant challenges to this perspective have been introduced in the real world, notably following the election of Barack Obama. These changes have implications for current discourse in leadership theory and practice such as authentic leadership (Goffee & Jones, 2005), distributed leadership (Diamond, 2007), and an aesthetic approach (Hansen & Koehler, 2005). For instance, what are the implications of authenticity for nontypical leaders like black, Asian, and minority ethnic (BAME) individuals? What are the implications for shared leadership in the context of power dynamics inherent in cross-identity group relationships? With increasing globalization, cultural and ethnic diversity, new leadership models ought to draw upon a wider notion of leadership, potentially encompassing a wider range of leadership styles from different societies and cultures.

CONCLUSION

It could be argued that, as a black person who has been socialized white, I have gained "unearned advantages that Whites, by virtue of their race, have over people of Color" (Leonardo, 2004, pp. 137–144). Such examples include access to resources, organizational structures, systems and processes which give credit and power to the white voice. I am constantly having to play down my experience of white privilege and justify my existence because my experience does not mirror the norm for many black people.

It gets even more complex, because even though I have numerous experiences of racism, I find myself minimizing these experiences. I find it difficult to connect with emotions when it comes to racism because I do not feel it is speaking to me or my inner socialized white self. It is only when black academics hear my story and their emotions have been stirred that I am able to recognize the extent of the racial experience encountered. Research suggests that people who have experienced complicated emotional trauma may repress, deny, or even develop their own strategies to deal with what others may view as a disconnect of emotions (Banks, 1992; Phoenix, 2009). Are such ways of thinking developed in a conscious or unconscious way?

When I reflect back, these bizarre situations occurred because of my "whiteness" and the need for people, like my black friend of Jamaican descent, to stop my progress because of the pain that society had placed onto him because of his blackness. I felt I had entered into a vacuum of guilt about my white privileged upbringing. This is the guilt that Jensen (2005) refers to about white people when they express remorse for slavery or about racism more generally. Being socialized white confers on me a burden which could be the same as "white guilt." The question I have to contend with is, does it include the same issues that other whites discuss, such as feeling personal responsibility for slavery, job discrimination, colonialism, and other crimes against racial minorities? To which I would say "no" because as Leonardo (2004) suggests, this "kind of guilt can be a paralyzing sentiment that helps neither Whites nor People of Color" (pp. 137–144), and I do not intend to be paralyzed by guilt.

REFERENCES

Banks, J. A. (1992). Multicultural education: Approaches, developments, and dimensions. *Cultural diversity and the schools, 1*, 83–94.

Bourdieu, P. (2001). Forms of capital. In M. Granovetter & R. Swedberg (Eds.), *The sociology of economic life* (pp. 96–111). 2nd ed. Boulder, CO: Westview.

Collins, P. H. (1998). It's all in the family: Intersections of gender, race, and nation. *Hypatia 13*(3), 62–82.

Cose, E. (1993). *The rage of a privileged class.* New York: Harper Perennial.

Diamond, J. B. (2007). Where the rubber meets the road: Rethinking the connection between high-stakes testing policy and classroom instruction. *Sociology of Education, 80*(4), 285–313.

Ellis, C., & Bochner, A. P. (2000). Autoethnography, personal narrative, reflexivity: Researcher as subject. In N. K. Denzin & Y. S. Lincoln (Eds.), *Handbook of qualitative research* (pp. 733–768). Thousand Oaks, CA: Scholar Commons.

Goffee, R., & Jones, G. (2005, December). Managing authenticity: The paradox of great leadership. *Harvard Business Review*, 87–94.

Gordon, E. V., & Yowell, C. (1999). Cultural dissonance as a risk factor in the development of students. In E. V. Gordon (Eds.), *Education and justice: A view from the back of the bus* (pp. 34–51). New York: Teachers College Press.

Hansen, R., & Koehler, J. (2005). Issue definition, political discourse and the politics of nationality reform in France and Germany. *European Journal of Political Research, 44*(5), 623–644.

Harris, A. R. (1993). Gender and race in the theory of deviant type-scripts. *Sociological Inquiry 63*, 166–201.

Jensen, E. (2005). *Teaching with the brain in mind.* Alexandra, Virginia: ASCD.

Johnson, S. K., Murphy, S. E., Zewdie, S., & Reichard, R. J. (2008). The strong, sensitive type: Effects of gender stereotypes and leadership prototypes on the evaluation of male and female leaders. *Organizational Behavior and Human Decision Processes, 106*, 39–60.

Le Guin, U. K. (1976). Is gender necessary? *Aurora: Beyond Equality*, 130–139.

Leonardo, Z. (2004). The color of supremacy: Beyond the discourse of "white privilege." *Educational Philosophy and Theory, 36*(2), 137–52.

López, G. R. (2003). The (racially neutral) politics of education: A critical race theory perspective. *Educational Administration Quarterly, 39*(1), 68–94.

Lumby, J., with Coleman, M. (2007). *Leadership and diversity: Challenging theory and practice in education*. London: Sage Publications.

Montecinos, C. (1995). Multicultural teacher education for a culturally diverse teaching force. In R. Martin (Ed.), *Practicing what we teach: Confronting diversity in teacher education* (pp. 97–116). Albany, NY: State University of New York Press.

Osler, A. (2006). Changing leadership in contexts of diversity: visibility, invisibility and democratic ideals. *Policy Futures in Education, 4*(2), 128–144.

Phoenix, A. (2000). Constructing gendered and racialised identities: Young men, masculinities and educational policy. In G. Lewis, S. Gewirtz, & J. Clarke (Eds.), *Rethinking social policy* (pp. 94–110). London: Sage.

Phoenix, A. (2009). De-colonising practices: negotiating narratives from racialized and gendered experiences of education. *Race, Ethnicity and Education, 12*(1), pp. 101–114.

Steele, C. M. (1988). The psychology of self-affirmation: Sustaining the integrity of the self. In L. Berkowitz (Eds.), *Advances in Experimental Social Psychology 21* (pp. 261–302). New York, NY: Academic Press.

Woodson, Carter G. (1990/1933). *The mis-education of the Negro* (1990 Africa World Press edition). Trenton, NJ: Africa World Press.

Section 5

WOMEN'S LEADERSHIP STORIES

Editor: *Jacqueline Oram-Shortt*

Chapter 21

Overview

Women's Leadership Stories

Jacqueline Oram-Shortt

Stories are the fabric of our lives; and stories reflecting the work of women educational leaders can encapsulate the in-depth details of how women lead. Through the work of Women Leading Education Across the Continents (WLE), women's leadership stories have been resonating with educators across the globe. The literature covering women educational leaders in the Caribbean, Asia, and Africa is sparse, hence the importance of the following stories in this section, which voice the experiences of women from Asia, Australia, Africa, and the United States.

The stories highlight women's views on leadership, the balancing act—being mothers and nurturers—versus their roles in the public spheres, as well as the impact of religion on leadership roles. Each story highlighted in this section emphasizes the impact of cultural beliefs on how women are perceived in education, as well as the challenges, joy, personal struggles, and barriers which they face in trying to lead educational institutions. The sharing of these stories is one important mechanism for disrupting the deficit storyline associated with women's leadership, and carving out space for celebrating what women bring to their leadership roles, in their many forms.

THE NATURE OF WOMEN'S LEADERSHIP

The stories of women educational leaders often detail the barriers and struggles they encounter. Harris, Ballenger, Hicks-Townes, Carr, and Alford (2004) identified two primary categories: marriage and family responsibilities and cultural stereotyping. Both impact on how women lead. However, these are not the only aspects of women's leadership, and understanding the complexities and even opportunities which arise from these experiences is important.

Coming to understand the complexities whereby women must constantly try to balance marriage and fam-

ily responsibilities and at the same time acknowledge the cultural stereotypes that often provide the framework within which they work, is essential to furthering women's leadership overall. This is not easy work. Grogan (2015) argues that women administrators are faced with many deterrents which are not experienced by men, with Hill and Ragland (1995) emphasizing the barriers to women's advancement in administration are entrenched in societal concepts and historical myths that act to "encumber female leadership visions and possibilities in many ways" (p. 7).

Barriers to educational leadership and administration, both internal and external, continue to be highlighted. Shakeshaft (1989) identified several models which have been posited to explain the origins of these barriers including the woman's place model, the discrimination model, and the meritocracy model. Other models discussed by Shakeshaft include socialization and sex stereotyping as well as organizational structure which shapes the behavior of its members. Shakeshaft identified the model which portrays the world as "male defined and male run" (p. 82) as providing a satisfactory explanation for the limits placed on female school administrators, and helps to solidify male hegemony as the dominant factor in all barriers to women accessing school administration. Shakeshaft disputed the literature which supports the internal barriers, which "blames the victim for her lack of achievement" (p. 83).

While traditional stories of women's experiences in educational administration have changed little over the decades, the contemporary stories in this section highlight the increasingly complex dichotomy of women leader's lives. The six authors in this section share personal narratives of leadership stories which give us deeper insights into the lives of educational leaders.

In her chapter, "Making Inroads and Making a Difference," Jill Sperandio explains that Madrasah schools are operated by the Ministry of Religious Affairs (MoRA) and brings to the forefront how female leadership is perceived in Indonesia. In the Indonesian society, the impact of religion on women's role in a predominantly Muslim society helps us to understand further, both the internal and external barriers discussed by Shakeshaft (1989). Seperandio shows in this contemporary study that the barriers which existed in previous decades still impact women's mobility into leadership roles.

Seperandio gives the history of Madrasah education in Indonesia, highlighting their early beginnings and how they help to maintain Muslim traditions and history. The women in the study explained what motivated them to become teachers or principals and what supported them in their leadership. Throughout the study the voices of the women also echo the barriers which permeate within the society, predominantly—traditional ideas, which state that men should be leaders. It is heartening however to note that despite the challenges and barriers that women face in the madrasahs, times are changing and the community is acknowledging that a woman can indeed become a leader based on her capabilities. Seperandio highlights that further training, support, and an encouraging environment can help women gain access to leadership positions which will help to dismantle gender stereotyping across Indonesia.

Shirley Randell's study "Celebrating Leadership Learnings in Education Across Continents: Experiences of an International Development Adviser," highlights the leadership work of women who hold significant positions in the public sphere. The participants in this research were five graduates from the first cohort of the Master of Gender and Development class in Rwanda.

From a strength-based perspective this study embraces themes such as resilience, the importance of family, empowerment, mentoring, and leadership. The participants have all embraced education, giving meaning to their lives and work presently; regardless of their backgrounds, whether they were raised in abject poverty or they were from middle-class backgrounds. Presented as case studies, the stories of each of the participants are intricately woven and respectfully presented, giving readers an in-depth look into the lives of these women from Rwanda.

Randell emphasizes how the stories of the leaders in her study provide strong parallels, emphasizing the value of supportive families, education, and the belief in social justice leadership. This study highlights the importance of cross-cultural, cross-gender, cross-border studies which can help us to understand how various *groups* across the globe access leadership roles and at the same time empower us in capacity building.

Yvonne Masters's narrative, "A Female Leader in a Man's World: Stories of Women Leaders of Catholic Schools," highlights the stories of women principals working in Catholic schools in Australia. She noted that, "women can be caught up in the binaries of mother and professional or in the male dominated hegemony of the Church, where the parish priest is often the employer." The stories of leaders in this chapter resonate with themes of patriarchal leadership, male hegemony compounded by the church being the employer and fulfilling the expectations of the parish priest, providing discourses of exclusion, ironically in a context which espouses strength through faith, fairness, and the giving of thanks (Caschetta, 2015).

Masters emphasized that the women leading these Catholic schools often experienced tension, especially in local communities, which upheld traditional views that women belong in the home. Hence problems would arise when the female principal had to balance family and work. However, the relationship between the parish priest and the female principals of the Catholic schools is a noteworthy theme. She discusses how important it is that the parish priest supports the work of the female principal, in instances where this is not the case, there is much more tension and stress in carrying out her role as principal.

The stories highlight the dichotomy of the roles of these school principals, serving in positions of leadership that they both loved and hated, where there are rewards as well as the feelings of being unappreciated and isolated.

Sarah Jean Baker outlined her dissertation journey in her chapter titled, "Leadingmamas—A Visual Ethnography." She describes how she was able to carry out a phenomenological study on a topic that embraced her lived experiences of being a mother and an educational leader. The women in Baker's study are all mothers with leadership roles in educational institutions. She explored what it means for women to identify with both the personal and the professional aspects of their lives. Often women's professional lives are discussed and documented, but the personal aspect is regarded as secondary and less open to scholarship. Hence for the most part women's private sphere is often not open to public scrutiny.

The women in Baker's study explored the impact of social media on how they reflect on motherhood, as well the biases in leadership roles. Baker noted, "No matter the topic of the focus group discussions and images—expectations, challenges, and the joys in our roles as mamas and leaders, the idea that these pieces of our identities were linked to each other was evident throughout our dialogue. . . . We desire to be good leaders and we desire to be good mamas."

Throughout the study the women's voices give readers their personal thoughts on motherhood, revealing the conflicts often faced by women with young children, and the barriers they encounter in their role as *leading mammas*. Baker explored in depth the concepts of *conflicted mothering* and *transpersonal mothering*; she explains *conflicted mothering* as encompassing the idea that women experience conflict in their roles as mothers and leaders. This is indeed an important development in contemporary literature on women's leadership roles, where women can explain honestly how they feel about motherhood, without feeling that they will be judged too harshly, and also engaging with social media to share women's leadership experiences.

In her chapter, "The Path of Leadership for Women in Pakistan: Critical Reflections," Abaida Mahmood provides reflection on the many challenges facing women from her home country of Pakistan. As a leader of a charity whose commitment is to education and career prospects for women, Mahmood is accustomed to the daily challenges women face to attaining the human rights her country's laws afford them. She describes the deeply held cultural values that perpetuate women's subservience to men in all aspects of society.

Mahmood examines the stereotypes of Pakistani female leaders and how gender roles of women affect their career choices and professional advancement. Even though broader society benefits from educated professional women, the price these women pay for success can be high in their personal lives and their contributions in the workplace remain undervalued. She emphasizes that women alone cannot tackle the deeply entrenched societal norms—that women need allies and advocates from male family members, suggesting that Pakistani society has work to do with sociocultural policies that lift up the other half of the country.

Concluding the section, in "Balancing the *Yang* and the *Yin* Through Source-fully Intelligent Education," Coomi Vevaina provides her model of source-full intelligence as a means to understand and experience our uniqueness as an individual and our oneness, or connection to others, simultaneously. The model helps individuals understand how they *are* both unique and part of a greater whole at the same time.

Vevaina remarks, "The deepest part of our self makes us aware that we are part of an unimaginably greater whole. The energy matrix or, as we say in India, our *chita* (life force), within which we exist, connects us, not only to every single being and thing on our planet but to the entire universe (and even universes). The result of apprehending the life force is a joy-filled, purpose-driven, selfless state . . . when All is Self and the dancer and the dance become one." In other words, the perfect whole is the amalgam of the self and the other.

CONCLUSIONS

The stories in this section emphasize the personal lives of leaders across several continents. The authors have explored themes which are often regarded as taboo—health issues, being conflicted between job and family, as well as sharing personal conversations often discussed in private. They have delved into the often-untouched territory of leaders' private lives and illustrated how important it is to consider women's leadership identities as multiple and evolving. Other scholars who have documented women's leadership stories have also highlighted similar developing "truths."

Grady, Curley, and LaCost (2008) in their article, "Women Leaders Tell Their Stories," also discussed the issue of how female educational leaders struggle with the balancing act. They cited the feedback of one participant in their study, "When I go home, from 3:00 until 11:00, I am mom. And once my kids go to bed, and then I put back on that superintendent hat. And that's when I do my work. And I thought, our male superintendents aren't doing that" (p. 290).

Grady, Curley, and LaCost also noted that, as the women discussed these relatively recent developments a participant summarized the situation as, "I think you can have it all. I just don't think you can do it all" (p. 290). Shakeshaft (2015) highlights the importance of understanding identity not just from our own perspectives, but also recognizing how that identity is framed by those we interact with.

Using stories to document female educational leaders' personal challenges and struggles provides a better understanding of their multiple and sometimes competing roles and identities. It is paramount that the stories of women educational leaders from the developing world continue to be explored to highlight the challenges, struggles, and inequalities they face. Embracing the complexities of women's leadership also allows the joy and motivating factors to be recognized and surfaced within these contexts also.

Comparative analytical stories will help policy makers to assess similarities and differences with their counterparts in the developed world, and ascertain how changes might be implemented to enhance the lives of women who aspire to lead educational institutions. The continued documentation of the life stories of women educational leaders across the continents will help us to further understand the themes which are explored in this section. Certainly, stories on women leading in many contexts can offer us many lessons and help us to understand the *real worlds* of women who lead.

REFERENCES

Caschetta, J. (2015). The four pillars of the Catholic church. Retrieved from https://4pillarsofthechurch.wordpress.com/2015/08/22/hello-world/

Grady, M. L., Curley, V. R., & LaCost, B. (2008). Women leaders tell their stories. *Journal of Women in Educational Leadership, 6*(4), 275–291.

Grogan, M. (2015). Re(considering) gender scholarship in educational leadership. In W. Sherman Newcomb & K. Mansfield (Eds.), *Women interrupting, disrupting and revolutionizing educational policy and practice* (pp. 3–20). Charlotte, NC: Information Age Publishing.

Harris, S., Ballenger, J., Hicks-Townes, F., Carr, C., & Alford, B. (2004). *Winning women: Stories of award-winning educators.* Lanham, MD: Scarecrow Education.

Hill, M. S., & Ragland, J. C. (1995). *Women as educational leaders: Opening windows, pushing ceilings.* Thousand Oaks, CA: Corwin Press.

Shakeshaft, C. (1989). *Women in educational administration.* Newbury Park, CA: Corwin Press.

Shakeshaft, C. (2015). Introduction: Where have we been? Where are we going? In W. Sherman Newcomb & K. Mansfield (Eds.), *Women interrupting, disrupting and revolutionizing educational policy and practice* (pp. vii–xx). Charlotte, NC: Information Age Publishing.

Chapter 22

Making Inroads and Making a Difference

Women Leading Indonesian Junior and Senior Secondary Private Madrasahs

Jill Sperandio

The leadership of privately owned and operated Islamic madrasahs in Indonesia provides a challenging environment for women. Madrasahs represent 18 percent of all schools in the national education system and have traditionally been owned, operated, and led by men, despite relying heavily on female teachers. This chapter examines the motivation and experiences of women who have taken principals positions in these schools at a time when traditional societies in Indonesia have become more accepting of female leadership, and the government of Indonesia is actively promoting the recruitment and training of women for educational leadership positions.

The overall pattern of underrepresentation of women in school leadership worldwide continues, but international studies indicate that carving out a career in school leadership has proved more challenging for women in some contexts than in others (Brunner, 1999; Coleman, 1996; Shakeshaft, 1989). A recent study of women in school leadership in Indonesia (POM/DFAT, 2016) included one such challenging context, the leadership of privately owned and operated Islamic madrasahs. These schools form an important and integral part of the national school system, serving many disadvantaged children, but are managed by foundations that have traditionally favored male leadership.

Indonesia, with the fourth largest education system in the world serving over 60 million students, has two educational subsystems: the general school education, under the administration of the Ministry of Education and Culture (MoEC) and the madrasah education, under the Ministry of Religious Affairs (MoRA). MoRA maintains oversight over both ministry-operated and private madrasahs throughout the country (OECD, 2015). Approximately 18 percent of all Indonesian schools (primary and secondary) are madrasahs, with the majority of these (90 percent) being privately operated and only 10 percent being directly controlled by MoRA. In 2013 approximately 13 percent of primary and secondary school students in Indonesia were enrolled in madrasahs.

Leadership of madrasahs has been traditionally male stemming from interpretations of the Quran that limit all leadership to men, and limit the public exposure of women (BAPPENAS, 2013; Dewi, 2015). While madrasahs that are now directly administered by MoRA have requirements for qualifications for both teachers and school principals that are similar to those of MoEC and promote a gender-neutral merit-based promotion system, private madrasahs can appoint their own teachers and leaders based on owner choice and justification rather than qualifications. As such, these schools have proved particularly resistant to appointing women to leadership, and prove challenging environments for women who have accepted appointments (Gaus, 2011). However, women are increasingly being recruited for private primary (MI), junior secondary (MP), and senior secondary (MA) leadership in the private madrasahs, mirroring patterns found in the general school system.

This chapter will present the findings from a study of the life histories of women teachers and leaders in the junior and secondary school level in private madrasahs with the overall purpose of establishing the causes of the ongoing underrepresentation of women in educational leadership (POM/DFAT, 2016). The challenges participants have faced and still encounter, and their beliefs regarding the contributions they can make to improving student outcomes in their schools are supported by contextual information collected from district education officials and community members. The chapter concludes with a consideration of the benefits of increasing female school leadership in private madrasahs from both the perspective of improving school quality, and of better utilizing female potential for leadership for the benefit of students and their communities.

HISTORY OF MADRASAH EDUCATION

Before a formal education system was introduced during the Dutch colonial period in Indonesia, the pesantren, an Islamic boarding school, was the only educational institution available. Usually situated in rural areas and under the direction of a Muslim scholar, pesantren were attended by young people seeking a detailed understanding of the Quran, the Arabic language, Islamic law, and Muslim traditions and history.

Students could enter and leave the pesantren at any time of the year and the studies were not organized as a progression of courses leading to graduation. With colonization and the introduction of European-style schooling with an emphasis on academics, Islamic education became marginalized and regarded as inferior. Independence brought moves to set up a state education system, and by 1975 Indonesian children could choose between state-run, non-sectarian public schools, and private or semi-private religious schools. Most of the latter were madrasahs, Islamic day schools established and supported by Islamic foundations and community organizations. The madrasahs were not a popular choice initially, but since government changes in 1998 they have increased in numbers and enrollment.

As madrasahs mostly serve poor rural students and attract more female than male students, madrasah education has played a crucial role in achieving the government's goal of universal nine-year basic education, and in achieving the Millennium Development Goals for education and gender equality. The Law on National Education (MOE, No. 20, 2003) formally integrated all madrasahs into the national education system, and they are now required to follow the national curriculum and education standards set by the government. However, according to a recent study, many madrasahs, particularly privately operated schools, offer low-quality education. They are neither able to meet the minimum standards for learning outcomes, nor provide an adequate teaching and learning environment (OECD/Asian Development Bank, 2015).

BACKGROUND TO THE RESEARCH

The study recorded and analyzed the professional life stories, beliefs, and opinions of seven female principals and 13 female teachers in junior and senior secondary madrasahs. In addition to providing demographic information charting their professional careers, participants explained their motivation to become a teacher or a principal, identified who inspired them and who mentored them, and discussed their sources of satisfaction in the classroom and principal's office. They discussed what they believed were the qualities of an effective principal and their perceptions of the differences in leadership styles between men and women who led schools. The teachers included those currently aspiring to be principals, those undecided, and those convinced they were not interested in the position.

Although each story is different, reflecting on the personal background, life chances, and unique features of the private madrasahs in which they served, the process of rereading, rewriting, and ultimately coding the interviews for key themes revealed interesting similarities. These similarities shed light on the factors that influenced participants' entry and progression through teaching to leadership. Interviews with focus groups of teachers and community members, key informant interviews with district office officials and supervisors, additional principal interviews with principals from MoRA-administered schools, and personnel from ministries and nongovernmental organizations (NGOs) provided collaborating data, depth, and different perspectives to the life history events provided by the study's targeted teachers and principals.

FINDINGS: KEY THEMES

Committed Educators

All teacher and school principal participants in the private madrasahs visited for the study noted the satisfaction they derived from teaching. This satisfaction came from the pleasure of passing on the knowledge they had acquired through their own education, and from helping their students become better in some way, either through knowledge acquisition or changed behavior and outlook. Typical comments included, "I'm very close to my students. School holidays are boring. The most beautiful moment in my life is when I meet my students every day" and "Madrasah is a workshop where people are changed from not good to good." Most also mentioned the challenges of teaching poor or dysfunctional children with very limited teaching resources. For the majority of participants in the study, teaching was clearly a vocation.

A Challenging but Changing Context for Women in Leadership

The common understanding of why so few women are principals in the madrasahs is that the majority and more classical interpretation of Islamic teaching defines leadership roles as assigned to men and that women lack the temperament and capability to lead. Further, religious beliefs require married women to seek the permission of their husbands to engage in any activities outside of the home and these activities will be limited to those that can be supervised by the husband or male relative, restricting work-related travel such as professional training or appearances at public events.

While there was plenty of evidence in this study that such views still impact the employment of women as school leaders, study participants also provided evidence that these views were changing. They suggested that interpretations of Islamic tenets were becoming more nuanced and liberal, and that the women school leaders in the public eye were themselves acting as change agents with regard to public acceptance of women's place and capabilities in Islamic communities. These subthemes are explored next.

Only Men Should Lead

Many of the study informants noted that patterns of male dominance of leadership in all aspects of Islamic life, and particularly in the environment of religious boarding schools, were rooted in a strictly literal interpretation of the Quran. This was explained by a school supervisor from the Makassar district in the following way: "based on the Quran men are superior to women. Arrijalu qowwamuna ala nisa" (men as leaders/rule over women), which the participant noted was the common local understanding. This interpretation was endorsed as being a contributing factor to low rates of female school leaders by a number of respondents.

One participant noted, "the belief that leaders are men is still strong in society . . . resulting in the small number of women who become the heads of junior and senior secondary madrasah," and another noted, "The obstacle (to women's leadership) thus far is the prevailing interpretation that the leaders must be men," and "pesantren tradition according to syariat Islam teaches this . . . men should be leaders and have leadership." Other participants, however, suggest that a more liberal interpretation now prevails, a view summarized by a respondent who explained "this interpretation applies only to the conditions of war and emergency conditions that require physical toughness."

Personal Bias

While the majority of participants agreed that there were positive changes in attitude at the societal level to women taking leadership positions, others were frank enough to acknowledge that traditional beliefs were still important and slower to change at a personal level. This, in turn, influenced individual and family decision making. One respondent noted, "If there are women who become leaders, there is always the question 'Is there no man who can become a leader?'" Another respondent stated, "Islam

recognizes women's leadership aspects, but nevertheless, it is still better for a man to become a leader," and another concluded, "Women have the same capacity to learn as men. This provides an opportunity for women to be leaders but if there is a man available, better the man leads."

A few respondents revealed ingrained sexual stereotyping. A chairman of a foundation, praising a local female principal, noted:

> At first I thought that Ibu H is not a Madurese, because it is difficult for Madurese women to have such (intelligent) ideas. Very few Madurese women have forward thinking on a par with men. Moreover, I personally still adhere to the belief that leaders must be men. Under the prevailing tradition, this school adheres to the belief that women should not stand out in public, because there are men present.

Stereotypes of Leadership Styles

Traditional stereotypes of the capabilities of women may be changing together with changes in cultural restrictions on their movement and behavior, and there was general agreement among study participants that women are both capable of leading and would not necessarily face restrictions or resistance if they chose to do so. However, there remains a clear perception by the majority of participants in the study that men and women lead in different ways. Women's leadership is described using terms such as meticulous, detail oriented, student focused, empathic to female students, approachable (especially to female teachers) and communicative. Women principals are seen as more collegial and consultative when it comes to decision making, but also weak and emotional. Men's leadership is described most frequently using the terms firm and decisive, rational; they make decisions quickly without consulting others, and they distance themselves from teachers' problems.

Participants rarely consider one leadership style preferable to another, rather noting the strengths and weaknesses of both and suggesting that a good principal will have self-knowledge that allows him or her to play to their strengths and minimize the effects of their weaknesses. Participants, when asked the characteristics of a good teacher, showed considerable similarity in their responses, typically including social skills of cooperation and consultation with teachers, the board/chairperson of the foundation, and the district office of religious affairs. Reaching out to parents and the community is an important private madrasah principal responsibility to help attract viable numbers of students and involve parents in the support of the school.

Managerial skills were recognized as equally important to ensure the smooth running of the school, fund raising and distribution, ensuring teacher attendance and student discipline, and careful oversight of all aspects of school functioning—descriptions very much in line with government standards for competency and private school leadership worldwide. Within the Islamic community, one focus group suggested that good principals reflected the leadership characteristics of the prophet Muhammad: shiddiq (truthful), amanah (trustable), tabligh (communicative), and fathonah (smart). These characteristics cannot be separated and are always mentioned as a unity.

Changing Attitudes

Many respondents noted changing attitudes, attributed to higher levels of education of both men and women, reduced isolation of communities, and government initiatives to sensitize the population to gender equality issues (Blackburn, 2004; Brenner, 2011; Noerdin, 2002; Parawansa, 2005). A female school supervisor for madrasah schools commented, "In the field of education, and in the structure of government, both women and men have equal opportunities to become leaders. The right of men and women to hold office in the structure of government institutions is equal. Now it is better recognized that there are many smart women."

Regional differences in attitudes, connected to economic issues, such as low-income areas where female labor outside the home is a necessity, or in matriarchal cultures, or those with exposure to many cultural traditions, were suggested as influencing acceptance of female leadership. A focus group participant explained, "The community in Bangkalan regency tend to be more open and their views about the need for a man to be the leader have changed. The present coastal culture has allowed women to lead, which is quite different from communities in the inland areas."

A district office official stated, "Islam recognizes equality . . . recognizes women's leadership aspects . . . does not absolutely reject female leadership, particularly if she has the capability and power to lead." This change of attitude was also noted by some madrasah leaders, with one commenting, "In general, society is already accepting (of women leaders) . . . they are smart and (communities) no longer demand a male leader. If a woman meets the criteria, she will surely be appointed." Others echoed this opinion. A focus group participant explained, "given the current development, if women are able to demonstrate their capacity as leaders, the environment would accept them happily."

A female supervisor from the Madura region first noted the continuing unwillingness of men to be led by women that inhibited women from considering leadership positions, but then concluded, "though, actually, if a woman demonstrates that she has the ability as a leader, then the public will acknowledge it."

Challenges to Successful Female Leadership

Just as the study revealed perceived differences in leadership styles between men and women principals, perceived differences in the challenges they faced also became apparent. A number of participants commented to the effect that male principals in the private madrasahs, because they were supporting families and salaries were often low, frequently worked two jobs. This resulted in their spending the minimum time at school, leaving as soon as school finished, and demonstrating less involvement than women, who would typically be more directly involved in the hands-on management of the school. Women, however, because of family connections and restrictions on mobility, had fewer opportunities to attend meetings and trainings in some areas, or go to events that required a male relative to accompany them.

The additional burden of domestic responsibility was seen as a challenge that women but not men had to face, as was the need for family support/permission to take on leadership positions. Women were seen as having a more challenging time dealing with senior male teachers and teenage boys—although clearly not the woman principal who noted that when she walked round the school the boys whispered to each other, "Look out, here comes the boss!"

Overall, while participants noted these limitations for women they were quick to note that the challenges could be overcome if an aspiring principal, male or female, was determined and well organized. One female madrasah supervisor noted, "there used to be a saying in Madurese, wherever a woman goes, she will end up in the kitchen again." However, she continued, "now that women are seen to be founding madrasah schools, chairing foundations, and are appointed as principals, there has clearly been a change in popular understanding." Successful women leaders are an important element in changing ingrained societal beliefs about gender roles and equality of opportunity, and provide role models to inspire other women to take on leadership positions.

Attitudes to Women Developing Careers

Focus groups of teachers and school community members were asked to comment on whether it was acceptable for women to plan careers. A group from Sumenep agreed that a career is acceptable for a woman, if she can balance her career and household responsibilities. Further, they noted that with the removal of barriers to girls being educated, girls now outnumbered boys in gaining entrance to tertiary training and education, and Sumenep "will have a Pilkada (election for mayor) where the winning candidate is expected to be a woman. This means the community has no issues about women having a career. This is a change from the past." A group from Bagkalan noted, "it's the era for career women."

With increasing educational opportunities and the opportunities these offer to create a better life, women had an expectation to develop a career, but a married woman must be prepared to gain her husband's approval and demonstrate she can balance career and family. These themes emerged from each of the six focus group discussions held in private madrasah school communities. They encapsulate the tensions between traditional views of the gender division of labor in the home that reflect both religious beliefs and teaching about the relationships between men and women together with deep-rooted cultural understandings, and the increasing recognition that with educational equality, women have the potential to increase family income and well-being together with self-actualization.

Yet even on the subject of a husband's permission for a woman to work, the views expressed by several male focus group participants illustrated a changing world. The traditional view—that women's place was in the home—was put forward by a male teacher from Bangkalan. He explained that he would not allow his wife to work outside of the house, and this was not because of the "R principle" (an Indonesian saying that refers to a woman's place being the kitchen, well, and mattress) that was the common statement of women's inferior position in relation to men, but because he believed it was his role as husband to take care of his wife and children, "I support members of my family who want to have a career as long as it does not go beyond their nature as a woman. However, for my own family, according to my religious beliefs, I cannot allow my wife to be involved in public interactions (that could cause scandal or accusations of infidelity)."

However, two male school committee members from Maros took a different view, stating that there should be no difference in the challenges that men and women face developing their careers. They acknowledged that the problems faced by married women with children were the problems of their husbands too—husbands had the obligation to support their wives' careers and should not limit their wives' professional development, "I would feel guilty if I didn't support my wife's career advancement." They noted that a career woman was making a great contribution to the family economic situation, reducing the male burden to provide for the family. "For me, if my wife is getting a promotion, I will be very happy, Alhamdulillah! She will reduce my burden as head of the family."

The two men also addressed a concern voiced by women in the study that men would find it unacceptable to have their wives holding higher positions than themselves. For example, one aspiring female teacher stated she would not take a principal's position even if it were offered if it meant she was higher in rank than her husband and it would make him uncomfortable. The men noted, "Maybe there is a concern from the husband that he will be belittled if his wife becomes more successful than himself. But as long as the couple manages to maintain respect, there should not be a problem."

Few Women Aspire to Leadership

Interviews were conducted with 13 female teachers in the madrasahs to establish the reasons for their desire to progress, or otherwise, to leadership positions in the schools. Given the lack of a formal career path in the private madrasah where principal appointments are made by the madrasah foundation and require no formal qualifications or experience, aspiring women can do little other than demonstrate competence and express an interest in a position. Given traditional preferences for male leadership, the study was expected to find that women were simply not offered positions.

The reality, however, was that a number of the women interviewed had been offered leadership positions and rejected the opportunity. Of the seven teachers who were clearly not interested in becoming principals, two were holding leadership positions as vice principals of curriculum and found the responsibilities and distraction from teaching with no additional remuneration burdensome to the point where they were both waiting to relinquish these positions and return to full-time teaching. Others noted they would not be able to cope with the responsibility of being a principal given existing family commitments.

Other nonaspiring teachers expressed a strong desire to remain as teachers because teaching was their passion. One MoRA-certified teacher expressed it this way: "Ah no [I don't want to be a principal], I love it better being a teacher. It has been my childhood dream. I love teaching and being close to the children." Another noted she enjoyed the collegiality with her fellow teachers: "I prefer to be a regular teacher, blending with colleagues, no gap." One teacher in stressed economic circumstances, a single divorced parent with two children working two jobs, stated, "I want to improve school quality but this doesn't mean I want to be a principal. I am satisfied to support the principal. I am happy just being a teacher."

However, she noted that she would need a master's degree, which she couldn't afford to get, before being considered for a principal position, and would have to consider transport costs if a position was offered. Another teacher noted that earlier in her career she had ambitions to be a principal and a position was offered, but at the time she would have been required "to pay" to be appointed, so she declined. She states that now "I am not the ambitious type and am satisfied to just teach."

Another teacher explained her lack of interest in being a principal was in part due to her belief that she lacks the experience needed. Several teachers noted that they might be more interested if they had civil servant status: "if I were a civil servant, I could pursue a career. However, as only a teacher appointed by the foundation, I have to think it over." Across the group there was considerable confusion about the actual qualifications needed to be a principal and a generally held belief that they were in some way not qualified to undertake the role.

Nurturing Further Aspirations for Leadership

A teacher who expressed her interest in school leadership noted a problem she would face was that she would not want to hold a higher position than her husband who is a vice principal in another madrasah. She noted, "I don't want to create a gap in my family. My husband might say that he is OK with the situation, but when we are in a formal environment where I'm a principal but my husband is not, he will be upset." However, she went on to say that if she was given the mandate to be a principal, she would be ready, but only if there were no other people available.

Others were more proactive. Ida explained that she needed to improve her school management skills, but "if one day the foundation trusts me to lead, I will do it seriously and wholeheartedly." Maulidah, after experiencing leadership opportunities provided by the foundation for which she worked, has gone from not considering being a principal to actively acquiring the skills and knowledge she understands she will need for the position. Nadziratul, the youngest of the teacher participants, in her late 20s and a novice teacher, nevertheless had clear ambitions to progress, "Of course, I don't want to stay being a teacher; every human being wants to have a higher position at work." She has already considered the chances of moving up, noting that because her husband is the son of the foundation chairman, she would have to look for a principal's position in another school, and also contend with the "like and dislike" factor from her colleagues and the internal seniority competition that she claims exists in every school. She already has ideas for changing and developing the madrasah in which she works and which she finds conservative and closed to new ideas.

Confidence, Vision, Self-Promotion

Previous studies of female principals and supervisors in Indonesia note that women rate themselves lower than men on many leadership skills and lack confidence in their ability to lead. Several participants and key informants perceived this to be the case and offered possible explanations. The Head of the Ministry of Religious Affairs of one regency in the study suggested, "What frequently hinders women is their lack of confidence before trying something new, easily giving up, just like surrendering before going to war. They should have courage, not plain boldness but having mental preparedness." He noted that women had no problem managing elementary schools, but it was just lack of confidence that stopped them applying to junior and senior secondary schools.

A male head of a private foundation noted that women were often too modest regarding their capacity to lead. He suggested, "Sometimes a woman does not want to show off her authority in the way men do." He expressed his opinion that women needed to show their strengths in leadership on the one hand, even while remaining modest on the other. Another madrasah chairman noted the tendency of women to give up chances of leadership in deference to their male colleagues.

These views were confirmed by several women in the study. A woman well qualified to take on a principal's role and confident that she could do it but holding back because it would place her in a higher status position than her husband noted, "Female principals are as able to manage a school as a male principal. However, the feelings of inferiority of the female could be a barrier for her to increase her capacity as a leader. It's not about women's skills and capacity, but women's mentality always to prioritize men, limiting women's own development—it happens to me too."

A woman principal, who had herself refused the principal's position on several occasions when she knew there were qualified male candidates available, suggested that it was not so much a matter of confidence, but the social/religious conditioning that women received to defer to men in all situations. Women could not contemplate competing with men for a position, but would take the position when it was offered and it was clear there were no qualified men with an interest in it.

These views were supported by a number of female teachers who explained that they would be interested in becoming principal and would be duty bound to accept if they were asked. Taking a proactive or self-promotional approach by advertising that they were interested was not something they perceived as necessary or likely to enhance their chances of success. This is in contrast to a male teacher who, having decided that he was interested in becoming a principal, let his colleagues and the district MoRA office know and as a result received encouragement and support, and another who actively sought the vice principal's position to gain experience in the day to day running of the school.

Four of the 13 women teachers in the study had been offered principal positions and had turned them down, or had accepted reluctantly out of a sense of duty when no one else could be found to take the position. That this was not uncommon was confirmed by a key informant, the head of a prestigious government senior secondary school, who had been offered the principal's position twice before she finally accepted on a third occasion. Each time of offering she had the full support of her family and her colleagues at the school.

In addition, the second offer came with the promise of an opportunity to attend leadership training in Australia. When asked a third time, it was her husband who convinced her it was her duty to accept the position, noting she was actually doing the work of the principal while the male principals she worked for prepared themselves for upward moves to the ministry and beyond. She had gone on to use the position of principal to realize her vision of introducing an understanding of environmentally friendly "green" educational environments and gained considerable recognition for herself and the school for her leadership in this area. Understanding of how best to motivate women with clear leadership potential or demonstrated capability to lead is clearly a complex issue.

CONCLUSION

As the government of Indonesia continues to experiment with principal training schemes to improve school leadership and student outcomes throughout the country (ACDP-007, 2013a; ACDP-007, 2013b; Jala & Msthafa, 2001; Sofo, Fitzgerald, & Jawas, 2012), the leadership potential of female teachers in the private madrasah should not be overlooked. The voices and experiences of study participants, and the themes that emerge from their stories, suggest the need for training programs to draw more women into madrasah school leadership at junior and secondary school level. Leading secondary education in madrasahs presents challenges for women that are not experienced in either the MoEC or MoRA public schools, and the provision of training for them requires sensitivity to the religious and cultural constraints that may affect women in the madrasah communities with regard to travel and male instructors.

Within the schools the challenges of school improvement with limited funds, and working with disadvan-

taged children in many instances, appeals to a group of dedicated female teachers. For women who want to work close to home, who may not have the opportunity to gain the formal qualifications needed to progress along ministry-defined career paths, and who gain satisfaction from contributing to the community focused environment of the school, free of the constraints of being assigned to different schools as public school teachers may be, there is strong motivation to remain in the private madrasah. However, without encouragement, support, and training, few are likely to go forward to become principals. That more women principals are needed in the private madrasah is indisputable given the role they can clearly play in breaking down gender stereotyping and demonstrating gender equality for the sizable number of girls and boys, women teachers, and school communities spread across Indonesia.

REFERENCES

ACDP-007 Indonesia. (2013a, March). *School and madrasah principals and supervisors competencies baseline study.* ACDP Secretariat: Ministry of Education and Culture, Jakarta, Indonesia.

ACDP-007 Indonesia. (2013b, September). *Policy Brief: Gender equality in education in Indonesia.* ACDP Secretariat: Ministry of Education and Culture, Jakarta, Indonesia.

BAPPENAS. (2013). *Review of a decade of gender mainstreaming in education in Indonesia. Ministry of National Development Planning/National Development Planning Agency* (BAPPENAS) Jakarta, Indonesia.

Blackburn, S. (2004). *Women and the state in modern Indonesia.* Cambridge, England: Cambridge University Press.

Brenner, S. (2011). Private moralities in the public sphere: Democratization, Islam, and gender in Indonesia. *American Anthropologist, 113*(3), 478–490.

Brunner, C. C. (Ed.). (1999). *Sacred dreams: Women and the superintendency.* Albany, NY: State University of New York Press.

Coleman, M. (1996). Barriers to career progress for women in education: The perception of female head teachers. *Educational Research, 38*(3), 317–332.

Dewi, K. H. (2015). *Indonesian women and local politics: Islam, gender and networks in Post-Suharto Indonesia.* Singapore: NUS Press.

Gaus, N. (2011). Women and school leaderships: Factors deterring female teachers from holding principal positions at elementary schools in Makassar. *Advancing Women in Leadership, 31,* 175–188.

Jala, F., & Msthafa, B. (Eds.) (2001). *Education reform in the context of regional autonomy: The case of Indonesia.* Jakarta, Indonesia: Ministry of National Education, National Development Planning Agency and the World Bank.

Ministry of National Education. (2003). *Act of the Republic of Indonesia on National Education System* (No. 20/2003).

Republic of Indonesia: National Gazette 78. http://plani-polis.iiep.unesco.org/sites/planipolis/files/ressources/indonesia_education_act.pdf

Noerdin, E. (2002). *Customary institutions, Syariah law and the marginalisation of Indonesian women. Women in Indonesia: Gender, equity and development.* Institute of Southeast Asian Studies, Singapore.

OECD/Asian Development Bank (2015). *Education in Indonesia: Rising to the challenge.* Paris, France: OECD Publishing.

Parawansa, K. I. (2005). Enhancing women's political participation in Indonesia. In J. Ballington & A. M. Karam (Eds.), *Women in parliament: Beyond numbers* (pp. 82–90). Stockholm, Sweden: International IDEA.

POM/DFAT. (2016). *Female education personnel: A study of career progression. Report prepared by the Performance Oversight and Monitoring (POM) team of Australia's Education Partnership with Indonesia.* Jakarta, Indonesia.

Shakeshaft, C. (1989). *Women in educational administration.* Newbury Park, CA: Sage.

Sofo, F., Fitzgerald, R., & Jawas, U. (2012). Instructional leadership in Indonesian school reform: Overcoming the problems to move forward. *School Leadership & Management, 32*(5), 503–522.

Chapter 23

Celebrating Leadership Learning in Education Across Continents

Experiences of Women Leading in Rwanda

Shirley Randell

From 2009–2013 I worked in Rwanda where I was the Founding Director of the Centre for Gender, Culture and Development (CGCD) at the Kigali Institute of Education, now the Centre for Gender Studies at the University of Rwanda. This chapter showcases the life stories of team members I led and mentored in Rwanda who have been empowered to become leaders in their own country and abroad. This chapter illuminates the valuable contextual leadership stories of three graduates of the first cohort of the Master of Gender and Development (MGD) degree in Rwanda and illustrates the contextual leadership challenges and moments of celebration and success as each woman worked to enact change through her leadership.

Four years of civil war preceded the 1994 genocide against the Tutsi in Rwanda, which was a moment of cataclysmic rupture with the nation's previous history. Since, women have made striking gains, being elected to local and national governance bodies and entering the labor force in increasing numbers. In Rwanda, women have played a key role in democracy and development, and now top the world in political representation with 64 percent of parliamentarians being women. The presentation of three case studies of women leaders highlights the concepts of resilience, family resilience, empowerment, mentoring, and leadership and how they impact women.

This chapter commences with an introduction to the Rwandan context and reflection on the highly personal aspects of family resilience, empowerment, mentoring, and leadership and how they impact women. The research methodology is shared and case study methodology used to highlight the life stories of the women from Rwanda. The final section will propose some overall findings that focus on women, leaders, and education and making a difference in the world.

THE RWANDAN CONTEXT

Rwanda is a small, densely populated, landlocked country located in Central East Africa, surrounded by Burundi, the Democratic Republic of Congo (DRC), Tanzania, and Uganda. It is a member of both the East African Community and the Commonwealth. It is notorious because of the tragic 1994 genocide against the Tutsi in which nearly one million people were brutally murdered and nearly 500,000 women raped. General Paul Kagame, who headed the army that eventually liberated Rwanda from the genocidaires, has recently been elected for his third term as president. He has been a firm and popular leader inside Rwanda, with zero corruption and zero gender-based violence policies. Under his direction Rwanda has seen amazing economic growth, reduction in poverty, and significant improvement in health, education, and agriculture.

Rwanda is now a multiparty democracy with two houses of parliament: The Chamber of Deputies, in which 64 percent of parliamentarians are women, and the Senate, the upper house in which 36 percent are women. The government of Rwanda is committed to gender equality in all areas of public and private life and is proud of both long- and short-term development policies and strategies, which significantly address gender issues; for example, the National Constitution (Republic of Rwanda, 2015). There are also sector strategies in agriculture, health, education, and others; for example, the National Accelerated Plan on Women, Girls, Gender Equality and HIV in Rwanda, 2010–2014 (Republic of Rwanda, 2010) and the Girls' Education Policy (Republic of Rwanda, Ministry of Education, 2008).

Rwanda has almost achieved universal primary school enrollment and government policy is that all children should have compulsory, free secondary education to year 12. Initiatives to increase early childhood education and tertiary and vocational education and training are in place. Much of the remarkable trajectory of progress in Rwanda can be attributed to the contribution of women to reconciliation, peace, and reconstruction. Women not only hold a majority in Parliament but also are significantly represented in senior positions of the Ministry, the Judiciary, and the Public Service. Government departments, for many years, have supported gender focal points. In 2009 the need for gender theory to underpin the widespread gender practice was recognized through the establishment of an academic program at CGCD. The participants in this section are the 2011 foundation graduates of the MGD program.

Theoretical Underpinnings of Rwandan Women's Leadership Stories

The three case studies in this chapter are underpinned by the five key concepts of resilience, family resilience, empowerment, mentoring, and leadership, summarized. The women in this study have lived through traumatic experiences that they have overcome. As resilient leaders, they have demonstrated the ability to recover, learn, and grow stronger when confronted by chronic or crisis adversity (Patterson, Goens, & Reed, 2009).

The definition of resilience provided by Atkinson, Martin, and Rankin (2009) is "the ability to return to recover readily from the extremes of trauma, deprivation, threat or stress" (p. 137). A focus on resilience is consistent with the aim of promoting factors that allow individuals and communities to thrive (Sheldon, Frederickson, Rathunde, Csikszentmihalyi, & Haidt, 2000). What binds these definitions together is that they suggest there is an element of recovery of the individual from difficult events.

A separate body of research has since considered resilience as a family-level construct, in which the family is portrayed as an important unit of support (Patterson, 2002; Walsh, 1996). Family resilience has been described as how families use their strengths in times of stress (Hawley & DeHaan, 1996). Culture is also a vital aspect of family resilience (Boyden & Mann, 2005). The literature suggests that strong connectedness and being able to seek reassurance and safety are all factors that can help increase family resilience.

There are different forms of empowerment, including psychological, social, political, and outcome-oriented empowerment. Empowerment is inextricably related to, and relevant for, particular cultural and social contexts in which people live (Mohajer & Earnest, 2009). Freire (1999) describes the result of empowerment as a cultural synthesis, where all actors involved in the empowerment process undergo change and all knowledge is shared

equally. This knowledge has the power to enact social and cultural action and bring about change (Freire, 1999). Internationally, the term empowerment is used to describe a range of activities, including micro-credit and employment schemes, activities related to reproductive health and self-esteem for female adolescents, women's empowerment programs aimed at overcoming gender disparities, and spiritual empowerment activities of faith-based organizations.

Mentoring is mentioned as a vital contribution to a successful career, particularly for women. Mentoring has traditionally been defined as a one-to-one relationship in which an experienced, older career person guides and supports the career development of a new or early-career member. Sorcinelli and Yun (2007) have proposed a model that encourages a broader, more flexible network of support, in which no single person is expected to possess the expertise required to help someone navigate a career. In this model, robust networks are established by engaging multiple "mentoring partners" in nonhierarchical, collaborative, cross-cultural partnerships. These reciprocal partnerships benefit the "protégé" but also the "mentor."

In his autobiography, the great African leader Nelson Mandela compared leadership with shepherding. "He stays behind the flock, letting the most nimble go out ahead, whereupon the others follow, not realizing that all along they are being led from behind" (Mandela, 1997, p. 22). Linda Hill advocates for the importance of cooperation, building community, and harnessing people's collective genius—"creating a world to which people want to belong" (Hill, 2010). All members of the group then see themselves as contributing to results. One of a leader's roles as opposed to a manager is to influence and inspire staff, and much of that influence can come from knowledge gained by interacting with colleagues, employees, and customers. Courage, identified by Aristotle as the "first virtue," is another key characteristic of a great leader—courage to give voice to difficult decisions and give tough feedback, to take the hard and unpopular decisions, and to have confidence in others rather than always seeking to control (Treasurer, 2008).

The Research

This research used an exploratory, multiple, qualitative case study approach in a real-world setting. The overarching aim was to give a voice to the participants as it is important for their story to be heard in their own words. Therefore, a case study approach was the methodology of choice, as its main characteristics help bring the realities of the participant experiences to the reader and because it is a method which is now widely employed in social science research studies (Noor, 2008).

The cases under exploration are three women from Rwanda. They were approached to take part in the study as they are known to have made a difference to the institutions they work for, the communities they belong to, and had also played a role in empowering other women. Underpinned by the theoretical frameworks of resilience and empowerment, each person presented personal case narratives.

Jovia Kayirangwa: Consultant, Girl Effect Rwanda

Family Jovia is 42 years old, the third child and first girl in the family with three brothers and one sister, all born in Uganda. In 1959 Jovia's parents' families fled the civil war in Rwanda to Uganda and her father and mother met and married there. They were both teachers and urban refugees with minimal means but were nevertheless able to support their children in good schools where all were able to complete and graduate. Her parents taught many of the current leaders of Rwanda.

During her lifetime in Uganda, Jovia's parents were her role models—they provided the best they could for their children, lived in a good neighborhood, and never went without a meal. Most of Jovia's close relatives were outside Rwanda during the genocide—in Tanzania, Burundi, and the DRC. However, relatives who were still in Rwanda died during the 1994 genocide against the Tutsi, so the history of the country had an impact on all of them. Jovia is married to a very supportive husband and has three children, two girls and one boy.

Education and Professional Career When her family returned to Rwanda in 1995, Jovia enrolled at the reopened National University of Rwanda to study law and graduated in 2000. She suspended her MGD studies after completing the first semester in 2010 because she had to support her husband in diplomatic duties in South Africa. While there she learned more about women's issues; women faced rape, murder, and other forms of violence. This made Jovia realize that she needed to complete her studies in gender to find out why there was so much violence against women in different societies. After being away for three years, Jovia reenrolled in the MGD program at the CGCD in Rwanda which she completed with distinction. She learned to analyze all aspects of her life using a gender lens and from a gender perspective, including her own family, realizing that change needs to start from the smallest unit of society, which is the home.

Jovia also studied law and after graduating she had a variety of fascinating work experiences. She worked with the Minister for Justice in the Court of First Instance in Rubavu district as a public prosecutor; ActionAid Rwanda, as head of the administration, human resources and logistics department; United Nations Human Rights Council (UNHCR) in the protection department and the Butare field office as acting head, leading a Burundian refugee camp of 6,000 refugees; the First Lady's initiative in Rwanda—Imbuto Foundation; and in consultancy for Girl Effect Rwanda since 2015.

Mentors Jovia's mother was her biggest mentor and role model, who had a major impact on her life. Her mother pushed her to achieve her best, taught her how to work hard and to relate with everybody and how to love God above all. During her time at Imbuto, Jovia met her other role models, the First Couple of Rwanda. The First Lady, Jeanette Kagame, is zealous about her work in helping the most vulnerable families in the Rwandan community to get a better life. She is humble and loves excellence in all her work. She taught Jovia how to work with the local community and often commented, "Be humble and the most vulnerable will reach out to you." Her husband, H. E. Paul Kagame, the President of Rwanda, loves his country and his people with so much passion. They inspire her and she said she will always look up to them.

Leadership In Jovia's work as a public prosecutor, abused women would come to her as the only woman in the prosecution department where she helped them with legal challenges, learning from them and interacting with them. This inspired her to work with joy as a leader toward the empowerment of women in the society. She was among the first lawyers to review and pilot the Gacaca courts structure in Rwanda. On the UNHCR Gender Based Violence (GBV) committee that focused on protection issues for urban refugees, Jovia was able to help reintegrate many Rwandan returnee families, mainly female-headed households, to resettle in their country.

The biggest achievement of the team was to repatriate 4,000 Burundians back to Burundi and resettle over 80 families in other countries—Canada, Australia, and others, and to finally close the Burundian refugee camp. On a daily basis, Jovia supported refugees to organize their lives, supervised distribution of food and nonfood items, ensured children were enrolled in temporary schools, and organized refugee committees and governing bodies. Her inspiration during that time was how women refugee leaders managed cross-cutting issues around their complicated lives, working hard to uphold their families when their husbands had given up because of displacement and loss of their normal livelihoods.

These women took advantage of the Rwandan system and laws, which were fair and empowered them. At Imbuto Foundation, Jovia led an HIV/AIDS prevention program that focused on enabling HIV positive mothers to be mentor mothers at health centers. Jovia worked in 50 health centers across the country and closely supervised

80 HIV+ empowered women who gave testimonies to encourage expectant women to test for HIV and enroll in the Prevention of Mother To Child Transmission program with the aim of HIV+ women giving birth to HIV– babies.

Empowerment   At Girl Effect, Jovia has entered a new world by focusing especially on adolescent girls with the motto "educate the girl and you will have educated the world. Empower the girl and you will have empowered the woman of tomorrow." It is joyful leadership to see adolescent girls becoming empowered, making right choices around education, job opportunities, reproductive rights, and marriage, knowing that later this will have a positive impact on their lives, families, and society as a whole. With her gender expertise, Jovia is in position to continue to provide leadership in advising how gender can be mainstreamed to ensure equality and equity are attained.

Viviane Kalumire Furaha: Executive Director, IMARA Women Empowerment Foundation

Family   Viviane is 36 years old, third in a family of eight children, comprising four boys and four girls, with only two years age difference between each. She was born in Bukavu, a town in Eastern DRC and was raised in the Roman Catholic Church tradition. Viviane was very close with her siblings, and her big sister was her best friend. Her mother was very spiritual; a wonderful, loving, compassionate woman whose values built in Viviane her passion to advocate for vulnerable women and girls and thus led to her career in gender and development, while her father forged in her the "Go get it!" attitude.

Viviane's parents owned a business together and were incredibly hard workers. They did not have the chance for enough education, her father completing elementary school and her mother high school. However, they ended up building up a wholesale business and became successful, thus allowing their children to have the opportunity to study in very good schools, since they both believed that good education was the way to succeed in life.

Having successful entrepreneurial parents who had started from nothing gave Viviane the strong belief and confidence that nothing is impossible. Her father was very strict, especially with schools and the choice of friends surrounding them, monitoring everything his children did, and they had lots of restrictions. Her life was between the school, home, library, and church. "It was like we were in a soldier camp with the chief commander, Dad." He said, "I put you in nice schools but it depends on you to take advantage of the opportunities. It is your own life and you are responsible for it."

The first tragedy of her childhood was her first experience with domestic violence when her dad beat her

mother for the first time, ending up in hospital. That day changed the image Viviane had of her father. Despite all his restrictions in their education, she used to look at him as a role model and suddenly he was violent to her mother, that changed everything for her. Then from October 1996, her family experienced a tragic war and its consequences in DRC during which women and girls faced serious GBV, especially rape as a weapon of war. This was the end of Viviane's somewhat happy and stable childhood.

She lost close family members and experienced trauma that impacted on her health, family, and social life. The most life-changing was she contracted HIV from sexual abuse; after which she struggled to survive in a world controlled by men. These experiences impacted Viviane's adulthood terribly because she lost trust and confidence in men. In 2001, after graduating from high school, Viviane left DRC with her sisters and returned to Rwanda. She used silence as a coping mechanism in order to forget the terrible things that had happened to her. She did not talk and did not mention any of her traumatic experiences to her university friends. She pretended everything was ok and was living as a normal young woman. But it was not easy. Viviane is now a single mother with a six-year-old girl.

Education and Professional Career   Viviane completed elementary and high school and knew she had to perform very well and worked hard. Influenced by a family friend who was a pharmacist, Viviane decided to take biology and chemistry as her main subjects for her last three years in high school and went on to study pharmacy at the National University of Rwanda. She found that she enjoyed and learned more through tutoring her classmates and thus discovered the teaching talent that led later to her academic career.

Viviane's career life is divided between being a pharmacist, an academic, a researcher, a gender and development expert, and a social entrepreneur. Being one of the pioneers who established Rwandan Women Living with HIV/AIDS and Fighting Against It (FRSL+/RW) was a life changing experience for her. This was a great opportunity for Viviane to express her passion for adding value and empowering women and girls who have been in vulnerable situations like her. Since then she has been involved in many national and international bodies such as the African Community Advisory Board, an advocacy hub for fair, sustainable, and affordable pricing and access to HIV and tuberculosis treatment in sub-Saharan African countries.

Viviane relocated to the United States where she gained certification to practice pharmacy. She is also part of the John Maxwell Team as a trainer, speaker, and coach. She is planning to enroll for a PhD in Global Health. She is passionate about research tasks as research is a powerful tool that not only gives her and other participants a voice but also allows her to bring her contribution to science, inform policies, and serve as a tool of effective advocacy.

Mentors Viviane developed a love of reading books as a child and became inspired by the lives of her role models and heroes who were instrumental in her choice of subjects to study: sciences from Marie Curie, and how to deal with life issues and become a good leader from Nelson Mandela, Mother Teresa, Helen Keller, Maya Angelou, and Jeanne d'Arc. There are other multiple role models in Viviane's life that she reaches out to.

For her academic career, Professor Kadima Justin and Peter Sallah from the University of Rwanda are great role models and mentors. She always mentioned Professor Shirley Randell as her gender and development expert mentor, not a one-on-one style mentoring, but she follows Randell's work, publications, and social media and gets guidance from that. Lillian Mworeko, the International Community of Women Living with HIV (ICW) East Africa coordinator, is Viviane's one-on-one mentor as a woman living with HIV advocate. Having been blessed to be equipped by people who believe in her potential, Viviane wants to empower others. Yvonne Birungi from Rwanda, who graduated in social science at the National University of Rwanda in 2012, and Helena Nangombe, a young woman living with HIV and youth advocate from Namibia, are two of Viviane's mentees.

Leadership As a leader, Viviane wants to be a good influence in people's lives by adding value to them, and in order to do that she herself has to grow so that she can effectively give back. She thus continually invests in her personal development and every day makes sure that she grows "at least one percent better than I was yesterday." Reflecting and journaling help her to keep track of her growth and the influence she is having in people's lives. As a lecturer Viviane adds value to her students. As a grant writer, she secures funds for economic development and sees the positive result in women's lives through their empowerment. As a researcher, she informs policies and shares success stories.

Viviane's joy today is the establishment of the two great IMARA women empowerment organizations. Imara, from the Swahili language, means stable and comes from the Swahili saying "Simama Imara" which means "Stay Firm, Dynamic." These two organizations are inspired by her life story full of various inequalities and GBV and their consequences that affected her physical and psychological health and socioeconomic empowerment. However, inspired and encouraged by the brave and strong way many women face all the problems of life, Viviane has overcome those troubles. She has given her life meaning by becoming a strong entrepreneurial

passionate woman who can equip other women to stay strong and dynamic regardless of vulnerable situations, to regain control of their lives and move from victim to victorious in order to create a stable society where all women live in dignity and respect for their human rights.

Empowerment In 2006, psychologically and physically weakened by her double life and all the traumas she had been through since 1996, Viviane suffered severe depression with memory loss in her fourth year at university and was put into a psychiatric hospital for six months. She began to develop many HIV-related sicknesses and attempted suicide. While she was recovering, her counselors and social workers, one also a woman living with HIV, suggested she join a group of educated women leaders living with HIV. They founded the local nongovernmental organization (NGO), FRSL+/RW. These activities helped Viviane regain confidence in herself to taste life again. She felt useful for the society since she could speak out for the rights of people who suffered like her.

Her innovative global social enterprise, an authentic African fashion brand called IMARA Social Enterprise (ISE), empowers women socially and economically in sub-Saharan Africa to break through the intergenerational cycle of poverty by providing them with the tools and support to reclaim their own future and flourish as independent entrepreneurs driving development in their communities. In 2013 she also cofounded a NGO, IMARA-Women Empowerment Foundation (IWEF), to advocate for the social, economic, and cultural rights of vulnerable women and girls in DRC, essential to their dignity and empowerment. As a women's rights and health-for-all advocate she has contributed from September 2013 as a blog writer for the Inter Press Service News Agency to the Countdown to Zero stories on the global plan to eliminate new HIV infections and keep mothers living with HIV alive.

Josephine Mukakalisa: Country Manager, Right to Play Tanzania

Family Josephine Mukakalisa is 53 years old. She is the fifth born in a family of eight children, five girls and three boys in the Rusizi district in the Western Province of Rwanda. Although her mother never went to school, she was very intelligent, hard-working, and lived peacefully with neighbors and family members. Josephine's father was a teacher and inspired her to become a teacher in 1984, teaching at the same school as her dad. She liked to play volleyball at secondary school, which constituted one of the motivations for her to pursue university studies, where it was possible to develop her sport talents by participating in competitions and tournaments. That was achieved when she had the opportunity to be part of the first Rwandan national female volleyball team in 1989. Josephine was married in 1991 and has one child, a boy.

Education and Professional Career   Josephine was among the best in primary and secondary school and dreamed of becoming a teacher like her father. She completed secondary school at Nyamasheke, Institut Sainte Famille and started working as a teacher at Murehe primary school in a remote rural area. Although this was the achievement of Josephine's childhood dream, it was not sufficient. Her objective was to teach at secondary school. French and physical education were her favorite subjects and she wanted to do further studies and teach in French, a teaching language in secondary school. The application for university studies did not take long to be approved, and in 1985 Josephine won a scholarship to the National University of Rwanda, after only one year teaching at primary school. In 1990, she graduated with distinction in the Faculty of Education Sciences, majoring in School Psychology. Late in 2010 Josephine had the chance to join the CGCD to study for her master's degree.

Josephine has worked in different organizations, both national and international NGOs. This has been mostly in the area of reproductive health where she began in 1991 with the National Population Office after the completion of her university studies. She was responsible for the integration of population and development content, including sexual and reproductive health, in the national education curriculum for primary and secondary education.

From 1998 Josephine worked with Association Rwandaise pour le Bien-Etre Familial (ARBEF), the Rwandese Family Welfare Association, a specialized national NGO for sexual and reproductive health, and as a member of the International Planned Parenthood Federation. In ARBEF she occupied respectively the positions of responsibility for information, education and communication, director of programs, and director of advocacy and partnership. In 2005, Josephine joined IntraHealth International and had the responsibility of supporting the development of the curriculum of nurses and midwives being established for the first time in Rwanda.

In 2007, she was appointed national program manager for the Right to Play Rwanda Country Office and after excellent performance was promoted to country manager for Right to Play Tanzania. During all these years of experience, Josephine has been inspired by the need for promoting the well-being of families, most specifically children and youth. Her dream of becoming a university teacher is still alive and she is still watching for any opportunity to obtain access to a PhD program that will allow her to occupy confidently the position of university lecturer. During her professional life, Josephine was appointed to the board of the National Information Of-

fice of Rwanda from 1999 to 2009, and has been a board member and president of the Women Cooperative for Family Economic Development.

Mentors   Josephine describes her mentors as her role models, her work supervisors, and her lecturers. She mentors her staff and the sportspeople whom she coaches, and sees mentorship as an important part of her life and ongoing responsibilities.

Leadership   Josephine has developed her leadership skills since she was very young when she was appointed as class representative in secondary school but also when leading a volleyball team as assistant captain and then captain at secondary school and university. Her leadership skills matured when she was working with ARBEF as program director and in Right to Play as program manager. She has facilitated various training workshops and conferences for staff and partners of many organizations. Combining managing programs with managing people has not been an easy task but with patience, hard work, and determination, it became possible for her and led to the position of country leader in an international position in Tanzania. Josephine has joy and is satisfied any time she achieves her goals, and when she is with her family members, her son, and her husband, taking care of them, especially when she visits her mother and sees how she is still working hard despite being 85 years of age.

Empowerment   Josephine believes that her personal empowerment has come from different capacity-building opportunities, through training, experience sharing, traveling to different countries, and learning from other women's successes. Inspiration, good coaching from supervisors, who provided her with opportunities to take initiatives and decisions, have contributed to Josephine's growth, and she feels responsible for passing this on to the people she is coaching now. She will be pleased when a successor arises from the people she supervises at this moment.

Participating in sport has also made a big impact in Josephine's life. The skills she learned through sporting activities, teamwork, discipline, resiliency, respect for the rules, confidence, and striving to reach goals have contributed to her personal development and the leader she is today. These skills are central to the philosophy of her organization, Right to Play, which uses sport and play to educate and empower children and youth.

CONCLUSION

The narratives of the Rwandan women highlight strong parallels. All of the participants have supportive families, especially parents, who valued education and encouraged them to get a university education. The women are involved, passionate, and supportive community advocates. They display a strong social justice and human rights conscience. While the Rwandese women experienced the tragic consequences of the 1994 genocide against the Tutsi, all showed great resilience and involvement in the rebuilding of their country. They have taken on the challenge of accepting senior government, NGO, and academic positions both inside and outside their countries, often learning new skills on the way.

The findings resonate with the vital and uncontested importance of education, the desire to be empowered, the capacity to be resilient and adaptive and the importance of giving back to the community. They have greatly benefited from their role models and mentors, but are now themselves providing support to many mentees.

Core recommendations which arise from the exploration of these case studies include providing women with avenues to feel empowered, developing access to education at all levels (primary to tertiary), and also supporting women to further their studies in areas they see are needed. Offering adaptive structures and mechanisms that build resilience and grow strong communities where both men and women are engaged in a constant dialogue for growth is also important. Through transnational alliances and collaboration, women can cross borders to generate change, transform, and bring about capacity building in their communities, which in turn grows all communities.

REFERENCES

Atkinson, P. A., Martin, C. R., & Rankin, J. (2009). Resilience revisited. *Journal of Psychiatric & Mental Health Nursing, 16*(2), 137–145.

Boyden, J., & Mann, G. (2005). Children's risk, resilience, and coping in extreme situations. In M. Ungar (Ed.), *Handbook for working with children and youth: Pathways to resilience across cultures and contexts* (pp. 3–26). Thousand Oaks, CA: Sage.

Freire, P. (1999). *Pedagogy of the oppressed* (Rev. ed.). New York, NY: Continuum.

Hawley, D., & DeHaan, L. (1996). Toward a definition of family resilience: Integrating life-span and family perspectives. *Family Process, 35*(3), 283–298. doi: 10.1111/j.1545 -5300.1996.00283.x

Hill, L. (2010, Spring). Leading from behind. *Harvard Business Review*, 5.

Mandela, N. (1997). *Long walk to freedom*. Boston, MA: Little, Brown and Company.

Mohajer, N., & Earnest, J. (2009). Youth empowerment for the most vulnerable: A model based on the pedagogy of Freire and experiences in the field. *Health Education, 109*(5), 424–438. doi: 10.1108/09654280910984834

Noor, K. B. M. (2008). Case study: A strategic research methodology. *American Journal of Applied Science, 5*(11), 1602–1604.

Patterson, J. L., Goens, G. A., & Reed, D. E. (2009). *Resilient leadership for turbulent times: A guide to thriving in the face of adversity*. Lanham, MD: Rowman & Littlefield.

Patterson, J. M. (2002a). Integrating family resilience and family stress theory. *Journal of Marriage and Family, 64*, 349–360.

Republic of Rwanda. (2010). *National accelerated plan on women, girls, gender equality and HIV in Rwanda, 2010–2014*. Kigali: Republic of Rwanda.

Republic of Rwanda. (2015). *The Constitution of the Republic of Rwanda of 2003 as revised in 2015*, The Official Gazette no. Special of 24/12/2015. http://www.minijust.gov.rw/ fileadmin/Law_and_Regulations/Official_Gazette_no_Spe cial_of_24.12.2015__2___1_.pdf

Republic of Rwanda, Ministry of Education (2008). *Girls' education policy*. http://www.mineduc.gov.rw/fileadmin/ user_upload/Girls_Education.pdf

Sheldon, K. M., Fredrickson, B., Rathunde, K., Csikszentmihalyi, M., & Haidt, J. (2000). *Positive psychology manifesto*. Manifesto presented at Akumal 1 conference and revised during the Akumal 2 meeting. Retrieved from http://www .optimalfunctioning.com/featured/positive-psychology-man ifesto.html

Sorcinelli, M. D., & Yun, J. H. (2007). From mentors to mentoring networks: Mentoring in the new academy. *Change Magazine, 39*(6), 58.

Treasurer, B. (2008). *Courage goes to work*. San Francisco, CA: Berrett-Koehler Publishers.

Walsh, F. (1996). The concept of family resilience: Crisis and challenge. *Family Process, 35*(3), 261–281. doi: 10.1111/j .1545-5300.1996.00261.x

Chapter 24

A Female Leader in a Man's World

Stories of Women Leaders of Catholic Schools

Yvonne Masters

In this chapter, the stories of three Australian female principals of Catholic secondary schools are presented, not as complete stories in themselves, but as illustrations of the ways in which gender plays a role in the experience of principalship for these women. The stories of the female principals emerged as part of a larger study on the role of the Catholic school principal. The study used narrative inquiry (Clandinin & Connelly, 2000), and was conducted with the researcher being a coparticipant rather than an objective outsider. As such, the study was discussed using first person and this has been maintained in this chapter. This research specifically explored the lived (and living) role of the principal through principal narratives in order to understand more deeply how principals perceived themselves and their work.

Being a female school principal for the Catholic Church, a traditionally patriarchal system, has its challenges, but many female principals still find satisfaction and joy in their work. This became very evident as a group of principals told their stories during a research project which explored the nature of being a Catholic school principal in the Australian secondary school system.

Gender was a theme that had not been purposefully addressed in the project but became one which could not be ignored as the narratives of the female participants were analyzed. These school leaders described joy and fulfillment in their roles, poignantly mixed with discussion of the challenges they faced. Interestingly, many of these challenges could be related to their gender, but reference to gender was usually more implicit than explicit. Other studies reveal that this "silence" is not unusual, leading to the possibility of misinterpreting the subtle references that are made. This can engender a situation where "the difficulty is to work out what the silence is saying" (Grace, 1995, p. 188).

LEADERSHIP IN THE CATHOLIC SCHOOL MILIEU

There are indications of dissatisfaction with how the role of principal is perceived, particularly among women in other leadership positions in schools. The Leadership Succession for Catholic Schools in Victoria, South Australia and Tasmania (VSAT) Project reports on leadership succession for Catholic schools and makes comment on gender differences in terms of pathways to the principalship and in terms of time spent in other leadership positions and particularly in more than one school (Flagship for Catholic Educational Leadership, 2003, pp. 40–41).

The data from this research reveal that more women than men enter the position of principal without long-term leadership experience. The data also reveal that the position of principal is less attractive to women than men with 52.6 percent of women in other senior leadership positions being unwilling to apply for the role of principal compared to 24.6 percent for men with the researchers contending, "this under-representation of female applicants, given that females constitute the significant majority of staff in Catholic schools, is a critical issue and is worthy of further investigation by diocesan authorities" (Flagship for Catholic Educational Leadership, 2003, p. 44).

The report also suggests that disincentives, such as perceived male bias, recruitment problems, and the impact of the role of principal on family life, may all be responsible for these findings.

The majority of teachers are women, yet a minority of principals in Catholic schools, at least in Victoria (Catholic Education Commission of Victoria [CECV], 2002), are female. Brooking, Collins, Court, and O'Neill (2003) posit that this imbalance creates a structure that

156

is a disincentive to women joining the principalship or remaining within it.

While the restructuring of schools in the 1990s and introduction of self-managing schools in the Victorian government education sector has been discussed as providing an antithetical atmosphere for women principals (Blackmore, 1996), due in part to "the re-masculinisation of the centre or core" (Blackmore, 1996, p. 345), Power (2002) suggests that the male-dominated nature of the Catholic Church has been responsible for the oppression of women in Catholic education since its inception in the 19th century and that this domination has been based on religious truth for "maleness has been dignified by the theologians as the only genuine way of being human, thus making Jesus' embodiment as a male an ontological necessity rather than an historical option" (pp. 64–65).

Catholic schools belong to an idiosyncratic education system and, perhaps more importantly, they are a part of the institution of the Catholic Church. While the ownership of an individual school, for example, whether it is diocesan, parish, or congregational, has some effect upon how that school is governed, it is ultimately within the wider Church context that all Catholic schools function.

The Catholic Church is, perhaps, one of the most archetypal examples of hierarchical governance. The likelihood that women will be part of the Catholic clergy, and therefore the leadership, is very remote given that Pope John Paul II (1994) stated, "I declare that the Church has no authority whatsoever to confer priestly ordination on women and that this judgment is to be definitively held by all the Church's faithful (No. 4)."

This strongly worded statement refers directly to women in Church leadership. In terms of women and educational leadership within the Catholic tradition, while several orders of nuns have been responsible for setting up schools in various countries of the world, these orders have been answerable to the bishops and priests of the dioceses and parishes respectively. Power (2002) argues strongly that the male-dominated nature of the Catholic Church "relegates women to the margins of significance . . . it raises questions as to how it has affected the way women feel and are treated and how priests view women as leaders" (p. 178).

It is perhaps no surprise that the VSAT Project (2003) found "perceived male bias" to be one of the eight main disincentives to applying for principalship. The statistics (Catholic Education Commission of Victoria, 2007) regarding the gender of principals of Catholic secondary schools in Victoria make interesting reading in light of the patriarchal, and also, one is tempted to say, patronizing view of the Church regarding women in leadership. In 2005, there were 94 secondary schools (including two P–10 schools and one P–9 school) in the

state of Victoria, only three of which had co-principals. This equates to 97 percent of the Catholic secondary schools having sole principals and, of these, 66 percent were male.

The statistics are more interesting when the breakdown on type of school is made, with 83.5 percent of principals of co-educational schools being male and 100 percent of boys' school principals being male. The latter may not seem surprising, but, in comparison, 14.2 percent of principals in girls' schools are male (Melbourne Catholic Education Office, 2003). Furthermore, 75.8 percent of the female principals were sole principals of girls' schools and of the six female principals of co-educational schools (12.5 percent of the principals of such schools), three were religious principals. Only men lead the church, and, based on these statistics, men lead the church's schools in the state of Victoria, at least, and the statistics are probably repeated elsewhere.

Research Methodology

The purpose of the original research was to examine the experiences of educational leaders, both male and female, who held the position of principal within the Catholic School system. The stories of the female principals' experiences emerged from this larger study on the role of the Catholic school principal, revealing differences in experience from their male counterparts. Juxtaposing the gendered stories revealed a range of issues faced by the female principals that were either unknown to the male principals or glossed over as not important challenges. The intention of focusing on this group of participants was to use narrative inquiry (Clandinin & Connelly, 2000) to elicit the voices of educational leaders from within the Catholic School system.

The research was designed and conducted with the researcher (myself) being a coparticipant rather than an objective outsider. Purposive sampling was used as a means to engage participants from existing professional and social networks whereby trusting relationships were already established to more easily facilitate the sharing of information during the narrative encounters. The leadership narratives from each principal were crafted and analyzed through thematic analysis, and emergent core themes were analyzed, refined, and compared and contrasted across each individual participant's contributions.

Research Participants

Five principals, three females and two males, participated in the research journey with me. They were colleagues and friends, people with whom meals, joys, sorrows, and experience of the role of Victorian Catholic secondary school principal had been shared. One had been a principal in the diocese when I entered the role; one was a deputy principal in one of the schools when I arrived in the diocese, later leaving to become a principal interstate and then returning to the diocese as a coprincipal; a third was a teacher in one of the schools when I first arrived, who became a member of the Catholic Education Office before taking on the role of principal; and the others joined the diocese from other dioceses, taking up principal roles for the first time. Between us we had amassed over 36 years of experience as principals within the diocese. Pseudonyms are used in the presentation of their stories below.

Bridget

Bridget was principal of Alpha College, Acacia, a coeducational 7–12 parish school of approximately 800 students. When data collection commenced Bridget had been a principal for two and a half years and had just completed her first principal review. She was 38 years old when she took up this role, her first as principal. A short time after the data collection phase was completed, Bridget left the principalship and entered the Catholic Education Office as a consultant.

Mary

Mary had held the position of principal for five and a half years at Beta College in Banksia, a small tourist town. The population of the town was increasing when the data collection began and there were talks of the school changing from a 7–10 to a 7–12 college. Mary was a young principal, having been about 32 when she took on the role. Mary also had a young family, including three babies born while she was a principal.

Patrick

Patrick was principal of Gamma College in Hakea, a large regional center, for 13 years at the commencement of the data collection for my research. The college is coeducational and has approximately 1,200 students. It is a 7–12 school and the Mercy Sisters are its congregational leaders. In his late 50s, Patrick is an experienced principal with a range of other positions behind him.

Teresa and Thomas

Teresa and Thomas were coprincipals of another congregation-owned school, this time administered by the Brigidine Sisters. Delta College is another 7–12 coeducational school of 700 students, in Boronia, a rural city with a major tourist industry. Thomas had been a deputy in a college in the diocese, but left the diocese to take up the role of principal in a Catholic secondary college in New South Wales. He returned to the diocese when one of the coprincipals at Delta College retired. Teresa came to the diocese as one of the inaugural coprincipals, sharing the position with the person who had been principal of the college for five years as a sole principal prior to that. Both Teresa and Thomas were in their late 40s when they first became principals.

Findings

The leadership experiences and narratives shared by the participants highlighted numerous complexities and opportunities. These were located in the core aspects of balancing personal and professional lives, negotiating the Parish Priest relationship and experiencing ambivalence in their leadership roles.

Juggling Family and Career

Juggling family and career could be a tension for a principal of any school, regardless of system and regardless of whether primary or secondary. Any school principal with a family, whether a male or female principal, could be faced at some time, as I was on some occasions, with the dilemma of deciding whether to stay home with a sick child or partner or to attend the meeting at school. However, this dilemma could be exacerbated in the case of a female principal where the local community was traditional in its views. In traditional communities, as I experienced many times both as a deputy principal and also as a principal, there is often a contradictory belief that mothers should be home with their children and also a belief that school principals, regardless of gender, should be constantly available for meetings, sports carnivals, and other important school occasions. There appears to be no consideration of the fact that these two beliefs conflict when the principal happens to be a woman.

Of the three women principals, only Bridget had no children. Teresa's children had all grown up before the time of my research and she made very little comment about family as any source of tension for a principal. Because gender and family were not specifically addressed as themes within the open interviews that were conducted, but rather emerged as themes when the interviews were analyzed, it is not possible to say that Teresa had never experienced juggling family and career as a tension at any stage of her leadership career in schools. However, Teresa's overall silence regarding family could indicate either that, by the time she became a school principal, family was no longer an issue or that being a coprincipal alleviated any tensions that family might cause.

Bridget was far more open about gendered experience, particularly of family. She explained, "I have an easier run than a lot of other women because I don't have children and because I have a partner who's almost full time at home. And that means that I don't have the tension between juggling the good little woman while at home and being the professional."

Bridget's comment makes apparent that she was acutely aware of the tensions of being a wife/mother as well as professional and that balancing both can be problematic. However, while agreeing that being a mother and a principal at the same time is challenging, she also commented that having young children could be challenging for male principals as well. In discussing how the role of principal is not particularly family-friendly, Bridget described how a male colleague coped:

> He's managed; he manages because of the way he does his role. He'll often have his kids in at the school when he's doing the people stuff, or the public face stuff. I've watched him in operation there, and he'll be at an event and he'll have a kid sitting on his hip. He'll be carrying one of his children round and he'll be doing pressing the flesh sort of stuff, at a fete or at a sporting day or something like that.

What is not known is whether this approach would be accepted by a community, in the case of a female principal. My opinion is that, while carrying a child on one's hip reflects well on a male principal, showing him in the light of a good family man, for a woman to do this would not be so acceptable, where many would believe that a woman needs to prioritize rather than combine. Bridget explained that her male colleague's approach "endears him to the community," conjecturing that this was because he was the first lay-principal. Bridget commented that being accepted by the community had been difficult for Mary, "[she] suffered from that enormously when she went to Banksia. Because she replaced a man whose family was grown up and finished and Henry spent every waking moment in that school and had been there so long that the community just knew him and the fact that she went home—you know, at four o'clock some days—that was considered to be a mortal sin."

Mary had young children and she was the only female Catholic secondary school principal who, at least at the time of the interviews, had become pregnant while being principal. Others had children before taking on the role, but Mary was unique in having given birth three times during the course of her principalship. Mary's situation was therefore quite different from any of the other principals and, indeed, from any other principal in a Victorian Catholic secondary school. She described herself "as a woman who has tried to effectively juggle a family life with a working life and who has had babies as a principal which has not been an easy thing."

Mary's husband stayed home and looked after the house and the children. This switching of stereotyped gender roles was not commented upon by Mary, and I wonder whether she had ever been subjected to the same comments that I received regarding what others viewed as taking over the role of the man of the house! This is an entire area that would make a separate, and fascinating, research study.

Mary did reflect on how the diocesan culture of support had allowed her to be both mother and principal, where she stated that she could not have taken on the principalship without support at the systemic level. However, even with home and systemic support, the toll of juggling personal and professional was reflected in some of her statements where she acknowledged:

> Having a young family's not quite so difficult, but having a baby is absolutely exhausting. I've found it very, very hard at times. Part of it is just being tired all the time, functioning on probably three cylinders. The other part of it, though, is the demands of outside hours stuff. There's a very fine line between balancing your work and your family commitments. . . . I think it was still an area for people to be a little bit critical of me in my appraisal; 'why didn't you go to such and such?', 'why weren't you at such and such?' . . . So, even though I'm quite comfortable with it, I think that other people probably look at my role and probably think that I should be doing much more 'stuff' out there which I'm just not prepared to do at the moment.

Mary made clear that it was a struggle to balance all aspects of her life and to do well all that was required in each area. Bateson (1989) supports this view of struggle and, further, states that each individual struggle builds toward models that could assist others in situations similar to Mary's:

> Women today, trying to compose lives that will honor all their commitments and still express all their potentials with a certain unitary grace, do not have an easy task. It is important, however, to see that, in finding a personal path among the discontinuities and moral ambiguities they face, they are performing a creative synthesis with a value . . . that can sometimes be shared as models of possibility for men and women in the future.

Negotiating the Parish Priest Relationship

All school principals have to negotiate a wide variety of relationships; with students, with staff, with parents, with the community, and with school and system administrators. However, there is a unique relationship that has to be negotiated by those who are Catholic school princi-pals, the relationship between principal and parish priest.

Catholic schools are considered to be an integral and important arm of the institution of the Catholic Church. This means that Catholic schools, most particularly through the person of the principal are accountable to both secular (in the form of the state and Common-wealth governments who provide funding) and religious authorities. Within this context the parish priest holds an important position. In many schools, the parish priest is both the employer, and thereby the person ul-timately responsible for ensuring that the school fulfils all requirements of being a school, and the Canonical Administrator of the school, appointed by the Bishop, as the link between school and Church. As Power (2002) states, "Catholic Education is situated within this broad Catholic Church organization and the Catholic school's relationship to the church is mediated by the position of the Parish Priest" (p. 39).

Only Bridget and Mary discussed their relationship with the parish priest in their interviews. Both were prin-cipals of parish-owned schools and had been appointed after male principals who were considered successful. My own experience was similar, taking over from a male principal in a parish-owned school. For all three of us there was a need to negotiate how the relationship would occur and we all also had to renegotiate this relationship when the parish priest changed. Patrick, although in a jointly owned school, commented on the power of the parish priest as employer when he stated, "the parish priest can get rid of you," but he was also quick to point out that, at least as far as he was concerned, the parish priests that he had worked with "wouldn't have a bar of that." It appeared that Patrick experienced no relationship struggle with the parish priest. Thomas and Teresa also didn't comment in any way about the parish priest–prin-cipal relationship. However, as with Patrick, their school was owned by a religious congregation, the parish priest was not the employer.

Mary, when asked whether the parish priest and the caliber of the parish priest could make a difference to the tensions and frustrations of the principal, replied, "Mas-sive. Absolutely massive." One way she described was through the expectations of the parish priest. With her former parish priest, Mary stated, "I would never have gone into any formal or informal discussion or any meet-ing without scripting myself beforehand. I was very, very careful about how I did it, but because of that I never had any worries. I'd have had serious worries if I hadn't taken that much care beforehand though. I think my current parish priest is a little more forgiving."

Careful negotiation of her relationship with her parish priest has been necessary for Mary, particularly as the

relationship changed after the first parish priest left and renegotiation took place. Mary stated that she had learned how to "play" the relationship to ensure that she could continue to lead in her own way.

Like Mary, Bridget also commented on her differing relationships with two parish priests. When she was first appointed principal of Acacia College, Bridget found that she was working with "a parish priest who was pretty happy for the school just to get on and do what it needed to do, and he would sign off on anything. He used to say to me, 'Bridget, thank you for letting me know that and I'll just trust you to deal with it.'"

By contrast, the advent of a new parish priest saw changes for Bridget, "There was a new parish priest who wants the school to be very much a parish school and who wants to be present in the school, and who wants every-body to see the links and who wants to be the employer. So there's been a huge tension there for me, and it's re-quired a lot of work for me and the parish priest in coming to terms for what that means for both our expectations."

In my own case, I spent my first two years establishing credibility with my parish priest in terms of my ability to lead the school and also to handle the finances. The school had previously been run by nuns. This had led to the parish priest keeping the financial reins in his hands. The parish priest trusted the nuns to educate the students and to provide them with a safe and caring environment. However, he believed that if he left the finances in their hands that they would send the school bankrupt. I learned this only some years into my principalship after a good relationship had been forged and most of the financial decisions were mine. In the early years, I felt that I was going cap in hand for money and negotiating a very slip-pery relationship.

Over the eight years that I worked with the parish priest who appointed me, our relationship developed and deepened. By the end I felt both trusted and supported, but it had taken time and energy. However, after his death, I, like Mary and Bridget, was challenged to forge a new relationship with a person who had a very different view of the role of the parish priest in the school. In many ways, it was like going back to square one and my role became more difficult as a consequence. I finally found that sustaining my role in the light of the new relationship was untenable, and I chose to seek a new position.

The change in relationship that Bridget, Mary, and I encountered could be read as part of the natural ad-justment that is required with any change of personnel, rather than as a gendered experience. Where I believe the impact of gender does become apparent is in the silence of both Patrick and Thomas, both of whom experienced changes in parish priest at some time in their principal-ship, but felt no need to comment on the change as problematic, and also their silence about the role of the parish priest in their schools. Their relationship with their parish priest did not have to be so carefully negotiated as with the female principals. Power (2002) claims that a changing of parish priests can be problematic:

> Uncertainty regarding relationships can occur during a principal's term of office as the priest who employed that principal may transfer to another parish at any stage during a principal's contract. The incoming priest may act very differently. As one experienced female principal shared, "I think the Parish Priest can either be one of the most wonderful things to help you in a principalship, or can make your principalship hell." (pp. 275–276)

It is telling that her example is of the difficulties for a female principal.

Embracing the Ambivalence in the Role

It is clear that there are tensions in being a female principal of a Catholic school. Women in this role can be caught up in the binaries of mother and professional or in the male dominated hegemony of the church, where the parish priest is often the employer. The stories told by Bridget and Mary, in particular, reinforced by the literature about women in leadership, can easily be mistaken for tales of woe, where women are constantly battling and finding little joy in their positions. However, there is joy found in the role and other benefits as well. Mary states of the challenges in the role that, "I know I'm a very different person now from when I started up and I also believe I'm a better person now than when I started up. I reckon that they, in some ways, probably from a personal point of view, brought out the best in me . . . I don't always love what I do, but in the general sense I do."

Bridget also reveals that she finds joy in her role, tempered by ambivalence. "I love it, except when I loathe it!" Ambivalence is not unusual in discussions regarding school principalship, the position is both loved and hated; that there are times when principals feel isolated and unappreciated, and others where they are certain that there are rewards; that principals sometimes feel overwhelmed by the nature of the work that they do; and that principals wish to remain in the position, despite its responsibilities. Bridget, Mary, and Teresa all enjoyed their roles and felt great satisfaction in their performance as school principals but had moments of questioning. The greatest evidence of the emotional toll of the role for all of them was each commenting that they were not sure that they could sustain themselves in the role long term.

CONCLUSION

The complexities of women's experiences in leadership are frequently overlooked. Within the Catholic school system, traditional discourses related to women's positioning, hegemonic, and ritualized practices which position women in certain ways continue to reinforce women's experiences of male bias and lack of representation in leadership overall. However, under closer scrutiny, the experiences shared by the school leaders in this project highlight that while the Catholic school context can reinforce generic stereotypical expectations on women about leadership, core features such as balancing personal and professional lives, negotiating the parish priest relationship, and navigating the associated ambivalence linked to their leadership roles manifest as contextual and experienced through multiple sources.

It is well documented that the role of principal is multilayered, challenging anyone, regardless of gender, who inhabits that role. However, just as the female leaders in this project have observed and experienced, there are layers in the role that are largely unknown to their male counterparts. These experiences could be part of the reason that there are so few females applying for the position. However, within the stories the joy of leadership is also told by these women, revealing the drive to be part of Catholic school leadership. These strong women have the capacity to continue the move to change gender perceptions within the Catholic system.

REFERENCES

Bateson, M. C. (1989). *Composing a life.* New York, NY: Plume/Penguin.

Blackmore, J. (1996). Doing "Emotional labour" in the education market place: Stories from the field of women in management. *Discourse: Studies in the Cultural Politics of Education, 17*(3), 337–349.

Brooking, K., Collins, G., Court, M., & O'Neill, J. (2003). Getting below the surface of the principal recruitment 'crisis' in New Zealand primary schools. *Australian Journal of Education, 47*(2), 146–158.

Catholic Education Commission of Victoria. (2002). *Annual statistical report: Diocese of Ballarat, Melbourne, Sandhurst and Sale.* Melbourne, Australia: Catholic Education Commission of Victoria.

Catholic Education Commission of Victoria. (2007). *Annual report.* Melbourne, Australia: Catholic Education Commission of Victoria.

Clandinin, D. J., & Connelly, F. M. (2000). *Narrative inquiry: Experience and story in qualitative research.* San Francisco, CA: Jossey-Bass.

Flagship for Catholic Educational Leadership. (2003). *Leadership succession for Catholic secondary schools in Victoria, South Australia and Tasmania: The VSAT Project.* Melbourne, Australia: Australian Catholic University.

Grace, G. (1995). *School leadership: Beyond education management.* London: Falmer Press.

John Paul II. (1994), *Ordinatio Sacerdotalis: On reserving priestly ordination to men alone.* Rome, Italy. Retrieved from https://w2.vatican.va/content/john-paul-ii/en/apost_letters/1994/documents/hf_jp-ii_apl_19940522_ordinatio-sacerdotalis.html

Melbourne Catholic Education Office. (2003). *Directory of Schools.* Melbourne Catholic Education Office, Melbourne.

Power, T. (2002). *Dancing on a moving floor: Lay women and the principalship in Catholic education.* (Doctoral of Education dissertation). Geelong, Australia: Deakin University. Retrieved from http://hdl.handle.net/10536/DRO/DU:30023112

Chapter 25

Leadingmamas

A Visual Ethnography

Sarah Jean Baker

Using an emergent feminist poststructural method, this study explores how women who identify as educational leaders and mothers negotiate their identities in their everyday lives. Four participant collaborators employed visual ethnographic methods to create representations of their leader and mother identities and explored the meaning of these representations through focus groups and digital communication tools (Instagram, texting, and Facebook). The findings support other studies that suggest women struggle to meet the expectations of intensive mothering (Hays, 1996).

The study also reveals an associated struggle with the expectations of what has been named intensive leadership—a theory that mirrors the tenets of intensive mothering. In addition, the study discovered the theory of conflicted mothering—a space that the women occupied when trying to escape the ideals of intensive mothering, but have not yet been able to attain the theory of transpersonal mothering (Desai, 2014). Leadership and mothering identities are not separate from one another, but rather integrated in the everyday life of women.

The purpose of this study was to examine the lived experience of being a school leader and mother. The principal is recognized as a leader in charge of teaching and learning for the students (Ediger, 2014), as well as the teachers (Drago-Severson, 2012). The school leader not only has a role in high-stakes accountability but is also expected to manage the myriad complexities associated with changing student populations and technology advances, as well as increasing interactions with the community (Crow, 2006). And, the school leader must also not forget to share decision making (DeMatthews, 2014). Being a school leader has become more than a full-time job; there are not enough hours in the day to accomplish all that needs to be done.

Being a good mother, traditionally, has been viewed as a full-time job. Literature suggests that a good mother in Western culture is someone who is engaged full time

with her mothering role at home, typically white, middle class, and expects all her aspirations to be fulfilled by her mothering role (Hays, 1996; Johnston & Swanson, 2006). This definition of a good mother leaves out women of color, single parents, low-income, and lesbian mothers (Johnston & Swanson, 2006; Medved & Kirby, 2005). This traditional mothering ideology is preserved by cultural hegemony and those who are not privileged by the dominant culture experience failure in meeting the good mothering standards (Johnston & Swanson, 2006). When one is a mother, there are not enough hours in the day to accomplish all that needs to be done to care for the children and home. So, what happens when a woman is a school leader and a mother?

I am a school leader and a mother. I have personally experienced the impossible expectations of each of these identities. I have been subject to the views that women are still to be in charge of the children and home, even though I work outside of the home as a school leader (Okimoto & Heilman, 2012). As I shared my experiences of facing the impossible standards of being a school leader and a mother with my colleagues, who were also school leaders and mothers, I began to notice they had similar experiences to share with me. So, I began to wonder more about these two identities, identities that I value and yet struggle with daily as I try to meet the cultural expectations of each. Why does the struggle exist and what can be done about this struggle for women?

BACKGROUND TO THE RESEARCH

When I started the School Improvement PhD program at Texas State University my oldest son was four years old and my twin sons were two years old. In addition to being a mother and graduate student, I was working full time at a liberal arts university in the teacher education department. Prior to my assistant professor position, I was an assistant principal and teacher. Needless to say, I lost track of the number of times I received comments about having my hands full or the questions about how I was managing all my responsibilities. I thought that maybe I had finally taken on more than I could handle with graduate school.

One evening during a class break I had a conversation with a professor that forever changed my perspective about my research interests. The professor commented, "You make many connections with being a mother. I want you to know that's a valid research topic." As the words sank into me I felt a bit of disbelief—I had never considered that my research interests could include the identity that meant just as much to me as my professional one. I knew from that moment on that my dissertation study would include the complexities of motherhood—a place that I had found great happiness, but also my greatest challenges. It was an incredible experience to study a matter so important to me personally and professionally and to also be able to do the study alongside other women that were willing to open themselves to the research process by sharing some of their deepest struggles and joys of being a mama.

THE FEMINIST RESEARCH APPROACH

This was a qualitative research study which engaged visual ethnography to explore the mothering experiences of four women who were educational leaders and mothers (I was one of the participants). The purpose of the research was to examine the everyday life experiences of four women (April, Natalie, Tracie, and myself) and explore how we drew on visual observations and personal reflections to make sense of our experiences as we participated in the duality of roles through motherhood and leadership overall.

Visual Ethnography

This study utilized visual ethnographic methods. Visual ethnography utilizes images such as photographs, films, and social media to study cultures throughout the research process and analysis (Brace-Govan, 2007; Buch & Staller, 2014; Pink, 2008). Visual methods emphasize participation and collaboration throughout the research process between the researcher and participants (Hill, 2013; McCarthy, 2013; Pink, 2008, 2012, 2013). This study utilized photographs. There are numerous ways photographs can be used in research design.

Typically, there are three techniques; these include (a) researcher-created or collected photographs; (b) partici-

pant-centered, existing photographs; and (c) participant and researcher collaboration in the creation of photographs (Banks, 2007). The research design for this study employed the participant and researcher collaboration of creating photographs. The use of photographs for this study, "becomes a way of arriving at particular types and layers of knowledge or ways of knowing" about the research questions of the study (Pink, 2012, p. 7). This method allowed participants in the study to share their lived experiences about the research questions (Steyn, 2013).

Research Process

As a feminist, I intentionally involved my collaborative partners throughout this ethnographic research study. This meant that collaboration occurred at every step of the research process to allow for the needs and desires of my collaborators, as well as my own, to be fulfilled (Buch & Staller, 2014). The criteria for the collaborators of this study were that the women self-identified as educational leaders and mothers. The other criterion is that the women in this study were already in a relationship with the other collaborators; whether the relationship was professional or personal did not matter. The reason for this criterion was that the research design was focused ethnography. As such, focused ethnographic methods are data intensive and collected in a rapid manner (Knoblauch, 2005). This is not possible without familiarity between collaborators (Knoblauch, 2005). Therefore, the existing relationships between the women became essential. We shared and discussed our life experiences through text conversations, images, and focus groups. The research process occurred over four months.

The data collected included photographs as well as brief captions of the photographs taken by all members of the research group. Data also included text conversations, transcripts of the focus group sessions, and text messages sent between focus group sessions, and comments posted to Instagram and Facebook. We made sense of the data throughout the research process through our text conversations, as well as during our focus group sessions.

The analysis was comparative, because each collaborator was able to explore the focus statement (challenges of the identities, expectations of the identities, and joys of the identities) determined by the group in their own way (Pink, 2013). Therefore, in addition to coding for themes through the use of open and axial coding, we also reflected on the narratives of the images in terms of academic discourses (Pink, 2013). This reflection adds another layer of meaning given to the photographs by the collaborators and myself during the research process (Pink, 2013).

RESEARCH FINDINGS

The findings illustrated the complex and often challenging circumstances the women found themselves in, however, findings also illuminated the aspects of joy and pride which were central to both their personal and professional lives. It was difficult to separate the professional leadership aspects of identity from the personal aspects. The experiences in the personal and professional lives of the women leaders crossover and inform each other, and the duality of motherhood and leadership can provide important reflective moments for the women leaders. Two key areas of findings are shared in this chapter: The importance of surfacing, valuing, and learning from Leadingmama's[1] mothering and leadership experiences through metanarratives; and, leading through the different mothering identities (intensive, conflicted, and transpersonal).

Surfacing, Valuing, and Learning from Leadingmama's Experiences

The majority of the findings from the study came from the women sharing their experiences and perceptions about their mothering identity, more so than their leadership identity. This is important to note as the mamas identified they had little opportunity to share these aspects of their lives. The research provided an opportunity to do this, as one woman stated, "the established relationships and the collaborative nature of the research with each other allowed us to feel more comfortable sharing our authentic selves, because we were already a part of each other's communities."

I noted, "as mamas we often do not have a place where this part of ourselves can be shared openly with others, a place that recognizes the expectations and challenges we face, as mamas." The women identified that even schools do not allow Leadingmamas to fully integrate their full identities. This part of their identity was not to be brought into the school workplace, even though schools are places for children and families.

The findings highlighted the metanarrative around mothering, that women are the ones responsible and held "accountable for her children's health, the clothes they wear, their behavior at school, their intelligence and general development" (Rich, 1986, p. 53). This belief is well established in the literature (Brown, 2014; Huisman & Joy, 2014). Data collected also showed the metanarrative around schools, that leaders are the ones responsible for the success of their schools.

The images especially highlighted the metanarratives of mothering and leading, as we shared images around the challenges, expectations, and joys in being

Figure 25.1. Healthy Lunches

a leader and mama. And through the research process we found community and deeper connections with each other by sharing our everyday experiences of being a Leadingmama. For example, in figure 25.1, the women discussed the pressure to feed our children healthy meals for proper growth and development. This image shows the ideal of intensive mothering that the mother is ultimately the one responsible for the growth and development of her children.

The women also discussed the embarrassment felt when children are not behaving well. The behaviors of children indicate a mother's success or failure in her mothering identity. Good mothers have well-behaved children, all the time and in all circumstances. This is another tenet of the theory of intensive mothering (Hays, 1996). But as school leaders, we also know that there are many factors that can influence a child's development.

The women also shared ideas about the theory of intensive leadership. As leaders, we know that teachers and staff, students and families, are depending on us. We know and believe that the work we do each day can and will make a difference for students and families, so how can we not be at work? The stakes seem too high. Student success is the result of leading well (Leithwood, 2006) (see figure 25.2).

As valuable starting points for conversations, the women shared their visual artifacts to illustrate the important aspects of their mothering and leadership roles. Opportunities to talk about their artifacts and share their personal stories of mothering and leadership encouraged the women to reflect critically upon their personal and professional identities, which began to allow for the creation of different mothering narratives (Green, 2001). All the collaborators connected with the opportunity to broaden their views of being a leader and mama.

Sharing stories of joy about their work as Leadingmamas was an empowering process. During the first focus

Figure 25.2. School Improvement Results Are a Reflection of the Leader's Ability to Lead

group, Natalie remarked about "waiting for the texts and pictures" and that "it was super fun and I enjoyed it all week." Tracie echoed this sentiment by saying, "I don't have a lot of friends that have the same lifestyle that I am in right now in the same position, so it was neat to share with you, you know, that we're in the same season." The images shared and text messages became a way to support each other in being a mama, which in turn allowed mothering to become "an empowering rather than oppressive experience" (D'Arcy, Turner, Crockett, & Gridley, 2011, p. 31).

Leadership and Mothering Identities

The second core area of findings relate to the relationship between leading and professional lives as educators and

the ways the Leadingmamas made sense of their mothering identities. Three areas of mothering—intensive, conflicted, and transpersonal (table 25.1)—are core features of these findings.

Intensive Mothering

All women identified the challenges associated with motherhood and noted the pressure of expectations they felt were placed on them by others, themselves, and society. The complexities of balancing the role of being a mother and a leader were evident and the women explored aspects such as gender bias, career pathways, and societal expectations. The women became attuned to the need to critically reflect upon their experiences and April asked, "What kind of conversations can we have that change that?" This was her question to recognizing that we have been socialized into our roles of leader and especially being a mama.

Discussion highlighted thinking that there is no longer a gender bias in education and yet, it also supported that gender bias still exists for women in education. One woman said she purposely did not become a principal until she was older; she waited until her responsibilities at home had diminished. Women still make professional decisions based on their family situations, because women are still the ones who are in charge of the home (Faircloth, 2014; Huisman & Joy, 2014).

The women noted that the actions of some women can reinforce the gender expectations of what it means to be a mama and a woman leader (Chowdhury, 2009; Douglas & Michaels, 2004), and women recognize they can play an active role in shaping and being shaped by social pro-

Table 25.1. Types of Mothering

Domain	Intensive Mothering (Hays, 1996)	Conflicted Mothering (Baker, 2016)	Transpersonal Mothering (Desai, 2014)
Employment	Stay home to care for child; work only if income is needed; nonemployed is ideal	Makes decision to not work, even though would like to work	Mother may or may not work depending on a myriad of complex circumstances and mother's own aspirations
Responsibility	Childcare is mother's responsibility	Recognizes and wants equal support from a partner, but the conflicts to this desire result in mother being solely responsible	Responsibility of both parents supports by family, friends, and community
Protection	Protecting children from outside influences is mother's job; mother is ultimately responsible for how child turns out	Acknowledges myriad of factors that influence children's development, including the child's personality/genes; but still feels responsible for how child turns out	Responsibility of everyone including parents to protect all children from outside negative influences and environments
Self-Sacrificing	Mothers should always place children's needs before their own Being a mother is the most important thing a woman can be	Understands importance of self-care, but continues to consistently put children's needs before own needs Being a mother is a part of the self, along with other identities, but feels guilt with identities own needs	Mother's well-being is intimately intertwined with child's well-being so it is as important for mother to attend to her own needs as it is for her to attend to her child's needs

cesses. The women identified that as they play the role defined for them they also marginalize themselves as women. Furthermore, some actions result in marginalizing and even competing with other women with the findings even illustrating how women judge other women's performances within their identities of being a mama and leader, "she's hard core."

One participant, identified how as women, "We have just accepted our roles as mamas to be natural, to believe that we are the ones who are best suited to raising and caring for children." Yet another shared, "being a mama is not always natural for us as women." Faircloth (2014) similarly identified, "Early childhood is a period of high emotional and physical dependency. This is not just an invention of an intensive parenting culture. . . . The problem is not the fact of this requirement but rather that meeting this need has come to rest exclusively, and in insolation, on the shoulders of biological mothers" (Faircloth, 2014, loc 3401 of 6032).

The women perceived societal assumptions, where women are identified as central to the role of raising children, were further intensified through systems and structures in communities which reinforced such beliefs. One participant identified there were "very few structures in schools to support the families," another commented, "we believe this is the way it must be, that schools are workplaces where we cannot integrate our identities." Challenging systems that ignored women's experiences of motherhood was perceived as difficult and the women's lack of action to question systems within organizations that failed to support Leadingmamas was further reflected upon, "Because we don't even really ask the question. You know, what would we need to be in place for it to be better. So why don't we have better systems in place, so every time a woman gets pregnant we're not acting like our heads are cut off and we're running around like what are we going to do, now?"

Douglas and Michaels (2004) have extended the idea of intensive mothering to include the belief that women are not complete unless they have kids, and motherhood has been so romanticized that "the standards for success are impossible to meet" (p. 4). Intensive mothering has become the ultimate female Olympics, or is sometimes even coded as a war between groups of women (Douglas & Michaels, 2004; McHenry & Schultz, 2014). This may be the reason why the women did not post the images to social media they felt comfortable texting.

Conflicted Mothering

The conflicted mothering experienced by the Leadingmamas is characterized by Natalie feeling that she had no choice but to stay home with her first child when finding quality childcare became a barrier. April felt like she may not be ready for a principal's position because she has young children and they are her responsibility, and Tracie felt she couldn't share that she had experienced the death of an infant. And I am still feeling conflicted, after eight years, about my desire to work outside of the home, because this may not be good for my children, even if it is good for my well-being. We do not want to be women who are confined by the intensive mothering ideals and yet, when decisions or conflicts arise, we fall back on those ideals to make decisions.

So, why do we feel conflicted about our mothering, still? Hochschild and Machung (2012) discuss the stalled revolution for women noting the "strain between the change in women and the absence of change in much else" (p. 12). They also proposed, "Women have changed. But most workplaces have remained inflexible in the face of the family demands of their workers, and at home, most men have yet to really adapt to the changes in women" (p. 12). This stalled revolution contributes to the conflict we experience as Leadingmamas, because our workplace and schools have not made changes to structures or systems to support our work as Leadingmamas.

The possibilities of taking a leave of absence to have a baby remain an issue, with organizational structures and systems providing challenges for mothers. Arrangements such as working part time are often not considered a viable option, making a progressive return to work difficult. Schools continue to use structures and systems that put us in a place of conflict about being a Leadingmama. We also experienced conflict as Leadingmamas in our feelings toward our decision to be a mama.

We wanted and still want to be mamas; it is an important part of our identity. We also want to be leaders; it fulfills other parts of ourselves that being a mama is not able to satisfy. But, we have difficulty expressing these feelings out loud to others, because we believe we are supposed to love being a mama all . . . of . . . the . . . time. And if at times we do not find ourselves loving the experiences of being a mama, then there is something wrong with us. So, we do not share these feelings out loud to others and we even try to suppress these feelings to ourselves. We do not want to acknowledge they exist, so we ignore them.

As Parker (1997) illustrates, "None of us find it easy to truly accept that we both love and hate our children. For maternal ambivalence constitutes not an anodyne condition of mixed feelings, but a complex and contradictory state of mind, shared variously by all mothers, in which loving and hating feelings for children exist side by side" (loc. 397 of 4403).

We often look at our children and experience mothering through the lens of conflicted mothering. We shared the struggle of putting our needs aside, in order to address the needs of our children. Even during times that would call for our needs to be prioritized, such as when we get sick and need rest.

As women in this study we recognized our privilege: we are educated, middle-class women who have opportunities and access that others do not. If we find conflicted mothering to be an issue in our everyday lived experiences as Leadingmamas, than women who earn less, work at even less flexible, steady, or well-paid jobs, and are limited in finding affordable childcare options must find mothering and working all the more difficult (Hochschild & Machung, 2012). We need to recognize conflicted mothering if we want to arrive at transpersonal mothering. And part of this recognition is noting how the inflexibilities of the structures and systems in organizations continue to push against our desire for transpersonal mothering.

Transpersonal Mothering

Transpersonal mothering creates new dialogues and new views around the challenges faced by parents. It recognizes other influences on child development, such as child temperament, peers, and the media (Desai, 2014). This recognition alleviates the burden of having to be a perfect mother and being solely responsible for the child's well-being, because the complexity of child rearing and the imperfections which are part of mothering are acknowledged (Desai, 2014). No longer are the mother-child dynamics the only focus of raising children (Desai, 2014). As Kristin van Ogtrop so eloquently wrote, "I will love my children, but my love for them will always be imperfect" (p. 169). Just as importantly, "transpersonal motherhood enhances this recognition that we are dependent on each other and on the environment for our survival and wellbeing. This reflects a shift from I to We" (Desai, 2014, loc. 5534 of 6032).

One of the findings of the study was the challenge of balancing our identities or being a double agent, a term coined during the research process. "When I became a mom, I thought I could do this, be a mom and a leader, I'm going to be able to do both of these jobs and be doing both really well. And it's been one of the biggest, 'what was I thinking,' you know?"

Developing better policies and practices in our schools is needed, so Leadingmamas can be supported, integrate their identities, and no longer need to compartmentalize parts of their identity. Desai (2014) states, "By integrating various parts of her identity, the mother opens herself up to an experience of self that has expanded beyond the personal ego (I self) and the roles she plays (expansion of identity). The focus has shifted from these individual pieces to a synthesis until the whole is experienced" (loc. 5534 of 6032). Changing policies and practices in our schools will not only support teachers, leaders, and staff within a campus, it will also create schools that are more connected to students and their families within the school community.

From a transpersonal mothering perspective, parenting challenges that are encountered are not problems to be fixed or tragedies to despair over but are opportunities to access the greater potential within. Such a transformation often corresponds with the development of transpersonal values such as intuition, creativity, mindfulness, compassion, altruism, and forgiveness. These values reflect deeper awareness and connection to self, to others, and to nature. Transpersonal mothering recognizes motherhood is a multifaceted experience, and acknowledges mothering is a life-changing, transformative experience (Desai, 2014).

As Leadingmamas we "are looking for ways to create a new consciousness of motherhood, which as Radicalesbians suggests, is at the heart of women's liberation" (McHenry & Schultz, 2014, loc. 5462 of 6032). We believe we can create a space for women to encourage and support each other and to raise our consciousness around issues related to being a mama and a leader in schools. We can create our own culture around being a Leadingmama (Kinser, 2010). We, the collaborators and I, would like to create a website for Leadingmamas (www.leadingmamas.com).

The website would be a place that can create conversations in local communities around being a Leadingmama, to inspire groups of Leadingmamas to gather together and work collaboratively to create change in their local community. School leaders are also faced with distinct challenges in their leading compared to business leaders. For example, an elementary school principal often leads as many as 70 faculty and staff, in addition to supporting the learning needs of hundreds of students. As a committee member of my dissertation stated, "Schools are the only business that sees all their clients, every day, and at the same time." This reality for school leaders creates expectations and challenges that are exclusive to school leaders. So, the creation of a website for Leadingmamas will uniquely support and encourage Leadingmamas in their lived experiences as Leadingmamas. We cannot arrive at a new model of mothering without first acknowledging our current condition as Leadingmamas.

CONCLUSION

No matter the topic of the focus group discussions and images—expectations, challenges, and the joys in the women's roles as mamas and leaders, the idea that these pieces of their identities were linked to each other was

Figure 25.3.   Leadingmama

evident throughout our dialogue. They desired to be good leaders and they desired to be good mamas (Douglas & Michaels, 2004). They could not imagine not being mamas or leaders, they wanted to be Leadingmamas. As Tracie said, "I love both; I don't know how I'd ever just be one." With Sarah describing, "It is the conflict we live with each day." April later commented that part of the conflict is feeling like no matter the decision you make, "you can't win, you just can't win." This is a reminder that, "Theory is not an abstract intellectual activity divorced from our life, but is intricately linked with it" (Chowdhury, 2009, p. 32).

Figure 25.3 (photograph captured by my oldest son) was posted to Instagram and Facebook during the data collection period of the study. I was living the theory of intensive mothering and leading in this moment, thinking I can do it all and do it all well! By sharing my story, I hope I am helping others share their stories and think differently about our possibilities of being Leadingmamas. I also look at this image and have feelings of conflicted mothering; I am a woman, a Leadingmama, in the kitchen with my children. The irony of the image does not escape me.

This moment is an image of what life is like in our home these days—a babe who would rather be carried than walk, brothers who are growing bigger and seeking new learning. This moment combines with other moments to create my story and their story. And this image is a reminder of the joy I experience in being a Leadingmama.

NOTE

1. The term Leadingmamas was developed by the women in the research group through their interactions and discussions about their identities as mothers and as leaders.

REFERENCES

Baker, S. J. (2016). *#leadingmamas: A visual ethnography* (Unpublished doctoral dissertation). Texas State University, San Marcos.

Banks, M. (2007). Using visual data in qualitative research. London, England: Sage.

Brace-Govan, J. (2007). Participant photography in visual ethnography. *International Journal of Market Research, 49*(6), 735–750.

Brown, S. (2014). Intensive mothering as an adaptive response to our cultural environment. In L. R. Ennis (Ed.), *Intensive mothering: The cultural contradictions of modern motherhood* (loc. 488–849). Bradford, ON: Demeter Press.

Buch, E. D., & Staller, K. M. (2014). What is feminist ethnography? In S. N. Hesse-Biber (Ed.), *Feminist research practice: A primer* (2nd ed.; pp. 107–144). Thousand Oaks, CA: Sage.

Chowdhury, A. (2009). Historicizing, theorizing, and contextualizing feminism. *The ICFAI Journal of English Studies, 4*(1), 28–39.

Crow, G. M. (2006). Complexity and the beginning principal in the United States: perspectives on socialization. *Journal of Educational Administration, 44*(4), 310–325.

D'Arcy, C., Turner, C., Crockett, B., & Gridley, H. (2011). Where's the feminism in mothering? *Journal of Community Psychology, 40*(1), 27–43.

DeMatthews, D. (2014, Spring). Shared decision making: What principals need to know. *Principal Matters,* (100), 2–4.

Desai, F. (2014). Transpersonal motherhood: A practical and holistic model of motherhood. In L. R. Ennis (Ed.), *Intensive mothering: The cultural contradictions of modern motherhood* (loc. 5498–5833). Bradford, ON: Demeter Press.

Douglas, S. J., & Michaels, M. W. (2004). *The mommy myth: The idealization of motherhood and how it has undermined all women.* New York, NY: Free Press.

Drago-Severson, E. (2012). New opportunities for principal leadership: Shaping school climates for enhanced teacher development. *Teachers College Record, 114,* 1–44.

Ediger, M. (2014). The changing role of the school principal. *College Student Journal, 48*(2), 265–267.

Faircloth, C. (2014). Is attachment mothering intensive mothering? In L. R. Ennis (Ed.), *Intensive mothering: The cultural contradictions of modern motherhood* (loc. 3198–3465). Bradford, ON: Demeter Press.

Green, F. J. (2001). *Living feminism: Pedagogy and praxis in mothering* (Doctoral dissertation). Retrieved from Proquest Dissertations & Theses Global (Order No. NQ76730).

Hays, S. (1996). *The cultural contradictions of motherhood.* New Haven, CT: Yale University Press.

Hill, J. (2013). Using participatory and visual methods to address power and identity in research with young people. *Graduate Journal of Social Science, 10*(2), 132–151.

Hochschild, A., & Machung, A. (2012). *The second shift: Working parents and the revolution at home.* New York, NY: Viking.

Huisman, K., & Joy, E. (2014). The cultural contradictions of motherhood revisited: Continuities and changes. In L. R. Ennis (Ed.), *Intensive mothering: The cultural contradictions of modern motherhood* (loc. 1541–1853). Bradford, ON: Demeter Press.

Johnston, D. D., & Swanson, D. H. (2006). Constructing the "Good Mother": The experience of mothering ideologies by work status. *Sex Roles, 54*(7/8), 509–519.

Kinser, A. E. (2010). *Motherhood and feminism.* Berkeley, CA: Seal Press.

Knoblauch, H. (2005). Focused ethnography. *Forum Qualitative Social Research, 6*(3), Art. 44.

Leithwood, K. (2006). The 2005 Willower family lecture: Leadership according to evidence. *Leadership and Policy in Schools, 5*(3), 177–202.

McCarthy, L. J. (2013). It's coming from the heart: Exploring a student's experiences of 'home' using participatory visual methodologies. *Graduate Journal of Social Science, 10*(2), 76–105.

McHenry, K. A., & Schultz, D. (2014). Skinny jeans: Perfection and competition in motherhood. In L. R. Ennis (Ed.), *Intensive mothering: The cultural contradictions of modern motherhood* (loc. 5264–5491). Bradford, ON: Demeter Press.

Medved, C. E., & Kirby, E. L. (2005). Family CEOs: A feminist analysis of corporate mothering discourses. *Management Communication Quarterly, 18*(4), 435–478.

Okimoto, T. G., & Heilman, M. E. (2012). The "bad parent" assumption: How gender stereotypes affect reactions to working mothers. *Journal of Social Issues, 68*(4), 704–724.

Parker, R (1997). The production and purposes of material ambivalence. In W. Hollway & B. Featherstone (Eds.), *Mothering and ambivalence* (loc. 488–849). New York, NY: Routledge.

Pink, S. (2008). Mobilising visual ethnography: Making routes, making place and making images. *Forum Qualitative Social Research, 9*(3), Art. 36.

Pink, S. (2012). Advances in visual ethnography: An introduction. In S. Pink (Ed.), *Advances in visual ethnography* (pp. 3–16). London, UK: Sage.

Pink, S. (2013). *Doing visual ethnography* (3rd ed.). Thousand Oaks, CA: Sage.

Radicalesbians. (1997). The woman-identified woman. In L. Nicholson (Ed.), *The second wave: A reader in feminist theory* (pp. 153–157). New York, NY: Routledge.

Rich, A. (1986). Of woman born: Motherhood as experience and institution. New York, NY: W. W. Norton.

Steyn, G. M. (2013). Using visual ethnography to explore a principal's perceptions of innovations made in a South African primary school. *Africa Education Review, 10*(3), 554–578.

Van Ogtrop, K. (2002). Attila the honey I'm home. In C. Hanauer (Ed.), *The bitch in the house* (pp. 159–169). New York, NY: HarperCollins.

Chapter 26

The Path of Leadership for Women in Pakistan

Critical Reflections

Abaida Mahmood

Two roads diverged in a yellow wood
And I took the one less travelled by

—Robert Frost

The Chinese leader Mao Zedong once said women hold up half the sky, suggesting the value of women in the workplace. While it may be true that women make up half the sky demographically, it is far from the reality of many women's daily lives throughout the world with education and work. According to the patriarchal view of Pakistani society, males and females are assigned different roles, and individuals are always viewed through the lens of gender. If women attempt to be assertive or authoritative, then they are labeled "unfeminine."

Women leaders walk a tightrope to reach positions of influence and power. Lack of education and economic opportunities for women restrict the potential of women to embrace their rights. Furthermore, poverty and religious extremism are also roadblocks to Pakistani women becoming progressive and independent. Women in Pakistan are highly connected with society's view of what constitutes the honor of men. Men normally control women's movements and behavior, whether they are a father, husband, or brother. The women of Pakistan have to go a long way before they are able to realize their rights.

This chapter examines the stereotypes of Pakistani female leadership and how culturally driven gender roles of women affect their career choices and professional advancement in organizations. Those few women who have succeeded in achieving executive level or other comparable professional positions pay a price for such a success with personal sacrifices, including delaying motherhood or remaining childless. In developing nations such as Pakistan, women students sometimes earn more college degrees than men, but their abilities in the workplace remain undervalued. As a practitioner and leader of a charitable organization in Pakistan, I present my reflections on and recommendations for addressing the challenges of women in leadership.

No nation can rise to the height of glory unless your women are side by side with you.

—Mohammed Ali Jinnah

INTRODUCTION

When we talk about leadership and gender, the assumption in many people's minds is that the leader is likely to be a man. Women and leadership are still a rarity in the 21st century despite many nations' claims of giving equal opportunities to women. With females making up 49.6 percent of the world population, the leadership should reflect the ratio of the population. Despite all the feminine agendas and equal opportunities talk, women still make up only 3.4 percent of CEOs around the world (PricewaterhouseCooper, 2017).

The British Council director in Pakistan, Nishat Riaz (2015), laments that women do not exist in a vacuum. They are surrounded by men and fellow women, each of whom has perceptions driven by their culture, education, religion, and personal bias. Their resulting behavior affects our perceptions about gender roles. This starts at birth: in some parts of Pakistan, a girl's birth is mourned, not celebrated. Later on, boys are often given preference over their sisters when it comes to basic health and educational needs. And we can well imagine the gender bias grows with the passage of time.

According to the International Labour Organization's 2015 Women in Business and Management report,

Women CEOs today head more than 20 Fortune 500 companies. That's up from zero in 1995, but still only 5 percent of the total. More women sit on corporate boards, but hold less than 20 percent of seats. The larger the company, the less likely the head will be a woman. While more women own and manage businesses, it is still 30 percent of the world total. The gender pay gap still exists and is hardly shrinking. On average, women still earn 23 percent less than men worldwide. ILO estimates that at the current rate of change, there won't be pay equity between women and men for another 70 or more years. (p. 10)

All-male company boards are still common but are decreasing in number, with women attaining 20 percent or more of all board seats in a handful of countries. A global survey quoted in the study shows that Norway has the highest global proportion of companies (13.3 percent) with a woman as company board chairperson, followed by Turkey (11.1 percent) (International Labour Organization, 2015). Governments and gender diversity advocates alike have established that at least 25 percent of a company's leadership needs to consist of women in order to capitalize on the advantages that women in leadership positions bring.

NOT SO GRIM

Pakistan is a country of 180 million people; more than half of the population is female. Although female participation in the paid labor force is increasing, it is still at a low level. According to World Bank statistics, only 12 percent of women are in the workforce (International Labour Organization, 2015). Even so, Pakistan is slowly developing women's leadership capacity. In November 2007, history was made when Pakistan's premier business association, The Overseas Chamber of Commerce and Industry, appointed its first-ever woman CEO, Unjela Siddiqi. In 2008, Dr. Fehmida Mirza of the Pakistan People's Party was elected the first woman speaker of the National Assembly.

Recently, Ms. Nasrin Haq became the first woman to head the Karachi Port Trust (KPT) as its chief executive. She is the first civilian as KPT chief in 18 years. Another name that has changed the IT world for women is Jehan Ara. She is the mastermind behind PASHA (Pakistan Software Houses Associations). Her project, "Women's Virtual Network," has helped educated women deal with employers and other professional workers, giving them a chance to explore themselves in a world with rapid IT growth. Women like Roshaneh Zafar are setting trends for women. She is the managing director of the Kashf Foundation which educates and

funds women working in villages so as to better their economic conditions. Women, then, are leading in an array of sectors in civil society.

In Pakistan, 20 percent of the National Assembly and 18 percent of the provincial assemblies are comprised of women, but women's voices are still far from reaching the mainstream despite their numbers. Dependent on the nomination from their parties, they cannot perform and grow according to their talents and hence, have a limited role in policy and decision making. Imparting leadership skills to present and aspiring women parliamentarians will create examples for women in leadership. It will strengthen the faith of the Pakistani society in the leadership capability of women and will also inspire young women to step forward and lead the country.

BARRIERS FACING WOMEN TO REACH THE TOP: THE SURVEY

The study described in this section was undertaken to discover what barriers were stopping women from achieving leadership positions. A survey of perceptions of leadership roles was distributed to 100 women from various industries in Pakistan. Findings suggest approximately 50 percent of women perceived leadership as a trait that was exceptionally hard to achieve. This study also showed that in 90 percent of women, aspiration to lead existed, whether or not they take action and motivate themselves to advance for top management positions. However, barriers such as discrimination, family demands, prejudice, and stereotyping result in a sense of futility in many cases. The majority felt education and training could increase the preparedness of women for leadership roles. A positive association existed between a participative leadership style and organizational effectiveness. Our findings depict how culture and religion play a significant role in affecting women's ability to seek the path of leadership. The barriers divided into the ones that they could control and the ones they had no control over. The findings are summarized in table 26.1.

Table 26.1.   Pakistani Women's Leadership Barriers

Internal Barriers	External Barriers
Belief in one's self	Gender bias
Coming out of comfort zone	Lack of support
Asking for help	Organizational structure
Finding the right balance	Cultural barriers
Staying put	Religious barriers

DISCUSSION

In this section, I discuss in greater detail the internal barriers and external barriers that women face, In considering the internal barriers, we generated solutions to help women learn leadership skills. I present here some thoughts about the five areas of internal barriers: belief in one's self, coming out of the comfort zone, asking for help, finding the right balance, and staying put. The external barriers are gender bias, lack of support, organizational structure, cultural barriers, and religious barriers. These are likewise discussed.

Internal Structures

Belief in One's Self

Women are very hard on themselves. They need to be reassured that they are capable; they need to believe in themselves and their leadership capacity. They suffer from something which I have called "leadophobia." Leadership evokes fear for some women. Once we overcome that fear we can increase our ability to achieve our goals. Women need to think of themselves as leaders, imagine where they want to be, and then work toward their goal.

A growing body of evidence shows just how devastating a lack of confidence can be (Warrell, 2016). Success, it turns out, correlates just as closely with confidence as it does with competence. Despite women's progress, we are still woefully underrepresented at the highest levels, and a lack of confidence may be one factor. The good news is that with work, confidence can be acquired, which means that the confidence gap, in turn, can be closed (Warrell, 2016).

Bleidorn, Arslan, Denissen, Rentfrow, Gebauer, Potter, and Gosling (2016) found that the disparity in self-esteem between men and women is universal. The eight-year study analyzed data from over 985,000 men and women across 48 countries, from Norway to New Zealand, Kuwait to South Korea, asking them to rate the phrase, "I see myself as someone who has high self-esteem." The study found that across the board—regardless of culture or country, men have higher self-esteem than women. New evidence is emerging regarding how much our brains can change over the course of our lives in response to shifting thought patterns and behavior. If we channel our talent for hard work, we can make our brains more confidence-prone.

Coming Out of Your Comfort Zone

Pakistani women are frequently quite content with their surroundings. We are reluctant to move out of our comfort zones. After all, it's comfortable in there. Our comfort zone is familiar. We know the thoughts and feelings that reside in that zone. We know the kind of life that exists there. A comfort zone is like a bubble. It feels protective, but therein lies the problem: it also might be claustrophobic because it prevents change and growth. Leaving our comfort zone gives us a better understanding of who we are and what we like when we expose ourselves to new experiences.

A little anxiety can help us perform at our peak, psychologists have found. When we challenge ourselves, we tend to rise to the occasion. Sometimes, we're not even that comfortable in our comfort zone. But we still stay there. We worry that things outside our comfort zone will be worse. We worry about the unknown; women tend to fear the unknown more than men. According to Harvard Business Review research (cited in Groysberg, 2008), 35 percent of women do not want to take risks toward leadership. Stepping out means making a fool of ourselves, knowing that the worst thing that can happen when you try something new is that you might fail; facing our fears; becoming comfortable with taking risks (no alternatives for experience); and enjoying the unknown.

Asking for Help

Gone are the John Wayne leadership days of those who modelled or suggested we can have it all, fearlessly and without support, carving a glorified path for others to follow. The best leaders inspire the best in their people; they shape the path together. They ask for help as they know they cannot do it all themselves. Even the strongest of people need help.

We often feel like we cannot or should not ask for support or help with our career development. We think that by asking for support we are admitting that we fall short of the required standard. We believe that it can appear as a sign of weakness to our peers that we aren't ready for the next rung on the career ladder. We do not have to seek help from women only. Men can and do make equally good mentors. Women need to remember to be coachable and passionate; have many mentoring moments in their careers; surround themselves with encouraging and positive people; reach out to people they admire and not wait for a mentor to find them; and pay it forward by offering to help other colleagues.

According to a KPMG women's leadership study, 67 percent of women in leadership stated that they had learned the most important leadership lessons from other women (2016). Eighty-two percent believed that access to and networking with female leaders would help them advance in their careers (KPMG, 2016).

Balancing Act

Although women have been a more prominent presence in the workplace for over five decades, the struggles surrounding work-life balance still drive some women to opt out of career opportunities. Women now make up more than half of the populations at universities and in the workforce, yet they are not advancing into the highest positions at the same rate as their male counterparts. While nearly a quarter of all researchers in Pakistani universities are women and a quarter of all published peer-reviewed work now comes from women scholars in Pakistan, there is much room for growth (British Council, 2015).

Research shows that women are more likely to be successful at juggling multiple roles if their career is meaningful and fulfilling. Guilt is still a major factor for working mothers. Many women said that the most difficult aspect of managing work and family is contending with cultural expectations about mothering (Slaughter, 2012). We have been socialized to believe that the idea of a "good mother" is usually attentive to children, bakes cookies, keeps a clean house, and reads to her children 20 minutes each night. Everything requires time and attention, and dividing the chores with our partner would not only help to keep a balance but would help to strengthen family bonds.

The art of work-home balance as a female leader requires careful planning and prioritization. Enlisting trusted family members and friends to help us accomplish the things we cannot on our own is one of the best ways to achieve this. Having a support system at home, including a willing partner and extended family, can be a tremendous resource when women get caught with conflicting commitments between home and work.

Taking Risks

The years when women are at the top of their careers are a time of consolidation, solidification, and fulfillment. It is a time when women can stretch themselves or gain greater depth in areas of interest. For example, in business it can be directorships and in politics it can be senior policy making or other influential positions. Mentoring one another via peer relationships and networks can be very effective and satisfying. Having a close group of trusted friends and peers who can be frank, generous, and supportive of each other's success can be the thing that helps bring the goals that seem distant, even at the time, to become much more achievable.

Suggestions for success include mastering the art of delegation, asking questions, listening carefully but ignoring negative comments, accepting that you won't know it all, communicating often, creating goals for

yourself, and developing strong peer relationships. And, most importantly, you have earned this position.

EXTERNAL BARRIERS

Gender inequality is not only a pressing moral and social issue, but also a critical economic challenge. If women—who account for half the world's working-age population—do not achieve their full economic potential, the global economy will suffer. While all types of inequality have economic consequences, the 2015 report of the McKinsey Global Institute explains that for every 100 women promoted, 130 men are promoted (2015). In addition, external hiring is not improving the representation of women. At every level, companies hire fewer women from the outside than men, and this is especially pronounced in senior management.

According to the patriarchal view of Pakistani society, male and female genders are assigned different roles and the individuals are always viewed through the lens of gender. This includes the notion that men and women are fundamentally different in nature. This lens also provides a hierarchical structure whereby men dominate the public sphere while women are relegated to the private sphere. Thus, female leaders operating in a male-dominated sphere are deemed unfit due to their femininity.

Organizations need to monitor and measure promotion rates and address areas of underperformance—why are women less likely to be promoted into particular roles or departments? They can adopt a specific gender strategy and develop a targeted strategy with a strong business case on the proportion of women progressing through the organization (British Council, 2015).

Circumstantial Barriers

According to Anne-Marie Slaughter (2012), former Director of Policy Planning in the United States Department of State under the Obama administration,

> Women should think about the climb to leadership not in terms of a straight upward slope, but as irregular stair steps, with periodic plateaus (and even dips) when they turn down promotions to remain in a job that works for their family situation; when they leave high-powered jobs and spend a year or two at home on a reduced schedule; or when they step off a conventional professional track to take a consulting position or project-based work for a number of years. I think of these plateaus as "investment intervals." (p. 25)

Cathleen Benko and Anne Weisberg (2007) echo Slaughter's thoughts in their book *Mass Career Customization:*

Aligning the Workplace with Today's Non-Traditional Workforce, emphasizing that a career trajectory today is more of a series of adjustments over time.

In Pakistan the support that women need in the work place is denied to them simply because they are women. The interesting aspect is that it was the other women at home and at work who failed to support the women concerned, not the men. Men tend not to extend support openly, as those who want to help women at home are labeled feminists and those who extend a hand at work are termed flirtatious. All women who achieve educations and professional success have the support of their families, especially from the male members.

Cultural Barriers

Gender relations in Pakistan rest on two basic perceptions: women are subordinate to men, and a man's honor resides in the actions of the women of his family. Thus, as in other orthodox Muslim societies, women are responsible for maintaining the family honor. To ensure that they do not dishonor their families, society limits women's mobility, places restrictions on their behavior and activities, and permits them only limited contact with the opposite sex.

Lack of education and economic opportunities for women restrict the potential of women to think about their rights under the law. Education is the only way forward. Education encompasses teaching and learning specific skills, and also something less tangible but more profound: the imparting of knowledge, good judgment, and wisdom. It provides people with the tools and knowledge they need to understand and participate in today's world. Literacy provides girls and women with a greater understanding of basic health, nutrition, and family planning, as well as of their own potential. It helps them long term as educated women marry later, have fewer children, and receive better prenatal care.

Imaginary Religious Barriers

It is a fallacy to suggest that women do not need work and that men should have the primary responsibility to provide for their families. The role model of Prophet Muhammad's wife, Khadija, who was one of the most successful traders of Makkah, along with many other examples in the annals of Islamic history confirm that women in business are not frowned upon in Islam. Khadija was unable to travel with her trade caravans because of the social and cultural traditions of the Arabian Peninsula at that time, and had to rely on someone else, to whom she paid a commission, to act as her agent and to trade on her behalf. However, she continued trading this way, which confirmed that women were allowed to generate moneymaking activities, thus helping improve the economic state of the family and the community.

Pakistani society's inclination to effectively deny women the right to work on the basis of religion is an unrealistic and largely historical paradigm. In several areas of society, women have been denied the right to access an education even though Islam has made it compulsory for men and women to pursue knowledge. Islam has given women the right to own property, to own businesses, to keep their maiden name, to choose their spouse, to divorce, to hold political office, and to enjoy equality with honor and respect.

The right to work is also an inalienable right of women, which Islam has never prevented. If this right is denied, as it is, it will, as a consequence, deprive women of the ability to make choices in many areas and affect other interrelated rights such as mobility, decision making, and entering into politics. The key point worthy of consideration is that there is nothing in the Quran or in the hadith (sayings of the Prophet Muhammad) which prevent women from working outside the home. In fact, the Quran extols the leadership of Bilqis, the Queen of Sheba, for her capacity to fulfill the requirements of the office, for her political skills, and for the purity of her faith and her independent judgment (Qur'an 27:23–44, Oxford World's Classics).

If a woman is qualified and the one best suited to fulfill a task, there is no Quranic injunction that prohibits her from any undertaking because of her gender. The hadith literature is replete with women leaders, jurists and scholars, and women who participated fully in public life. Another hadith states that 90 percent of our sustenance comes from business. For those who are able and competent, Islamic society should encourage them to become entrepreneurs or to become actively involved with other types of business activities (al-Hibri, 1982). Because women are not given the right to education, they are made to believe in the cultural norms of the religion rather than the true meaning of Islam. The men, especially the religious leaders, are afraid that allowing women to read and write will lead to enlightenment and moral degradation.

An educated woman understands the true meaning of religion and takes leadership roles within the context of her set cultural boundaries. The government, the media, the communities and, in particular, the religious leaders, need to work together and see the importance of women's participation in all walks of life. Linda Babcock (2007), professor of economics at Carnegie Mellon University and the author of *Women Don't Ask*: *The High Cost of Avoiding Negotiation—and Positive Strategies for Change*, has found in studies of business-school students that men initiate salary negotiations four times as often as women do, and that when women do negotiate, they ask for 30 percent less money than men do. At Manchester Business School, in England, Professor Marilyn Davidson has seen the same phenomenon, and believes that it comes from a lack of confidence (2011). It's well known that women, on average, make 78 cents for every dollar a man makes in the same job. It should also come as no surprise that the pay disparity goes all the way up the corporate ladder. Female executives make around 18 percent less than male executives, according to a Bloomberg study (Suddath, 2017).

Due to the religious and cultural values in Pakistan, women who do try to enter the workforce are often pushed into the lower of the three employment structures. This structure level, unorganized services sector, has low pay, low job security, and low productivity. In order to improve this situation, governmental organizations and political parties need to push for the entrance of women into the organized services sector. Conservative interpretations of Islam have not promoted women's rights in the workforce, since they value women as keepers of the family honor, support gender segregation, and the institutionalization of gender disparities. Furthermore, women who do work are often paid less than minimum wage because they are seen as lesser beings in comparison to men, and "their working conditions vis-à-vis males are often hazardous; having long working hours, no medical benefits, no job security, subjected to job discrimination, verbal abuse and sexual harassment and no support from male oriented labor unions" (Sarwar & Abbasi, 2013, p. 214).

CONCLUSION

The most successful women in Pakistan have seized every opportunity afforded to them and have created opportunities for themselves, harnessing their fears and doubts as rocket fuel instead of rocks in their pockets. Some of the characteristics of successful women leaders, such as motivation, natural curiosity, courage, self-management, enjoying being stretched and rising to a challenge, personal will and fortitude, drive and flexibility, may be innate, but there is no doubt that these characteristics also need to be nurtured and encouraged.

Never settling, always being driven, and always seeking new experiences are the hallmarks of the most successful women leaders, and indeed of successful leaders who are men, in Pakistan and around the world. We must all play a part in helping young women succeed, as our countries, economies, and futures depend on their success.

REFERENCES

al-Hibri, A. Y. (Ed.). (1982). *Women and Islam*. New York, NY: Pergamon Press.

Babcock, L. (2007). *Women don't ask: The high cost of avoiding negotiation—and positive strategies for change.* New York, NY: Bantam.

Benko, C., & Weisberg, A. (2007). *Mass career customization: Aligning the workplace with today's non-traditional workforce*. Cambridge, MA: Harvard Business Review Press.

Bleidorn, W., Arslan, R. C., Denissen, J. J. A., Rentfrow, P. J., Gebauer, J. E., Potter, J., & Gosling, S. D. (2016). Age and gender differences in self-esteem—A cross-cultural window. *Journal of Personality and Social Psychology, 111*(3), 396–410. doi: http://dx.doi.org/10.1037/pspp0000078

British Council. (2015, January). *Defined by absence: Women and research in South Asia.* Retrieved from https://www.britishcouncil.org/sites/default/files/women_researchers_jan15_print.pdf

Davidson, M. J., & Burke, R. J. (2011). *Women in management worldwide: Progress and prospects.* Aldershot, England: Gower Publishing.

ILO Bureau for Employers' Activities. (2015, January 12). *Women in business and management: Gaining momentum.* Retrieved from http://www.ilo.org/wcmsp5/groups/public/—-dgreports/—-dcomm/—-publ/documents/publication/wcms_334882.pdf

International Labour Organization. 2015). *Share of women in wage employment in the nonagricultural sector (% of total nonagricultural employment).* Retrieved from https://data.worldbank.org/indicator/SL.EMP.INSV.FE.ZS?locations=PK

KPMG. (2016). *Women entrepreneurs: Passion, purpose, and perseverance.* Retrieved from https://assets.kpmg.com/content/dam/kpmg/pdf/2016/02/kpmg-women-entrepreneurs-passion-purpose-perseverance.pdf

McKinsey Global Institute. (2015, September). *The power of parity: How advancing women's equality can add $12 trillion to global growth.* Retrieved from file:///Users/ereilly2/Downloads/MGI%20Power%20of%20parity_Full%20report_September%202015.pdf

PricewaterhouseCooper (2017). Executive Directors Practices and Remuneration Trends. Retrieved from https://www.pwc.co.za/en/assets/pdf/executive-directors-report-2017.pdf

Riaz, N. (2015, March 6). *Why aren't there more women leaders?* Retrieved from https://www.britishcouncil.org/voices-magazine/why-arent-there-more-women-leaders

Sarwar, F., & Abbasi, A. S. (2013). An in-depth analysis of women's labor force participation in Pakistan. *Middle-East Journal of Scientific Research, 15*(2), 208–215. doi: 10.5829/idosi.mejsr.2013.15.2.2367

Slaughter, A. M. (2012, July/August). Why women still can't have it all. *The Atlantic.* Retrieved from https://www.the atlantic.com/magazine/archive/2012/07/why-women-still -cant-have-it-all/309020/

Suddath, C. (2017, June 21). *Why can't your company just fix the wage gender gap?* Retrieved from https://www .bloomberg.com/news/features/2017-06-21/why-can-t-your -company-just-fix-the-gender-wage-gap

Warrell, M. (2016, January 20). For women to rise, we must close the confidence gap. *Forbes.* Retrieved from https:// www.forbes.com/sites/margiewarrell/2016/01/20/gender -confidence-gap/#572947cc1efa

Chapter 27

Balancing the *Yang* and the *Yin* Through Source-fully Intelligent Education

Coomi S. Vevaina

Modern society has consistently favoured yang, or masculine values and attitudes, and has neglected their complementary yin, or feminine, counterparts. We have favoured self-assertion over integration, analysis over synthesis, rational knowledge over intuitive wisdom, science over religion, competition over cooperation, expansion over conservation, and so on. This one-sided development has now reached a highly alarming stage; a crisis of social, ecological, moral and spiritual dimensions.

—Fritjof Capra

In school, educators should encourage three types of thinking, serial, associative, and unitive, so that learners are able to understand life connotatively (symbolically) and denotatively (literally). To balance education, mathematics, pure sciences, social sciences, and the arts such as literature, painting, sculpture, music, and drama should be regarded as equally essential. Almost all countries of the world prioritize mathematics and the sciences and neglect art education. This chapter presents an argument for balancing learning in schools so as to provide a socially just, tolerant society. I propose source-full intelligence as a framework by which we can understand and experience our uniqueness as individuals and our oneness, or connection to others, simultaneously.

THEORIZING THE CRISIS IN EDUCATION

The alarming social, ecological, moral, and spiritual crisis that our modern world faces is, as Capra (1975) rightly indicates, caused by the devaluing of the feminine principle in all patriarchal societies which, being dominant globally, have caused damage to humankind as a whole. "Yang" values require to be balanced with "yin" values as we humans are an admixture of both "masculine" and "feminine" energies. Scholar, philosopher, and researcher Jean Houston points out that yin values have

been denied and suppressed for thousands of years and adds that their resurrection is vital to our very survival on this planet. Houston (2011) wrote,

For the first time in human history we are required as a species to extend ourselves into, radically new ways of being. Among these, I believe, is the restoration of the full dignity and the power of the Sacred Feminine, so that the sacred marriage of masculine and feminine, transcendence and immanence, clarity and passion, and wisdom and compassion can take place within our humanness and engender an inspirited, engodded humanity capable at last of co-creating and partnering with the Divine, a transformed world.

With the human feminine, *process* is more important than product, *being* rather than doing, *deepening* rather than producing and achieving, *circular investedness and sharing*, more important than hierarchy, *the art and science of making things work, cohere, grow* more important than the strategies of end-goaling, *eros* more important than logos, and the *subjective realm* given equal status with the objective one. And when you get to the Sacred feminine and the feminine face of God, all of these qualities are amplified. (p. 3)

As I have said in my book, *Source-full Intelligence: Understanding Uniqueness and Oneness Through Education* (2013), Houston's words cannot be understood in a simplistic manner to imply that "woman power" should replace "man power" for, as the French theorist Julia Kristeva cautions us, in no way is fascist matriarchy more desirable than fascist patriarchy. Houston's call, which is echoed by numerous educators throughout the world, is an invitation to bring, not stereotypical attributes of femininity, but "the feminine principle back into consciousness" (Bolen, 2005, p. 1) and merge the two principles to "parent" human beings through education.

Once the yang and the yin are balanced, other oppositional systems that are bred by the Manichean Aesthetics can also be rethought. The renowned feminist theologian

Rosemary Radford Ruether perceptively foregrounds the fact that yang-based patriarchal thinking must be balanced by Yin-based matriarchal thinking, for patriarchy mindlessly assigns to all subjugated groups the exact characteristics it assigns to women:

> A repressive view of the alien female was . . . the model for the inferiorisation of other subjugated groups, lower classes and conquered races. Subjugated groups are perceived through similar stereotypes not because they are alike, but because the same dominant groups (ruling class males) are doing the perceiving. All oppressed peoples tend to be seen as lacking in rationality, volition, and the capacity for autonomy. The characteristics of repressed bodiliness are attributed to them: passivity, sensuality, irrationality, and dependency. (Ruether, 1975, p. 118)

The end result of this kind of thinking is the oppression of the "Other." Racism, sexism, classism, casteism (in India), and ageism, to name only a few, have led to the creation of what Tagore called "narrow domestic walls," which have spawned wanton suffering and misery over centuries.

In Western societies the despair and existential angst triggered by World War II led to the rise of numerous resistance movements in the '60s of the previous century and a radical display of "incredulity towards metanarratives" (Lyotard, 1979, p. xxiv). The truth claims of several master narratives that we had unquestioningly regarded as axiomatic came to be revisioned and deconstructed. Among those which came under the scanner was education.

It is common knowledge that thinkers as diverse as Jean-Jacques Rousseau, William Blake, William Wordsworth, Rabindranath Tagore, Maria Montessori, Rudolf Steiner, Jiddu Krishnamurti, Michel Foucault, Sir Ken Robinson, and, more recently, Prince Ea (whose video titled, "He Just Sued the School System" was extremely popular) have severely critiqued the educational system for unwittingly ensuring that students come out of school and college and even university "magnificently unprepared" to meet the challenges of life and deal with their own frustrations, anger, fears, desires, boredom, aggression, and suffering.

Though education is touted as preparing learners for the future, by teaching *what* to think rather than *how* to think, it fails to nurture the capacity to think clearly, ethically, and wisely. Krishnamurti (2011) convincingly argues that modern education "has not solved a single human problem, be it poverty, war, injustice, inequality, cruelty or corruption . . . [It has] led to incredible technological progress but it has failed to create a world where human beings can live in peace and happiness" (n.p.).

He also believed that proper education and self-knowledge go together in developing high sensitivity to everything, for the highest form of sensitivity is the highest form of intelligence. Krishnamurti (1995) felt that for change to happen, problem-solving skills and creative thinking are necessary, but in no way do schools support them and allow young people to "grow in freedom with a deep sense of inner order" (p. 9).

Like Krishnamurti, Sir Ken Robinson also believes that far from nurturing innovative and creative thinking, educational systems everywhere "kill" it. In one of his educational videos, "Do Schools Kill Creativity?" Robinson (n.d.) insists that children are wonderfully secure in their own imagination, but it is we adults who instill in them the fear of being wrong.

Citing a real-life event to support his view, he tells us that, a few years ago, a primary school teacher noticed a little girl totally absorbed in drawing at the back of the classroom. This surprised the teacher, for the little girl normally did not pay much attention in class. The teacher walked up to her and asked her what she was drawing. Without taking her eyes off her work, the little girl replied, "I'm drawing a picture of God." This surprised the teacher who said, "But nobody knows what God looks like" to which the child replied, "They will in a minute."

The unfortunate truth is that instead of respecting children for their freshness of thought and feeling, we reprimand them, put brakes on their thinking and, worse still, impose our thinking on them. Such lapses of understanding on our part cause students to feel powerless to determine their own lives and while some meekly succumb to their victim status, others rebel, and still others develop strategies to subvert the "authority" of the overbearing adults who claim to know everything about them.

Robinson (2009) reminds us that mass education emerged in the 18th century because of the Industrial Revolution in Europe and the United States. The factory model of education, which still exists today, organized the school day similarly—bells ringing, discrete units of time for each subject, tightly structured classes based on age (Robinson, 2009). Robinson grants that this system has worked for many people whose real strength is conventional academic work, but most others are deeply dissatisfied by it.

Children today have all the information they could possibly want available on computers, smartphones, and other electronic devices. Under such circumstances, is it realistic to expect them to "pay attention," learn, and recall the often-irrelevant things we teach in schools? More importantly, in our current knowledge-based society in which nanotechnology and neuroscience are creating the most unimagined changes, do we need to continue using systems that were created to meet the requirements of bygone ages?

In his book, *The Element*, Robinson narrates numerous real-life "epiphany" stories and says that each one of us should be encouraged to discover our Element and become achievers in our own unique way. The Element, according to him, is "the meeting point between natural aptitude and personal passion" (Robinson, 2009, p. 21). In order to facilitate this discovery, schools should encourage creativity and innovation for we are all, without exception, gifted with extraordinary capacity for creative thinking.

As children, we all start our school career "with sparkling imaginations, fertile minds, and a willingness to take risks with what [we] think" (Robinson, 2009, p. 15). In one of his many educational videos, Robinson talks about a sustained study of creativity in children. As kindergarten children, the capacity of the group for creativity was found to be 98 percent. Five years later, it fell to 50 percent and by the time they were 12 or 13, it plummeted to around 30 percent.

Robinson concludes that original thinking is so greatly discouraged that children get educated out of creativity and are forced into adopting the herd mentality. By creativity, however, he does not mean divergent thinking. Unlike Edward de Bono, he distinguishes between the two forms of thinking and says that creative thinking is "the process of having original ideas that have value" (Robinson, 2009, p. 67), while divergent thinking is the capacity for creative thinking.

Rejecting the idea of standardized testing, Robinson says that "intelligences" are so diverse, dynamic, and distinctive and so rich and complex that there can be no quantifiable evidence to prove their existence. Since we are potentially or actually intelligent in our own unique way, both Robinson and Howard Gardner (who pioneered the theory of multiple intelligences) urge us to reframe our question and not ask: "How intelligent is person A?" but "How is person A intelligent?" By rethinking intelligence with the openness that the yin point of view permits, learners could be led to discover their Element.

One of the most fascinating of social thinkers of the previous century, Michel Foucault (whose work on the relations between power and knowledge won him international recognition) strongly insists that, like other social systems, the educational system imprisons rather than liberates minds and is itself modeled on a prison building, a Panopticon. In his seminal work *Discipline and Punish: The Birth of the Prison* (1975), Foucault discusses Jeremy Bentham's architectural design of the Panopticon as a means to exercise power and enforce discipline and extends this metaphor to speak of "Panopticism" as a social phenomenon used to discipline work forces through covert strategies.

According to Foucault, a Panopticon "is polyvalent in its applications; it serves to reform prisoners, but also to treat patients, to instruct school children, to confine the insane, to supervise workers, to put beggars and idlers to work . . . [Its] modes of intervention of power . . . can be implemented in hospitals, workshops, schools and prisons" (1977, p. 205). With the aim of producing "normal" subjects it marks out a whole finely graduated realm of deviances and under the guise of discipline, "produces subjected and practised bodies, "docile bodies" (1977, p. 138).

Foucault regards the school system as illustrative of Panopticism where, in the name of educating children to become future citizens, the jailers (the authoritarian adults) coerce the prisoners (young learners) into accepting those knowledge systems that they deem necessary to replicate their social systems and retain power. In this space the individual prisoner is placed in a state of permanent visibility and is keenly aware of the unseen gaze of authority.

Shoshana Zuboff, in *In the Age of the Smart Machine: The Future of Work and Power* (1988), contextualizes Foucault's discussion in an age where the work culture uses information and communication systems (ICT) extensively for surveillance. She calls such a structure an "Information Panopticon." With CCTV cameras installed in the rooms of those in positions of authority, school children and both the teaching and nonteaching staff are placed in a state of continuous and rigorous surveillance.

The greatest advantage of Information Panopticons is that "freed from the constraints of space and time, [they] do not depend upon the physical arrangement of buildings or the laborious record keeping of industrial administration. *They do not require the mutual presence of objects of observation*" (Zuboff, 1988, p. 322). In this manner, technological advancements have made it possible to exercise power even more effortlessly, efficiently, and selectively than ever before. More often than not, the subject may even be unaware of the fact that (s)he is being observed. In this sense, the Information Panopticon is like the modern-day upgrade of Bentham's Panopticon.

Albert Einstein believed that every single individual is a genius and, more recently, Howard Gardner (1993) also says that we are all born with at least three intelligences of the nine intelligences that he could detect in humans. By disrespecting children, whose intelligence configurations are different from those demanded by the prison authorities, individuality, creativity, and innovative thinking are trampled upon and, as Prince Ea metaphorically says, such fish are forced to climb trees, climb down trees, and do a 10-mile run.

Undoubtedly it would be incorrect to say that the school system fails to nurture every single student. A few fit in by virtue of their dominant intelligences but millions are left out in the cold. Unfortunately, however, most of those who fit in and make the grades, remain fiercely individualistic "traditional intellectuals." Rarely do such traditional intellectuals (even if they hail from the lower economic strata) assume social responsibility, dare to step out of their comfort zones and evolve into what Antonio Gramsci (1996) calls "organic individuals," which are individuals who determinedly counter hegemony in its various guises and direct the aspirations of the class to which they belong.

Elaborating on Gramcsi's concept of an organic intellectual, Gayatri Spivak (1996) observes: "When the subaltern 'speaks' in order to be heard and gets into the structure of responsible (responding and being responded to) resistance, he or she is on the way to becoming an organic intellectual" (p. 271). Since this rarely happens, most educated intellectuals are not useful to society.

Perhaps the greatest casualty of the mainstream education system is the dismally low happiness index. In most schools and colleges, the teaching-learning process is essentially a joyless one. Research done by psychologists such as Margaretha J. Markesleijn and others reveals that several learning disorders are caused by the distress that students experience in joyless Apollonian classrooms. Markesleijn (2002) considers ADD as a symptom which is often suffered by Dionysian learners in Apollonian classrooms for "Apollo teaches us distance, while Dionysus teaches us proximity, contact and intimacy with ourselves, nature, and others" (p. 213).

Besides Dionysus, the God of epiphany, we also need to welcome Eros, the God of Love and Hermes the God of Liminality into our classrooms. Eros can help us work with a sense of interconnectedness while Hermes could help us think in nuanced ways and rest content in paradoxes and ambiguities instead of demanding logical explanations to every single thing. Educational systems rooted in this awareness could easily transform yang-dominated Apolloian education into creative and joyful, yin-balanced Aphroditean education. It could make learners feel and believe in interconnectedness and see themselves as not merely Cartesian citizens belonging to specific nations but Gaian citizens of the world.

A POSSIBLE SOLUTION

The crisis in the educational system merits a radical overhauling. Not only should education engage learners by making them see the relevance of the knowledge imparted but also enhance self-esteem. The famous psychologist Abraham Maslow, who pioneered positive psychology and studied the greatest achievers of all times, created a model which he called "Mankind's Hierarchy of Needs." Each human being must start from the bottom and fulfill the four basic needs—physiological, safety, love/belonging, and esteem—before moving further upward to the higher need for self-actualization.

By nurturing what I call "Source-full Intelligence," we can help learners feel safe, loved, and valued for *who they are* and not for *how they perform on standardized tests* and help them move toward what Maslow calls self-actualization and Jung calls individuation. The obvious question is, "What is Source-full Intelligence?" *Source-full Intelligence is the dual capacity that we humans have of understanding and experiencing our uniqueness and our oneness simultaneously.*

We may wonder how we can possibly be both unique and one at the same time. How is it possible to combine spirited individualism with unitive thinking? The answer is simple. The upper layers of the mind in the Jungian paradigm—Consciousness and the Personal Unconscious—encourage us to think of our uniqueness while the Collective Unconscious and the transpersonal Deep Self encourage us to think of our oneness.

To put it differently, Source-full Intelligence is our dual awareness of our individual self and higher self. With this kind of intelligence, we can consciously move from oppositional thinking of the *Self-versus-Other* kind to a *Self-and-Other* consciousness and finally to an awareness of a unitary cosmology where there is no Other and *All is Self.*

Our entire social system promotes competition and encourages us to think in terms of Self-versus-Other. By encouraging competition, which strengthens such a consciousness, we as educators make students vulnerable to the manipulations of consumer society and cause damage to their self-esteem. Those who do not make the mark feel worthless while those who do cling to external markers of self-worth which are in themselves mere delusions.

Parents with this kind of consciousness who obsessively talk about how clever or talented their children are and how they stand head-and-shoulders above others of their age, force their children to live up to their expectations rather than accepting their children as they are. Worse still, their children understand that by failing to live up to their view of them, they will be reprimanded and labeled losers. Undoubtedly, a little bit of competition may be necessary to motivate learners to excel, but too much of it is detrimental to their emotional, mental, and physical well-being and their self-worth.

Numerous studies in psychology and sociology tell us that we humans actually prefer cooperation to competition. When we routinely respond with love, compassion, kindness, empathy, and other higher qualities, we move away from the survival of the fittest mentality of the Self-versus-Other consciousness toward a Self-and-Other consciousness. Our selfless, noble acts have their origin in this consciousness.

The deepest part of our self makes us aware that we are part of an unimaginably greater whole. The energy matrix or, as we say in India, our *chita* (life force), within which we exist, connects us, not only to every single being and thing on our planet but to the entire universe (and even universes). We begin seeing ourselves as waves in the cosmic ocean and become Source-fully aware of both our individuality and oneness.

The deep self is a boundless ocean and though scientists are actively involved in researching it (under different names), we humans, as yet, can only catch glimpses of it, but even those glimpses result in an expanded consciousness which leads us to rejoice in all of existence. This awareness, however, does not promote lethargy or a state of passivity but joy-filled, purpose-driven, selfless activity reaching a state when All is Self and the dancer and the dance become one.

It is important to realize that, with increasing self-awareness, we may choose to respond with higher consciousness but, since our shadow and our negative aspects do not disappear completely, we may lapse into low road consciousness and display negative emotions from time to time. If, however, we are committed to our growth, the negative will reduce with each passing day.

Interestingly, the movement from *Self-versus-Other* to *Self-and-Other* to *All is Self*, is the exact trajectory followed by science in the 20th century. Albert Einstein's belief that we are essentially passive observers living in a universe already in place, reflects the *Self-versus-Other* awareness. John Wheeler, who insisted on shattering the plate glass between us and the universe, voices the *Self-and-Other* consciousness, for he believed that we are not observers but participants in the cosmic dance of the universe.

David Bohm, one of the most respected scientists in the latter part of the century, came up with a near holistic view of the universe and our role in it. According to Bohm, the things we see and touch and which appear separate in our world, are examples of the *explicate order*, but they are all linked in a deeper reality which constitutes the *implicate order*. Unmistakably, Bohm reflects the *All is Self* consciousness which results from our connection with our deep self.

Once educators arrive at the *All is Self* or at least *Self-and–Other* state of expanded consciousness through self-exploratory techniques (such as those outlined in my book *What Children Really Want*, 2017), they can transmit this consciousness to the learners using what I call "Technopoiesis."

Technopoiesis involves balancing the use of technology and left-brained techniques with "poiesis"—poetry, myth, the arts, and right-brain learning—to enable learners to develop both parts of the brain. This results in the cultivation of Source-full Intelligence, which helps us perceive both uniqueness and oneness. Technopoietic learning can free our children from the "Cogito ergo sum" ("I think therefore I exist") stalemate and move to valuing thinking, feeling, intuition, and sensation equally.

Figure 27.1 illustrates the steps for arriving at Source-fully Intelligent, Technopoietic Learning lesson plans. At each stage, technology should, ideally speaking, be combined with poetry, music, art, architecture, sculpture, storytelling, and myth.

Step one, *Relevance*, involves an attempt to make learners feel that what they are about to learn is going to be helpful, here and now. Once students see the relevance of the unit of knowledge, it is easy to elicit their active participation in the learning process.

Step two, *Analysis*, involves intense engagement with the key concepts and issues. If a poem or a science concept needs to be learned, it is necessary at this stage to break it into bite-size pieces and plan activities which will make the learners respond in thoughtful ways.

Step three, *Skill Development*, refers to the development of competencies in the various disciplines. For instance, when reading a poem, we use our literary competencies or prior knowledge of the different types of poems, the rhyme scheme, rhythm, imagery, and so on, to add to our appreciation of the poem. Similarly, when attempting to understand ocean currents in geography, our geographical competencies, with reference to the pressure belts, help us understand how and why the currents move in predictable ways. The first three steps of Technopoiesis focus on each learner as an individual and therefore promote the *Self-versus-Other* consciousness.

Step four, *Interlinking*, attempts to cut across barriers of the various disciplines and see knowledge as whole. The arts, sciences, social sciences, and even wisdom literature could be shown as essentially interconnected to help learners develop a more nuanced understanding of the unit and of life.

Step five, *Probing and Reflection*, turns the spotlight on the way in which the learners process the learning as individuals and share their reflections with others.

Step six, *Action*, encourages students to be proactive rather than reactive. This is a necessary and deeply empowering stage. Steps four, five, and six of Technopoiesis help learners move to a *Self-and-Other* awareness. The final step, *Awareness of Oneness*, helps learners dip into the collective unconscious and the deep self to glimpse the essential unity that lies under differences and evolve an *All is Self* consciousness.

Step 7: Awareness of Oneness

Step 6: Action

All is Self

Step 5: Probing and Reflection

Step 4: Interlinking

Self and Others

Step 3: Skill Development

Step 2: Analysis

Step 1: Relevance

Self vs. Others

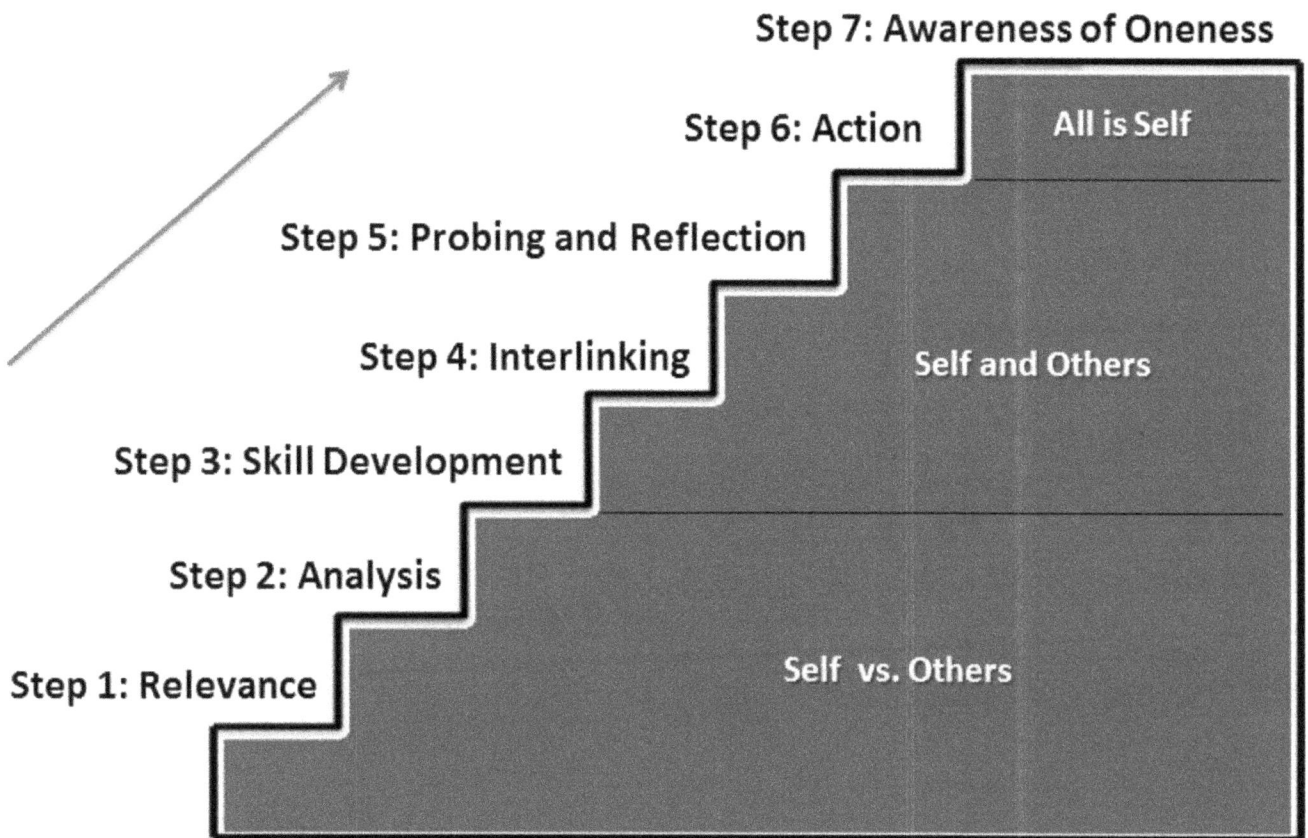

Figure 27.1. Steps for arriving at Source-fully Intelligent, Technopoietic Learning Lesson Plans. Source: *Sourceful Intelligence* by Coomi Vevaina (2013)

In a powerful manner, Technopoietic Learning relates to what we educators know as the Four Pillars of Learning. In 2000, a team of educators came together under the leadership of the French educator Jacques Delors (1996) and designed a report for UNESCO titled, Learning: The Treasure Within. The educators insisted that healthy personal and social development of every child is possible if education is based on what they called "the Four Pillars of Learning"—Learning to Know, Learning to Do, Learning to Live Together, and Learning to Be.

Learning to Know refers to the type of learning that is concerned less with the acquisition of structured information than with the mastery of learning tools such as concentration, memory skills, mind mapping, and the ability to think independently. Learning to Do considers the manner in which we can make education more innovative and application-based. Learning to Live Together involves celebrating (not merely respecting) differences and coexisting peacefully with others. This pillar is deemed crucial to the survival of humanity. The final pillar, Learning to Be, refers to living life to one's full potential. This fourth pillar corresponds to Maslow's need for self-actualization that I discussed earlier in the chapter.

True to the holistic vision of the designers of the Delors Report, *Source-fully Intelligent Technopoietic*

Learning includes all the Four Pillars of Learning. Relevance, Analysis, and Skill Development, the first three steps of Technopoiesis, correspond to pillars one and two, Learning to Know and Learning to Do refer to the nurturing of individual intelligences. The next three steps of Technopoiesis, Interlinking, Probing, and Reflection and Action, which seek to cultivate interpersonal and intrapersonal intelligences and encourage learners to live together, correspond to the third pillar Learning to Live Together. The final pillar, Learning to Be, involves developing unitive thinking and spiritual intelligence through an Awareness of Oneness.

Such yang-and-yin balanced Source-full Education would, to go back to Capra's words, make us value self-assertion and integration, analysis and synthesis, rational knowledge and intuitive wisdom, science and religion (or better still, spirituality), competition and cooperation and expansion and conservation equally. This kind of education also helps develop the three types of thinking that we are capable of.

We humans are intellectual, emotional, and spiritual creatures with the capacity for serial, associative, and unitive thinking which have three different neural systems. Our logical, rule-bound, linear, and dispassionate thinking (which gives us our IQ—Intelligence Quotient),

Learning to know   **Learning to do**   **Learning to live together**   **Learning to be**

Step 1: **Relevance**
Step 2: **Analysis**
Step 3: **Skill Development**

Step 4: **Interlinking**
Step 5: **Probing & Reflection**
Step 6: **Action**

Step 7: **Awareness of Oneness**

3. **All is Self**

2. **Self & Others**

1. **Self vs. Others**

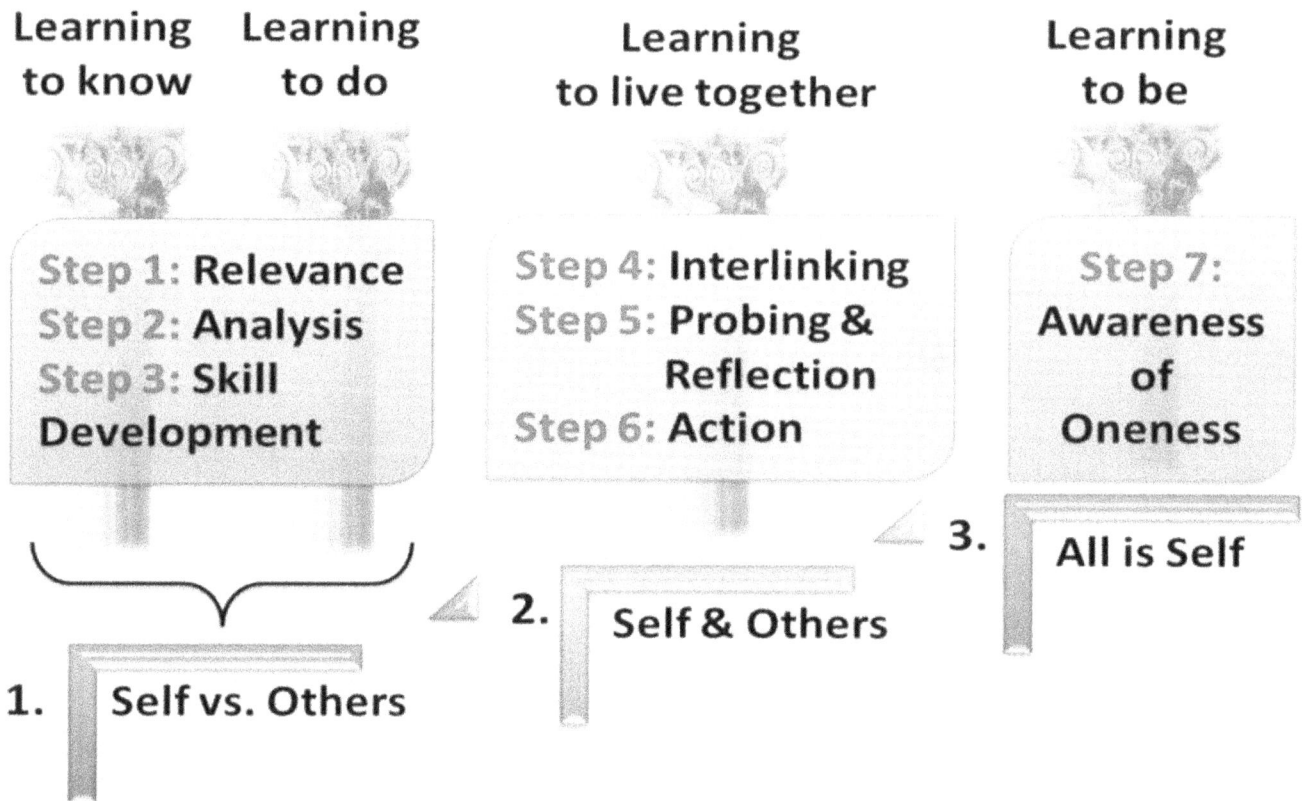

Figure 27.2. Source-fully Intelligent Technopoietic Learning. Source: *Sourceful Intelligence* by Coomi Vevaina (2013)

is caused by *serial* neural wiring in the brain. The neural tracts are wired according to a fixed program as a result of which, though it is accurate, precise, and reliable, it does not permit nuance.

For instance, if we hear someone say that 2 + 2 = 7, we will jump in to point out that it is wrong because our brain is hard-wired to accept only one answer and that is 2 + 2 = 4. Similarly, if we hear someone say, "Cat a mat on sat" we once again point out that it is wrong because the sentence structure hard-wired in our brain is, "A cat sat on a mat." When we think in such serial ways, computer graphs show geometric patterns.

In contrast, our pattern-recognizing, *associative* thinking (which gives us our EQ—Emotional Quotient) is far less rigid and can be rewired with dialogue and experience. This type of thinking is able to accommodate ambiguities and paradoxes and is flexible. Though less precise than serial thinking, it makes relearning possible without reprogramming. Serial thinking requires language but associative thinking is not connected with our language facility.

However, serial and associative systems interact constantly and support each other. When we think in such associative ways, computer graphs show tree-like patterns. The third type of thinking is *unitive* in nature and is linked to our need for meaning, vision, and value

in life. By bridging the gap between interpersonal and intrapersonal intelligences, our unitive thinking gives us our SQ—Spiritual Quotient. Unitive thinking is our creative, insightful, rule-making, rule-breaking thinking which, as Danah Zohar and Ian Marshall (2000) tell us in their ground-breaking book *Spiritual Intelligence, the Ultimate Intelligence*, is the highest kind of thinking that we humans are capable of.

It is extremely important that we nurture all three types of thinking—serial, associative as well as unitive—or only then will our learners be able to understand life connotatively (symbolically) and denotatively (literally). For this to happen, mathematics, pure sciences, social sciences, and the arts—literature, painting, sculpture, music, drama—should be regarded as equally important. The unfortunate trend in almost all countries of the world is to prioritize mathematics and the sciences and neglect arts education. The arts are vitally important, for they help develop all three forms of thinking and enable our children to understand things in a deeper way.

With well-developed Source-full Intelligence and the meta-ability of empathy (with which we are all blessed), young people can be helped to open their hearts "to feel and enjoy another as oneself" (Perry, 1993, p. xxiv) and realize that "[w]ithin the reality of our universal inadequacy, uncertainty and blindness lies a limitless capacity to reach out to one another, to hold one another, a limitless energy, a limitless empowerment which is available and accessible directly in our finite limited condition" (Kogawa, 1990, p. 21).

The indigenous people of the Americas believe that for 500 years the eagle (which represents the yang energy) is in ascendance and for the next 500 years the condor (which represents the yin energy). The eagle represents the wonders of the intellect and mind, while the condor, the wonders of the natural world. The prophecy is that the eagle and the condor will fly together and the way of the mind will coexist with the way of the heart and spirit to cocreate a nondualistic world which will be technologically advanced, environmentally sustainable, spiritually fulfilling, and socially just.

REFERENCES

Bolen, J. S. (2005). *Gather the women, save the world.* Boston, MA: Conari Press.

Capra, F. (1975). *The Tao of physics* (3rd ed.). London, England: Flamingo Press.

Delors, J. (1996). *Learning: The treasure within.* Paris, France: Presses Universitaires de France. Retrieved from http://www.unesco.org/delors/fourpil.htm

Foucault, M. (1975). *Discipline and punish: The birth of the prison* (Alan Sheridan, Trans.). New York, NY: Vintage.

Gardner, H. (1993). *Multiple intelligences: The theory in practice.* New York, NY: Basic Books.

Gramsci, A. (1996). *Selections from the prison notebooks.* (Quintin Hoare and Geoffrey Nowell Smith, Ed. and Trans.). Madras, India: Orient Longman.

Houston, J. (2011). *Partnership spirituality.* Retrieved from http://www.jeanhouston.com/

Kogawa, J. (1990). Audience Discussion. Panel Two. In S. Lee, L. Maracle, D. Marlatt, & B. Warland (Eds.), *Telling it: Women and language across culture.* Vancouver, Canada: Press Gang Publishers.

Krishnamurti, J. (1995). *Krishnamurti on education.* London, England: Krishnamurti Foundation Trust.

Krishnamurti, J. (2011). *A word to the young. Does school prepare you for life?* Chennai, India: Krishnamurti Foundation India.

Lyotard, J. F. (1979). *The postmodern condition: A report on knowledge* (G. Bannington & B. Massumi, Trans.). Manchester, England: Manchester University Press.

Markesleijn, J. M. (2002). *Attention deficit disorder: A depth psychological perspective* (PhD thesis). Pacifica Graduate Institute.

Perry, F. (1993). *When lightning strikes a hummingbird.* Santa Fe, NM: Bear & Co.

Robinson, K. (2009). *The element: How finding your passion changes everything.* New York, NY: Viking Penguin Books.

Robinson, K. (n.d.) *Do schools kill creativity?* Retrieved from https://www.youtube.com/watch?v=iG9CE55wbtY

Ruether, R. R. (1975). *New woman, new earth: Sexist ideologies and human liberation.* New York, NY: Seabury.

Spivak, G. (1996). Translator's preface and afterword to Mahasweta Devi, Imaginary Maps. In D. Landry & G. Maclean (Eds.), *The Spivak reader* (pp. 267–286). New York, NY: Routledge.

Vevaina, C. (2013). *Source-full intelligence. Understanding uniqueness and oneness through education.* Bloomington, IN: AuthorHouse Press.

Vevaina, C. (2017). *What children really want.* New Delhi, India: Maniken Press.

Zohar, D., & Marshall, I. (2000). *Spiritual intelligence, the ultimate intelligence.* London: Bloomsbury.

Zuboff, S. (1988). *In the age of the smart machine: The future of work and power.* New York, NY: Basic Books.

Afterword

Upoko whakakapi: Mana Wāhine

Rachel McNae and Elizabeth C. Reilly

Mana Wāhine
He wahine, he wahine
He whenua, he whenua
E ngaro ai te tangata Hi!

Without the nourishment women give,
Humanity would be lost
Joyful Leadership

On August 28, 2015, in Hamilton, New Zealand, the ground shook and the walls vibrated as the air filled with a cacophony of singing and stamping which rose from a guttural, warrior-like chant. Across the room, women's eyes—steely and wide—stared ahead, their voices strong, powerful, and unleashed, connected in unison, chanted and performed a haka, a traditional Māori dance, choreographed and written specifically for those attending the 5th International Women Leading Education Conference.

The meaning behind the chant illuminated the essential and nourishing roles women and the land fulfill in communities, without which humanity would not survive. Te Mana Rollo choreographed the piece with movements that not only acknowledged the importance of women in society, but also the burden they carry from this responsibility. In her explanation of the whakatauki (Māori proverb), she spoke of the many expectations placed on women and how the demands of each role they fulfill are complex. She identified the competing demands which were often intertwined across each role, as women sought to balance the expectations of being practitioners and teachers with their leadership as daughters, mothers, aunts, wives, and sisters, with each experience being unique and distinct.

As with previous Women Leading Education (WLE) conferences, this conference offered women leaders around the globe a place to stand, a place to listen, a place to contemplate, and a place to connect with others. In New Zealand, in Māori culture this is often described as Tūrangawaewae: tūranga is a standing place and waewae are feet. As a concept Tūrangawaewae describes a place where we feel especially empowered and connected, acknowledging our foundation, our place in the world, and our home (Te Ara, 2017).

At each of these gatherings over the years, since the first WLE Conference in Rome in 2007, a range of emotions has surfaced—pride, anger, sorrow, guilt, and sadness, to name a few. As we stood together singing, we were able to acknowledge these feelings, letting them wash over us as we paused, joyful and united in our beliefs and hopes for women's leadership, and considered that things could be better.

There is a part of women's leadership we hear very little about: the hope and joy in leadership. Because of this, we announced the conference theme of "Harnessing Joy in Leadership" with the intention of focusing attention on these positive and affirming aspects of leadership. What initially seemed a relatively straightforward task was anything but straightforward. The call for papers signaled the theme, yet submissions often failed to embrace this important element. This raised many questions for us. How can we surface joy in leadership and highlight these stories and experiences when they are so difficult to identify and write about? What are we afraid of? What makes talking about hope, joy, and enjoyment in leadership so difficult? What expectations, cultural and societal discourses frame leadership in ways that cause women to find it difficult to acknowledge this element in their work?

Glancing around the room that day, joy was everywhere. It was on faces as women sampled Hangi—traditionally cooked food, wrapped in leaves and steamed in sulphur springs underground over hot rocks; it emanated in sounds as women laughed together, debated topics with passion, and sung their waiata (song); it radiated as they greeted old friends; it was present in their dances as they claimed space on the floor. Joy was evidenced as a powerful presence in women's leadership. How might we embrace and demonstrate this concept more readily in our leadership practices, organizations, and lives? What can help us to identify and reclaim it?

KOTAHITANGA: VALUING UNITY

According to the founding Chair of Women Leading Education Across the Continents, Helen Sobehart, "WLE is founded on the fire of passion and the light of truth" (2015, p. ix). Fundamentally, the lack of diverse voices addressing women in educational leadership becomes the driver for the work, and in particular, for the establishment of a biyearly conference convened with the purpose of addressing social justice. The first conference convened in Rome in summer 2007. Scholars, practitioners, and graduate students participated and shared research. The inspiration for the conference came from the words of a 13th-century nun, Hildegard of Bingen, Germany, for whom light and flame were inspirations. Hildegard would have a recurring vision of a woman that represented wisdom. She observed that, "the woman was in the flame but not consumed by it, rather it flowed from her" (2015, p. x). The story continues to serve as inspiration for the members of WLE.

Since 2007, we have convened for five other conferences: the University of Augsburg in Germany (2009), the University of Thessaley, Volos, Greece (2011); the University of Education, Winneba, Accra, Ghana (2013); the University of Waikato in New Zealand (2015), whose presentations served as the chapters of this book; and Universidade do Estado do Rio de Janeiro in Brazil (2017). Either a book or a journal result from each of the conferences and feature as many as 40 authors from across the world. Members have extended their influence over the years through numerous collaborative research investigations, presentations, and publications internationally.

TITIRO WHAKAMUA: LOOKING FORWARD

The contributions throughout this book illustrate the powerful nature of women's leadership and the importance of surfacing and acknowledging women's experiences and voices within and across the contexts they lead. The chapters highlight women's experiences of leadership within different contexts and each section has the breadth and depth to stand alone, but also contribute to supporting the development of ideas across each section. Opportunities to reflect on the status of women in educational leadership from various global perspectives has illustrated not only the commonalities with regard to

leadership experiences, but also importantly, the highly diverse and distinct contextual narratives which call for an acknowledgment that culture and context must be key considerations when exploring women's leadership as a global phenomenon.

Speaking about women leaders as a homogeneous group does little to acknowledge these critically distinctive experiences and powerful perspectives and as Blackmore (2008) argued, "The popularization of women's ways of leading discourse treats women as a homogeneous group without differences in race/class/gender or in beliefs" (p. 57) and fails to take into account "the diverse contexts in which women lead" (Torrance, Fuller, McNae, Roofe & Arshad, 2017, p. 30). It is through examining these unique and culturally located stories that we can uncover the various factors that continue to influence women's access to and success in leadership, however that success might be defined.

If changes in the field of women leaders are to occur, then heeding Blackmore's (2008) advice, the conversation requires an extension beyond simply the numbers that illustrate the ways women are represented in core leadership roles. Making sense of the social and cultural architectures associated with being a woman leader and embracing wholeheartedly the ways in which women make sense of and demonstrate their leadership across the many different contexts they engage in is critical to shifting the conversation forward. Vongalis-Macrow (2016) encourages researchers to examine how gender is perceived, constructed, created, and enacted in the context of work, as she believes, "this has as much to do with women's perceptions and women's interactions that are changing and context dependent as it has with the obstacles of masculine culture that prevent more women from achieving leadership" (p. 100).

We encourage more nuanced lines of inquiry that examine the intersection of women in leadership with other factors such as race and ethnicity, religion, sexual orientation, and gender identity. Moorosi, Fuller, and Reilly (2016), for example, examined the intersection of race and gender with black women principals in South Africa, the United Kingdom, and the United States. Other intersections that emerged in their investigation included the impact of apartheid, colonialism, and slavery on the women's experiences. Their three-country comparative work has charted new territory on women in educational leadership when much of the literature has focused largely on white middle class women, leaving black women's experiences on the periphery—even in contexts where they are in the majority. The omission of black female leadership narratives, together with the lack of adequate understanding of the contexts in which leadership has been or is successful, has constrained the ability to contribute to ways that improve schooling experiences and advance lives in communities that are poor and disadvantaged (Murtadha & Watts, 2005).

As frustrating as it may seem for some to revisit old ground that has been covered, Shakeshaft (2014) argues the research pattern associated with women's leadership in education is not a straight line and more like an interstate highway, "with all of its exits and return ramps" serving the purpose of moving forward more understanding and circling back to update old notions" (p. xi). In her work, she underscores the importance of doing this, even though at times the whole effort may appear laborious and repetitive. She argues that just because issues have been documented once, does not mean they have gone away. There is an obligation to connect women to the findings of the research, to expose the multiple realities in their various forms, to acknowledge evolving patterns, shifts, and stagnations along with changes in the research findings and disrupt oppressive mechanisms that stifle women's leadership.

HUMANITY AND LEADERSHIP—TE IRA TANGATA ME TE RANGATIRATANGA

Carving Space for Joyful Emotion

Activism within organizations and deviance from organizational norms is frequently problematized in leadership literature. Sameness and status quo is championed over diversity and to stray from the mainstream culture can be viewed in a negative light, resulting in the silencing of women's stories and a lack of attention to women's lived experiences. Women's presence in educational change is paramount if the social, cultural, and political architectures are to shift and women are to flourish in their leadership. Positive deviance can play a key role in developing and sustaining leadership.

The work of Lyman, Strachan, and Lazaridou (2012) draws on the work of Aristotle, illuminating the concept of Eudaimonia, a flourishing state, while at the same time demonstrating the highest form of humanity. Eudaimonia in leadership can involve leading for the greater good, along with doing and living to full potential. However, "Eudaimonia is experienced not constantly in our lives, but in moments when we experience a euphoria of the soul born of the sense that we matter and are doing just what we are meant to do" (Bullough & Pinnegar, 2009, p. 246). The tension remains within organizations when structures, discourses, and organizational cultures prevent positive emotions, specifically joy, from surfacing, positioning women as participants within a system, vulnerable to discourses which do not necessarily recognize, celebrate, or even acknowledge women's ways of lead-

ing. Coming to understand the burden of vulnerability might provide opportunities to reevaluate architectures which fail to support human flourishing.

There is a whakataukī that helps us consider how to look forward with hope and joy. "Ēhara tāku toa i te takitini, he toa takitahi: My success would not be bestowed onto me alone, as it was not individual success but success of a collective." Aimee Ratana's artwork "takitini" on the front cover of this book references women's multiple and complex roles, and the significance of women existing as a collective. The work of this group which has collaborated to bring this project to conclusion is a working example of this in its entirety. This whakataukī (Māori proverb) captures the ability to work together as a team or group to accomplish something great. It also refers to sharing achievement or success with other people rather than self-advancement. Within the WLE community, it is time together which strengthens our resolve to make a difference for other women leaders. In the spaces and relationships that we have created, new members, new possibilities, and new hope surfaces for what lies ahead. It is time to share this joy, passion, and renewed strength to continue the valuable work for women and with women in leadership around the globe.

> Wāhine ātaahua
> Kei roto kei waho
> Wāhine mana nui
> Kei roto kei waho
> Ahakoa ko wai no whea
> He manukura ki mua
> Tika rawa a Te Puea
> Mahia te mahi
> Hei painga mo te iwi!

> The beauty of a woman
> Is reflected inwards and outwards
> Women have pride and a rich heritage
> That is felt inwards and shown outwards
> No matter who you are or where you are from
> You are a leader that leads from the front
> True are the words of Te Puea Herangi
> Get on with the work
> For the good of all people!

REFERENCES

Blackmore, J. (2008). Re/positioning women in educational leadership: The changing social relations and politics of gender in Australia. In H. Sobehart (Ed.), *Women leading education across the continents: Sharing the spirit, fanning the flame* (pp. 73–83). Lanham, MD: Rowman & Littlefield Education.

Bullough, R., & Pinnegar, S. (2009). The happiness of teaching (as eudaimonia): Disciplinary knowledge and the threat of performativity. *Teachers and Teaching: Theory and Practice, 15*(2), 241–256.

Lyman, L., Strachan, J., & Lazaridou, A. (2012). *Shaping social justice leadership: Insights of women educators worldwide*. Lanham, MD: Rowman & Littlefield Education.

Moorosi, P., Fuller, K., & Reilly, E. C. (2016). A comparative analysis of intersections of gender and race among black female school leaders in South Africa, United Kingdom, and the United States. In P. Miller (Ed.), *Cultures of educational leadership: Global and intercultural perspectives*. London: Palgrave Macmillan.

Murtadha, K., & Watts, D. M. (2005). Linking the struggle for education and social justice: Historical perspectives of African American leadership in schools. *Educational Administration Quarterly, 41*(4), 591–608.

Shakeshaft, C. (2014). Introduction: Where have we been? Where are we going? In Sherman Newcomb & K. Cummings Mansfield (Eds.), *Women interrupting, disrupting and revolutionizing educational policy and practice* (pp. ix–xxi), Charlotte, NC: Information Age Publishing.

Sobehart, H. (2015). Foreword: Becoming the beacon. In E. Reilly & Q. Bauer (Eds.), *Women leading education across the continents: Overcoming the barriers* (pp. ix–xi). Lanham, MD: Rowman & Littlefield.

Te Ara. (2017). *The encyclopedia of New Zealand*. Retrieved from https://teara.govt.nz/en

Torrance, D., Fuller, K., McNae, R., Roofe, C., & Arshad, R. (2017). A social justice perspective on women in educational leadership. In P. Miller (Ed.), *Cultures of educational leadership,* (pp. 25–52). London, UK: Palgrave Macmillan.

Vongalis-Macrow, A. (2016). It's about the leadership: The importance of women leaders doing leadership for women, *NASPA Journal About Women in Higher Education, 9*(1), 90–103. DOI: 10.1080/19407882.2015.1114953

Index

AASA. *See* American Association of School Administrators

affirmative action, 124; Canada's definition of, 122; competency and, 126–27; educator knowledge of, 104, 126; legislation obscurity of, 104; Malaysian Muslim women academics and, 107, 108, 109, 112; PPM 102 and, 104; proponents and opponents of, 123; pros and cons of, 126–27

Afghanistan: community development in, 12; complex geopolitical circumstances in, 9; cultural values and norms transformation in, 11; decades of conflicts in, 9; freedom of women in, 8, 11; gender equality and women's empowerment in, 12; international community partnerships of, 12; journalism in, 9; Malaysia and Indonesia as role models for, 9; opium economy in, 9, 12; Pakistan and Iran influence in, 9; principle challenges in, 8; proverb of, 6, 12; Rabia Balkhi tale in, 7; road toward equality in, 11; rural communities in, 9; shame prospect in, 12; two critical priorities for, 9; universal human rights debate in, 12; women and leadership in, 11; women's plight in, 7, 13

Afghan National Assembly, 7

Afghan women: gender injustice in educational leadership of, 4; plight of, 7, 13; politics impact on, 7; Taliban's violence against, 7–8

Akao, S., 15–16, 23

American Association of School Administrators (AASA), 40, *40*, 85

American Psychological Association (APA), 38

Anglican Church of Melanesia, 16

Anjuman, Nadia, 11

Aotearoa New Zealand: as bicultural island, xv; British shared governance in, xv; children's enjoyment in, xviii; colonialism in, xx; community engagement in, xx; community values in, xviii; cultural responsibilities shared in, xviii; designated character school principal in, xx; first settlers of, xv; historical trauma and mental illness in, xvi, xx–xxi; leadership between genders in, xviii; motherhood and family in, xix; other employment opportunities in, xviii–xix; place and people connection in, xviii; pressing noses ritual in, xviii; resident tribal groups origin in, xviii; schooling in, xviii; social ills of, xix; store managing in, xviii; Treaty of Waitangi and, xv; welcoming ceremony in, xviii; women callers and male speechmakers in, xviii.

See also Māori culture; Māori learning; Māori medium education; Wāhine Māori (Māori women's) leadership

APA. *See* American Psychological Association

Ara, Jehan, 172

Aristotle, 118, 150, 189

assistant superintendent for instruction (ASI), 70; career anchors definitions in, *81*; career anchors in, 80; career orientation factor of remainers and ascenders in, 84–85; career orientations and career plans of, 80; career orientation scale for remainers and ascenders in, 83; career orientations scale scores in, *84*; career plan and orientation relationship analysis in, *85*; COI mean scale scores in, 82–83; COI research instrument use in, 81; data analysis in, 82; data collection and response rate for, 81; demographics in study of, 82; dominant orientations in, 84; female career plan frequencies in, *83*; female race and ethnicity frequencies in, *83*; female remainers and ascenders in, 83; findings in, 83–84; gender and career plan results of, 85; gender association in, 80; general managerial competence orientation of, 84–86; male and female career plan differences in, 83; NCLB responsibility of, 80, 84; need-based orientations in, 84; service-to-a-cause orientation in, 84; study questions in, 80–81; superintendent role aspiring of, 80; talent-based orientations in, 84; technical functional competent orientations of, 85–86; value-based orientations in, 84; women remainers and ascenders orientation and plan in, 85–86; women total number of years worked as, *82*

Babcock, Linda, 175–76

Baker, Sarah Jean, 138–39

Bang, S. C., 35–36

Barakzai, Shukria, 7

Barbour, Karen, 70

Becker, Anne, 118

Benko, Cathleen, 174

Blackmore, J., 14, 89, 113, 188

Bogesi, G., 15–16

Bohm, David, 182

Branson, Chris, 77

Brown, M., 15, 23

Butterworth, Joanne, 77–78

About the Editors

Rachel McNae

Title: Director and Associate Professor of Educational Leadership
Institution: University of Waikato, Hamilton, New Zealand
Email: rachel.mcnae@waikato.ac.nz

Rachel McNae (PhD) is an associate professor of educational leadership and is director of the Centre for Educational Leadership Research at the University of Waikato in Hamilton, New Zealand. She is also the national president of the New Zealand Educational Administration and Leadership Society in New Zealand, and co-founder of *The Good Human Project*—an organization supporting young people to flourish in educational settings.

Rachel's research agenda is founded on a firm belief for social justice, and her numerous research projects span the fields of women and leadership, student voice and agency, youth leadership, and leadership innovation and curriculum generation. Rachel has developed, taught, and coordinated a range of postgraduate and higher degrees in educational leadership. Her recently published books include *Realizing Innovative Partnerships in Educational Research* (2017) and *Educational Leadership for Social Justice in Aotearoa New Zealand* (New Zealand Council for Educational Research, 2017). She is an active member of the International Women Leading Education group and the International School Leadership Development Network. In 2016 Rachel was awarded the position of New Zealand Educational Leadership Society Visiting Scholar and was the recipient of the International Emerald-European Foundation for Management and Development Outstanding Research Award for Leadership and Strategy. In 2015 Rachel received the Meritorious Service Award for her service to leadership in New Zealand and was awarded the New Zealand Education Administration and Leadership Society Presidential Research Award for her work with young women leaders in schools.

Elizabeth C. Reilly

Title: Chair and Professor
Institution: Loyola Marymount University, United States
Email: elizabeth.reilly@lmu.edu

Elizabeth C. Reilly (EdD) is chair and professor of educational leadership and administration for the School of Education at Loyola Marymount University (LMU) in Los Angeles, California. In the years preceding her appointments in higher education, Dr. Reilly served as a classroom teacher and educational leader in K–12 school districts. A recognized international scholar investigating women in educational leadership, with graduate students and fellow scholars she presents and researches globally on leadership; organizational culture and change; and women in leadership. She works with leaders of multinationals, government, nongovernmental organizations, and education on five continents. As a scholar, Dr. Reilly has conducted investigations in numerous countries including Afghanistan, China, India, Ghana, Russia, and Rwanda with the goal of highlighting the voices of those whose stories deserve to be told. In 2016, AERA's Leadership for Social Justice SIG honored Dr. Reilly as its recipient of the "Bridge People Award" that recognizes people whose work "creates a bridge between themselves and others" through scholarship and research. For the 2016–2017 academic year, LMU honored Dr. Reilly as one of its notable professors She is the author and co-author of numerous books, book chapters, and journal articles on education and on leadership in a global society.

About the Section Editors

Alice Kagoda

Title: Professor
Institution: Makerere University
Email: musano2009@gmail.com

Alice Kagoda (PhD) is professor of education at the College of Education and External Studies at Makerere University in Uganda. Alice's doctoral research (University of Alberta, Canada), focusing on international and intercultural education, combined with over 25 years of teaching experience spanning her career, had led to her interest and commitment to girl child education. Her interest in gender in education allows her to integrate this aspect into her teaching. Her work extends beyond academic and theoretical components and she is an active community member, supporting young women to develop their entrepreneurial activities of craft making so that they can earn a living. Alice is currently the representative for the School of Education in the University Senate and a member of the senate committee revising the university curriculum programs. She coordinates a scholarship program for girls from Buyende District, a remote poor district, sponsored by Graduate Women International based in Geneva.

Sister Chrispina Lekule

Title: Lecturer
Institution: St. Augustine University of Tanzania
Email: chrispina.lek@gmail.com

Sister Chrispina Lekule (PhD) is director of Postgraduate Studies, Research and Consultancy at St. Augustine University of Tanzania. She holds a PhD in Educational Leadership and Policy Studies from the University of Windsor in Ontario, Canada. She also earned a master's degree from St. Cloud State University in Minnesota, United States. She serves as a lecturer in the Faculty of Education where she teaches graduate courses in educational leadership and management. Prior to pursuing graduate studies, she served as a teacher and school principal in Zanzibar-Tanzania for seven years. Her recent publications focus on school culture and leadership models.

Pontso Moorosi

Title: Associate Professor
Institution: University of Warwick
Email: P.C.Moorosi@warwick.ac.uk

Pontso Moorosi (PhD) is an associate professor of educational leadership and management at the Institute of Education, Warwick University, in Coventry, England. She lectures in educational leadership and research methods that include practice-based research for school leaders. Her research interests examine issues of gender and educational leadership and leadership development broadly. Her PhD investigated challenges and constraints of female school principalship in South Africa with an interest in gender and career development, constructions of success in leadership and in addressing issues that concern equity and equality in school leadership. Pontso questions the way women (and women in education in particular) use their position of (dis)advantage to empower themselves (and others) in taking their place of leadership in society against oppressive cultural, race, and gender regimes. She has recently completed a school leadership development study involving four African countries with publications on school leadership development, gender and school leadership, and feminist leader identity construction.

Jacqueline Oram-Shortt

Title: High School Social Science teacher
Institution: Homestead Senior High School,
   Miami, Florida
Email: js_9192@yahoo.com

Dr. Oram-Shortt is a former Fulbright scholar and pursued a PhD in educational administration at Illinois State University. Jacqueline specializes in multicultural education, gender studies, and qualitative research approaches. For her PhD dissertation, *The Joan Wint Story: Biography of a Principal Whose Leadership for Social Justice Transformed a Rural Jamaican High School*, she was awarded the Distinguished Dissertation Award by Illinois State University in 2010. She served as the Dean of Graduate studies at the Mico University College for a number of years and presently resides in Florida.

Michelle Young

Title: Professor
Institution: University of Virginia
Email: Mdy8n@virginia.edu

Michelle D. Young, (PhD), is a professor of leadership at the University of Virginia. Dr. Young's scholarship focuses on feminist critical policy analysis and the preparation and practice of educational leaders. Young seeks to understand how leaders and policies can ensure equitable and quality experiences for all school community members. Young is the recipient of the William J. Davis award for the most outstanding article published in a volume of the *Educational Administration Quarterly*. Recently Young edited *Critical Approaches to Education Policy Analysis: Moving Beyond Tradition* and the *Handbook of Research on the Education of School Leaders*, 2nd Edition.

About the Contributors

Sarah Jean Baker

Title: Assistant Professor/Department Chair of
    Teacher Education
Institution: Concordia University Texas
Email: sarahjeanbaker@gmail.com

Sarah Jean Baker (PhD) is a recent graduate from the School Improvement PhD program at Texas State, where she also earned her master's in educational leadership. Before her position at Concordia University, Texas, she was an early childhood teacher and assistant principal in the Central Texas region. She was recently recognized as an emerging scholar through the Clark Scholar program of the American Educational Research Association. Her research interests include: teacher and educational leadership preparation and development, early childhood education, mentoring support, and women's issues in schools. She is also a mama to four children, three sons and a daughter.

Karen Barbour

Title: Associate Professor
Institution: University of Waikato
Email: karenb@waikato.ac.nz

Karen Barbour (PhD) is an associate professor at The University of Waikato, Hamilton, New Zealand. She is committed to fostering qualitative dance research, specifically in feminist choreographic practice, site-specific, and digital dance. Karen has published in a range of academic journals including *Cultural Studies*, *Critical Methodologies*, *International Journal of Arts in Society*, *Brolga and Emotion*, *Space*, and *Society*. Karen is editor of the journal *Dance Research Aotearoa* (http:www.dra.ac.nz), author of *Dancing Across the Page: Narrative and Embodied Ways of Knowing* (2011), and the edited book *Ethnographic Worldviews: Transformations and Social Justice*. Karen is a member of the World Dance Alliance-Asia Pacific branch, the World Alliance for Arts Education, and Congress on Research in Dance. In New Zealand she is a committed member of Dance Aotearoa New Zealand and the Tertiary Dance Educators' Network New Zealand Aotearoa. Karen contributes to numerous dance performances, research projects, and education opportunities, particularly through notions of feminist contemporary choreography, creative practice, digital dance, autoethnography/narrative writing, site-specific, and environmental dance practices.

Sharon Campbell

Title: Lecturer
Institution: University of Waikato
Email: sharonc@waikato.ac.nz

Sharon Campbell holds the position of lecturer in Te Hononga—School of Curriculum and Pedagogy, in the Faculty of Education, University of Waikato, Hamilton, New Zealand. Sharon is an experienced rumaki reo Māori teacher and principal in the Māori medium schooling sector within Aotearoa New Zealand. Her teaching philosophy considers holistic education underpinned by language, culture, practices, and values to enable ongoing emancipation and transformation through education for whānau, hapu, and iwi. Sharon's master's research considered ways of strengthening whānau (family) engagement and succession in Kura-ā-iwi (tribal schools). Kaupapa Māori theory and methodology are integral to her current and future research engagements. Working in the area of preservice teacher education Sharon is passionate about Māori education and fostering future teachers who are culturally competent and committed to advancing nationhood. She considers honoring Te Tiriti o Waitangi and culturally responsive practice and pedagogy essential for all current and future teachers in Aotearoa New Zealand.

Mku Chitra

Title: Assistant Professor
Institution: Madurai Kamarj University, India
Email: chitraeconometricsmku@gmail.com

Mku Chitra (PhD) is an assistant professor in the Department of Econometrics, School of Economics, Madurai Kamaraj University, Madurai-Tamil Nadu-India. She has taught and researched in higher education since 1992 across various institutions within India and Asia (Bhutan and Indonesia). Her areas of interest are health economics and economics of education. She has published six books. Two are reference books in health, one in education, and three textbooks. She is a life member of the Indian Health Economic Association, Indian Economic Association, Tamil Nadu Economic Association, and Regional Association for Women Society. Under her guidance three candidates have been awarded their PhDs and she recently submitted a report to the funding agency Malcolm Elizabeth Adiseashia Trust under the title "Economic analysis on Street Children in Dindigul District-Tamil Nadu." Mku believes the application of mathematics in economics is important for women's success in their communities and her work seeks to recognize the important role women play in the economic contribution to society.

Frances Edwards

Title: Senior Lecturer
Institution: University of Waikato
Email: frances.edwards@waikato.ac.nz

Frances Edwards (PhD) is a senior lecturer in the Faculty of Education, University of Waikato, New Zealand, teaching primarily in postgraduate programs and preservice teacher education. Her background includes working in New Zealand and in the Pacific region as a secondary school teacher, senior school leader, regional school adviser, educational consultant, and lecturer in initial teacher education. Frances' research interests include assessment, curriculum, pedagogy, Pacific Education, teacher professional learning and development, educational leadership, and educational change. She has taught in most curriculum areas, although her areas of curriculum expertise are science and mathematics education, and additional languages education Frances is particularly enthusiastic about helping educators develop themselves to be the best they can in their own contexts.

Katie Higginbottom

Title: Special Education Teacher
Institution: University of Toronto
Email: k.higginbottom@mail.utoronto.ca

Katie Higginbottom (PhD) is a Women in Leadership Educator & Consultant in Ontario, Canada. Katie's research interests include social justice leadership and women in leadership, two areas that Katie understands to be deeply interwoven and evidenced in her work with *Project Empowerment*. Supported by Ontario Graduate Scholarships and University of Toronto Scholarships, Katie's doctoral research examined how women directors of education in Ontario manage pressures associated with others' social expectations of them.

Wafa Hozien

Title: Assistant Professor
Institution: Central Michigan University, United States
Email: Hozie1w@cmich.edu

Wafa Hozien (PhD) is an assistant professor at Central Michigan University. Her work in the areas of ethical decision-making practices among school leaders has contributed to her research agenda in the area of exploring the ethical decision-making practices of minority school principals in urban school districts. Wafa teaches doctoral level courses in the school administrator preparation program and education research methodology in the Department of Educational Leadership and has created online courses, and blended learning environments and modules for graduate students. Recently, she has been studying education from a social justice perspective to examine how Muslim female public school students negotiate their Islamic religious values at home and a secular Western culture at school.

Tamara Jones

Title: Research Assistant
Institution: University of Auckland, Aotearoa
    New Zealand
Email: tell005@aucklanduni.ac.nz

Tamara Jones is a primary-trained teacher with 17 years' experience. During this time she has held various leadership roles, writing contracts for the Ministry of Education in Aotearoa New Zealand, and developing schoolwide programs with international agencies in Asia. Tamara completed her MEdLd (Hons) in 2014 while on a TeachNZ Study Award. Her research explored theories of risk-taking which may influence women to shape the educational environment. Tamara is currently a provisional doctoral candidate and working part time as a research assistant and visiting practicum lecturer in the Faculty of Education at the University of Auckland.

Deidre Le Fevre

Title: Senior Lecturer
Institution: University of Auckland, Aotearoa
   New Zealand
Email: d.lefevre@auckland.ac.nz

Deidre Le Fevre (PhD) is a senior lecturer in the Faculty of Education and Social Work and Co-Director of the Narrative and Metaphor Special Interest Network at the University of Auckland, New Zealand. She teaches graduate courses in educational leadership, organizational change, and professional learning. Deidre is interested in innovative strategies for professional learning and has worked in universities, businesses, and schools undertaking research and teaching in the United States and Aotearoa New Zealand. Her recent research examines the role of women in leadership, perceptions of risk in processes of change, and the interpersonal communication of leaders engaged in challenging conversations.

Linda McGinley

Title: Assessment Coordinator and Consultant
Institution: St. John Fisher College, United States
Email: lmcginley@sjfc.edu

Linda McGinley (EdD) is an assessment coordinator in the School of Education at St. John Fisher College in Rochester, New York. She has also served as an adjunct instructor in the Master of Science Program in Educational Leadership and the Doctoral Program in Executive Leadership. She holds an EdD in Executive Leadership from St. John Fisher College and a master's in education from the University of Rochester. Linda currently provides educational consultation services to K–12 school districts. Prior to consulting, she served as assistant superintendent for instruction, elementary principal, and special education teacher in the West Irondequoit Central School District, Rochester, New York.

Susanne Maezama

Susanne Maezama (PhD) (Sohi Pelo is her indigenous name) is from the island of Santa Isabel, Solomon Islands. Susanne trained to be a teacher of home economics and taught for a number of years in the Solomon Islands before winning a scholarship to study for her master's degree at the University of Waikato in Aotearoa New Zealand. On her return to the Solomon Islands she gained a position lecturing at the Solomon Island's College of Higher Education. Susanne went on to become the Head of School. She won a Commonwealth Scholarship and returned to the University of Waikato to study for her PhD which she successfully completed in 2016. Her PhD focused on women's leadership in Santa Isabel. After recently retiring from the Dean of Education role at the Solomon Islands National University, Susanne passed away in early 2018 after a sudden illness. She leaves behind her devoted husband and three adult children.

Abaida Mahmood

Title: Teacher Educator
Institution: Qurban & Surraya Educational Trust, Pakistan
Email: abaidamahmood@gmail.com

Abaida Mahmood is a voluntary teacher trainer from the United Kingdom who settled in Lahore, Pakistan, with the vision of imparting quality teacher training at her institute. She believes that teachers are the basic players in the field of education and they need the best of coaching. She is a trustee of Qurban & Surraya Educational trust and her voluntary services are reaching beyond her institution. Her work has empowered and engaged hundreds of girls to transform themselves from dependent women into contributing members of the family and society. She travels extensively and has presented many papers nationally and internationally.

Yvonne Masters

Title: Adjunct Senior Lecturer
Institution: University of New England, Australia
Email: ymasters@une.edu.au

Yvonne Masters (PhD) is an adjunct senior lecturer of Professional Classroom Practice in the School of Education, University of New England, Australia. She has 30 years' experience in secondary schools including in the roles of deputy principal and principal. Yvonne's recent research focuses on teacher education and policy, undergraduate research, professional experience, and virtual worlds, with a particular focus on distance education students. In the last few years she has gained, in collaboration with other researchers, several school of education research grants, a $200,000 Australian Learning and Teaching Council (Office of Learning and Teaching) grant, and in 2015 lead an OLT project to develop resources for preservice teachers to prepare them for online teaching. She is also the incoming editor of the International Academic Forum *Journal of Education.*

Samantha Mortimer

Title: Assistant Principal
Institution: Te Aroha College
Email: samanthamortimer70@gmail.com

Samantha Mortimer is assistant principal at Te Aroha College in Hamilton, New Zealand, and a doctoral candidate at the University of Waikato, New Zealand. Her research focus explores how school culture and leadership influence the development of beginning teachers' professional identities. Originally from the United Kingdom and with experience in the New Zealand and US education systems, Samantha went on to complete a master's in women's studies and Certificate of Secondary Teacher Education. Samantha also recently completed her master's of educational leadership at the University of Waikato. As a school leader and doctoral student, she is especially interested in social justice, effective teachers, restorative practice, and educational leadership.

Diane Reed

Title: Associate Professor and Director of
   Graduate Education
Institution: St. John Fisher College, United States
Email: dreed@sjfc.edu

Diane Reed (EdD) has served as associate professor and director of the Graduate Education Leadership Department for the last 10 years at St. John Fisher College in Rochester, New York. She has fulfilled a variety of leadership roles as superintendent, assistant superintendent, and elementary school principal. Along with working in the master's degree program in educational leadership, Diane chairs and serves as a member of a number of dissertation committees and is an active member of the College's Graduate Program Council and Institutional Research Review Board. Diane has published exten-sively on the topic of leadership resiliency and gender differences. Her recent work focusing on women and leadership was presented at the WLE Ghana conference and is available in the special issue of the *Planning and Changing* journal published by Illinois State University.

Kerry Robinson

Title: Assistant Professor
Institution: University of North Carolina, Wilmington
Email: robinsonkk@uncw.edu

Kerry Robinson (PhD) is an assistant professor in the Department of Educational Leadership at the University of North Carolina, Wilmington (UNCW). Prior to her appointment at UNCW, she was an assistant professor at the University of Tennessee. Previously, she worked in K–12 schools for 17 years in New Jersey and Virginia as an exceptional education teacher, building-level administrator, and district-level administrator. Kerry's primary areas of research include women in leadership, the superintendency, and leadership preparation. She is also very active with a number of special interest groups for the American Educational Research Association, including Leadership for Social Justice, Stress, Coping and Resilience, and Research on Superintendency, for which she is the current chair-elect.

Arceli Rosario

Title: Associate Professor
Institution: Adventist International Institute of
   Advanced Studies, the Philippines
Email: rosarioa@aiias.edu

Arceli Rosario (PhD) is an associate professor of the Adventist International Institute of Advanced Studies, the Philippines, where she teaches educational administration classes and is chair of the Education Department. She served as an English teacher in three secondary schools, principal and vice president for academic affairs, and president of a higher educational institution. One of her advocacies is helping women develop their leadership potential, find their voice, and make positive contributions to society.

Charol Shakeshaft

Title: Professor
Institution: Virginia Commonwealth University
Email: cshakeshaft@vcu.edu

Charol Shakeshaft (PhD) is a professor of educational leadership at Virginia Commonwealth University, United States. She has been studying equity in schools for four decades. She was elected an American Educational Research Association (AERA) fellow in 2015 and also received the 2015 AERA Distinguished Contributions to Gender Equity in Education Research Award. Charol is the author of three books and over 200 refereed articles and papers. Her research focuses on three strands: gender and leadership, sexual abuse of students by adults employed in schools, and the effectiveness of technology for learning, particularly for students of color.

Jane Strachan

Email: strachanjane89@gmail.com

Jane Strachan (PhD) is a feminist activist and retired academic. Her academic research and teaching career at the University of Waikato, Aotearoa New Zealand, focused on feminism, educational leadership, social justice, and Pacific education. She has been involved in the WLE group since the conference in Rome (2007), attending all the biennial conferences except for Brazil. She assisted Rachel McNae in organizing the 2015 conference in New Zealand. Jane spent the last 10 years of her academic career working in both Vanuatu (women's human rights policy development) and the Solomon Islands (teacher education program development), work she found deeply rewarding. In retirement Jane enjoys her family, friends, reading, walking, biking, traveling, movies, and, sometimes, academic contract work.

Shirley Randell

Title: Independent Consultant
Institution: SRI Public Sector Reform Pty Ltd., Australia
Email: mail@shirleyrandell.com.au

Shirley Randell (AO, PhD, Hon.DLitt, FACE, FIML, FAICD), is conjoint professor of education in the Faculty of Education and the Arts, at the University of Newcastle, Australia. A prominent expert in education, gender mainstreaming, and human rights, she has been a leader in providing specialist technical assistance in 25 countries in the Asia Pacific Region and Africa over the last 20 years. From 2006–2013 she worked in Rwanda as a gender and education specialist and was Founding Director of the Centre for Gender, Culture and Development, now Centre for Gender Studies, at the University of Rwanda. She is the author of numerous journal articles and books and is a renowned international speaker.

Saeeda Shah

Title: Reader
Institution: University of Leicester, United Kingdom
Email: sjas2@le.ac.uk

Saeeda Shah (PhD) is reader at the University of Leicester, England, teaching/supervising on master's and doctoral programs. Saeeda is also program leader for the PhD program, Chair of the College of Social Sciences Equal Opportunities Committee, and member of the International Strategy Forum. She has published widely on leadership, diversity, gender, and Islam and society, and is an internationally recognized scholar in the field. In addition to her responsibilities at the University of Leicester, Saeeda holds many external positions including visiting professor of education at the University of Derby, Fellow of the Higher Education Academy, and member of editorial boards of different prestigious international journals.

Victoria Showunmi

Title: Senior Lecturer
Institution: Maynooth University School of Education and University College London, United Kingdom
Email: v.showunmi@ioe.ac.uk

Victoria Showunmi (EdD) is a senior lecturer at Maynooth University while taking an extended career break at the Institute of Education, University College London. Victoria draws on experiences gained in further and higher education, the public sector, and corporate organizations to shape her work and research in the areas of gender, identity, race, and class. Her current research focuses on identity and leadership and black girls and black young women and their well-being. She uses such interests to critique societal discourses which marginalize and minoritize women in areas such as educational leadership and gender policies.

Jill Sperandio

Title: Associate Professor
Institution: Lehigh University, United States
Email: jis204@lehigh.edu

Jill Sperandio (PhD) is a graduate of the doctoral program of the University of Chicago and associate professor at Lehigh University in Pennsylvania, United States. After a long career as teacher and school leader in international schools worldwide, she now teaches and researches in the Educational Leadership Program of Lehigh's College of

Education. She has published widely on the education of girls, and women in educational leadership, in the United States and abroad. Jill's recent publications on women in educational leadership in Indonesia are the result of a study funded by Australian Aid to Indonesia for which she was lead researcher.

Rogena Sterling

Title: Researcher
Institution: University of Waikato, Aotearoa New Zealand
Email: rps1@students.waikato.ac.nz

Rogena holds a bachelor of arts and has taught English, established an English language school, and set up an oriental medical college. Rogena then went on to complete the LLB and LLM programs at the University of Waikato and a PhD in law with a focus on "Intersex, Identity, International Law, and State Obligations." At the University of Waikato Rogena tutors in the area of Jurisprudence and Administrative Law and has published work in the area of clinical legal education. Rogena has also presented papers at numerous conferences and been on panels with the New Zealand Human Rights Commission focused on the topic of Intersex.

Coomi Vevaina

Title: Director
Institution: Centre for Connection Education and Management
Email: csvevaina@gmail.com

Coomi Vevaina (PhD) is director of the Centre for Connection Education and Management and retired professor and head of the Department of English, University of Mumbai, India. She has two PhD degrees to her credit—one in literature and the other in Education—and has published nine books and 58 papers that have appeared in refereed national and international journals and critical anthologies. Her most recent book on education was declared one of the 18 best books published in the United States in that category. Her current areas of interest in literature include poststructural theory, gender studies, children's literature, ecocriticism, ethical criticism, cultural studies, spatial criticism, and new literatures in English.

Daisy Warsal

Title: Consultant
Institution: Qualao Consulting, Vanuatu
Email: daisywarsal09@gmail.com

Daisy Warsal is an independent educational consultant and holds a master's degree in the area of educational leadership from the University of Waikato, Hamilton, New Zealand. Her research interests include exploring the cultural elements of leadership, specifically, the impact of culture on women educational leaders in Vanuatu Secondary Schools. Daisy has co-authored academic publications in the area of women's leadership in Melanesia. She is employed as the gender and community participation specialist for Qualao Consulting, spending much of her time consulting for the Asian Development Bank through the Port Vila Urban Development Project.

www.ingramcontent.com/pod-product-compliance
Lightning Source LLC
Chambersburg PA
CBHW080236270326
41926CB00020B/4261